Christian Reconstruction

Christian Reconstruction

R. J. Rushdoony and
American Religious Conservatism

Michael J. McVicar

The University of North Carolina Press
Chapel Hill

Set in Minion
Manufactured in the United States of America

The paper in this book meets the guidelines for permanence and
durability of the Committee on Production Guidelines for
Book Longevity of the Council on Library Resources.

The University of North Carolina Press has been a member
of the Green Press Initiative since 2003.
Cover illustration: Promotional photograph of Rousas John
Rushdoony taken circa 1965 during the formative years of the
Chalcedon Foundation. (Courtesy of the Chalcedon Foundation)

Complete cataloging information can be obtained online
at the Library of Congress catalog website.

ISBN 978-1-4696-2274-3 (pbk: alk. paper)
ISBN 978-1-4696-2275-0 (ebook)

For Mary

Occupy till I come.

—Luke 19:13 (King James Version)

CONTENTS

ILLUSTRATIONS

ACKNOWLEDGMENTS

This history of Christian Reconstructionism and the ministry of Rousas John Rushdoony would not have been possible without the kindness and openness of the Chalcedon Foundation in Vallecito, California. Chalcedon's current president and R. J. Rushdoony's son, Rev. Mark Rousas Rushdoony, took a certain risk in allowing an unknown graduate student totally unfettered access to his father's personal papers and unpublished manuscripts. The archival backbone of this book is formed from thousands of digital images taken during two separate visits to Rushdoony's rambling library. Mark Rushdoony provided thoughtful comments on drafts of this project and saved me from making significant errors regarding his father's legacy. Christopher J. Ortiz, former communications director of Chalcedon and editor of *Faith for All of Life* (*FFAOL*) helped me get this project rolling by suggesting numerous leads and helping me make contacts with other Christian Reconstructionists. Chris also encouraged me to publish some of my preliminary research findings in *FFAOL*. Those early articles—the embryonic forms of the first three chapters of this book—offered me the opportunity to receive valuable feedback from Chalcedon staff members and the loyal readers of *FFAOL*. Finally, Martin G. Selbrede, vice president of the Chalcedon Foundation, offered helpful feedback on many aspects of this project. While Messrs. Rushdoony, Ortiz, and Selbrede will likely find much in this project with which to disagree, it is a better work because of their help and insight. The interpretations contained herein—and any factual errors—are mine alone.

To compliment the holdings of R. J. Rushdoony's library, I relied on archival resources across the United States. I would like to thank the staffs of the Louis Round Wilson Special Collections Library at the University of North Carolina at Chapel Hill; the Special Collections and University Archives at the University of Oregon; the Institute for Humane Studies at George Mason University; the State Historical Society of Missouri; the Digital Collections and Archives at Tufts University; the Rare Book and Manuscript Library at Columbia University; the Historical Center of the Presbyterian Church in America; the Superior Court of California; the Billy Graham Center in the Wheaton College Archives and Special Collections; the Hagley Museum and Library; the Tyler, Texas, Public Library; and the Intercollegiate Studies Institute. Finally, Political Research Associates (PRA) in Somerville, Massachusetts, deserves special thanks for opening its library to me. Chip Berlet gave generously of his time and wisdom, while Abby Scher kindly encouraged me to publish the results of my research in the PRA's *Public Eye* journal.

During key phases of research, several people gave generously of their time and resources to contribute to this project. Kenneth Templeton provided pancakes, Jack Daniels, and extensive memories of his time at the William Volker Charities Fund. Brian Doherty gave me a small treasure trove of documents that provided color to chapter 2. John Whitehead read parts of the draft and talked with me about his memories of Rushdoony and Francis Schaeffer. Gary North provided key background material in several lengthy e-mails and helped me make sense of the end of the Volker Fund. I'm grateful to Chris Smith for helping me track down Rushdoony's FBI files. A surprise e-mail and blog post from Jerusha Lofland fundamentally altered my thinking about chapter 1. Randy Booth provided last-minute insight into the later ministry of Greg Bahnsen. In many ways, this book is a footnote to an extended conversation I've been having with Brandon Sutherland for about fifteen years. He'd probably be surprised to know how much his ideas and random e-mails have contributed to this project. Myra Immell helped whip the manuscript into shape.

I would also like to thank Hugh B. Urban, Tanya Erzen, and Philip Armstrong in the Department of Comparative Studies at the Ohio State University (OSU). Hugh encouraged my idiosyncratic interests and taught me to love the field of religious studies. I can't imagine a more capable or fun guide for graduate study. Tanya helped convince me to pursue the topic of Christian Reconstruction, and she offered candid advice that helped turn a bloated manuscript into viable book. Philip clarified my thinking and theoretical approach throughout the project. He also provided moral support and crucial advice at several key points in my graduate education. I also must thank several other Comparative Studies folks. Chairs David Horn, Eugene Holland, and Barry Shank kept me in the program and kept the funding rolling. Thanks to Dan Reff for harassing me throughout the years, and to Lindsay Jones for tough love in his theory courses. Marge Lynd, Wen Tsai, and Lori Wilson helped me out of more jams than I can list here. Many thanks to Damon Berry, Keith Padgett, Beth Shively, Rita Trimble, and Lee Wiles, who were wonderful conversation partners and contributed directly to making this a better project. Keith pointed me to one of Rushdoony's greatest quotations—he'll know which one. Finally, in the wider OSU community, I owe endless gratitude to Alan Beyerchen in history and John Champlin in political science. I would not have completed college, let alone graduate school, without their help.

To academics known and unknown, I owe so much. I presented portions of this research to graduate student conferences at Ohio State, Florida State, and Indiana Universities and at national and regional meetings of the American Academy of Religion and American Studies Association. Feedback from these forums proved invaluable. Diane Winston read an early draft of this project and convinced me to do something with it. Thanks to Julie Ingersoll for reading versions of the project and for allowing me to read her own manuscript on Reconstruction. Brian Auten shared valuable tips and leads. Karl Baughman answered random questions about ancient Christianity. UNC Press's anonymous reviewers provided feedback that dramatically reshaped this project for the better. Elaine Maisner has been an ideal editor, helping me shape the manuscript and patiently shepherding me through the tangled process of academic publishing.

Special thanks to the Chalcedon Foundation, Covenant Media, the Montgomery Library of the Westminster Theological Seminary, Joel Pelletier, Paul Turnbaugh, and John Whitehead for generously providing permission to reprint the images in this book. The *Missouri Historical Review* and *Journal of Religion and Popular Culture* allowed the use of research originally published in their pages.

My new colleagues in the Department of Religion at Florida State University have been especially welcoming and supportive of this project. Thanks to everyone who provided critical feedback during two faculty colloquia on draft chapters of the book. The graduate students in my course on conservatism and evangelicalism challenged me to rearticulate key parts of the argument in this book; thanks for an engaging term. Special thanks to Amanda Porterfield and John Corrigan for all of their help, patience, and support as I've transitioned into my new role as junior faculty. Also, thanks to chair John Kelsay for supporting me with the department's resources and offering his kind advice. Florida State's generous First Year Assistant Professor program provided the time and funding necessary to finish this project.

Finally, I couldn't ask for a better family. To my folks, Keron and Eldon, and in-laws, Denise and Bob, thank you for being patient and supportive of my odd career choice. Finally, this book is dedicated to Mary—wife, best friend, and joy of my life. Without her love and support, I doubt that I would have finished this project.

Christian Reconstruction

Children of Moloch

Christian Reconstruction, the State,
and the Conservative Milieu

To surrender children to the state is to turn them over to the enemy.
For the surrendered children . . . to turn on the society that begat them
and to destroy it is a judgment on the Moloch worship of their elders.
—R. J. RUSHDOONY, *Institutes of Biblical Law*, 1:40

Whosoever he be of the children of Israel, or of the strangers that
sojourn in Israel, that giveth any of his seed unto Molech; he shall surely
be put to death: the people of the land shall stone him with stones.
—Leviticus 20:2 (King James Version)

In 1945, on the isolated Duck Valley Indian Reservation in Nevada, a young Presbyterian missionary named Rousas John Rushdoony had an idea. He believed that the troubles of the reservation's Paiute and Shoshone inhabitants were directly linked to the poor education they received in the reservation schools. He called his flock together to discuss the matter. During the meeting, "[i]t was decided that the present government-controlled school board was highly unsatisfactory."[1] One of the church's elders was "the sole Indian on the Board," so Rushdoony suggested that another tribal elder should run. But the reverend's goals were more ambitious than simply placing another Indian member of his church on the school board. "A Christian principal is our objective," he told the meeting, "plus a Christian staff, all willing to work with the Church on a broad Christian communal program."[2] Rushdoony reckoned that education based on Christian principles would not only help save the souls of the enrolled children but, over time, would also change the culture of the reservation and lead to the spiritual redemption and regeneration of the entire reservation. Since the area was so isolated, Rushdoony knew that his mission did not face the "usual competition most Churches face" from non-Christian diversions.[3] He also believed that federal officials would turn a blind eye to his proposed curriculum, which would include "temperance education, information against the strong peyote cult, facts on smoking, and the like."[4] On the reservation, Rushdoony realized that the weaknesses of the federal government afforded Christians an opportunity to break down the boundaries between church and state and use education to raise up a generation of godly children.

Four decades later, on a witness stand in Texas, Rushdoony, now seventy-one years old, testified as an expert witness in the case of *Leeper et al. v. Arlington ISD et al.* After the Texas Education Agency (TEA) declared that homeschooling did not satisfy the state's compulsory education requirements, Gary and Cheryl Leeper initiated litigation that eventually developed into a class-action lawsuit against all 1,060 public school districts in the state. They and other parents demanded the right to educate their children at home. Rushdoony's heated testimony in the case hinged on the question of the ability of Texas's school districts "to cover every square inch in the state."[5] The state's attorney insisted that Texas had an absolute right to enforce its educational prerogatives through legislative and judicial mechanisms. Under cross-examination, Rushdoony confounded the attorney by highlighting the historical inability of western states to administer large parts of their territory in the early 1900s, when the Texas law was written. At every turn, he provided anecdotes and historical facts to illustrate how gaps in the state's presence traditionally opened spaces for citizens' autonomy—including the ability of families to found homeschools and educate children according to their beliefs.

The forces behind the *Leeper* case represented an insurgency among a small group of Christian parents dedicated to resisting the intervention of the state in the regulation and governance of their families.[6] In 1987 a watershed ruling in the *Leeper* case struck down the TEA requirements. *Leeper* became one in a long string of victories that made homeschooling legal in all fifty states.[7] Little more than a decade before *Leeper*, in 1970, compulsory education laws made homeschooling nearly impossible in many states; by the middle of the 1990s, every state—most quite reluctantly—had relinquished their stranglehold on education. Texas had been one of the last major holdouts against homeschooling. Shelby Sharpe, one of the Leepers' attorneys, later recalled that Rushdoony's testimony proved decisive in the case: "His testimony was way beyond anything I'd hoped for. It was one of the few times in my career that I ever saw a witness destroy the attorney who was trying to examine him."[8]

Rushdoony had, in the intervening decades since plotting to take control of Duck Valley's school board, helped build the extensive network of parents, lawyers, and nonprofit parachurch organizations that wrought this revolution in national educational policy.[9] After leaving the Duck Valley Reservation in the 1950s, he labored tirelessly, first to carve out a legal space for home education in the United States and then to mobilize theologically and socially conservative evangelical Protestants to political action through grassroots organizing. In 1965 he founded the Chalcedon Foundation, a tiny Christian think tank with a modest budget and few staff members, to advocate for a specific model of Christian education organized around small family units. Pedagogically, he developed a model of education that insisted on teaching the factual truth of the entire Bible and using it as a primary guiding source for home-education curricula.

At the height of the Cold War and throughout the tumultuous final decades of the twentieth century, R. J. Rushdoony traveled the United States telling small churches and parents' groups that they must free themselves and their children from state-funded schools. Anything less than total emancipation from compulsory state education amounted to "Moloch worship." This ancient cult of the Ammonites, Rushdoony told audiences, "affirmed, not the sovereignty of the God of Scripture, but the godhead of the state and its ruler. Passing children through the fire of Moloch was human sacrifice. . . . They belonged to the state, to be taught the faith of the state, to die for the state, to work for the state, and, in all things, to be the creatures of their king, Moloch."[10] An institution as seemingly benign as public kindergarten represented parents' sinful desire to liberate themselves from the burden of their children. "Kindergarten," Rushdoony wrote, "has proven to be in part *a polite and oblique form of infanticide*, one which hypocritical women can indulge in while getting credit for solicitous motherhood."[11] Christian parents had an obligation to starve Moloch by refusing to offer up their issue to this false god and resist the indirect infanticide embodied in public schools.[12]

Rushdoony offered this stark message in an era of increasing standardization in primary and secondary education. Seismic shifts in American demographics saw the majority of the American population shift from rural to urban and suburban environments. Homogenization and routinization in the service of the post–World War II Cold War state dominated American educational policy. The United States needed engineers and scientists, not classically educated Christians who focused on biblical study or freethinking enemies of the military-industrial complex. Parents from across the political and religious spectrum began pushing back against uniform educational policies emanating from state and federal bureaucracies.[13] Among these many competing voices, Rushdoony distinguished himself by fusing a militant Christian Gospel with a visceral antipathy to the modern state. As he helped build the homeschooling movement, Rushdoony became one of the most controversial ministers of the twentieth century. He not only advocated that parents abandon public schools but also articulated a social project that called Christians to "take dominion" over all spheres of human society—including the state—and turn them toward explicitly Christian purposes. By 1980, Rushdoony was a folk hero among conservative Christian homeschoolers.

Christian Reconstruction

This book tells the story of the rise and fall of one of the most controversial and poorly understood religious and political movements to emerge in the United States during the twentieth century: Christian Reconstruction. The narrative details the intellectual and organizational history of Reconstructionism, a theological project situated at the juncture of religious practice, educational reform, and political action. Christian Reconstruction posits a radical reordering of the relationship between human beings and the Christian God. It seeks to "reconstruct" individual men through a form of Christian governance that, if implemented in the daily lives of U.S. citizens, would fundamentally alter the shape of American society, culture, politics, and economics.[14]

Rushdoony outlined the Reconstructionist project in his mammoth work, *The Institutes of Biblical Law*. The *Institutes* notoriously insisted that "a Godly order" would enforce the death penalty for myriad lawbreakers, including homosexuals, witches, and incorrigible children.[15] Published in 1973, the nearly 800-page first volume of the *Institutes* introduced the "dominion mandate" to a generation of Christian activists hungry for a theological foundation for their political engagement. Rushdoony's Christian Reconstructionism appeals to Genesis 1:26–28 to establish the role a Christian must play in governing other human beings and in ruling the earth. There, God creates Adam and Eve and blesses them.

> And God said, Let us make man in our image, after our likeness: and let them have dominion over the fish of the sea, and over the fowl of the air, and over the cattle, and over all the earth, and over every creeping thing that creepeth upon the earth. So God created man in his own image, in the image of God created he him; male and

female created he them. And God blessed them, and God said unto them, Be fruitful, and multiply, and replenish the earth, and subdue it: and have dominion over the fish of the sea, and over the fowl of the air, and over every living thing that moveth upon the earth.[16]

According to Rushdoony, this "creation mandate" is a commandment to "subdue all things and all nations to Christ and His law-word."[17] By adhering strictly to biblical law, Christians could reverse the curse of the Fall and "take dominion" over the planet and "reconstruct" all of life in Christ's image.[18] Ultimately, as these reconstructed dominion men fill the planet, they will replace ungodly, secular forms of governance with decentralized theocracies and rule as Christ's vicegerents on earth. Because of this focus on the reconstruction of men through the practice of dominion under biblical law, Rushdoony referred to his ideas synonymously as Christian Reconstruction or theonomy, from the Greek *theos* (God) and *nomos* (law).

As implausible as the vision of a reconstructed United States might seem, over the past fifty years, Reconstructionism and its more widely known variants, "dominionism" and "dominion theology," have steadily crept into America's popular religious and political consciousness. Not surprisingly, Reconstructionism's open call to conquer the world for Christ and execute evildoers is highly controversial. For decades, Rushdoony was largely unknown outside of a small but highly influential circle of Protestant theologians, education reformers, political activists, and lawyers. Beginning in the 1970s, observers in American evangelicalism uneasily recognized Rushdoony as an important actor at the intersection of religion and politics in American culture. No less a publication than Billy Graham's *Christianity Today* declared Rushdoony to be one of the "most impressive" political theologians of his generation.[19] The writings of Rushdoony and his disciples caused a significant amount of nervous hand-wringing and forceful denunciations among socially and theologically conservative Protestants. As one anonymous activist confided to an interviewer, "Though we hide their books under the bed, we read them just the same."[20]

This closeted, sometimes deliberately secretive, adoption of Reconstructionist ideas has prompted nearly obsessive attempts on the part of some to uncover links between Rushdoony and current political realities, especially by observers who identify Rushdoony not only as a major influence on the Christian Right but also as the movement's most dangerous patriarch. By 1981, recognition of Reconstructionism had crept beyond evangelical circles, with *Newsweek* pointing to Rushdoony's Vallecito, California–based Chal-

Joel Pelletier's satirical 2004 painting *American Fundamentalists (Christ's Entry into Washington in 2008)* vividly captures concerns over the threat of "dominionism" to American democracy. Based on James Ensor's protoexpressionist *Christ's Entry Into Brussels in 1889* (1888), Pelletier's massive 8'4" x 14'1.5" canvas depicts the Christian Right invading Washington, D.C., and marching under the banners of John Winthrop, John Nelson Darby, John Calvin, R. J. Rushdoony, and Francis Schaeffer. Rushdoony's son-in-law Gary North, in black glasses and pointed jester's hat, marches ahead of the banner. Courtesy of Joel Pelletier, http://www.joelp.com and http://www.americanfundamentalists.com.

cedon Foundation as *the* think tank of the Religious Right.[21] Since then, a growing number of popular media sources have detected Rushdoony's influence on everything from the rise of the Christian Right to the assassination of abortion doctors and the presidency of George W. Bush.[22] More recently, reporters in national venues have pointed to the influence of Christian Reconstruction in the complex network of ideas behind the rise of the Tea Party and even in the field of candidates contesting the 2012 Republican presidential nomination.[23] Media outlets, including NPR's *Fresh Air*, the *New York Times*, and CNN, warned audiences that Minnesota congresswoman Michele Bachmann and Texas governor Rick Perry were supported by a shadowy group of Christian theocrats who hoped to use the GOP to foist a Reconstructionist agenda on an unsuspecting nation.[24] Ominous reports warned of Reconstructionism's harsh theocratic vision of a nation "reconstructed" by the literal application of Old Testament law on all aspects of modern life. Reconstructionists would dismantle the modern federal state

Detail of Joel Pelletier's *American Fundamentalists (Christ's Entry into Washington in 2008)*. Courtesy of Joel Pelletier, http://www.joelp.com and http://www.americanfundamentalists.com.

in favor of decentralized fiefdoms run by an elite order of male Christian property owners. Education would be a private good, not a public good—the sole duty of families, not the state. Finally, reconstructed Christians would toil patiently and deliberately to build up Jesus Christ's Kingdom on earth. Even as the presidential aspirations of Bachmann and Perry faded, critics warned that Reconstructionism's influence over the American Right remained undiminished, especially in the Tea Party, raising serious questions about the origins, influence, and relevance of religious conservatism in contemporary culture.

As a result of this shallow, but nonetheless popular, interest, beginning in the early 2000s, Rushdoony became one of the most frequently cited intellectuals of the American right wing. Yet Rushdoony and Reconstruction remain understudied and fundamentally underappreciated in the religious, political, and cultural history of the twentieth century in the United States. Building on nearly two decades of groundbreaking historical research into the long history of the development of the so-called Religious or New Christian Right, this study of Christian Reconstructionism fills a significant void by tracing the complex relationship between contesting religious, intellectual, and political histories. While recent studies by American religious history scholars such as Lisa McGirr, Darren Dochuk, and Molly Worthen (among many others) have paid careful attention to the interrelationship between religion and intellectual production on the right, it is striking that Reconstructionism has received scant attention from historians.[25]

This lack of historical research into the origins of Reconstructionism and its relationships to other conservative religious and political movements is due, in part, to the fact that Reconstructionism developed through networks of activists and institutions that have left few traces in the kinds of archival collections upon which professional historians rely. Reconstructionism spread through living rooms, church meetings, Bible studies, homeschools, and small conferences organized by faithful adherents to the movement. Such events rarely left the written evidence necessary for the production of historical narratives. Further, Rushdoony, in the early years of his ministry, circulated in highly secretive circles—such as the William Volker Charities Fund and the John Birch Society—that actively dissimulated the extent of their activities. Finally, the documentary traces Reconstructionists did leave, in the form of a massive literary output and cantankerous engagement with other Protestants, tell a confounding tale, one at odds with many of the standard historical and political narratives of the twentieth century. The result is that Reconstructionism does not easily fit into conventional historical narratives documenting, for instance, the political influence of Billy Graham and his neoevangelical coalition or the mobilization of the machinery of the Religious Right during the Carter administration.[26]

When Rushdoony and other Reconstructionists do slip into standard histories, they usually make brief cameos as outsiders, misfits, or extremists with little connection to the central narrative.[27] Yet, as media scholar Heather Hendershot has noted, while historians recognize the important roles "extremists" played in building the post–World War II American conservative and evangelical movements, to date there have been few detailed histories of the so-called extremists "who ultimately had to be swept aside for the conservative movement to shift into the mainstream."[28] Likewise, as historian D. J. Mulloy has noted in his history of the John Birch Society, small, seemingly marginal movements such as Reconstructionism are historically significant because they "can generate new ideas, or give a renewed lease of life to old ones; they can pioneer innovative modes of political activity or communication; they can embody—and give voice to—some of the central tensions or conflicts of the time . . . ; they can attract millions of sympathizers and supporters to their cause; and they can leave behind a substantial legacy—positive and negative—for others to examine and learn from."[29] Following Hendershot and Mulloy, this study offers an alternative history of the rise of conservative evangelical activism. It unapologetically focuses on the "extremes" to explore how a movement now widely regarded as marginal and extremist simultaneously shaped and was shaped by its interaction with mainstream elements of the American conservative intellectual movement and traditional strains of evangelical and fundamentalist theology.

The Conservative Milieu

This study intervenes in three interconnected historiographic fields. It engages recent histories of the rightward list in American culture. Next, it explores the contested intellectual histories of American conservatism. Finally, it connects these histories of conservatism as an intellectual and political project with the diverse literature on the social and intellectual histories of evangelical fundamentalism.

The narrative engages a range of studies documenting the complex relationship between evangelical Christianity, laissez-faire economics, and political conservatism following World War II. It follows the trails blazed by researchers such as Lisa McGirr, Matthew D. Lassiter, John G. Turner, Darren Dochuk, Michelle M. Nickerson, and others who have situated the rise of contemporary conservatism within the context of the seismic shifts in American society and culture following World War II.[30] Through unique access to Rushdoony's vast personal library, the present narrative situates Rushdoony within this broader historiographic field while simultaneously using his ministry to reinterpret the standard narratives of the postwar rise of the American conservative movement. It uses the intellectual project of a singular individual to explore a much broader set of social and political developments that other scholars have neglected or ignored.[31]

Scholars have spilled much ink struggling to define the contours of evangelicalism and fundamentalism in U.S. culture.[32] Similarly, "conservatism" as an ideological and intellectual project remains an especially contested term with scholars, movement insiders, and critics battling for control of the concept.[33] This book sidesteps much of the scholarly uneasiness over categorical creation and deployment—*What is fundamentalism? How should we define evangelical? What is religion? Is Rushdoony a "real" conservative?*—by using Rushdoony's ministry as a lens to focus the narrative on how he and his interlocutors called these categories into being through their own histori-

cally situated and discursively coconstructed battles over intellectual production and organizational utility.[34] That is, rather than relying on categories
such as "evangelical" or "conservative" to mobilize the narrative, these terms
appear in the story because Rushdoony and his interlocutors used them. As
such, there is little utility in prescriptively defining them. Instead, the narrative treats these categories as troubled, unstable, quasi-objects that cannot
be defined in principle as the "referent of an ostensive definition," and it
traces how historical actors defined them in practice.[35] Thus, rather than an
ostensive or stipulative definition, it is more useful to explore the organizational networks that facilitated the intellectual production of categories
that emerge from attempts to create a salient and robust social structure.
As a result, overlapping, often contradictory and paradoxical formulations
occupy the same space. Yet this reflects the contentiousness that developed
as self-described evangelicals and fundamentalists (and Catholics and Jews,
for that matter) contributed to and resisted certain formulations of "conservatism" as a strategic ideological position.

Finally, this intellectual history of Reconstructionism is situated at the
nexus of Protestant theology and the emergence of various "conservative"
political projects in the wake of the New Deal. Rather than treat these theological and political categories as distinct, this study approaches them as
mutually coconstructing discursive structures that shared intellectual and
organizational resources while remaining heuristically distinguishable. The
central argument is that Rushdoony's Christian Reconstructionism resonated with a wider conservative milieu determined to address the interconnected problems of religion and governance that emerged in U.S. culture in
the middle of the twentieth century.[36]

The result is an extended study of Rushdoony's unique contribution to
American culture: Christian Reconstruction, a project of social reorgani-
zation that advocates for the continuing relevance of Old Testament biblical law to contemporary American society. By placing this religio-political
project within the wider context of twentieth-century U.S. culture, this
study refuses to reduce Reconstructionism to the aims of a madman or to
the machinations of some dangerous revolutionary conspiracy. Instead, in
this broader inquiry into the ways in which "religious conservatives" constructed oppositional identities rooted in certain Christian modalities of
conduct and governance, Reconstructionism becomes neither an extreme
aberration nor a sui generis fringe phenomenon. Through a history of Christian Reconstructionism, this book tells the complex story of the ways in
which certain expressions of Protestant evangelicalism helped constitute the

boundaries of a conservative revolution in late twentieth-century U.S. culture that was simultaneously endorsed and decried by America's political and cultural elites.

A Very Fallible Man

For better or worse, the history of Christian Reconstruction is entangled with the ministry of R. J. Rushdoony. His life dominates the study that follows. In spite of his centrality, however, the book purposefully avoids any attempt to provide a deeper assessment of Rushdoony's character or his emotional and psychological states. Readers will find no Freudian insights into Rushdoony's latent desires. Nor will they encounter an attempt to offer a convincing portrait of the "real" Rushdoony. This approach will likely frustrate many readers, but the narrative remains in such an ambivalent state because, while he is the central figure in this story, Rushdoony is not its real focus. The narrative traces the development of Christian Reconstructionism as a theological and social movement. As such, it leaves the story of Rushdoony's inner life to others and instead focuses on sketching the contours of a movement that is inseparable from him, but not reducible to him.

This book relies heavily on a largely unfettered access to Rushdoony's personal library. Through his correspondence, journals, and unpublished papers, it reassembles the complex institutional and intellectual history of Reconstructionism. Surprisingly, these sources allow a remarkably unintimate glimpse into the inner workings of Rushdoony's psyche. They present a singularly focused, almost mechanical man driven by an all-consuming ambition to build "a world-wide ministry through writing."[37] Beginning in the late 1940s and continuing every day until the late 1990s, when he grew too ill to write, Rushdoony meticulously recorded every book he ever read, every letter he ever wrote, and every idea he ever penned. His drive was monomaniacal, and his work ethic was second to none.

In contrast to the exhaustive details of his life as a writer, his journals depict a man with seemingly only two emotional states: spitting rage and tender, fatherly love. Rushdoony's diaries disproportionately recount his confrontations with theological critics, intellectual ne'er-do-wells at academic conferences, battles with Presbyterian officials, or run-ins with ignorant laypeople. Inevitably, these clashes left Rushdoony enraged, sleepless, or generally vexed. The result is a written record that displays a man more likely to note anger over personal slights and the perceived intellectual vapidity of his enemies than he was to document the happier moments of his life.

The exception to this tendency, however, related to Rushdoony's moving tenderness toward his children and grandchildren. While he was uninterested in recording most of the emotional details of life, he regularly indulged in documenting anecdotes related to raising six rambunctious children. His earliest journal entries about his children read like a theocratic parody of Bil Keane's *Family Circus* comic strip. Rushdoony mirthfully recounted his oldest daughter Rebecca damning a local stray cat as a "heretic" for its peripatetic behavior. In another case, Joanna, his second-oldest daughter, angrily condemned a failed imaginary bakery session as a "perversity." When a class bully kicked Rushdoony's adopted son, Ronald, "in the penis," the boy responded by telling his assailant, "I love you." "The way of the world," Rushdoony drily noted.[38] Other examples abound. He recounted every aspect of the births of daughters Sharon and Martha and son Mark. He regularly sketched the emerging personality of each child—Ronny was a kind and caring big brother to his younger siblings; Rebecca was smart and defiant; Joanna was the model of good behavior; Sharon often exclaimed "goddam!" when angry, a habit learned from a profane family friend in Nevada; Martha was ever the doting youngest sister; and Mark, an affectionate little boy, fascinated his dad.[39] Years later, Rebecca recalled her father's absentminded habit of reciting the names of his children. As he worked in his study, he softly repeated, "Rebecca, Rebecca, Rebecca . . ."[40]

For those outside of Rushdoony's family, much of his appeal came from his ideas and from his writings. Numerous personal friends close to Rushdoony have testified to his brilliance as a writer and generator of theological insights. None of these testimonies, however, indicated that people were drawn to Rushdoony because of his charm or personal charisma. Physically, he was a striking character—a stocky, barrel-chested man with a baritone voice and the conservative but nonetheless carefully cultivated fashion sense of a minister, complete with dark flannel suits, wide ties, and the beard of a biblical patriarch. As many of his recorded lectures and sermons indicate, Rushdoony was a restrained speaker. His ideas and sharp thinking often sparkle in his recorded lectures, but his delivery was, at best, professorial and workmanlike, with little flare and only hints of passion. The dedication he engendered was for adherence to an intellectual cause, not loyalty to a man. This will become clear later in the narrative, but it is worth noting at the outset that Rushdoony often surrounded himself with smart, dedicated people who found his ideas singularly compelling. Over time, many of his closest confidants had sudden, irreparable disputes with him as their ideas diverged. The resulting conflicts could be savage. These dramatic personal ruptures reveal a figure less concerned with cultivating intimate friendships than with building a movement of ideas.

The point here is to highlight at the outset that the image of Rushdoony that appears in this narrative is necessarily one-sided. Rightly or wrongly, Rushdoony the cultural warrior dominates this book. The father and husband appear only fleetingly. Those who knew him as a father and grandfather readily attest to his love and affection. But this side of the man is not always evident in his activism or the writings documented here. This should not efface the fact that Rushdoony was a complex man with a rich emotional life.

Critics of Rushdoony and the movement he started are likely to find much in this narrative that reinforces their negative sentiments. Rushdoony frequently vocalized openly bigoted and prejudiced positions related to women, racial and sexual minorities, and non-Christians. Readers searching for such anecdotes will not be disappointed. Conversely, those sympathetic to Rushdoony and conservative Protestantism will find glimpses of a godly man who, despite his failings, was a thinker of deep insight, a man of great charity, and a lover of his kith and kin. More temperate readers will likely find Rushdoony to be something of an enigma—at once intellectually deep and emotionally distant, a complex mix of hubris and humility.

Rushdoony was neither a saint nor a monster. He described himself as "a very fallible man."[41] That assessment of Rushdoony is about as clear-eyed and honest as one could manage. Readers can draw their own judgment from the narrative that follows.

Preparation for the Future

The following chapters provide a study of the emergence of Christian Reconstructionism and its complex, oppositional relationship to the intellectual and political expressions of conservatism and evangelicalism in twentieth-century American culture. Chapter 1 opens with the brutal violence of the Armenian Genocide in Turkey during World War I, providing a vision of R. J. Rushdoony's Old World heritage while also introducing the central themes of the uses and abuses of state power that appear throughout the narrative. As a young missionary on the Duck Valley Indian Reservation in Nevada in the 1940s, Rushdoony built remote connections with a surprisingly diverse body of intellectual figures—including Protestant historian George Huntston Williams, political theologian Ernst H. Kantorowicz, and the Dutch American Reformed thinker Cornelius Van Til—who fundamentally shaped the project of Christian Reconstruction. As he engaged with these thinkers, Rushdoony refused to constrain his intellectual development to a narrow disciplinary horizon and instead aspired to use the entire arch of Western Christian tradition to illuminate contemporary religio-political problems, including the threats of fascism and communism and the closing of the American frontier as embodied in the reservation system. The first chapter places Rushdoony within the interwar and postwar periods in U.S. intellectual history and sets the tone for following chapters by introducing the critical theological problems facing Reformed Presbyterians that would dominate Christian Reconstructionism during the latter half of the twentieth century.

The second chapter focuses on the coalescing conservative milieu of the mid-twentieth century. It pays particular attention to the emergence of the "mainstream" or "fusionist" intellectual wing of the American conservative movement during the 1950s and 1960s. It explores how this coalition developed at the expense of religious conservatives such as Rushdoony and other committed sectarians determined to purify politics through a specific religious vision. Rushdoony, after leaving Nevada for a pulpit in Santa Cruz, California, initially tried to develop a political agenda within the structure of the Presbyterian Church (U.S.A.), only to abandon the denomination for the friendlier world of ideological activism. In the late 1950s, a small but robust network of nonprofit groups and think tanks were looking to assemble a "remnant," a tiny minority of right-thinking men who might, through a new model of education, turn the United States away from its ruling liberal cabal. Through a history of Rushdoony's connections with Spiritual Mobilization, the William Volker Charities Fund, and the Center for American Studies, the chapter lays the foundation for a broader argument that illustrates how these understudied, but highly influential, midcentury organizations and conflicts over sectarian religion helped form the ephemeral but nonetheless sociologically robust conceptions of "mainstream" versus "extreme" (or "radical") conservatism.

Chapter 3 outlines Rushdoony's connections with the emerging grassroots infrastructure of the Southern Californian conservative movement, with its epicenter in Los Angeles and Orange County. Situating Rushdoony firmly in this grassroots matrix, the chapter details his relationship with Women for America, Inc., a patriotic women's study group that offered Rushdoony the necessary capital to turn his attention away from the pulpit and toward full-time writing and lecturing. In 1965 he used this support and help from other financial backers, such as Walter Knott, founder of Knott's Berry Farm, to found the Chalcedon Foundation. With the creation of Chalcedon, Rushdoony began to articulate an intellectually rigorous, philosophically sophisticated, and practically accessible familial project designed to relocate the discipline and governance of human beings from the state to the family. This project, which he first called a "Christian renaissance" and then "Christian Reconstruction," found an audience among women and men sympathetic to the John Birch Society and other contemporary action groups seeking a coherent religious foundation for their political ideas.

Biblical law is the central theme of chapter 4. Christian Reconstructionism grew out of Rushdoony's hostile relationship with the editors of *Christianity Today*, most notably Carl. F. H. Henry, as he tried to challenge other conservative Christians to see Mosaic law as the antidote to the perceived lawlessness of the 1960s. After failing to create an expedient alliance with businessman and philanthropist J. Howard Pew in an attempt to influence *Christianity Today* and the neoevangelical coalition it represented, Rushdoony turned his attention to fully articulating his vision of biblical law as an alternative to the "law and order" discourse emerging among his fellow conservatives. He argued that biblical law could provide the necessary mechanism to reconstruct America into a neofeudal Protestant state that would eventually usher in Christ's second coming.

As Rushdoony's ideas spread in conservative Calvinist circles, a second generation of "dominion men" flocked to his ministry. Chapter 5 documents the growth of Christian Reconstruction into an intellectual and political force during the 1970s and 1980s. It details the relationship between Rushdoony's work as an education and legal reformer and a wider trend on the part of evangelical Protestants to engage in direct political activism. The narrative expands far beyond the legacy of Rushdoonian Christian Reconstruction to explore diverse expressions of the movement cultivated by his son-in-law Gary North, theologian Greg L. Bahnsen, and lawyer-activist John W. Whitehead. By tracing the interconnected work of these activists and many others, the chapter highlights the practical aspects of Reconstructionism by following its influence in politics, seminaries, and court cases across the United States. These Reconstructionist-inspired activists marshaled grassroots Christian revolts in local politics, in Christian higher education, and against America's system of compulsory state education.

Chapter 6 closes the narrative with an assessment of the fracturing of Reconstructionism into a decentralized movement without a central organizational or intellectual leader during the 1980s and 1990s. As the movement grew, a greater number of theologically and socially conservative Christians became aware of its agenda. This wider awareness of Reconstructionism inspired both emulation and contempt. Charismatic Christians adopted aspects of Rushdoony's "dominion" rhetoric and gave his books wider readership. Some evangelicals condemned the movement as a dangerous, tyrannical expression of false Christianity. Other activists associated with the New Christian Right read Reconstructionism's carefully argued theological manifestos. In these documents, a small circle of organizers and preachers found theological arguments to support their political engagement. Meanwhile, a second generation of Reconstructionists heavily influenced by the antistatist sentiments of Rushdoony's system developed separatist communities in Texas and elsewhere. These church-centered groups created their own closed economies built around guns, gold, and bomb shelters designed to protect Reconstructionists from the imminent collapse of the federal government. In the midst of it all, Rushdoony continued his efforts to make homeschooling legal, even as the movement he founded fractured and became the topic of intense debates in both evangelical and secular media outlets.

From Rushdoony's earliest warnings in the 1940s about the growing danger of the centralized federal government to his excoriation as a hate-filled theocratic homophobe in the 1990s, Christian Reconstruction cuts straight to the heart of a century bedeviled by questions of religion and its proper relationship to American society. In the 1950s and 1960s, men like Rushdoony created an alternative to what they termed "liberal" American culture. They shaped a conservative milieu assembled from a diverse set of interests, ideas, and organizations. In the 1970s and 1980s, Christian Reconstruction emerged simultaneously with the Christian Right. By the 1990s, Reconstructionism had become a Rorschach test for the social anxieties of any number of progressives, conservatives, secularists, and even evangelical Christians. No longer simply a prominent reflection of right-wing anxieties, Reconstructionism has become a screen upon which critics and supporters project competing interpretations about the place of religion in American society and its relationship to "conservative" ideas.

In the end, this study of Christian Reconstruction provides a unique opportunity to map these complex screenings. It brings into sharp focus contemporary anxieties about the rise of a seemingly omnipresent federal bureaucracy that threatens to reach deeper into the private lives of ordinary citizens. Reconstructionism anticipated the politics of the Tea Party by more than a half century and helped write the script for popular revolts against public education most recently embodied in fights over the Common Core State Standards Initiative. Reconstructionism provides an occasion for reflecting on the ways that scholars, journalists, and average Americans conceptualize the boundaries between religion and politics in the United States. Finally, this book emphasizes the inherent complexity of the American conservative movement and highlights the interpenetrations and disjunctions between Christian Reconstruction, the Christian Right, and the victorious Reagan Revolution of 1980. It unsettles the histories of American evangelicalism and conservatism by highlighting the complex, recursive milieu from which both movements emerged.

CHAPTER ONE

The Glory Is Departed

Political Theology, Presuppositional Apologetics, and the Early Ministry of Rousas John Rushdoony

Nearly all of the wisdom we possess, that is to say, true and sound wisdom, consists of two parts: the knowledge of God and of ourselves.
—JOHN CALVIN, *The Institutes of the Christian Religion*, 1

For the weapons of our warfare are not carnal, but mighty through God . . .
casting down imaginations, and every high thing that exalteth
itself against the knowledge of God, and bringing into
captivity every thought to the obedience of Christ.
—2 Corinthians 10:4–5 (King James Version)

"Only a lazy son-of-a-bitch wants rights," Pete, a twenty-eight-year-old Pai-ute Indian, declared to Presbyterian missionary Rousas John Rushdoony. "A man wants freedom and justice, and he can take care of himself," Pete angrily concluded.[1] On New Year's Day 1946, Reverend Rushdoony had accepted a dinner invitation from Pete and his younger sister and brother. The small, parentless family lived in a humble two-room adobe and log cabin on the Duck Valley Indian Reservation near Owyhee, Nevada.

After dinner, Pete and Rushdoony talked long into the night about the problems facing Native Americans on the reservation. As the night wore on, Pete opened up to Rushdoony. He denounced his fellow Paiutes as lazy prisoners of the United States, and he insisted that white men were no better. As Pete saw it, "the Indian was fit only for Reservation life," and the "white man" was "ripe for the reservation . . . waiting for some superior man to drive him there."[2] Intrigued by Pete's point, Rushdoony added that "the white man, with his increasing predilection for a dictated economy, was rapidly bent on turning the world into a Reservation."[3] Pete agreed vigorously, insisting that although "the German and the Japanese" failed to put the "white man" on a reservation, "the next people might succeed."[4]

R. J. Rushdoony's conversation with Pete was a microcosm of the central problem that haunted the missionary's early ministry; namely, how might he help cultivate the "freedom and justice" necessary for a Christian man to thrive, especially when America's constitutional system no longer seemed to provide for either? Rushdoony began asking this question while serving as a spiritual leader to the Paiute and Shoshone Tribes of Nevada.[5] As a young missionary to Native Americans in Nevada, Rushdoony became convinced that only a rigorous, intellectually self-aware Christianity could provide a viable response to such oppressive state mechanisms. His intellectual approach to healing a nation by regenerating mind and spirit laid a foundation for how Rushdoony and his ideas would later play a significant role in the fusion of libertarian ideology and conservative Protestant theology that would eventually come to dominate some spheres of the American Right. While Rushdoony's precise formulation of this new form of Christian governance—Christian Reconstruction, as he later named it—would not come until the late 1960s, its broad contours were already evident in his missionary activities of the 1940s.

Rushdoony's commitment to resisting state oppression with Christianity began in his college years, as he struggled to integrate his secular education at the University of California, Berkeley, with his conservative theological perspective. At Berkeley, Rushdoony encountered the "political theology" of German historian Ernst Hartwig Kantorowicz.[6] Kantorowicz's lectures exploring the relationship between the law and divine revelation convinced Rushdoony that the political and the juridical are always essentially religious. Through a chance encounter with the writings of Cornelius Van Til, a Reformed theologian teaching at Westminster Theological Seminary in Philadelphia, Rushdoony connected Kantorowicz's political theology with emerging trends in fundamentalist Christian philosophy. Van Til argued that all ways of knowing the world are founded on a philosophy's presuppositions. If one presupposes the existence of a Christian God, Van Til argued, one will get a very different result than if one presupposes many gods or no gods at all.

By joining Van Til and Kantorowicz, Rushdoony concluded that as humans work to understand the world, they simultaneously strive to control it. If humans attempt to synthesize knowledge and power without a proper understanding of God, the outcome will be disastrous. In the wake of World War II, the growth of state-centered solutions for social problems was, Rushdoony argued, grounded on a faulty understanding of humanity's relationship (or lack thereof) with God. A proper theory of knowledge—or epistemology in philosophical terms—would recenter God in the lives of men and ultimately lead to a limited, even *libertarian*, view of the state. Rushdoony's concern with epistemological self-awareness led him to develop a program for reforming Christian education starting with the church and expanding to the wider world. These two interconnected intellectual themes—political theology and the Christian philosophy of knowledge—formed the central concerns of Rushdoony's early ministry, but they also formed the backbone of his later activism, research, and educational efforts.

"Can You Be Trusted to Be Loose in Society?"

On April 20, 1915, Ottoman forces laid siege to Van, an ancient walled city of some 80,000 Muslim and Christian Armenian residents.[7] Situated in the shadow of snow-capped mountains on the shore of Lake Van, the city had long been a hotbed of Armenian nationalism and revolutionary anti-Ottoman sentiment. For much of the late 1800s and early 1900s, Van and its surrounding countryside were plagued by brutal tit-for-tat outbreaks of violence as the local Turkish, Kurdish, and Armenian populations vied for political and cultural control over the region.[8] With the outbreak of World War I, Armenian separatists turned to Russian support for their cause, while Turkish officials looked for an opportunity to settle the Armenian problem once and for all. With the subsequent explosion of ethnic, religious, and nationalistic violence, the Armenian population paid a heavy price.

The Old World...

Present during the eruption of the violence was Yeghiazar Khachadour Rushdouni, the future father of Rousas John Rushdoony.[9] Y. K. Rushdouni could, according to family lore, trace his descent back through the ages to the first Armenian noble families to convert to Christianity after Gregory the Illuminator evangelized the area in A.D. 301. From that date onward, it was traditional for noble families such as the Rushdouni clan to send at least one son into the priesthood, thus creating a more-or-less unbroken priestly succession within their line until the late 1800s.[10] As a child, Y. K. Rushdouni played among the gravestones of his small village's church. There, he memorized the names of his ancestors, many of whom had served in the clergy of the Armenian Church, some even martyred by Muslims for their Christian faith. Y. K.'s connection with the ancient Armenian Apostolic Church ended abruptly in 1896, when Turkish forces killed most of his family. The violence left Y. K. orphaned and homeless. He found refuge in the nearby city of Van in an orphanage established by an American Presbyterian missionary, Dr. George C. Raynolds.[11] Under the influence of Raynolds, Rushdouni converted from Armenian Orthodox Christianity to Presbyterianism. Raynolds sent the young Armenian to the University of Edinburgh and New Mound College in Scotland to study. After completing his education in 1914, an Armenian Presbyterian church in Fresno, California, offered Rushdouni its pastorate.[12] He declined and instead returned to Van to aid Raynolds in his missionary work. There, he wed Vartanoush Gazarian, the daughter of a local merchant. Their first child, Rousas George, was born at Raynolds's mission hospital that same year.[13]

With the outbreak of violence in Van, Rushdouni wrote vivid eyewitness accounts for newspapers in England and the United States. He reported that tensions between Turkish soldiers and the Armenian residents of Van turned violent on April 20, when a group of Turkish soldiers "tried to seize some village women on their way to the city" of Van.[14] When two Armenian men came to the women's rescue, the response, according to Rushdouni's accounts, was immediate: "The Turkish soldiers fired on the Armenians and killed them. This served as a signal. The booming of cannons and rattle of rifles began from every side, and it was realised that the Armenian quarter [of Van] was besieged. In the evening houses in the Armenian quarter could be seen burning in every direction."[15] Turkish artillery devastated the wood and mud-brick homes of Van. Armenian men took to the city walls and began digging trenches and building other makeshift fortifications in the city's Armenian neighborhoods.[16] Rushdouni's journalistic accounts attest to the Armenians' stubborn defiance: "The spirit of the fighters was enough to inspire those that were in despair. I have seen young men who had fought the enemy day and night, without sleeping. . . . While the shrapnel was raining down upon Van, the Armenian children were playing soldiers in the streets."[17] Unfortunately for Rushdouni and his wife, three days before Turkish forces lifted the siege in order to resist a Russian offensive to their rear, Rousas George succumbed to measles and whooping cough, the consequences of the squalid conditions in the besieged city.[18] He was eleven months old.

When the Russian army marched into Van in May 1915, troops requisitioned Rushdouni's house and, in return, gave him a lame cavalry horse. Rushdouni used the horse to ferry his wife, now pregnant with their second child, to safety. He then made several dangerous return trips to the city to rescue family members and the aged and infirmed.[19] Once safely in Russian territory, Y. K. used the remainder of his wife's dowry to secure passage, first to the port city of Archangel in northern Russia and then to New York City. In the United States, Y. K. entered the clergy and adopted "Rushdoony" as the standardized Anglicized spelling of his family's surname. In 1916, shortly after the family's arrival in New York, Vartanoush, now known by the English translation of her name, Rose, gave birth to their second son, Rousas John. The Rushdoonys then moved to Kingsburg, California, a small farming community southeast of Fresno, where Y. K. started the Armenian Martyrs' Presbyterian Church. His son was baptized in Los Angeles.[20]

. . . and the New World

During the first two decades of the twentieth century, Kingsburg saw a steady influx of Armenian families. Many settled in the area because of its proximity to larger urban immigrant communities in nearby Fresno.[21] By 1922, there were twenty-one Armenian households in the area, just enough to support Y. K. Rushdoony's small church.[22] Evidence suggests that the tenaciously independent California Armenian diaspora community favored Republicans politically. As one observer noted, this trend was, in part, related to the community's memory of persecution in Turkey: "The lessons of centuries of powerlessness and oppression have suggested to them that survival is most likely on an 'old-fashioned liberal' model of living that stresses little contact with and no dependency on government; individual hard work, initiative and self-sacrifice; in-group inter-dependency and reciprocity; asking little assistance from others to discourage anti-Armenian sentiment."[23] When the Kingsburg church began to lose membership in subsequent decades, Rushdoony and his congregation resisted attempts to remove "Armenian" from the church's name, an indication of the deep relationship between the community's religious and ethnic identities.

In the political, religious, and ethnic mix of the Armenian-American community, Rose and Y. K.'s family grew. A sister, Rose, and brother, Haig, followed Rousas. Armenian was their primary language at home, but the new generation of American Rushdoonys learned English through Bible lessons and in the public schools. Rousas learned to read English by poring over the King James Version of the Bible under the kerosene lamps of his family's old farmhouse. Years later, R. J. recalled, "By the time I reached my teens, I had read the Bible through from cover to cover, again and again and again, half a dozen times or more."[24] When Y. K. told a local Congregational minister of his son's singular reading habits, the minister quizzed the boy on some of the racier parts of Scripture and confirmed that the child had read them. In response, the minister wondered aloud, "What's going on in that little head of yours? Can you be trusted to be loose in society?"[25] For his secular education, Rousas John attended public elementary schools in Kingsburg and in Detroit, where his father briefly accepted the calling of another Armenian congregation in 1925. Y. K.'s bad health forced the Rushdoony family to return to California in 1931, and there, Rousas completed his schooling in Kingsburg and eventually enrolled at the University of California in Berkeley. During his university years, R. J. resolved to put all of his intensive Bible reading to good use and follow his father's example to become a Presbyterian minister.

During his tenure as a university and divinity school student, Rushdoony evolved from a political and theological "liberal"—or even leftist—into a determined political and theological conservative. He graduated from Berkeley with an undergraduate degree in English in 1938, followed by a master's degree in education in 1940.[26] His time at Berkeley exposed him to modernist trends in literature, philosophy, historiography, and educational theory. He started his undergraduate career as a member of the American Civil Liberties Union and supported labor unions. At Berkeley, Rushdoony poured himself into his studies, but he recoiled in horror from what he saw as a degenerate and dangerous anti-Christian humanism lurking in the texts he encountered. He would enroll in classes and then drop out, "with or without a grade," after he learned what he wanted.[27] He began to push back against the leftist ideas he encountered and quarreled with faculty.

Even with this "rebellious" and "independent attitude," he graduated with honors and then turned his attention to divinity school.[28] He took his divinity degree in 1944 from the Pacific School of Religion (PSR) in Berkeley, a theologically and politically left-leaning institution far removed from the orthodox centers of American Presbyterianism. Rushdoony came to believe PSR's faculty was more interested in Karl Marx than in Jesus Christ.[29]

As he wound down his career as a student, Rousas John wed Arda June Gent in San Francisco on December 19, 1943. Their union came in Rushdoony's final year at PSR. Gent was the daughter of English immigrants who settled in Colorado in the late 1800s. She attended Whitworth College, a Christian liberal-arts school in Washington State.[30] In college, she was a member of the school's Volunteer Fellowship and active in the Protestant churches in the Spokane, Washington, area. The two likely connected over their shared religious values and desire to serve as missionaries.[31]

"First Owyhee and Then the World"

On May 14, 1944, Rev. George Huntston Williams delivered an ordination sermon in honor of his friend, Rousas John, at the Chinese Presbyterian Church in San Francisco. Williams's sermon connected Rushdoony's ancient lineage to his current calling as a missionary. "It is thus a moving and very fitting gesture, that you of this congregation . . . should provide the setting and occasion for the ordination of this scion of an ancient Christian house as an Evangelist, to be sent forth to still another people, the Paiute and Shoshone Indians in the mountains of Nevada."[32] In Rushdoony, Williams saw an "heir of a great national Christian heritage" who would "enunciate anew the Gospel which seems to have been forgotten for a season."[33]

Williams, who went on to teach at Harvard University and author the now-classic historical study *The Radical Reformation* (1962), met Rushdoony at the University of California in Berkeley, where they studied under Ernst H. Kantorowicz. At Berkeley, they formed a fast friendship that served as the foundation for Williams's highly personal sermon. Williams's address captured the complex ethnic and national identity of the young, ambitious clergyman at the outset of his long, prolific career. At twenty-eight, Rushdoony was the product of the Old and New Worlds. His parents had suffered greatly at the hands of a Muslim ruling elite in a country riven by political and religious upheaval as it transitioned from a religious empire into a secular, democratic state. His brother was dead, a tragic human sacrifice to these sweeping global transformations. Yet Rushdoony and his family survived precisely because of these very changes: revolutions in transportation, industry, and political freedom allowed a generation of Armenians to flee the Ottoman Empire and thrive in the United States. Born in New York City and baptized in Los Angeles, this New World man retained his father's faith in the almighty power of Christ and longed to serve in the priesthood, just as generations of Rushdoony men had before him. Also like his father, Rushdoony aspired to missionary work, through which he could similarly focus his ministry on politically and culturally marginalized populations. But whereas Y. K. sought to bring Protestantism to his own oppressed people in Armenia and then to their diaspora communities in the United States, R. J. spent his college years working with Chinese immigrants in the San Francisco slums. With his ordination, Rushdoony resolved to turn his religious energies to two of America's most marginalized populations: the Paiutes and Shoshones of Nevada.

R. J. Rushdoony in a traditional Native American headdress on the Duck Valley Indian Reservation, ca. 1950. Courtesy of the Chalcedon Foundation.

A Harsh and Ruthless Ministry

Shortly after Rousas's ordination, he and Arda packed up his "considerable and well-mounted library" into a large truck and moved to Owyhee, Nevada, to serve as Presbyterian missionaries on the Duck Valley Indian Reservation.[34] Owyhee, located in the northeastern part of the state just south of the Idaho border, was a tiny, isolated community of Paiutes, Shoshones, cowboys, and miners. Rousas and Arda found themselves in a land of extremes: harsh weather, lawlessness, and, paradoxically, constant government intervention in the day-to-day life of the reservation community. In his early correspondence from Owyhee, Rushdoony often commented on the stark splendor of the isolated mission. "We are beautifully situated here," he wrote to one of his former professors at Berkeley, "surrounded by high mountains and cradled in a small high valley."[35] The beauty enchanted Rushdoony, a young man who had grown up in a rural farming community but who had also spent part of his later childhood in urban Detroit and his college years in the San Francisco area. The former seminarian and philosophy student took up hunting and fell in love with fishing, often wandering off alone on lengthy, isolated fishing trips.[36] The rural setting of Owyhee prompted him to conclude, "I love it here and would gladly remain all my days if God so wills."[37]

For all of its physical beauty, however, Owyhee also brought severe hardship. Heavy snow and frigid temperatures dominated from fall until spring. During the Rushdoonys' first fall in Owyhee, the snows began in November and continued until Christmas. "We have had snow for a month and a half now," Rushdoony wrote in December 1944. "Our hills and mountains are wonderfully white. . . . On Sunday mornings I track through the clean snow to the Church to tug at the bell rope, with the joyous anticipation of hearing the clear ringing of the bell blend into the frosty stillness."[38] The harsh winters limited travel, while spring thaws unleashed torrents of water that destroyed bridges and turned roads into an impassable, muddy soup. Mail was always delayed for one reason or another, and electronic communication—telephones and telegrams—operated at the whims of the weather and the hapless bureaucrats in Owyhee and nearby Mountain City, Nevada. Only summers allowed for free travel and easy communication.

In addition to the difficulties imposed by the severe climate, the young minister discovered that the mission posed challenges he had not anticipated. When Rushdoony arrived in Owyhee, he found a mission in "deplorable" condition: "a collapsing building, cracking walls through which snow drifts, and general disrepair with no prospect of financial assistance."[39] Worse still, he believed that the degradation of the mission served as an analogue for the moral condition of the locals. "Lawlessness prevails," Rushdoony wrote a friend, reporting "extensive drinking, gambling (legalized), fornication, rape, adultery, and extremely widespread illegitimacy."[40] The "lawlessness" cited here is significant because many of the "crimes"—drinking, gambling, and illicit sex—were in fact legal on the reservation; Rushdoony was appealing to the higher demands of his religious office and saw it as his duty to enforce God's laws, not man's—a calling that would dominate his entire life.

For her part, Arda found the reservation an awkward fit for her own personal and social aspirations. She left no personal record of her time as a missionary, but Rushdoony frequently recorded her activities in his personal journals. She played a prominent role in the community, serving as a teacher at the reservation school, the leader of the local Girl Scouts troop, the coach of the girls' basketball team, and a Sunday school teacher. To all of these duties, Arda also added the role of mother to an ever-expanding young family. Early in their ministry, Arda and Rousas adopted their first child, Ronald Haig (b. September 12, 1945), an orphaned Native American from the reservation. Four daughters of their own quickly followed: Rebecca (b. March

1, 1947), Joanna (b. September 21, 1948), Sharon (b. March 26, 1950), and Martha (b. March 8, 1952). A son, Mark (b. February 21, 1954), was born after they left the reservation for Santa Cruz, California, in 1953.[41] The result was an endless succession of the pleasures and pains of domestic life—illnesses, messes, squabbling siblings, little achievements, and sweet anecdotes—all made more acute by the extreme environment of the reservation.

As the family grew, the responsibilities of running a mission and caring for the children put considerable stress on Rousas and Arda's relationship. Arda struggled with mission life and, according to Rushdoony's journals, did not enjoy the domestic routines of housework and caring for the mission's manse and chapel. She preferred making social calls and working with children through the Girls Scouts and other civic programs. Her social activities led Rousas to regularly lament the amount of child care and domestic work he had to do because he believed it impeded his studying and writing.[42] Eventually, however, the Rushdoonys came to some sort of peace over these issues. References to domestic tensions in Rushdoony's journals eventually gave way to anecdotes of his joy in being a father and to accounts of the more mundane matters of administering the mission. In part, their harmony may have emerged from Arda's health troubles. Rushdoony's letters to family friends indicated that Arda was often ill due to a misdiagnosed thyroid issue.[43] He also noted that Arda was exhausted by reservation work, and he frequently sent her to visit family in California for recuperation.[44]

Regardless of their private tensions, the moment the Rushdoonys set foot in Owyhee, they asserted themselves as a public moral and legal force in the community. Letter after letter from Rousas's time on the reservation tells of his and Arda's efforts to turn the locals away from drink and fornication. In one compelling instance, Rushdoony summarized a particularly eventful Saturday night:

> The gambling house is the center of all evil here. My wife was out until 9:30 p.m. clearing the girls off the streets and then I took over. We brought in one 7th grade boy, dead drunk, and laid him out in the front study for the rest of the night, sent a drunken 8th grader home in the care of an elder, slightly drunk but repentant boy. Others, very drunk, were carried off into the willows out of my reach. At midnight, I summoned the government superintendent to the manse, to burn his ears with an account of conditions. . . . At 2:30 [A.M.], a fierce fight broke out in the Owyhee Club (the gambling house), and knives were drawn. . . . At 5:30, another bad fight,

in which two boys I covet for Christ were involved. . . . Then home for sleep from 6:00 to 7:00, dressed and lying on the day-bed.[45]

He would preach his Sunday sermon in a few short hours.

Rushdoony reported that his sermons met this lawless environment with an uncompromising Gospel. To Orval Clay, a friend from his PSR days, he summarized the key themes of his reservation sermons: "Atonement, justification by faith, the two natures of Christ and His virgin birth, the congenital evil inherent in all civilizations and culture, the despair of man, the Church Triumphant and the Church Militant." It all added up, he told his friend, to "a harsh and ruthless ministry" that "wage[s] war in God's name."[46] In short, Rushdoony saw himself as a holy warrior crusading on the very frontiers of Christianity and using as his weapon the most traditional and fundamentally orthodox Protestant message he could muster. If the evil of the reservation sought to grind him down with its harsh environment and ruthless lawlessness, then Rushdoony would respond with an unsparing Gospel that laid bare the sinful depravity of man. Owyhee required the full attention of a young, hearty minister willing to endanger his family's spiritual and physical well-being for the Gospel. If Rushdoony described his ministry as "harsh and ruthless," then his message was perfectly suited for the natural and social realities of Owyhee.

Visible Sovereignty

As Rushdoony struggled to grow his outpost of the church, he also eagerly awaited word from the University of Chicago Press regarding his first major book manuscript. As mentioned previously, while he was a student at Berkeley, Rushdoony studied under Ernst Hartwig Kantorowicz.[47] Kantorowicz, a renowned German-Jewish intellectual forced to vacate his chair at the University of Frankfurt by Nazi policies, came to Berkeley in the late 1930s. According to one biographer, Kantorowicz "had a small following of carefully selected, enthusiastic students, who were thoroughly aware of the uniqueness of their teacher's qualifications and of their own unequaled opportunity" to study under his guidance.[48] While it is not clear if Rushdoony was among the most elite members of the Kantorowicz clique, he was certainly a hanger-on and a close friend of George H. Williams, one of Kantorowicz's more elite protégés.[49] Further, Rushdoony and Kantorowicz were close enough for Kantorowicz to guide Rushdoony's research projects.

In Rushdoony's last years at Berkeley, Rushdoony and Kantorowicz began collaborating on a project that emerged from their discussion of Kantorowicz's recently published essay, "The 'King's Advent.'"[50] As the pair sat in the locally crafted rattan porch furniture Kantorowicz used in his bay-side apartment, Rushdoony pointed out an occasion in Cromwell-era England in which James Naylor, a Quaker, had used pageantry typically associated with a king's advent to enter the city of Bristol and declare himself a messianic figure.[51] The professor had been unaware of the event and was so delighted by Rushdoony's account that he excitedly explained that he would write a piece to demonstrate how this event marked the democratization of the king's advent by expanding it into the realm of political protest against the king. Suddenly, Kantorowicz paused and sighed, "Oh, but I can't do it. This is outside my period."[52] Not concerned with such disciplinary limitations, Rushdoony began researching the event and many others under Kantorowicz's supervision. Rushdoony compiled the research into a book manuscript, entitled "Visible Sovereignty," and shipped it off to the University of Chicago Press.

Rushdoony saw the book as his ticket into academia. Throughout letters authored between 1944 and 1945, he cited the "interim living" imposed on him by the press's editors.[53] He noted that if the Chicago press accepted the manuscript, he would need to leave the reservation to revise it. At times, he implied he might not return to missionary work if the manuscript went to press.[54] "Visible Sovereignty" represented an important pivot in Rushdoony's religious life. Throughout this period, he pondered pursuing a Ph.D. and seeking faculty positions at various colleges, a series of options that could have led him down a very different career path.

In March 1945 John Scoon, a University of Chicago Press editor, rejected the project. Scoon wrote that the press could not publish the text because, due to the war, it "cannot get from the mills even the small amount of paper which we are allotted by the government."[55] Also, the editor worried that the manuscript's focus on England might make it more suitable for a non-American press: "[Y]our manuscript is almost entirely devoted to England and we feel that some other organization such as the Oxford or the Cambridge Press would not only do a better job with it but would have a larger sale, because of their tradition and the audience they reach."[56] In this ironic twist, wartime government rationing and a study of European Protestantism undid a man who eventually became infamous as a critic of government intervention in the economy and known primarily for his influence on American Protestantism.

Even with this rejection, Rushdoony hoped that he might find a publisher for the work. At this point in his intellectual development, he considered himself a Kantorowicz disciple. Writing to Kantorowicz, Rushdoony wondered if the professor might be interested in publishing one of his studies alongside Rushdoony's work and another by George H. Williams: "It requires temerity on my part to think in terms of coupling my work with yours and George's, but the three do represent a single strand and a product of the Kantorowiczian School."[57] Rushdoony's receptivity to the "Kantorowiczian School" of history had a long-term influence on his intellectual development.

Kantorowicz was a German nationalist with deeply ingrained strains of European romanticism and idealism. As medievalist Norman F. Cantor has noted, Kantorowicz's early research—specifically his biography of Frederick II—played a pivotal role in post–World War I German historiography. Kantorowicz sought to "put models of charismatic leadership before the beaten, confused, and impoverished postwar German people so that the *Volk* would rise up again under some Nietzschean and Wagnerian heroic figure."[58] Perhaps because of his own unfortunate experiences with a certain Austrian corporal, Kantorowicz arrived in Berkeley having already abandoned his search for national messiahs. Instead, he began to focus his attention on the influence of theological models of kingship and sovereignty in medieval European society.[59] This new project—dubbed "a spiritual history of European monarchy" by one reviewer—resonated with Rushdoony's own search for the Christian roots of all human experience.[60] From Kantorowicz's methods, Rushdoony learned to see the "centrality of theology to politics and the state."[61] This focus on the ideological and religious form of history taught Rushdoony to distrust studies that overemphasized the importance of individual men in history and emphasized material context over spiritual content.

During this time, Rushdoony was looking for an alternative to the forms of secular historiography that dominated mid-twentieth century American universities.[62] Modern historical research, with its focus on archival minutia and the evacuation of the divine foundation underlying human toil, deeply disturbed Rushdoony. Prominent historiographic methods in the 1940s betrayed the influence of the materialist philosophy of Karl Marx and the biology of Charles Darwin. Historians who focused on these materialist and naturalistic methods of historical research often also sought to integrate Freudian psychological insights into biographical assessments. Humanity, in Rushdoony's appraisal of modern historiography, had become the measure of mankind; human beings no longer were seen as derivative agents of God's sovereignty. Rushdoony believed that Kantorowicz's work challenged this trend toward a disenchanted world by calling historians' attention to the ways in which abstract theological conceptions of God and man had concretized into the political infrastructure of the medieval and modern worlds.

On a more personal level, the manuscript's failure forced Rushdoony to reassess his career goals and made it clear that he would not find work easily in academia. If his goal had been to follow Kantorowicz and Williams into academia, he quickly abandoned this path. Instead of throwing himself into a revision of the manuscript, Rushdoony abandoned the text and became increasingly pessimistic about his own abilities, about his missionary work, and about the entire Christian church. In fact, at this point in his ministerial development, Rushdoony became increasingly convinced that Christians were losing the war they waged in God's name.

Blessed Is the Name of the Government

With the failure of "Visible Sovereignty" and the exhausting Owyhee environment, Rushdoony's personal correspondence from the late 1940s took on a deeply pessimistic, even elegiac, tone. In a letter to Williams, Rushdoony described his emotional state as "distressed and disturbed."[63] He located "the source of my distress" in a simple question: "Where is the Church, that I might find it?" Throughout the mid-1940s, this concern for the location of the church in Western culture emerged as the central problem that Rushdoony would devote the rest of his ministry to addressing. How, he began to wonder, might one revitalize Western Christendom so that it could not only regenerate the souls of the Indians of Owyhee but also the world as a whole? The church, he believed, was rotting from the inside out. So, rather than proselytize a dead culture with the message of a dying church, Rushdoony began looking for ways to rebuild the church so that it might one day regenerate the entire world. And through this godly work, Rushdoony might also give renewed purpose to his diminished station in life.

Before Rushdoony settled on the need for the global regeneration of humanity, he first had to account for the place of the church on the Duck Valley Indian Reservation. Hinting at his later vision for the global triumph of Christ, Rushdoony consistently conflated the general state of Christendom and the failure of the church with his activities at the mission. He identified the rise of the modern secular state and the development of modernist theology as the two major factors undermining the church in Owyhee. He believed that the unchecked rise of the state had eroded the Christian foundations of the American republic, while a misguided theological modernism rendered American churches incapable of combating the threat posed by the secular state. The Indians on the Duck Valley Reservation provided Rushdoony with a framework for understanding the cultural implications of statism and modern theology for all Americans. The state ruled the reservation: "[The state] is the giver of all things, the source of power, of land, and (having built a reservoir for irrigation here) even of water. . . . The government hospital delivers the children, and the government army taketh them away, and blessed is the name of the government each Memorial Day and Fourth of July."[64] If the federal state stood as the giver and taker of life, then it usurped the sovereignty of Christ. In governing men, the state denied them the freedom to govern themselves as Christians according to the laws of God. Although this was only a latent theme at this point in his career, Rushdoony was beginning by fits and starts to focus on the problem of the state and its relationship to the laws of God. Slowly, the question would come into focus: how do men govern themselves and others in a properly organized Christian society?

In summarizing the sorry state of the reservation, Rushdoony used the physical location of Owyhee—located in the heart of a long-dormant volcanic ridge—as synecdoche for the entire Western world: "Both Church and State are located at the base of an extinct volcano, a true symbol of their condition. Ichabod, the glory is departed. Both Church and State live on the dead embers of their true sovereignty and power while striving hungrily to gain visibility through bastard sources. So it is, but this outpost of the Church shall not do so."[65] Similarly, on more than one occasion, he linked the situation in Owyhee to the complete arc of Christian history. "In government men and Indians," Rushdoony wrote, "I have the full range of the problems of Church and State, and all the concerns of Church History. I am facing the problem in its concentrated form, so that rather than a romantic adventure, Owyhee is in every aspect a studied assault on a thousand and one problems confronting the Church of Christ."[66] Rushdoony saw his Owyhee mission as one moment in the timeless struggle between humanity's desire to exercise sovereignty independently of the kingship of Christ and the church's battle against this sin. This battle manifested itself in the two sides facing down one another at Owyhee. On one side stood the federal agents who claimed authority to rule all aspects of reservation life. On the other huddled a defeated and dominated race that saw nothing to admire in their conquerors. Instead, they turned to degenerate forms of ersatz salvation: peyote, booze, illicit sex, nature worship. Only Christ could mediate between these two groups and return the state to its biblically constrained limits while allowing Native Americans to encounter true salvation through the atoning sacrifice of Christ. This, for Rushdoony, was a microcosm of the human drama of Christianity.

In a 1949 article in the *Westminster Theological Journal*, Rushdoony pulled together his scattered observations on Owyhee and bundled them with his general reflections on Indian missions. He argued that the failure of the missions reflected a deeper crisis within Western Christendom.

> Hence Indian missions are of central relevance to the church. If contemporary Christianity has lost its relevance to the central problem of Indian life, it has lost its relevance to the developing problem of Western civilization. Crisis has then ceased to be its opportunity and becomes its defeat. It must be conceded this is already the case. The weakness of Indian missions is merely the symptom which indicates the church's ailment as well, while government policies simply communicate the contemporary failure of Western culture.[67]

For Rushdoony, his mission work became part of a much larger network of theological and cultural issues that not only pointed to modern Christianity's inability to proselytize, but it also exposed its failure to offer Christian alternatives to an all-powerful state determined to usurp the ability of men to govern as Christians first and as citizens second.

At Owyhee, Rushdoony gleaned an important lesson about the relative strengths and weaknesses of the Christian Gospel as he struggled to spread it across nearly unbridgeable cultural boundaries. He became convinced that Western Christendom was such a weak and ineffectual culture that even the populations it had previously subjugated did not respect it. "Hence the dilemma," he concluded. "Indian culture is dead, Western culture is dying, and the Indian lives on the dregs of both in abject spiritual poverty and degradation."[68] His article registered all of his major concerns of the late 1940s. From his personal pessimism—perhaps even depression—to his deep existential angst about the state of Christianity, the article was an accretion of nearly a decade of despair. But for all of the gloom shrouding this period of his life, Rushdoony also harbored a rare kind of ambition and a maddening work ethic. "First Owyhee, and then the world: such is my dream," he wrote to a friend shortly after arriving in Nevada. He quickly qualified this sentiment, noting: "In many respects, I am seriously handicapped here."[69] Regardless of the handicaps and troubles of Owyhee, the mission was an important step in Rushdoony's development. The harsh social and physical environment of the reservation exhausted the young minister, while the isolated location hampered his intellectual growth.

Every Thought Captive

Although many of Rushdoony's early Owyhee letters implied that Christianity was a spent cultural force, by the late 1940s and early 1950s, a new set of optimistic themes emerged in his letters. A chance encounter with a book precipitated his theological shift. In March 1946, while traveling back to Nevada from an extended trip in the East, Rushdoony stopped in a small Colorado town to visit another minister. During the visit, Rushdoony ran across a copy of Cornelius Van Til's *The New Modernism* (1949) in the minister's library.[70] Van Til was a professor at Westminster Theological Seminary, which Presbyterian theologian and churchman J. Gresham Machen founded as a conservative alternative to what he perceived as the liberal theological trends at Princeton Theological Seminary. Intrigued, Rushdoony thumbed through Van Til's book. Noting Rushdoony's interest, the minister said, "You want it? Take it."[71] Rushdoony did and began reading it on his return trip. In a train bustling with troops returning home from the war, Rushdoony hardly noticed the commotion around him as he consumed the book. "When I reached Denver," Rushdoony told an interviewer decades later, "I had to wait several hours in the railroad station. I just sat there and didn't take the time to go and eat. I was there five or six hours" reading Van Til's study.[72]

In Denver, the rapt Rushdoony read a dense, carefully argued rejection of the theology of European Protestant thinkers Karl Barth and Emil Brunner. The book would have been notable to Rushdoony because it was one of the only sustained critical works published in the United States on the theologies of Barth and Brunner for Reformed audiences.[73] But if the subject matter lured Rushdoony in, it was the theological project that hooked him. Today, Van Til's text is perhaps best known as the first book-length exposition of his presuppositional apologetics.[74] The presuppositional method developed in the text soon became a facet of Rushdoony's intellectual and theological project. As an apologetic method, presuppositionalism insists that the relationship between God and His creation provides an important foundation for reassessing the nature of human knowledge. In a nutshell, if God created the universe, then he also created the means for interpreting it. A presuppositional apologetic works by demonstrating that another philosophical system has no real foundation and is therefore either essentially meaningless or actually rests on Christian premises.[75] Either way, the result is the same: the Christian God is the source of knowledge. To try to think independently of God is not only impossible; it also is the ultimate human temptation that leads to sin in its very essence.

Rushdoony's chance encounter with *The New Modernism* precipitated his rapid departure from a pessimistic, existentially fraught post-Christian perspective toward a positive—albeit highly critical—view of the Reformed church's ability to offer an alternative to theological modernism and statism. After reading Van Til in March, Rushdoony immediately adopted Van Tillian themes and terminology in his April 1946 correspondence. In a letter to a Presbyterian Mission official, Rushdoony offered the first clear exposition of Van Tillian ideas without directly mentioning Van Til:

> I have been doing considerable studying since my coming here and am increasingly convinced that without a doubt our present day Biblical studies are grounded, not on sound scholarship but on philosophical presuppositions and are thus unrelated to fact. And those elements in the Church which do cling to Scripture do so without the sound study and scholarship it requires: hence the prevalence of the premillennial view which is, I believe, a misreading of both scripture and the Second coming.[76]

Instead, Rushdoony explained that the faithful look at scholarship with skepticism because it seems to deaden their encounter with God. "To most young men . . . scholarship seems to belong to doubt and ignorance to faith, and the fact that this equation seems to be true, superficially, indicates the tragedy of the situation."[77] Rushdoony believed Van Til rectified this tragic situation with a theological system that acknowledged that scholarship is an essentially religious activity. In short, Rushdoony had come to the traditional Calvinist perspective that knowing is the supreme act of being a fully realized Christian. Van Til further suggested that such knowledge is essentially political because it recognizes God's absolute sovereignty over His creation.

Reformed Theology

Behind Rushdoony's enthusiastic reception of Van Til's text lay nearly half a century of institutional and theological infighting in American Presbyterianism. The American tradition of Presbyterianism developed from the complex interaction of various strains of Swiss, French, Scottish, Irish, and English Reformed theology. With their emphasis on first "reforming" the institution of the Roman church and then addressing perceived shortcomings in other Protestant factions, Reformed theologians—no matter however complex or seemingly arcane the issues they addressed—traditionally understood their theology as practical and grounded in the nitty-gritty of anthropological realism.[78]

As historians Randall Balmer and John R. Fitzmier have noted, since the writings of Calvin, Zwingli, and many other sixteenth-century theologians, "Reform divines have acknowledged the essential connection between humanity's quest for the knowledge of God and its quest for the knowledge of itself. For them, the study of the divine leads to human self-knowledge, and, conversely, the study of humanity leads to the contemplation, if not saving knowledge, of the divine."[79] This Reformed theological tradition and the churches that nurtured it have had a profound influence on American cultural and intellectual history. From its critical relationship to the political and religious motivations of many of the European populations that settled New England, the Middle Colonies, and other parts of the American frontier—notably Dutch immigrants in the upper Midwest—to its influence in twentieth-century debates related to the relationship between science and religion, many of the major intellectual trends in the United States bear witness to the long legacy of Reformed theological traditions in the American mind.

During the first half of the twentieth century, the intellectual significance of Reformed theology was particularly apparent as it played a pivotal role in forming the thinking of preachers, public intellectuals, and parishioners regarding a host of high-profile cultural lodestones. Most significant to Rushdoony's reception of Van Til were the struggles between the so-called liberals and conservatives. These two sides battled over the use of modern literary theories to interpret the Bible and the influence of Darwinian evolutionary theory to explain human origins. With the theologically conservative fundamentalists arrayed on one side and the liberal Modernists on the other, liberal minister Harry Emerson Fosdick famously wondered why the "great mass of new knowledge" revealed by modern science should not lead to "strange new movements in Christian thought."[80] Meanwhile, the conservative fundamentalist J. Gresham Machen readily conceded the point but noted that these "strange new movements" in thought amounted to a new religion and not orthodox Christianity.[81]

By following his father into the mainline Presbyterian Church in the United States of America (PCUSA), Rushdoony entered a denomination divided by the fundamentalist/modernist controversy. As Rushdoony came of age during the 1920s, the PCUSA had become one of the primary sites in what historian Barry Hankins has termed the first "culture war" of the twentieth century between theologically conservative elements in the church and liberalizers and reformers determined to drag American Christianity into the twentieth century.[82] While Y. K. Rushdoony cared little for these battles, preferring instead to focus his ministerial energies on his exiled Armenian flock, the younger Rushdoony wanted to jump headlong into these theological and institutional fights. Van Til's book had such a jarring effect on Rushdoony's thinking because it marked a radical departure from thinkers whom Rushdoony had read at PSR and encountered in conversations with his peers in the American Presbyterian and Reformed communities. *The New Modernism* provided a model for engaging in such intellectual struggles while also affirming the romantic, idealist conception of theology that Rushdoony inherited from Ernst Kantorowicz.

Knowledge and Being

Van Til's book manifested many of the significant intellectual and institutional struggles taking place within American Presbyterianism during the first half of the twentieth century. In 1929, after nearly a decade of infighting between theological fundamentalists and modernists, Princeton Theological Seminary, the primary institutional force behind Reformed theology in the United States, reorganized its board of trustees in an effort to build unity and compromise between the various factions. When the reorganized board seated two modernists who signed the liberal 1923 Auburn Affirmation, J. Gresham Machen and four other faculty members—including Van Til—resigned in protest.[83] Machen organized Westminster Theological Seminary to carry on the traditions of the "Old" Princeton theology and asked Van Til to fill its apologetics chair.[84]

Although hired to continue "Old" Princeton's mission, Van Til developed a new apologetic method. His method marked a sharp break from the then-dominant Reformed tradition of evidentialist apologetics.[85] Evidentialist apologetics grew out of the Scottish common-sense philosophical tradition that American intellectuals adopted and adapted during the eighteenth and nineteenth centuries.[86] According to historian Mark A. Noll, American evangelicals generally highlighted three key but simplified aspects of common sense philosophy. First, American evangelicals traditionally emphasized an empiricist theory of knowledge that asserted: "[O]ur perceptions reveal the world pretty much as it is."[87] Second, they argued that human beings can infer certain ethical standards from their nature, thus suggesting a normative anthropological project that assumes universal standards for moral behavior.[88] Finally, evidentialists advanced their intellectual and anthropological project through a vaguely Newtonian scientific methodology that, according to Noll, "encouraged evangelicals to believe that the end product of theology was a system of certain truths, grounded on careful induction from simple facts, eschewing hypothetical flights of fancy, and providing a universal and unvarying picture of God and his ways."[89]

Van Til broke with this centuries-long tradition in American Protestantism to offer what he believed to be the restoration of a proper Calvinist epistemology, or theory of knowledge. Van Til, an immigrant from the Netherlands, was influenced by his Dutch Reformed heritage. Specifically, he adopted the teachings of nineteenth-century Dutch theologian and statesman Abraham Kuyper.[90] In the United States, Kuyper is remembered as the father of neo-Calvinism, a theological and social movement whose adherents view Calvinism as a comprehensive, coherent Christian worldview capable of resisting the social, cultural, and political advances of the Enlightenment and modern theology.[91] "Kuyper," according to Van Til's biographer, "insisted on the absolute separation, or 'antithesis,' between the Christian and the modern worldview that came to prominence in the French Revolution."[92] Kuyper encouraged Calvinists to draw sharp distinctions "between Christian approaches to social issues and those supported by non-Christian or 'apostate' thought."[93] Only Christians, he argued, could be self-conscious. In fact, non-Christians could not think in a consistently non-Christian manner, because such a project would ultimately lead to utter meaninglessness. All meaning and knowledge for non-Christians was therefore "borrowed" from the non-Christian's dull apprehension of King Jesus.

Van Til embraced Kuyper's concept of the antithesis and rigorously developed it through his wide-ranging engagement with modern continental philosophy. The thinking of the eighteenth-century German philosopher Immanuel Kant especially influenced the young theologian. Kant argued that pure, unmediated empirical observation is not sufficient for comprehending the world. Instead, empirical knowledge is structured by preexisting mental categories that shape human reasoning. By the early twentieth century, Kant's ideas had challenged most epistemological philosophies and influenced academic theology. Careful engagement with Kant and his critics convinced Van Til that common-sense evidentialism and its related apologetic methods were at best naïve and, at worst, leaving conservative Christians unequipped for philosophical battle in the twentieth century. In response to Kant's ideas, Van Til developed his "pioneering insight" into the nature of Christian apologetics. He concluded that the "given presupposi-

Cornelius Van Til (1895–1987), professor of theology and apologetics, teaching in 1965 at Westminster Theological Seminary. On the chalkboard is Van Til's famous circle diagram of a "theocentric" conception of the universe. The big circle depicts God, while the smaller circle represents His creation. The circles do not touch, leaving "no ontological bridge" between the two. One flimsy line overlaps the perimeters of each loop, forming a narrow but perceptible bridge of grace between the Creator and His created. Courtesy of Montgomery Library, Westminster Theological Seminary.

tions of any philosophical position predetermined and governed much of its later outworking."[94] This focus on "presuppositions" over evidence ultimately became the distinguishing characteristic of Van Til's "presuppositional" apologetic method.

By engaging philosophical theories of knowledge more directly than many of this conservative Reformed peers, Van Til recognized that modern thought "is largely preoccupied with the theory of knowledge"; therefore, he surmised that Christians needed to meticulously expound how their theory of knowledge differed from non-Christian systems of thought. This led him to appropriate aspects of Kantian thought to expand Kuyper's concept of the antithesis. By adopting and developing the antithesis of Dutch Reformed Calvinism, Van Til declared war on any system of thought that did not accept the authoritarian prescriptions of Scripture as its own a priori foundation for knowledge. Within the context of the early twentieth-century fundamentalist/modernist controversy, Van Til's ideas made him one of the most radical thinkers in the fundamentalist camp. He insisted that traditional common-sense empiricism presumed the autonomy of a human being's intellect in relation to God. This presumption undermined the Calvinist emphasis on the absolute sovereignty of God over all aspects of humanity—including thought. Building on this point, Van Til insisted that human beings could not think a single thought independently of God.

This theory of knowledge rested on Van Til's understanding of the nature of the Christian God. Van Til argued that the Holy Trinity—Father, Son, and Holy Spirit—is the only proper starting point for understanding reality; therefore, being and knowing—ontology and epistemology, in philosophical terms—are fundamentally interrelated in Van Til's apologetic strategy. Van Til believed that Christianity, rightly understood, posited a two-layer theory of reality.[95] The being and nature of the first layer, God, is "infinite, eternal, and unchangeable."[96] The second layer is the created universe, which is finite, temporal, and constantly changing.[97] Between creator and created, there is an insurmountable gulf that cannot be bridged by any willful means of a created being. Instead, the only bond between God and His creation is grace. The recognition of this chasm between God and creation is, in Van Til's mind, the essential presupposition upon which orthodox Christianity must be founded. Christians must presuppose this separation in order to correctly apprehend the nature of God and creation. Any attempt to collapse God into creation or to subsume creation into the nature of God is a false, non-Christian presupposition.

Sin and Sovereignty

Although the philosophical foundations of Van Til's apologetic method may read like abstract theological sophistry, to the Owyhee-bound Rushdoony, they were simultaneously a revelation and a revolution. Presuppositional-ism, he reckoned, had immediate implications for his place as a missionary seeking to unite two seemingly unbridgeable civilizations. It also gave him a renewed sense of hope: change a Christian's intellectual presuppositions and you could change the church. Here were the seeds of the answer to his question, "Where is the Church?" The answer lay on a presuppositional foundation of educational reform that would empower Christians to capture and re-Christianize any and all social institutions that threatened to undermine a Christian educational system. By 1947 Rushdoony began encouraging his friends to read *The New Modernism*, and by the early 1950s, Rushdoony dropped the last vestiges of his liberal PSR education to embrace a systematic Reformed perspective based on Van Til's presuppositional apologetics. Further, during this period, Rushdoony recognized in Van Til's ideas the hope for a wide-ranging American cultural renewal rooted in epistemological self-awareness. By developing this focus on knowledge and its origins, Rushdoony launched his earliest attacks on non-Christian education.

To understand why Rushdoony believed that Van Til's insights could change the world, it is essential to understand how they related to the Christian concepts of sin and sovereignty. Van Til's philosophy begins with the presupposition that God is the origin of all creation. Since "all aspects" of the universe are "equally created" by a sovereign God, then "no one aspect of reality may be regarded as more ultimate than another. Thus the created *one and many* may in this respect be said to be equal to one another; they are equally derived and equally dependent upon God, who sustains them both."[98] Humanity can never have exhaustive knowledge of this creation by attempting to reduce one aspect of nature to another or by trying to subsume the particulars of nature into an abstract totality. Instead, as theologian and former Van Til student John M. Frame summarized, "Insofar as we can know the world, it is because [God] gives us revelation and the ability to repeat his thoughts on an analogical, finite level. And insofar as we cannot know the world, we can trust that the world is nevertheless an intelligible whole. Things that are mysterious to us do not spring from an ultimate chaos or meaninglessness; they spring, rather, from the wonderful riches of God's thought, which transcends our understanding."[99] The plurality and unity of creation are an analogue for the plurality and unity of the Trinity. Just as God can no more be reduced to a single person of the Trinity, no aspect of nature can be reduced to another. Similarly, just as the persons of the Trinity only have meaning in relation to one another, so too do all aspects of nature.

For Rushdoony, Van Til's great revolution was his insistence that human beings sin when they attempt to apprehend reality independently of God's revelation without acknowledging our finite, subordinate relationship to God. As Van Til outlined, God gave Adam and Eve—humanity's "first parents"—a prescriptive path "marked by love and obedience" if they "led their lives in the direction he indicated to them."[100] Rather than follow this path, they instead listened to Satan, who told them "how free he had become since declaring his independence of God." Van Til's Satan explained to Adam and Eve that "[t]o be self-determining . . . man must surely be able to decide the 'nature of the good'—regardless of what God says about it." Adam, after listening carefully to Satan's appeal and weighing it against God's plan, concluded: "You are right Satan, I must first decide whether such a God as often speaks to us (1) knows what the 'good' for us is, (2) controls history so that he can determine what will happen if we disobey him, and (3) has the right to demand obedience from us. After I decide these issues, and if the answer is 'yes,' then I shall obey him. Certainly not before."[101] While one might wonder exactly how Van Til grasped Adam's thought process in all of its logical rigor, most Christians agree on what happened next: Adam and Eve sinned precisely because they succumbed to Satan's temptation to "be as gods, knowing good from evil." At that precise moment, human beings asserted the primacy of their intellect over that of God's.

A desire to reason independently from God's authority precipitated humanity's fall into sin. Accordingly, humanity's pretense to independent knowledge became a matter of rebellion against God's plan because "[d]eep down in his mind every man knows that he is the creature of God and responsible to God. Every man, at bottom, knows that he is a covenant-breaker. But every man acts and talks as though this were not so."[102] For human beings, the image of thought must be God's Word. As historian Wesley A. Roberts noted in his summary of Van Til's philosophy, "Van Til insists that all knowledge that any finite creature would have must rest upon the revelation of God. Thus the knowledge that we have of the simplest objects of the physical universe is based upon the revelation of God."[103] Scripture is the objective yardstick by which all human thought must be measured, and, when found lacking, by which it must be disciplined. In Van Til's words, "if man is not autonomous . . . then man should subordinate his reason to the Scriptures and seek in the light of it to interpret his experience."[104] Frame clarifies this point by observing, "revelation in the form of scripture governs our interpretation of experience,"[105] but in turn, humans learn of this revelation by experiencing it: "We learn about God by reading the Bible . . . and by observing his handiwork in creation and in ourselves. That is, we receive revelation through experience."[106] Thus, for Van Til, Scripture authorizes human experience and constitutes it—whether we recognize it or not.[107]

From his isolated perch in Nevada, Rushdoony immediately realized that Van Til's system would allow him to rewire the relationship between his oppressed charges and the state that dominated them. Since thinking is an explicitly religious activity, Rushdoony reasoned that this knowledge had political implications: thinking is a matter of kingship, power, rebellion, and, in the final analysis, warfare. Either human thought recognizes God's sovereignty, or it does not. There is no middle ground, no compromise. Consequently, Rushdoony embraced Van Til's theology partly because of its political implications: Van Til's antithesis between Christian and non-

Christian forms of knowing justified educational separatism and secession as strategies for the political reformation of a rapidly changing American republic. Van Til's antithesis posited a war between those who think God's thoughts after Him and those who do not. If Rushdoony could persuade Christians to reject any form of education that emphasized state sovereignty over God's sovereignty, then he could start a reform movement that would fundamentally reorganize all human relationships.

Conclusion: From Owyhee to the American Conservative Movement

Rushdoony developed this new educational project as he began looking for a pastorate that would reconnect him with the wider Presbyterian Church. During his time in Owyhee, he spent much of his effort cultivating relationships off the reservation. He wrote, lectured, and preached all over the West, and he even made frequent trips to the East Coast. Although committed to the reservation and his planned educational reforms, his flirtation with publishing and efforts to engage in academic theology pointed to his loftier ambitions. Rushdoony believed that the grand battles between modernists and fundamentalists had been settled prematurely and unsatisfactorily. He wanted to remake American Presbyterianism, but he knew he could not do it in Owyhee. After some searching, Rushdoony accepted a call to the pastorate of Trinity Presbyterian Church in Santa Cruz, California, in May 1952.[108] The 300-member church was affiliated with the mainline PCUSA.[109]

The isolation of Owyhee and the transition back to the city took its toll on Rushdoony's personal and professional life. On a personal level, Rousas and Arda, now both in their late thirties with six children, struggled to keep their marriage together. Arda left no surviving record of her time spent with Rousas, and he wrote very little about their relationship as they transitioned from the reservation to Santa Cruz. In fact, their relationship seems to have been mostly happy until 1956. After moving to Santa Cruz, Rushdoony frequently noted little anecdotes involving his children—Ronny playing in the school band, family trips to see fireworks on July 4, Sharon catching caterpillars with Martha, the birth of Mark Rousas—and mentioned Arda as he recounted the quotidian details of their domestic life.[110]

Beginning in late 1956, Rushdoony's happy notes about family life gave way to a series of increasingly disconcerted journal entries documenting Arda's behavior. Arda—at least according to Rushdoony's account and subsequent church proceedings—underwent a severe and sudden psychological breakdown. Rushdoony recorded several incidents in which Arda lashed out at him verbally. On multiple occasions, she accused Rousas of infidelity and drug use.[111] She also insisted he was possessed by a demonic force.[112] Eventually, the accusations escalated into violence. Rushdoony recorded numerous instances in which Arda hit him, ripped off his suits, or physically assaulted him. In the early cases of violence, he indicated that he retreated to his study and barred the door.[113] As the abuse intensified, he called on church members to intervene.[114] Eventually, the church elders and Rushdoony decided to seek professional psychiatric intervention. After multiple evaluations, Arda was committed to Agnews State Mental Hospital in Santa Clara, California.[115] After her release from Agnews, she sued Rushdoony for divorce.[116]

Existing court records of the divorce make no reference to Arda's mental state and provide little information regarding the motivations for each party in the breakup. The Rushdoonys officially separated in 1957, and the court finalized their divorce in 1959. The initial settlement gave Rushdoony custody of their six children. The judge awarded Arda $1 per month of alimony.[117] In 1962 another ruling gave Arda custody of Ronald, Rebecca, and Joanna, the three oldest children, while the three youngest, Sharon, Martha, and Mark, remained with their father.[118] In court documents, Arda accused Rousas of "extreme cruelty" and claimed he "wrongly inflicted upon her grievous mental suffering."[119] Rushdoony, aside from his previous references to Arda's violent outbursts, stopped commenting on the divorce and remained silent on the matter.[120] Whatever the exact circumstances surrounding the divorce, it left lingering questions that Rushdoony refused to address publicly and that dogged him through much of his ministry.

Even as his personal life fell apart and his family fractured, Rushdoony began making fitful progress toward developing his professional career as a writer, lecturer, and churchman. Through his travels away from the mission, Rushdoony started building connections with a rogue's gallery of political activists concentrated in California and on the East Coast. In the early 1950s, he met with representatives from Spiritual Mobilization (SM) and the William Volker Charities Fund, both based in California, along with the Foundation for Economic Education (FEE), located in New York State. These three organizations represented the vanguard of a movement working to link free-market economic policies with basic Christian principles. They insisted that centralized state control of the economy was leading the United States to ruin.

Rushdoony's time on the Duck Valley Indian Reservation had led him to the same conclusion. Because of his own personal history as a descendant of an oppressed ethnic minority and his work with Native Americans who were less than a generation removed from forced relocation and genocide, Rushdoony was particularly sensitive to trends in governance that could lead to the intensification of ethnic and religious persecution. At Berkeley, he learned from Ernst H. Kantorowicz that ancient Christian theology had a profound influence on the political and social realities of modern Western civilization. His time on the reservation convinced him that modern Christianity needed to relearn this lesson because it had abdicated its responsibility to address the very problems of political theology that it had bequeathed to the modern world. The Paiutes and Shoshones had lost respect not only for their own history but also for the religion of the culture that had conquered them. At the same time, Rushdoony watched with increasing alarm as postwar American society rushed to reject its God-given Christian liberty for government management of all sectors of human life.

When combined, Rushdoony's personal history, his education, and his missionary work led him to question the role the state plays in the lives of individual people. Further, he became increasingly concerned with Christianity's proper relationship to the state. His exposure to the writings of Cornelius Van Til convinced him that Christians in the United States could address these theological and political problems by adopting a self-conscious Christian epistemology. Only through a rigorously developed educational agenda rooted in a Calvinist criticism of modernity would Christians free themselves from the twin tyrannies of modern theology and oppressive statism.

In leaving Owyhee, Rushdoony set aside missionary work in favor of an urban pastorate and began building connections with a shadowy and amorphous network of midcentury American conservative activists, intellectuals, and educators. Building on his interconnected concerns of political theology, epistemological self-awareness, and antistatism, Rushdoony approached the blossoming conservative movement with a unique religious, political, and cultural agenda. His certainty and intellect impressed many of the businessmen and activists he encountered. By the beginning of the 1960s, Rushdoony found himself working with right-wing political activists who were building a new movement that was at once rooted in the traditional structures of American Christianity and yet fundamentally opposed to them.

CHAPTER TWO

The Anti-Everything Agenda

Sectarianism, Remnants, and the
Early American Conservative Movement

Conservatism . . . is . . . the political
secularization of the doctrine of original sin.
—PETER VIERECK, *Conservatism Revisited*, 81

For though thy people Israel be as the sand of the sea,
yet a remnant of them shall return: the consumption
decreed shall overflow with righteousness.
—Isaiah 10:22 (King James Version)

On August 10, 1964, a staffer at the William Volker Company handed Federal Bureau of Investigation special agent Warren W. Richmond a copy of Rousas John Rushdoony's personnel file. The FBI had taken a keen interest in Rushdoony. He was ethnically Armenian, and his family—displaced by World War I—had escaped through Czarist Russia and sought refuge in the United States. Rushdoony subscribed to *People's World*, a communist daily. He received mailings from the Christian Knights of the Ku Klux Klan.[1] He claimed to be a preacher and public lecturer.

The FBI liked keeping tabs on figures like Rushdoony because, as one memorandum put it, they might be one of the many "'illegal' agents" dispatched by "Soviet intelligence services" to "establish themselves as legitimate Americans by obtaining genuine documents."[2] Rushdoony's file was only one of more than 500,000 domestic intelligence dossiers the FBI collected from 1960 to 1974.[3] During this period, the bureau expanded its domestic surveillance beyond tracking down potential Soviet agents to investigate a wider array of domestic targets ranging from the Ku Klux Klan to civil rights leaders. In this era of increasing domestic tensions, the metastasizing federal bureaucracy began to fear its own citizens as much as foreign agents. Citizens with unusual ethnic backgrounds, tenuous connections to the Klan, novel political affiliations, and strange career choices often drew the FBI's attention.[4] Rushdoony combined all four features into an interesting bundle.

The William Volker Company's personnel file revealed Rushdoony's educational background and his ties to American Presbyterianism. Further investigation by FBI special agent Orville N. Molmen revealed that Rushdoony had a spotless credit record. Also, Rushdoony had recently lectured at the Santa Cruz Kiwanis Club on "The Public and Law Enforcement." An unnamed source at the Santa Cruz sheriff's office informed Agent Molmen that "it was a good talk generally in favor of law enforcement. Reverend Rushdoony commented that the Communist[s] were trying their best to get the public against law enforcement and public apathy toward law enforcement was playing into the hands of the Communists."[5] The only blemish on Rushdoony's record seemed to be a divorce from his first wife, who had "experienced severe mental illness"—an unfortunate but understandable outcome given the circumstances, the file implied. Content with Rushdoony's American *bono fides*, the agents concluded that "the identity of this Subject is satisfactorily resolved and no further action is contemplated by this office."[6]

While the FBI dutifully vetted Rushdoony's status as a citizen, Rushdoony was undergoing a different kind of vetting within the structures of American conservatism. After leaving his Owyhee mission in 1952, Rushdoony began a circuitous trek through the coalescing institutions of the conservative and libertarian movements in the United States. In the early 1950s, both libertarianism and conservatism, as coherent political ideologies and cogent intellectual agendas, were in their most embryonic stages of development. Everything was up for grabs in these movements—including their religious identities and the very definitions of "conservative" and "liberty."[7] As intellectual historian George Nash noted, before 1945, "no articulate, coordinated, self-consciously conservative intellectual force existed in the United States."[8] Instead, Nash argued that the few intellectuals and activists who today might be retrospectively labeled "conservatives" or "libertarians" were little more than "scattered voices of protest, profoundly pessimistic about the future of their country."[9]

While Nash's thesis has come under scrutiny from historians who note that there were indeed self-consciously conservative forces in the United States before 1945, his description does capture something of the spirit of how many intellectuals viewed themselves following the war.[10] The apparent postwar triumph of liberalism and the ascendancy of command economies left many conservative-minded, free-market intellectuals feeling embattled, disillusioned, and disconnected. This perception of failure and defeat left many business leaders and intellectuals across the United States scrambling to find what they conceptualized as a "Remnant" of right-thinking individualists dedicated to resisting the rise of modern centralized state bureaucracies, or "statism" in the parlance of the midcentury. Eventually, this self-styled Remnant coalesced into the networks of America's elite postwar conservative establishments in the form of think tanks, colleges, and private nonprofit operations of all descriptions.

From his Santa Cruz pulpit, Rushdoony watched as this emerging conservative infrastructure came together in Southern California. The Golden State had seen a large wave of immigration during the Depression years and massive spending from the public sector—most notably, in the form of defense contractors—following World War II. These demographic changes, coupled with a postwar housing and economic boom, brought big business to the forefront of California culture. No longer isolated in Nevada, Rushdoony set about building relationships with some of the most powerful and wealthy California-based benefactors bankrolling the production of "conservative" ideas. He reached out to like-minded business leaders and activists with his unique Christian vision of a world reordered by a specific model of Protestant education.

Initially, Rushdoony found many supporters fascinated by his vision, but as his reputation grew and his potential allies became more familiar with his religious views, many grew uneasy. As one ally-turned-critic fumed, Rushdoony was "an extreme right-winger" who stood against everyone and anything that failed to acknowledge his narrow, sectarian vision of Christian regeneration.[11] With the very categories of "conservative" and "libertarian" up for grabs, even the "extreme right-wingers" mattered as much as the "moderates" or "mainstreamers" because oppositional self-definition would constitute the contours of the developing movement.

Who was Rousas John Rushdoony? Was he an extreme right-winger? A religious zealot? A sectarian, anti-Catholic bigot? Or was he, as he described himself, a *true conservative* struggling to purify a faltering movement willing to sell its soul to a bland, inconsistent form of Christianity? In the 1950s and 1960s, all of these positions were intellectual battlegrounds over which much sweat and ink were spilled. Many powerful activists and business leaders on the emerging right wanted to build a big-tent movement organized around "traditional" Judeo-Christian American values, individual liberty under a constitutional order, and anticommunism. Others, such as Rushdoony, longed for a much smaller movement built on ideological and religious purity. To the winners of this fight over the size and inclusive scope of the movement would go intellectual and organizational legitimacy, and to the losers, political and institutional exile.

Spiritual Mobilization

Rushdoony's path out of Owyhee was paved by the rise of the infrastructure of the American conservative movement. As Rushdoony rallied to his own self-styled banner of Christian self-awareness, an analogous trend was percolating within the elite social circles of America's oligarchs. This movement was founded on a desire to make Americans aware of the implications of their national traditions, but the focus was primarily economic and political, not religious. Influential business titans from General Motors, the DuPont Company, and innumerable smaller corporations and firms cultivated an environment of experimentation, improvisation, and the eclectic free play of multiple religious perspectives—secular and spiritual; theologically liberal and conservative; Catholic, Protestant, and Jewish; heterodox and orthodox.[12] At its base, this movement worked to equip Americans to defend the market economy with a generically Christianized biblical rhetoric and helped capitalists understand that their profits were, in fact, Christ's business. In this complex milieu, simplified theology and muscular capitalism merged, melded, and disintegrated, providing a rich environment for enterprising, thoughtful, and synthetically minded intellectual and religious leaders. Not surprisingly, Rushdoony thrived in this context.

Rushdoony's association with religiously inflected probusiness advocates developed on the heels of nearly two decades of cooperation between religious and business leaders. During the 1930s and early 1940s, a wide variety of business, intellectual, and religious interests formed a loose coalition of institutions to attack President Franklin D. Roosevelt's New Deal policies. Groups ranging from the American Liberty League and the National Association of Manufacturers to protolibertarian, antiwar isolationists who would eventually form the America First Committee warned that FDR's economic policies and clear trend toward interventionism in Europe threatened to drag America closer and closer to a socialized welfare state.[13] Those who emphasized the sovereignty of the individual citizen-subject, resistance to a centralized bureaucracy, and the benefits of unfettered free-market capitalism eventually formed the components of the conservative and libertarian movements of the mid- and late twentieth century. In the 1940s, these anti–New Deal forces built alliances with Protestant religious leaders determined to resist "socialistic" tendencies within the church. The discursive contours of this midcentury project influenced several generations of American Christians and helped create a political and religious environment in which it has become common sense to suggest that theologically conservative Christians are also economically and politically conservative. The revolt against the New Deal succeeded in creating an intellectual foundation for a small cadre of thinkers and activists who were eager to reinterpret capitalism in terms of Christ's Gospel.

Although many organizations were formed to address these concerns, Mobilization for Spiritual Ideals played an especially important role in the Southern California context. Founded in 1935 by Congregational minister Rev. James Fifield of Chicago, Mobilization for Spiritual Ideals became a primary clearinghouse for probusiness religious material through printed media such as its widely distributed journal, *Faith and Freedom*. Beyond publishing and mass mailings, the organization also served an important networking function. It brought together religious leaders ranging from such well-known national figures as Norman Vincent Peale, author of the immensely popular *The Power of Positive Thinking* (1952), to minor regional actors like Rushdoony.[14] Popularly known as Spiritual Mobilization (SM), Fifield's operation earned the fiscal and advisory support of such anti–New Deal philanthropists as J. Howard Pew of Sun Oil Company, Jasper Crane of DuPont, Southern California Edison chairman William C. Mullendore, B. E. Hutchinson of Chrysler, and department-store mogul J. C. Penney.[15]

Fifield and his financial backers made their chief target the Social Gospel, which intellectual historian David A. Hollinger has succinctly defined as "a broad movement of American Protestants seeking, in the name of religious duty, to reform society along the lines of the ethics of Jesus."[16] Like many Americans in the Progressive Era, a period of religiously motivated social reform that stretched from the late 1800s to World War I, the Social Gospelers believed that government regulation could change America for the better by changing the nation's degenerate and dangerous social environment. Rooted in the postmillennial expectations of the late nineteenth century, optimistic reformers focused their attention on everything from temperance and hygiene to poverty and birth control.

Although the Social Gospel lost much of its driving dynamism following World War I, popular and clerical interest in the tradition lingered until the Great Depression of the 1930s reignited some commitment to (and much criticism of) the movement's underlying theological concepts. While the movement did not experience a full-fledged rebirth during the Depression, its renewed influence among some clergy in mainline denominations troubled business leaders and probusiness Protestant clergy such as Fifield. Facing the daunting task of resisting nearly five decades of entrenched Protestant teaching and the harsh reality of the Depression, Fifield sought to reach preachers and laypeople eager to criticize the massive redistribution of wealth they saw in President Roosevelt's New Deal.

Spiritual Mobilization made a simplistic but effective appeal. American clergy needed to start preaching the eighth commandment: "Thou shalt not steal." In this commandment, Fifield and his supporters believed they found the biblical basis for private property and a divine limit to the government's ability to redistribute wealth, tax, and otherwise impede commerce.[17] SM identified itself as an explicitly "libertarian" organization; its flagship magazine, *Faith and Freedom*, beginning in its fifth volume (1953), proclaimed itself "a voice of the libertarian—persistently recommending the religious philosophy of limited government inherent in the Declaration of Independence. The chief intent of the libertarian is . . . the further discovery and application of the Creator's changeless principles in a changing world."[18] With heavy subsidies from wealthy backers, Fifield built an organization of nearly 17,000 clerical representatives from "all faiths" to undermine the "present-day Goliath, the totalitarian state."[19] SM argued that clergy and laity needed to focus on the spiritual causes of poverty rather than on the social and political programs advocated by secular social reformers in Washington and the recently resurgent advocates of the Social Gospel.[20] "Man," SM's founding *Credo* insisted, "being created free as a child of God, has certain inalienable rights and responsibilities: the state must not be permitted to usurp them; it is the duty of the church to help protect them."[21] The New Deal and the later conflicts with the Nazis and the Soviets were manifestations of humankind's rejection of God's grace for the false salvation of a centralized bureaucracy. An all-powerful bureaucracy, SM warned, usurped the "Christian principle of love" and replaced it with the "collectivist principle of compulsion."[22]

At Spiritual Mobilization's peak in the mid-1950s, its Christ-centered free-market ideas reached nearly 50,000 pastors and ministers via *Faith and Freedom*.[23] Many of the publication's subscribers used its stories and reporting in sermons and in public outreach.[24] Under the dynamic leadership of James C. Ingebretsen, a Los Angeles–based attorney and former Latter-day Saint, and editor William Johnson, *Faith and Freedom* published the rhetorical flare of such libertarian luminaries as the Congregationalist minister Edmund A. Opitz, the Austrian economist Ludwig von Mises, and the atheist anarcholibertarian Murray Rothbard.[25] Many issues featured the writings of British writer and philosopher Gerald Heard, who was the confidant and spiritual guru of popular novelist Aldous Huxley and an early LSD enthusiast.[26] More often than not, the publication's self-identified libertarian authors completely avoided any discussion of religion in their articles. In spite of—or perhaps, precisely because of—the journal's freewheeling spiritual eclecticism, *Faith and Freedom*'s provocative journalism moved many pastors to embrace SM's antitax, noninterventionist, antistatist religio-economic model. Fifield's organization helped a generation of politically and economically (although not necessarily theologically) conservative clergy to find an alternative to the Social Gospel, the New Deal, and communism that resonated with their traditional values, probusiness sympathies, and Christian faith. SM's permissive, ecumenical brand of pop theologizing appropriated aspects of Norman Vincent Peale's popular midcentury positive-thinking, "mind-cure" prosperity gospel and melded it effortlessly with an antisocialist, procapitalist vision.[27]

A Tendency toward Rigidity

While in Owyhee, Rushdoony began receiving *Faith and Freedom* and reading it with interest. When its editor, Johnson, offered Rushdoony an opportunity to review the publication, he responded with an effusive note. He cited his predisposition toward "any publication which takes the stand yours does," specifically noting its support of private property and free enterprise as his principal points of agreement.[28] In his letter, Rushdoony noted that many clergy with whom he had spoken regarding *Faith and Freedom* rarely attacked its merits but instead denounced its "tendency toward rigidity" in its economic and political positions.[29] *Faith and Freedom* insisted that clergy see government as a problem, not a solution. Rushdoony shared this sentiment and eventually contributed articles to *Faith and Freedom* that outlined the ways in which government intervention on Indian reservations destroyed Native American culture.[30]

Aside from its rigid tendency regarding economic issues, Rushdoony's letter to Johnson also noted that, in some important ways, the magazine did not go far enough on many issues. As a foreshadowing of fights to come, Rushdoony argued that *Faith and Freedom* needed to attack the Christian church as a whole, observing, as was his wont, that it was not Calvinist enough. On the former issue, Rushdoony lamented *Faith and Freedom*'s timidity in directly accusing various denominations of hypocrisy on economic matters, warning that the chief danger to Americans was "the lack of an independent church press," which "has crippled the cause of freedom."[31] On the issue of Calvinism, Rushdoony argued that "the American republic was the product of two streams of thought, classical liberalism . . . and Calvinism."[32] *Faith and Freedom* ably embodied the first stream of thought, Rushdoony claimed, "but the Calvinist objection [to collectivism and statism] needs stating also."[33] In short, for Rushdoony, the publication was correctly rigid on economic issues but flaccid and promiscuous in its theological orientation.

Rushdoony's laudatory, but nonetheless candid, comments must have caught someone's attention, because in July, SM invited him to attend a conference at Carleton College in Minnesota. The conference marked a major turning point in Rushdoony's ministry because it brought him into contact with some of the leading libertarian activists and organizers of the 1950s. At Carleton, Rushdoony met representatives from the William Volker Charities Fund, a secretive philanthropic charity, and the Foundation for Economic Education, a well-funded free-market advocacy organization. These, along with other contacts he made at the conference, embodied a vanguard of militantly probusiness activists all searching for religious ideas to support their economic convictions.

At Carleton College, Rushdoony circulated an idea for an independent newspaper aimed at conservative Presbyterian laypeople and pastors. The project grew out of his sectarian criticisms of *Faith and Freedom* and his missionary work at Owyhee. As he had indicated in his analysis of the importance of Fifield's periodical, Rushdoony believed that the lack of critical journalism within all major Protestant denominations imperiled the church. Further, as he explained to the participants at Carleton, his time as a missionary had convinced him that clergy could no longer effectively link the profound theological realities of Christianity with the lived reality of laity. Inspired by both the strengths and weaknesses of *Faith and Freedom*, Rushdoony proposed his own publication, the *Westminster Herald*, to attack mainline liberalism.

From the outset, Rushdoony's sectarian religious tendencies drove the proposed journalistic project. He dreamed of the *Herald* refighting battles long settled in theological circles: it would attack theological liberalism using the tools of Van Tillian presuppositional apologetics to educate Reformed Christians on the finer points of theological orthodoxy. As he talked about the *Herald* to the other Carleton conference attendees, Rushdoony warned that ecumenism and liberal theology must be abandoned "because it is basically a body of sentimentally held and conflicting ideas. It is naive syncretism."[34]

Starting a Dogfight in the Presbyterian Church (U.S.A.)

When Rushdoony pitched his new journalistic endeavor to the Carleton participants, he did so to a rogues' gallery of secular libertarians and religious mavericks. Representatives from the William Volker Fund and the Foundation for Economic Education, along with Spiritual Mobilization's James C. Ingebretsen, were Rushdoony's most vocal supporters. On one hand, Herbert Cornuelle, a liaison officer at the Volker Fund, was sympathetic to Rushdoony's theological conservatism, explaining in a letter: "I am much intrigued by the idea outlined [at Carleton] regarding a publication for ministers and laymen in the Presbyterian Church."[35] While this hardly amounted to a ringing endorsement of Rushdoony's version of Reformed Christianity, Cornuelle did open avenues for support from other libertarians associated with the Volker Fund and the Foundation for Economic Education. Through the Volker Fund and FEE, Rushdoony met F. A. "Baldy" Harper, a former Cornell University marketing professor who had turned to probusiness activism and was interested in Rushdoony's religious ideas. Like Cornuelle, Harper stopped far short of offering financial support for the *Herald* project. Instead, he offered a stark warning, cautioning, "Your church 'hierarchy' will be grossly unpleased, in the main, with your project."[36] On the other hand, Ingebretsen, a Mormon turned Aldous Huxley and Gerald Heard disciple, made a halfhearted effort to stir up support for the *Herald* by pitching it to several of SM's major financial backers, including Southern California Edison chairman William C. Mullendore and former DuPont executive Jasper Crane, but he ultimately recognized that public support for the *Herald* would prove a distraction from his duties at SM.[37] "When it comes to raising money," he wrote apologetically, "my primary obligation and interest is in the direction of providing more resources for Spiritual Mobilization."[38] When Ingebretsen encouraged Rushdoony to reach out to wealthy donors such as Crane, Rushdoony dismissed the suggestion. "Frankly," Rushdoony wrote, "I don't feel too sure of the reactions of men like Crane, etc., who probably represent a vague, urban Presbyterianism. Their political and economic thinking is not derived from certain root and branch Presbyterian concepts, but from American liberalism."[39]

Rushdoony's search for support outside of the emerging libertarian and conservative networks converging at Carleton had better results. He found some support for his periodical among young clergy and laity from predominantly rural areas with connections to highly conservative institutions. In contrast to the "vague, urban Presbyterianism" of men like Crane, one nineteen-year-old student at South Carolina's Southern Presbyterian College wrote a long, excited note to Rushdoony regarding the *Herald*: "I have been investigating the possibilities of organizing the faithful in our Church in order to present a united witness for the Faith and combat the spiritual wickedness. I felt that the most urgent need was a militantly conservative journal, for only after the laymen are informed will there be any hope of restoring a believing leadership and pure clergy in our beloved Church."[40] Summarizing the sentiment of this letter and others like it, Rushdoony noted that "the interest is mainly among the young men"[41] who live "in the town and country areas, where Presbyterian thinking and tradition are strongest."[42] Not only did these rural supporters prove capable of resisting the siren song of theological modernism, but they also were anchored from the alluring pull of that other urban horror: communism. "Communists," Rushdoony reasoned, "are products of our rootless urban culture, [and] are rarely found in the rural areas."[43] Even if his rural supporters were inoculated against the twin threats of theological liberalism and messianic statism, they were neither wealthy nor intellectually sophisticated. It was a cruel catch-22 for the aspiring editor.

Not surprisingly, Rushdoony found far fewer supporters for the *Herald* in the church's hierarchy. Many conservatives in the Presbyterian Church familiar with the project tried to dissuade Rushdoony from moving forward with it. Warning of the disastrous consequences to both his ministry and his wallet, they argued that Rushdoony was picking a fight against a liberal establishment that would not be dislodged by a small publication like the one he proposed. In response to one such letter that registered support for Rushdoony's ideas but urged him to end the project, Rushdoony replied, "I thoroughly share your feeling about starting a dog fight in our denomination. I am by nature averse to such things, and it was only after long and prayerful consideration that I was ready to make this present step. . . . The fight is already being waged against us, and there is no evading that point. I do not want to respond in kind, but I do feel that our fundamental principles need re-asserting, that we need to put up our own candidates, and take up patient, Christian action."[44]

While Rushdoony vowed to keep fighting, his Presbyterian supporters urged him to understand the awkward position into which he was pulling them. They also warned of the dire personal consequences of his actions.

As he later observed in a forlorn note to Ingebretsen, "The more prominent ministers, like senators, will play safe until they feel that open support is politically expedient. I have received very enthusiastic letters from a number, written immediately on receipt of the *Westminster Herald*, promising help, but, as the days go by, they seem embarrassed by their outburst and find themselves 'too busy' to do much."[45] Most prominent men in the church recognized that Rushdoony was hankering for a dogfight, whether he admitted it or not. As a result, they gave their support privately and kept their wallets and mouths firmly closed.[46]

Although he failed to gain much support for the *Herald*, Rushdoony did succeed in raising his profile in the Presbyterian Church. His constant appeals for the publication made him a controversial regional figure among Presbyterian clergy on the West Coast. His connections to the Volker Fund, FEE, and SM also exacerbated tensions between regional presbytery officials and the more-conservative members of Rushdoony's congregation.[47]

Rushdoony's new notoriety made his life difficult as he transitioned in 1952 from Owyhee to a new pastorate at Santa Cruz's Trinity Presbyterian Church. The *Herald* troubled Rushdoony's tenure at Trinity from the outset. In spite of strong support from some in the church, many in the congregation disliked his activities outside of the church. Rushdoony angered many of the laity when he solicited their financial support for his struggling journalistic project and voiced his unwavering support of Van Til's controversial ideas.[48] Making matters worse, his controversial attacks on the PCUSA's hierarchy angered many in the region. Complaints about Rushdoony went all the way to the top of the PCUSA, with one former general-assembly moderator condemning Rushdoony as "devil-possessed." Rushdoony took the admonishment as a compliment, sardonically noting that the statement "indicates a return to conservative theology. . . . Perhaps having recognized the devil's existence, he may even admit God's!"[49]

In this fraught environment, things became much worse when "certain family problems," including his divorce from Arda, compelled Rushdoony to take a leave of absence.[50] In 1957 the church forced Rushdoony to take an involuntary leave and severely reduced his salary.[51] With Arda absent, Rushdoony had to raise six children alone. He relied on loyal members of the Trinity Church to provide free food and small cash gifts. Humiliated and impoverished, Rushdoony turned to his network of libertarian activists to seek work outside of the church.

During Rushdoony's leave, the presbytery appointed a substitute minister who was supposed to provide a counterbalance to Rushdoony's preaching and undermine his controversial parachurch activities. This step prompted a group of Rushdoony's fiercest loyalists to petition in 1958 for separation from the PCUSA. At least sixty-six members split from the mainline church and joined the Orthodox Presbyterian Church (OPC), a secessionist church founded by J. Gresham Machen.[52] They called Rushdoony to the newly created pastorate. He grew the new congregation steadily and was active in the intellectual community of the California Presbytery of the OPC.[53]

Although far more socially and theologically conservative than the mainline PCUSA, Rushdoony nonetheless found that his political and economic views did not fit well with the OPC either. When he produced a filmstrip criticizing the Federal Reserve System, several OPC pastors condemned his theological reasoning and asked the presbytery to investigate Rushdoony's political activities.[54] Exasperated by the open hostility to his message, Rushdoony confided in his journals: "Discouraged; all doors are closed to me. Does the Lord have any purpose for me, or are my beliefs concerning my calling only a false hope? Lord God, have mercy. Make me to know mine end that I may serve Thee."[55]

Rushdoony further complicated relations with the OPC when he married his second wife, Dorothy Barbara Kirkwood. The origins of his marriage to Dorothy are murky. According to a marriage license issued in West Virginia, Dorothy Barbara Ross married Thomas Gilbert Kirkwood on August 1, 1932.[56] They had one son, Thomas Jr., who was often in trouble and had several brushes with local law enforcement.[57] The Kirkwoods were prominent members of the Trinity Presbyterian Church and staunch supporters of Rushdoony. Thomas Sr. remained loyal to Rushdoony during the 1958 dissolution of the Trinity congregation and went on to serve as an elder in the new OPC congregation.[58] It is not clear what happened between Dorothy and Thomas, but Rousas and Dorothy wed in 1962.

That same year, Rushdoony's search for a full-time research career finally paid off when he landed a consulting and research position with the William Volker Charities Fund. In leaving his OPC pastorate, Rushdoony set aside work as a minister and missionary in favor of the shadowy and amorphous world of midcentury American conservative activism, research, and education.[59] With his alienation from the PCUSA and the OPC, Rushdoony needed to reach beyond the pulpit and disseminate his ideas through other channels. To reach this wider audience, Rushdoony exploited the connections he had made at the Carleton College conference to obtain the position at the Volker Fund. "The opportunity to study, write, and speak to the glory of God. Thanks be to God!" he gushed in his journals.[60]

Rushdoony had reason to be happy: with millions of dollars on hand, the Volker Fund was one of the wealthiest private foundations in the United States. Funding conservative and libertarian activities, it was also a highly secretive organization dedicated to remaking America's entire economic and educational infrastructure. When Rushdoony went to work for the fund in 1962, he intended to mold its charitable outreach with his Reformed vision.

Dedicated Minorities

The William Volker Charities Fund was the brainchild of William Volker, a wealthy Kansas City philanthropist who amassed a fortune selling window blinds and home furnishings throughout the Midwest. Born in Hanover, Germany, in 1859, Volker and his family immigrated to Chicago, where he started a home furnishings business before relocating to the less-competitive environment of Kansas City, Missouri.[61] As his wealth grew, Volker began giving away much of his fortune. Prompted by the Gospel of Matthew's admonition "do not your alms before men,"[62] Volker gave all of his gifts anonymously and insisted that recipients of his charity tell no one of his generosity. The practice eventually earned him the nickname "Mr. Anonymous" and, paradoxically, made him a legendary figure in Kansas City.[63] In 1932 he set aside millions of dollars into the William Volker Charities Fund, which operated on a model of "aggressive philanthropy" that "never waited for opportunities [for giving] to appear but went in search of them."[64] Under Volker's direct leadership, "aggressive philanthropy" meant giving money to community members in immediate need, supporting public welfare organizations, and donating to charities that could immediately affect the broader community. As he aged, Volker relinquished control of his company to his nephew, Harold W. Luhnow, and focused on his charitable activities.

When Volker passed away in 1947 at the age of eighty-eight, Luhnow took control of both the company and the charitable fund and started channeling a significant amount of the fund's $15 million away from its typical targets in Kansas City and toward a different one: intellectuals. Under Luhnow, "aggressive philanthropy" morphed into an ideological project favoring charities, educational programs, and academicians dedicated to Luhnow and his staff's hostility toward government-subsidized social programs and support for the proliferation of unregulated markets.

Even as Luhnow shifted the focus of giving, he continued Volker's habit of anonymous giving. He did so by channeling money through front organizations and by requiring grant beneficiaries to not disclose the source of their funding. Where Volker had justified his giving based on a vaguely "conservative" ideological model rooted in scriptural precedent and bootstrap individualism, Luhnow quietly developed the fund into a major supporter of antistatist intellectuals.

The fund was especially receptive to critics of secular education—particularly state-sponsored education at all levels. From 1952 to 1962, the fund gave away more than $7 million to fund educational research.[65] A significant portion of the money went to traditional outlets in higher education to fund building programs and institutional development. But much of it found its way to events like the Carleton College symposium, which the fund secretly subsidized for Spiritual Mobilization. These events were part of the Volker Fund's strategic goal of locating like-minded intellectuals who could be integrated into a wider network of conservative scholars and their supporting institutions. By connecting Rushdoony with any number of other scattered libertarian and conservative activists, the fund was building an elect "Remnant" of thinkers dedicated to undermining statism in the United States.

Remnants

Luhnow and his staff's hunt for a Remnant of antistatists coincided with a growing consensus that critics of big government and collectivist ideas needed to play a more active role in shaping the American intellectual landscape. The cultivation of a generation of self-conscious conservatives became the cause of many on the American Right during the 1950s and early 1960s. Unfortunately for Luhnow and many of the other business leaders seeking a sound theoretical foundation for their probusiness convictions, the intellectuals and activists they hoped to assemble were few and far between. In the 1940s and early 1950s, there was the collective sense that no discernible, coherent cohort of critical academics voicing conservative sentiments existed.[66]

In response to this perceived intellectual vacuum, under Luhnow's direction, the Volker Fund's staff members spent more and more of their time quietly and methodically locating and connecting intellectuals who shared a nominally libertarian or conservative philosophy. As Volker's staff sought out scholars, they began creating a network of thinkers and activists who, in most cases, had no idea that like-minded right-wingers existed. The fund's staff recognized that their mission was both unprecedented and trailblazing. "These efforts to spin webs of communication among this scattered band of ideological outliers, helping them find each other," reported libertarian journalist Brian Doherty, "thrilled Volker's employees, and they all remember it with great affection decades later."[67] Although they focused much of their efforts on recruiting free-market economists, they also financed the research of cultural conservatives who criticized collectivism and any form of state-sponsored coercion.[68]

The eschatological language of the Remnant adopted by Volker Fund staffers at midcentury grew from the contrarian writings of Albert Jay Nock.[69] A muckraker and anarchist-tinged essayist, Nock prophesied that an antistatist "Remnant" existed despite the nation's infatuation with socialism during the New Deal era.[70] In a 1936 essay, Nock imagined a comic conversation between God and the prophet Isaiah in which God commands Isaiah to tell the people (or masses) "what a worthless lot they are."[71] God then concludes: "The official class and their intelligentsia will turn up their noses at you and the masses will not listen. They will all keep on in their own ways until they carry everything down to destruction, and you will probably be lucky if you get out with your life."[72] The frustrated prophet then wonders aloud why God would send anyone on such a silly, pointless mission. In response, Nock's God tells Isaiah: "Ah . . . you do not get the point. There is a Remnant there that you know nothing about. They are obscure, unorganized, inarticulate, each one rubbing along as best he can. . . . Your job is to take care of the Remnant, so be off now and set about it."[73]

Nock's little parable highlighted a stark distinction between the "masses"— a homogenous "majority" within a society that is either too dumb or duped by the "intelligentsia" to see past the current state of things—and the Remnant, "who by force of intellect are able to apprehend these principles, and by force of character are able, at least measurably, to cleave to them."[74] Buried deep within Nock's Remnant philosophy of the 1940s was an antipathy to statism, which he identified as the enemy of the Remnant.[75] The masses yearn for state domination for a simple reason: whether rich or poor, the masses seek "the material gains accruing from control of the State's machinery" because it "is easier to seize wealth than to produce it."[76]

Less than a decade after Nock's death in 1945, a key group of journalists, authors, and activists embraced the Remnant concept to sanctify their self-perception as an embattled minority within U.S. culture. Novelist-philosopher Ayn Rand developed in *Atlas Shrugged* the apocalyptic tale of John Galt, who called a remnant of superfluous individualists to a secluded gulch in Colorado.[77] Ed Opitz organized the Remnant, a group of conservative and libertarian-inspired ministers who embodied Nock's "alien spirits." William F. Buckley Jr. explicitly took up Nockian rhetoric to describe *National Review* as "superfluous," "standing athwart history, yelling Stop, at a time when no one is inclined to do so."[78] Like his contemporaries, R. J. Rushdoony developed an explicitly religious notion of the Remnant designed to combat the ecumenical, secular, and even atheistic forms imagined by his peers on the Right. While Rand, Opitz, and Buckley tried to imagine more-or-less inclusive concepts of a Remnant, Rushdoony attacked his peers for being too open and insisted that the true Remnant needed to be much, much smaller.

Hard Core

If Nock had used Scripture to tell an eschatological parable about resisting the expanding New Deal state, then mid-twentieth-century conservative organizations such as the Volker Fund turned that fable into an organizing principle for a loosely affiliated network of intellectuals, business leaders, and activists. Ironically, for a tale drawn from Old Testament prophecy, Nock's vision and its organizational implementation were strikingly nonreligious. With the general concern for the Remnant circulating among Volker Fund beneficiaries, this opened a space for Rushdoony to offer a *Christianized* response to the problem of the fragmented nature of the developing conservative movement. If, as Rushdoony insisted, "basic to sound action is a sound faith," then he needed to convince his peers that Nock's Remnant was meaningless without its Christian foundation.[79] Rushdoony believed that the concept of the Remnant confused liberty as both a *truth* and *end* in and of itself. In contrast, since the ultimate truth is the reality of the Christian Trinity, then liberty must be a fruit of this truth and cannot be presupposed without Christ. It is in this distinction between liberty as *truth* and liberty as a *fruit* of the truth of Christ that Rushdoony located the uniqueness of his own social and political mission.

Rushdoony first developed this distinction between the truth and end of liberty while assessing the intellectual viability of F. A. "Baldy" Harper's Institute for Humane Studies (IHS). The IHS was an extension of the educational work of the Volker Fund and its search for the Remnant in academia. Harper took the search for the Remnant seriously. After coming to the Volker Fund in 1958, he proposed the IHS as a separate tax-exempt "institute devoted solely to promoting research and education in support of individual liberty across the full range of contemporary scholarly discipline."[80] Echoing Nock, Harper conceptualized these scholars as the "hard core" of liberty-loving intellectuals who, through their ideas, might induce broad societal changes. "Every successful social revolution," wrote Harper, "has apparently sprung from a philosophical well-spring of ideology."[81] In a series of meetings on the proposed IHS, early supporters of the institute similarly situated it within the Remnant paradigm. Economist Murray Rothbard, one of the IHS's most vocal supporters, told Harper: "An intellectual 'hard core' has been [the] well-spring of *every* intellectual and spiritual 'revolution' in history."[82] By converting money from wealthy donors into intellectual production, the IHS developed into a liaison between business interests and the academy capable of "speed[ing] up the development of pro–private property analysis" and "advanc[ing] the research and careers of scholars with whom we work, and all the time enjoy[ing] a growing influence on public opinion."[83]

Harper's vision of a "hard core" of academics capable of generating ideas for the ages had a profound influence on Rushdoony and forced him to articulate a religious response to the problem of the hard core. While respectful of Harper's vision and the enthusiasm of his supporters, Rushdoony politely challenged all involved to more clearly define "the basic perspective of the Institute."[84] Any organization dedicated to cultivating a hard core for protecting liberty must focus neither on the Remnant nor on liberty as its primary goal. It must focus on the foundational truth on which the Remnant must stand in order to defend liberty.

Rushdoony elaborated this problem in "The Strategy of Fabian Socialism," an unpublished but influential memorandum from his brief stint at the Volker Fund.[85] The memo circulated among a small network of business leaders, clergy, and intellectuals, many of whom viewed it as a lucid call to revolutionary action. Emerging from a conversation with former Cornell University economist Ivan R. Bierly in the fall of 1961 or winter of 1962, the essay briefly outlined the history of the Fabian Society, a British organization formed in 1883 that seeks to progress socialism via a gradual war of attrition against capitalism.[86] Rushdoony's essay analyzed the Fabians' strategies that eventually led to the rise of the Labour Party in Britain and, in Rushdoony's eyes, to the injection of socialism into mid-twentieth-century American culture.

Rushdoony argued that the Fabians' success in converting both "the ruling class of Britain" and some 2,000 "upper administrative officers in Washington" to socialism was attributable to its status as a "thought-and-action group" that provided "thinking and nurturing action among their followers."[87] The Fabians forbade "socialist inter-party battles on method"[88] and embraced a pragmatic approach that favored using the mechanism of democracy and capitalism to further socialism in the long term, even if such action temporarily undermined the cause. The Fabians recognized the necessity of committed leaders, an elite who directed not only government but also society as a whole. They achieved this goal, Rushdoony argued, by developing a coherent philosophy of government that ensured that Fabian principles survived in British bureaucracy regardless of Labour electoral success.

To many of Rushdoony's readers, especially those not familiar with the history of gradualist socialism, his summary of Fabianism was undoubtedly a minor revelation. His real insights, however, appear at the end of the essay, where he focused on the conservative movement forming around him. He reflected on the infrastructure of conservatism and criticized some of the major organizations working to counter the Fabian strategy—Fifield's Spiritual Mobilization, Leonard Read's Foundation for Economic Education, Howard E. Kershner's Christian Freedom Foundation (CFF), Fred C. Schwarz's Christian Anti-Communist Crusade (CACC), and William F. Buckley and Victor Milione's Intercollegiate Society of Individualists (ISI). Although each of these groups was on the vanguard of the conservative movement, Rushdoony noted that they all fell short on one half of the "action-and-thought" model pioneered by the Fabians. For example, both the CFF and the CACC were action groups with weak philosophical foundations, while SM and FEE focused on ideas but erroneously posited anarchist and Enlightenment thought to "champion a Reformation cause."[89]

Rushdoony's comments on FEE, which was founded by Read in 1945 with $30,000 of Volker Fund money, are especially illuminating because at the time, it was seen as one of the most effective and powerful organizations on the Right.[90] Read was a Nock disciple and prominent figure in the California business community. By the late 1930s, he had risen to the head of the Los Angeles Chamber of Commerce, the largest business group in the state. After leaving the chamber, Read moved to Upstate New York and founded FEE to search for America's liberty-loving Remnant. In contrast to Harper's much younger IHS, which focused on providing an institutional home to the scholarly Remnant, FEE's mission revolved around finding and educating a popular Remnant. Read would, according to Doherty, "try to find [Nock's] Remnant, whoever they might be, through excessive travel and speaking, usually set up for him by local friends and FEE supporters." Mollifying the hard, pessimistic edge of Nock's tale, Read believed that with the right ideas, anyone "could have incalculable effects for the cause down the line."[91] The result was that Read worked tirelessly to expound FEE's "freedom philosophy" "by all available media of communication, whether written, spoken or pictorial."[92] As a significant clearinghouse of conservative economic literature, FEE distributed free copies of Austrian economist F. A. Hayek's *Road to Serfdom* (1944), popular business journalist Henry Hazlitt's *Economics in One Lesson* (1946), and other titles that merged serious economic scholarship with heated invective or popular appeal.

Although FEE's efforts reached thousands of Americans and helped shape the thinking of a generation of conservative and libertarian thinkers, the organization's eclectic ideological mix of populist rhetoric, free-market capitalism, religious ecumenism, and philosophical openness left Rushdoony deeply dissatisfied. Despite FEE's stature as a highly successful conservative group, it was, to Rushdoony, a schizophrenic, inconsistent mix of an anarcho-Protestantism. The result of this ideological hodgepodge? "Today," wrote Rushdoony, "almost any given conservative group is likely to include Protestant, Catholic, atheist, positivist, Ayn Randian egotist, anarchist, utilitarian, and more. There is little common purpose and much uncommon trouble. It is necessary therefore to define the underlying premises carefully in order to have both unity and freedom. To attempt this will automatically leave many behind—but it will provide the anchor which many today, especially young people, are seeking."[93]

This prescriptive narrowing of the conservative movement on a religiously inflected philosophical foundation seemed to Rushdoony a logical process for encouraging common action based on shared assumptions. He knew the winnowing would leave many behind, but the remaining tiny minority of religious conservatives would have the world to gain. "History," he comforted his readers, "has never been commanded by majorities but only by dedicated minorities, and the need today is a strategy for the development of that minority into an instrument of thought and action power."[94] The need, then, was for Rushdoony to convince conservatives that they required something akin to the London School of Economics. This project dovetailed nicely with the goals of the principals of the Volker Fund, who were in the process of turning the anonymous charitable organization into a "new type of educational institution" intended to create a space for the cultivation of a vanguard of religiously inspired champions of limited government and free-market economics.

A New Type of Educational Institution

Through the early 1960s, the Volker Fund's many staffers worked in an explicitly cooperative framework to bring as many conservative and libertarian scholars together as possible. As intellectual historian George Nash has emphasized, throughout the 1950s and early 1960s, the fund represented "healthy cooperation" between various factions on the American Right.[95] The fund merged three major and highly factious elements of the rising Right: (1) "classical liberals," or "libertarians," who emphasized Austrian economics and individualism; (2) "traditionalists," or "new conservatives," who looked to European and American history as sources for a modern identity rooted in Christian values and aristocratic pretenses; and (3) "militant" anti-communists standing against foreign and domestic enemies.[96] This tripartite division of the emerging conservative consensus became popularly known as "fusionism" in the pages of William F. Buckley Jr.'s *National Review*. Through the writings of Frank S. Meyer, Will Herberg, Garry Wills, and many others, *National Review* popularized a form of big-tent conservatism built around the *fusion* of conservatism with economic libertarianism. The fusionists disagreed on much but concluded they must work together to defeat the twin threats of international communism and domestic liberalism.[97]

In practice, the Volker Fund embodied these fusionist tendencies before the 1960s. The network of relationships and secret funding orchestrated by Luhnow and his staff profoundly shaped midcentury political and intellectual history. While the fund's staff generated few original intellectual ideas, the fund supported a series of notable academic ventures. Of central importance was the William Volker Fund Series in the Humane Studies, an edited book series with fifteen scholarly volumes published under the fund's auspices by 1963. The series published laissez-faire economists alongside cultural conservatives. The fund also secretly sponsored the National Book Foundation (NBF), an organization that provided free copies of conservative-themed books to academic libraries. Designed to look nonideological, the NBF selected several books a year for the program and distributed thousands of copies over the course of nearly a decade. Librarians would likely have overlooked many of these books, but with well-designed information cards featuring glowing reviews, the NBF found a home for texts in important academic collections across the country.

The fund also supported a number of anti-Keynesian economists who attacked New Deal–era and post–World War II economic policies. Most notably, Luhnow used the fund to support the academic careers of controversial Austrian-born economists Ludwig von Mises and Friedrich A. Hayek. Mises and Hayek were leading proponents of the Austrian school of economics, which emphasizes the activity of individual economic agents, downplays collective action and state intervention in the economy, and advocates for laissez-faire. Volker resources also funded the first meeting of the Mont Pèlerin Society, which in the words of historian Kim Phillips-Fein was an "elite intellectual organization devoted to the development of an economics and a worldview critical of the welfare state and economic planning."[98] Today, historians and economists generally view that meeting as a major turning point in economic history that eventually laid the intellectual foundation for the reemergence of conservative, free-market economic principles in American and British governance during the end of the twentieth century. Ultimately, the Volker Fund supported the early research careers of many noted free-market economists, five of whom later won Nobel Prizes.[99]

In spite of the organizational success of the Volker Fund, by the early 1960s, Luhnow came to believe his staff was insufficiently Christian, and he decided to terminate the fund and replace it with "a new type of educational institution" built on a solidly religious foundation. In a February 1962 staff meeting, Luhnow opened with a discussion of his religious views, noting that he possessed a unique but unspecified spiritual power.[100] "The power I have may enter even Khrushchev," Luhnow told his staff. "The step is to tune in on this power and let it work."[101] If this revelation perplexed the fund's staff, it also heightened religious tensions between various factions at the Volker Fund. Luhnow had become aware since the late 1950s that many of the staffers did not share his appreciation for Christianity. He responded by aggressively insisting on the importance of Christianity as the foundation of the American social order. He stressed that Volker employees must themselves be committed Christians and became suspicious of many of his longtime staffers.

In the early 1960s, the increasingly erratic Luhnow came under the sway of Ivan R. Bierly. A convicted Christian, Bierly convinced Luhnow that the Volker staffers were a pack of atheists and anarchists and warned against their influence on the fund.[102] Bierly had himself experienced something of a religious reawakening after encountering Rushdoony's ideas in the late 1950s. Before Bierly, staffers had traditionally avoided discussing religious issues because they attempted to recruit and cultivate intellectuals of very different religious backgrounds. In the 1950s, the fund comfortably supported known atheists such as Murray Rothbard and reached out to Catholics associated with organizations such as the ISI and the *National Review*.

Harold W. Luhnow (center in vest) and his staff at William Volker & Co. headquarters in Burlingame, California, ca. 1956. Morris Cox, who succeeded Luhnow in the 1960s and negotiated the fund's merger with the Hoover Institution, stands at Luhnow's right. Kenneth S. Templeton Jr., courtesy of the author.

In contrast to this ecumenism, Bierly actively antagonized atheists and made his preference for Protestantism obvious. Shortly after the strange February 1962 staff meeting, Luhnow produced a memorandum declaring the termination of the Volker Fund.[103] He announced his intention to fire most of his staff and reorganize the Volker Fund into the Center for American Studies (CAS).[104] Luhnow sent his staff packing and, with Bierly, recruited new, sufficiently religious personnel.

With the precipitous dissolution of the fund in 1962, Luhnow unloaded what remained of the Volker Fund's commitments to social charities in Kansas City and replaced them with a new mission to provide a physical and intellectual home for conservative and libertarian scholars.[105] Luhnow also hoped the name change would enhance fund-raising efforts.[106] He and Bierly proposed a "new type of educational institution" that would be oriented toward a unified religious vision.

"The intent of the Center," Luhnow stated in a press release, "is to bring a renewed appreciation of Americans to the firm convictions of the founding fathers in the reality of God, and the necessity of looking to Divine Providence for the proper direction of our government."[107] An internal memo circulated to center staffers made this commitment even clearer: "No individual will ever be employed by the Center of American Studies who does not have an admitted dedicated commitment to God. . . . In our daily contacts we hope all staff members might clearly demonstrate their Christian convictions but nevertheless our activities, particularly our printed literature, will stress the spiritual foundations rather than using the word Christian. . . . We sincerely hope that every contact of the staff members of the Center for American Studies will leave no doubt of our sincere dedication as Christians."[108] With this focus on Divine Providence and a stated dedication to Christian commitments, the CAS became a Christian organization, and over time, it became clear that "Christian" meant "Protestant."

On this new religious foundation, Luhnow and Bierly endeavored to build a stable ideological institution by recruiting a new staff. One of their first hires was Rushdoony. Bierly had met Rushdoony while serving as a FEE staffer. In the intervening years, the two corresponded regularly. Rushdoony's fervent religious commitment and strong antagonism with public education convinced Bierly that the minister could play an important role in the new organization. For his part, Rushdoony came to the CAS with the ambition of molding it on the philosophy of Van Tillian presuppositionalism; he saw it as an opportunity to start a Christian college.

Along with Rushdoony, Bierly and Luhnow also hired William T. Couch and David L. Hoggan. Couch, former director of the University of North Carolina and University of Chicago Presses and editor in chief of *Collier's Encyclopedia*, came to the center to edit the "Encyclopedia of Americana."[109] Bierly and Luhnow hoped the project would generate revenue for the CAS, but it never found supporters beyond the confines of the center. Hoggan was a Harvard-trained historian who despised the New Deal, adored Hitler, and would, Bierly and Luhnow hoped, serve as the lead scholar on a team of revisionist historians dedicated to correcting the collectivist and anticapitalist bias of a generation of U.S. historians. This dream team of religiously, economically, and culturally conservative scholars was supposed to reform the American university and, with it, American culture. Instead, Rushdoony, Bierly, Couch, and Hoggan could not agree on the religious identity of CAS, and their infighting helped destroy the new center.

"Is There Room for a Roman Catholic in the Movement Which Is Rooted and Grounded in the Protestant Theological Perspective?"

When Rushdoony came to the Volker Fund as it transitioned into the Center for American Studies, he worked as a researcher, speaker, and writer, composing internal memos on various topics and traveling to conferences. Before joining the CAS as a speaker and researcher, Rushdoony had received a grant from the Volker Fund that allowed him to finish *Intellectual Schizophrenia* (1961), his first attack on the philosophy underlying modern education.[110] The Volker Fund had long maintained a keen interest in criticisms of public education, and Rushdoony's writings boiled with vituperative contempt for state-supported schools. It was a match made in heaven. Bierly had read drafts of the work, heard Rushdoony lecture, and recruited him to the fund based on his educational philosophy.[111]

During his brief stint at the CAS, Rushdoony made religion a central problem by consistently demanding that all fund employees demonstrate their commitment to orthodox Christianity. Further, he aggressively pushed the CAS and its principals to accept the Van Tillian presuppositionalism he advocated in his writings. Not surprisingly, this push toward a specific strain of orthodoxy angered the many Catholics, non-Presbyterian Protestants, and atheists associated with the center. Consequently, as Rushdoony pushed the fund to accept his interpretation of Van Til's presuppositionalism, many otherwise sympathetic supporters of the CAS withdrew their backing in the belief that the center had no interest in objective scholarship because it had interpreted all facts in advance.

The hiring of Rushdoony resulted in several unintended consequences for the CAS and its employees. First, although it is unclear whether Bierly appreciated it or not, in hiring Rushdoony because of his criticism of public education, he also got Rushdoony's Calvinism in the bargain. The two—educational criticism and sectarian religious commitment—were inseparable in Rushdoony's mind. Further, Bierly was not only getting an unapologetically zealous sectarian; he also was hiring a Christian apologist whose commitment to Van Til's apologetic strategy guaranteed conflicts between Rushdoony and others at the fund. Most interestingly, Bierly's encounter with Rushdoony's ideas seems to have sparked a renewed interest in religion for Bierly himself.[112] In a series of letters and discussions, Bierly quizzed Rushdoony on the theological foundations of Calvinism. Over time, Bierly began reading Van Til and adopting aspects of his apologetic rhetoric. Rushdoony encouraged the transformation by drafting lengthy annotated bibliographies as primers for Bierly. Bierly responded with questions that pushed Rushdoony to elaborate on the practical aspects of his theological position. Bierly was fascinated with Van Til's presuppositionalism and its implications for politics and economics, but he seems to have been much less interested in Rushdoony's specific Reformed commitments. As a result, Bierly never fully adopted Rushdoony's religious worldview; however, he did end up defending Rushdoony against charges of sectarianism.

Nowhere was Rushdoony's destabilizing sectarianism more evident than in a series of exchanges between Bierly and Richard M. Weaver. Weaver was a highly respected English professor at the University of Chicago who in 1948 published *Ideas Have Consequences*, the "fons et origo of the contemporary American conservative movement."[113] Weaver's book captured the mood of an era and potently encapsulated the primary argument made by many American conservatives in the "fusionist" paradigm that the societal ills of the United States can be boiled down to bad ideas and not the structural inequities created by industrial capitalism, racism, gender, and the like.[114] In his exchange with Bierly, Weaver attempted to protect his friend and confidant Victor Milione, the Catholic leader of the ISI, from an effort by Bierly to force the ISI to distribute a "sectarian" Protestant work.[115]

In the early 1960s, Milione's ISI was a small but important conservative organization that distributed conservative literature to college students and professors free of charge. The Volker Fund had traditionally provided large subsidies to ensure that the ISI could continue its book program. In 1961–62, for instance, the fund contributed nearly $50,000 to underwrite the ISI's book-distribution plan, and it made annual contributions of $1,500 to the institute.[116] Traditionally, the ISI had ties to anticommunist Catholics, most notably William F. Buckley Jr., who served as its first president. Milione, also a devout Catholic, carefully guarded his religious commitments and was reluctant to concede ground to conservative Protestants.

In 1963, as the Volker Fund transitioned to the Center for American Studies, Milione sent a worrisome note to Weaver expressing his fear that the fund was supporting "sectarian" literature and might try to force out anyone who resisted efforts to distribute such work. The work that Milione brought to Weaver's attention was an early draft of Rushdoony's *This Independent Republic*.[117] After reviewing Rushdoony's manuscript, Weaver wrote to Bierly, concluding: "I have to agree with Vic that distributing matter of a sectarian nature would be quite beyond the scope of the ISI. . . . I should add, as a matter of candor, that it would be a distressing thing to me if the Fund were to limit itself to a much narrower field than it has the ability and the means to operate in."[118] Weaver's note and Milione's worries about his future as head of ISI indicate that both men sensed the change in direction and purpose at the Volker Fund. The letter also indicates that Volker's intentions with the organizations it funded were sometimes less than benevolent. Weaver politely, but nonetheless forcefully, chastised Bierly for trying to pressure the ISI to distribute sectarian material. If the Volker Fund truly valued the autonomy of the groups it sponsored, this example may be an aberration. But this seems unlikely since Bierly's comments make it clear that he was more than ready to remove Milione, whose faith was an impediment to Volker's goals.

Bierly's response to Weaver's accusations also make it clear that Rushdoony was the central issue in the dispute. Specifically, Weaver distrusted Rushdoony's Calvinism and feared it would steamroll Catholics such as Milione and less-committed believers in Weaver's mold. Bierly responded to the charges by suggesting that both Weaver and Milione had confused a religious discussion with a sectarian one. Further, Bierly noted that Milione was well aware of the nature and content of Rushdoony's Calvinistic take on American history because the ISI had sponsored a series of lectures by Rushdoony in 1962. Bierly then tried to turn the tables on Weaver by suggesting that the real sectarians were Milione and the Catholics who dominated the ISI. "In fact," Bierly charged, "Vic made it very clear that it was his own personal difficulty here that was really disturbing him, 'Is there room for a Roman Catholic in the movement which is rooted and grounded in the Protestant theological perspective?'"[119] Contrary to Bierly's protests, Milione's concerns were not misplaced. As William Couch reported to another Rushdoony critic, "I have seen Rushdoony talking in the most amicable way with Roman Catholics that he was using for his own purposes at the same time that he was supporting other people who were making the most vicious attacks on Roman Catholicism."[120] Milione's resistance to distributing *This Independent Republic* was a reflection not only of his assessment of Rushdoony's ideas but also of the Reformed minister's public behavior.

Weaver countered Bierly's assertions by noting that he had once considered reviewing Rushdoony's *Intellectual Schizophrenia* in *Modern Age*, an explicitly conservative academic journal helmed by Weaver and conservative political theorist Russell Kirk, but had concluded:

[D]espite the brilliant passages it contains, the book was too sectarian for our columns. This was two years before the current issue came up. I must say that my response to the lectures is pretty much the same. I agree with Rush on lots of points, and I wish that millions of people could be brought to see those points. But at the same time, in the midst of matter very sensible and defensible, I come on things that seem to be pulled out of the wild blue—things that really do not emerge from his facts or his reasoning. This makes the work very hard to defend as a scholarly performance, even when one is prone to agree with him, and a sound basis in scholarship is a necessity for our position. So, my present feeling is one of doubt—wanting to be convinced, but not quite convinced.[121]

In Weaver's mind, the things Rushdoony "pulled out of the wild blue" were directly related to his Calvinist worldview and presuppositionalist approach to history. Not content to accept the Chicago professor's assessment of Rushdoony's scholarship, Bierly demanded: "Could you indicate things that 'seem to be pulled out of the wild blue?'"[122] Pushing even harder, Bierly then suggested that perhaps Weaver's vaunted work would wither under similar scrutiny: "I could send *Ideas Have Consequences* to fifty professors of English and Philosophy and get almost as severe criticism as you have leveled at Rush's lectures. Does this mean that your book has or has not passed the 'scholarship' test?"[123]

When Bierly ran the issue by Couch, Couch further aggravated the situation by siding with Weaver, noting: "If I understand the situation, I believe you have the choice of either giving Milione stuff he feels he can use effectively or, if you have enough power, of replacing him with someone who shares your ideas."[124] Couch suggested the latter would be a poor decision and agreed with Weaver's assessment that he would find it difficult "to think of an ISI without Vic Milione." On Rushdoony's sectarianism, Couch argued: "I think he cuts down sharply on his effectiveness by connecting his argument with particular doctrines that separate him from persons who otherwise would be in agreement with him."[125] Couch recognized that Rushdoony's entire theological project was founded on separation and not connection and understood it would have catastrophic consequences for the type of big-tent conservatism and probusiness agenda to which the Volker Fund aspired.

Outnumbered and out-scholared, Bierly eventually dropped the issue. He ceased agitating for Milione's ouster at ISI, and the organization never distributed Rushdoony's text. Bierly eventually put the issue to rest by noting that he did not really understand the issues involved. "I am conscious," he wrote, "of the fact that my own lack of a firm grasp of the history of Christian doctrines puts me in a position from which I am not qualified to judge one view from another—and thus I'm anxious and concerned that different views on some of these matters have an opportunity of a voice in educational circles that has been substantially denied them for many years—at least I can say from personal observation in the classroom and on a university faculty and in my present capacity that very few scholars are willing to give hearing to any viewpoint that gives emphasis to the relevance of Christian faith."[126] This reversal and plea to his own ignorance leads one to wonder on what basis Bierly had assessed Rushdoony's text as worthy of distribution in the first place.

Our Christian Faith

Soon after fending off Bierly's attempt to pressure Milione into distributing Rushdoony's writings, Couch found himself battling Rushdoony and David L. Hoggan and their newly hired followers for control of the CAS. In Rushdoony, Couch saw a "literate Fundamentalist"[127] and "congenital liar"[128] who was using his position at the center to forward an "anti-Catholic, anti-Semitic, anti-Negro, anti-just about everybody and everything" agenda. Hoggan, Couch rightly believed, was a "Nazi sympathizer" and "apologist." Couch also wrongly believed Hoggan was cooperating with Rushdoony to start a "neo-Nazi movement" in the United States; whatever Rushdoony was, he was not a neo-Nazi. For a year, from 1963 to 1964, Couch struggled against this united Rushdoony/Hoggan front.[129] The conflict left Couch "deeply distressed," leading him to conclude his only real option was "to quit and get away just as quickly as I could."[130] Although he eventually persevered and succeeded in getting both men fired, he did so at a high personal and professional cost; the struggle created intense antagonisms and an environment of mutual distrust among CAS board members, staffers, and academic supporters. The resulting paranoia and hostility directly contributed to the center's eventual implosion.

Couch, unlike Rushdoony and Hoggan, was a notable and respected American academic who was no stranger to controversy and political infighting.[131] But his timing at the CAS could not have been worse. He found himself in the midst of an intense struggle to define what it meant to be a "conservative" in post–World War II America. As Couch churned out memo after memo attacking Rushdoony and Hoggan's religious project, he found himself in the trenches of this much broader nationwide fight to define the constitutive boundaries of the American right wing. While Couch himself had yet to self-consciously adopt the moniker of "conservative," his tenure at the center was coterminous with the fight over the place of religion in American conservatism.

Even though Couch and Richard Weaver temporarily managed to settle the tension between Rushdoony's Calvinism and the largely Catholic identity of the ISI, by May 1963 tensions over religion reemerged within the CAS staff. No longer targeting the center's Catholic surrogates, Rushdoony and his supporters at the center now focused their attention on purifying the religious commitments of all CAS staff members. The first calls for theological purification emerged in a draft version of the new center's "Statement of Purpose." C. John Miller, one of Rushdoony's Reformed allies at the center and a future Presbyterian pastor and theologian, outlined a three-part "Perspective" that he assumed all center staffers would share. First, he cited the generic notion of "patriotism." Next, all at CAS would strive for a hazily defined ideal of impartial "scholarship." The third perspective of "commitment" was much more specific: "A respect and commitment to the great creeds, faith of orthodox Christianity as represented in the Apostles' creed, the Nicene creed, the Augsburg Confession, the Belgic Confession, the Westminster Confession, and the Declaration of Savoy."[132] The latter four, of course, are all essential to Reformed Christianity. In the margins of the draft statement of purpose, Couch scribbled: "[Point three] would exclude me."[133] Rushdoony, through his proxies, was effectively drawing the limits of the new organization—and the ire of other staff members.

Adding insult to intellectual and religious injury, on the same day, Couch received another memo from David L. Hoggan. Hoggan's memo explicitly appropriated the contemporary rhetoric of the budding conservative movement, titling it "The American Conservative Concept in Relation to the American Studies Program." Hoggan's memo is notable for two reasons. First, he enumerated twelve points that he argued are the "minimum condition" upon which all staffers at the program must agree. Four of Hoggan's points are interesting for their religious specificity: "1) That the United States was and is a Christian nation. 2) That belief in the Trinity is indispensable to an individual Christian Faith. . . . 11) That instruction about American traditions cannot be meaningful unless it includes an adequate emphasis on the Christian Origins of these United States and the American Federal Constitution. 12) That further emphasis on Christian values is required if higher education is to meet the challenge of the materialistic creeds."[134]

As a whole, Hoggan obviously intended the twelve points to designate the boundaries of the center's religious and political commitments. If adopted as policy, the points would have excluded all but the most committed Christians from the center's staff. Less obviously, Hoggan's points demonstrated a growing conviction among some activists that the American "conservative concept" is fundamentally a Christian concept. The list began with historical foundation—"the United States was and is a Christian nation" based on the doctrine of the Trinity—and terminated with the ethical implications of these theological presuppositions. Through Miller's and Hoggan's memos,

Rushdoony succeeded in translating the presuppositional philosophical position of Van Til into an institutional shibboleth designed to identify only the most fervent of Christians willing to presuppose the reality of God's agency in shaping American history.

Immediately after receiving the two memos, Couch produced his own angry memo. Entitled "Sectarianism in the Center," it clearly attacked the Miller-Hoggan-Rushdoony alliance. The memo charged that "three members of one denomination were proposed for major positions on the staff of the proposed graduate school. This denomination is Calvinistic."[135] Further, Couch noted that when a Roman Catholic was suggested as editor of an important series of publications for the center, "the appointment . . . was objected to on the ground that he is a Roman Catholic."[136] Couch suddenly found himself in the same place as Vic Milione—a religious outsider aware that the Calvinist clique led by Rushdoony would not cooperate with a nominal Christian such as himself.

Couch needed to convince Bierly that any invocation of specific religious doctrines would lead to two problems for the CAS. First, since all of the documentation regarding the religious convictions of the center's staff ultimately pointed toward Calvinism, Couch concluded that any reference to "our Christian faith" or "Christian nation" "could reasonably be taken to mean Calvinism" to the exclusion of any other form of Christianity.[137] If this was the case, Couch himself would have to resign from the center since "to represent my Christian faith as Calvinism is to falsify."[138] Second, Couch asserted, "'our Christian faith' could be taken by men like Ludwig von Mises as a slap in the face."[139] In short, the insistence on Reformed Christianity threatened to alienate both non-Calvinist Christians and more-secular individuals.

The central question for Couch was whether Bierly, and ultimately Luhnow, would reject Rushdoony's attempt to drag the CAS into an exclusively Calvinist religious position or whether Couch would encourage the kind of ecumenism favored by other conservatives. The answer to the dilemma came quickly. During a staff meeting on July 5, 1963, Bierly insisted on changing the language in the controversial statement to reference only a shared reverence for "God" without a direct appeal to the orthodox creeds and confessions cited by Miller. Rushdoony responded angrily to Bierly's change, arguing that such an "alteration of Mr. Miller's statement was a change to a deistic doctrine."[140] As tempers flared, Rushdoony insisted that he alone understood the intentions of Luhnow and that Bierly did not have the authorization to make such changes.[141] This audacious and specious claim sealed Rushdoony's fate with the CAS. Couch saw it as final evidence that "Mr. Rushdoony is determined to control the work of the center or to make continual trouble, and then make it appear that others are the trouble makers."[142] Bierly, who was superior to Rushdoony within the CAS hierarchy and also had Luhnow's ear, similarly saw it as a direct threat and moved to clamp down on Rushdoony's activities in the center. Couch convinced Bierly that Rushdoony aspired to take over the operation of the CAS with his "allies and disciples"—including Hoggan and Miller, along with researcher Fred Andre and summer intern Gary North. "Fortunately," Couch later wrote a friend, after persuading Bierly of Rushdoony's intentions, "Rushdoony became too sure of himself and took positions that others had to oppose or let him run everything. This brought his separation and that of his allies—through whom he still tried to run the place after he had left."[143]

In an effort to regain control over his staff, Luhnow acknowledged Couch and Bierly's concerns and settled the matter by issuing a statement that clarified "various discussions on our statement of spiritual foundations."[144] All staffers would be expected to affirm the center's "intent . . . to bring a renewed appreciation of Americans of the firm conviction of our Founding Fathers in the reality of God and the necessity of looking to Divine Providence for the proper direction of government."[145] While the statement did not depart from the center's generic desire "to awaken interest in the American tradition, which . . . has its roots in the Judaeo-Christian tradition," it clearly deviated from Rushdoony's religious vision for the center.[146]

In September 1963, the CAS terminated Rushdoony's employment but allowed him to remain temporarily on the payroll. In this interim period, Bierly issued warnings to Rushdoony regarding his use of CAS travel accounts "since your present relationship is that of independent contractor and not employee."[147] In December of that year, Bierly ended Rushdoony's ability to use the center's library to send books out to friends and associates as he saw fit.[148] Finally, in January 1964, the CAS officially terminated its ties with Rushdoony with a $2,475 check. All total, paperwork filed with the Internal Revenue Service indicated that the center paid Rushdoony $30,000 for "research and writing" independent from his advisory role. The center's disbursement to Rushdoony was the second-largest grant the CAS made to an individual researcher in fiscal year 1964.[149] Only Sister Mary Margaret Patricia McCarran, the daughter of Nevada's aggressively anticommunist senator Pat McCarran Sr., merited a larger grant of $35,000 for her work to arrange her late father's papers.[150] For comparison's sake, it also is worth noting that such conservative luminaries as *National Review*'s Brent Bozell and Frank S. Meyer grabbed $5,000 and $20,000, respectively. Despite the acrimony, Rushdoony's separation from the center was gentle and generous, giving him the necessary resources to write two more books.

Conclusion: An Extreme Right-Winger

After firing Rushdoony, Couch and Bierly worked hard to earn intellectual and institutional legitimacy for the CAS. At first, they tried to build an alliance with the Hoover Institution at Stanford University. Representatives from Hoover were initially quite receptive, as they stood to gain almost $10 million from the deal. But when Bierly and Luhnow pushed for an unacceptable level of autonomy for the center, the deal started to crumble. Matters became worse when rumors spread of personnel problems related to Rushdoony's sectarianism. The final straw came when stories in the international and domestic media revealed David Hoggan's ties to neo-Nazi groups and anti-Semitic Holocaust deniers in Germany and the United States.[151] Luhnow, now very ill from a series of strokes, no longer could manage the center or the Volker Fund's remaining money. The Center for American Studies closed down in 1963, and the Volker Fund's remaining money eventually went to the Hoover Institution following a murky out-of-court legal settlement reached in 1978.[152]

If Rushdoony's aggressive pursuit of theological purity had already alienated him from his church's hierarchy, then the potential of working in a well-funded nonprofit environment with sympathetic intellectuals must have seemed an appealing option. As one of the most controversial casualties of the CAS's implosion, Rushdoony suddenly found himself on the losing side of yet another public dispute; the emerging mainstream of American conservatism essentially had fired Rushdoony because of his exclusivist religious convictions. The combined failures of his *Westminster Herald* and the CAS effectively ended the second stage of Rushdoony's development as a missionary, minister, journalist, and academic organizer. They forced his separation from many of the most influential and moneyed conservative organizations that emerged in the early 1960s.

Although Rushdoony failed to remake the CAS into a clearinghouse for theologically conservative political and social theory, his time at the center proved invaluable for his development as an organizer and gave him the time and resources necessary to hone his ideas to a sharper edge. In contrast to Hoggan, who turned to substance abuse and cultivated a relationship with American Nazi Party founder George Lincoln Rockwell, Rushdoony remained patient and as intellectually prolific as ever. Disciplined and methodical, Rushdoony carefully developed his theologically rigorous, religiously exclusive form of conservatism. He would wait nearly two decades before any significant portion of the "mainstream" of American conservatism would take his work seriously again; eventually, however, it would enjoy a wide audience among a network of grassroots activists, educational reformers, and theologians.

Even if the conditions among conservative activists in the 1960s were conducive for William Couch to dismiss Rushdoony as "an extreme right-winger," that certainly did not mean that Rushdoony was alone on the "extreme" fringes of the Right. The conservative milieu of the late 1950s and early 1960s was a dynamic jumble of integrative and disintegrative organizations, leaders, and ideas. In this disorienting environment, articulate leaders with a consistent message who could impose order and intellectual clarity on what it meant to be an "American" and decipher the seemingly chaotic international environment of the Cold War were hot commodities capable of commanding both local and national attention. From Robert Welch's John Birch Society to Billy James Hargis's Christian Crusade ministry, demand was high for information and education from a "traditional" Protestant perspective that could explain a complex world. Rushdoony's presuppositional epistemological perspective may have alienated academics and movement activists in search of more-practical organizing principles, but he found its niche with a dedicated minority of Christian conservatives who longed to fundamentally redraw the boundaries between individuals, families, the church, and the state.

CHAPTER THREE

A Christian Renaissance

The Chalcedon Foundation, Families, and the War against the State

History has never been dominated by majorities, but only by
dedicated minorities who stand unconditionally on their faith.
—R. J. RUSHDOONY, *Newsletter* no. 1, October, 1965

Stand fast therefore in the liberty wherewith Christ hath made
us free, and be not entangled again with the yoke of bondage.
—Galatians 5:1 (King James Version)

Shortly after being fired from the Center for American Studies, Rushdoony asked Gary North, a college intern at the center and Rushdoony's future son-in-law, to pray for Harold Luhnow, the center's ailing chief. "Confidentially," Rushdoony wrote North, "be in prayer with respect to the Center. Mr. Luhnow has been seriously ill, enough to endanger the future of the Center, and has been turning his thoughts towards orthodox Christianity more and more. I believe that if he truly accepts the faith, great changes may ensue. His illness is more or less a secret."[1] But Rushdoony did not wait for prayer—or conversion—to heal Luhnow. He set out to pick up where his failed project with the Volker Fund and the CAS had left off.

Undeterred by his dismissal from the CAS for sectarianism, Rushdoony reached out to many of the groups and individuals with whom he had made connections while lecturing and researching at the libertarian organization. He continued to impress upon his audiences the importance of Van Tillian presuppositionalism and its necessity within any orthodox system of Christian thought and action. In 1965 Rushdoony's post–Volker Fund hustling paid off when a group of conservative Christian women from the suburbs of Los Angeles heard him speak. They were so engaged by his analysis of contemporary events that they made him an offer: if he would move from Palo Alto in Northern California to the Woodland Hills area near Los Angeles, members of Women for America, Inc., a patriotic women's group, would pay him a small stipend to lead them in weekly Bible study sessions.[2] So in August 1965, Rushdoony, his family, and fourteen tons of books arrived in the L.A. metropolitan area about a week after the Watts Riots had destroyed vast swaths of the city.

The story of how Rushdoony and his family came to the attention of Women for America is part and parcel of the history of the emergence of postwar American conservatism as a grassroots, populist movement with its epicenter in Southern California. Rushdoony's association with Women for America tapped the familial resources of a tight-knit community of activist housewives and their middle-class, professional husbands. In them, he found an audience hungry for a Christian message that not only explained the troubles facing modern America but also offered practical, Bible-based solutions to those problems. Through his association with Women for America, Rushdoony gained access to an array of businesses and schools, churches and political offices, and nonprofits and bookstores, all staffed with people eager to hear his ideas, debate them, and open their wallets to register their support. With the resources of this network, Rushdoony would establish a new type of educational institution of his own: the Chalcedon Foundation. Rushdoony envisioned the Chalcedon Foundation as the institutional backbone of a unique Christian college devoted to instilling in its students an orthodox Christian education based on the philosophical system of Cornelius Van Til. Fittingly, Rushdoony's gateway into this vast network of conservative organizations was a book.

Of Books and Bookstores

Books molded the contours of R. J. Rushdoony's life. When he and his family moved from Palo Alto to Woodland Hills, the transportation of his massive library required a considerable amount of planning and a certain amount of sacrifice. As his son Mark Rousas Rushdoony recalled years later, "When we moved to Los Angeles to start Chalcedon in 1965, Dad was forty-nine. We had to enclose a large screened-in patio to house the books. Still, they took up much of the rest of the house and the garage."[3] A decade later, when the Chalcedon Foundation was a fully functioning nonprofit, no single room or house could contain Rushdoony's collection, so he built a freestanding 1,300-square-foot library to house his nearly 40,000 volumes.

Rushdoony's library was a lifelong obsession. He scavenged for books wherever he could and squirreled them away, but he was no collector. He preferred hardcovers; he found paperbacks "distasteful" because of their "disposable nature."[4] Each new book was a joy and a pleasure. When Rushdoony was a missionary on the Duck Valley Reservation in Nevada, an approaching book—so rare and wonderful to him in that isolated outpost—forced the expectant reverend to wait for the stage of weekly mail. "After he received it from the driver," remembered a member of his congregation, "he would return to the house by crossing the road and then across the footbridge and in the yard without looking up. This weekly event took on a life of its own as several folks wouldn't miss it if their lives depended on it."[5] As he focused his attention on writing and lecturing, Rushdoony depended more and more on books, and he carried them everywhere. Any time he had to pause or wait, he cracked a book. He took a briefcase full of them on every trip and returned with many read and annotated.[6]

Books disciplined Rushdoony. And, in return, he organized them carefully, making each book ripe for future use in his research and writing projects. He wrote in his books, indexed them in a compulsively neat fashion, imposing his formidable, if idiosyncratic, intellect on them:

> When he read a book, he would use a six-inch ruler and a pencil. He would neatly underline, using the ruler (never freehand), an important piece of information. Sometimes he would double-underline something of particular importance. Longer passages he would mark with a single (or double) line in the margin parallel to the edge of the page. An exclamation mark, or an "x" in the margin would denote a particularly significant passage or statement. He then would write a reference to the marked passage in the back of the book.[7]

He noted the date and location where he finished reading every book and logged the title of each completed volume in his journals.

Rushdoony's discipline went far beyond marginalia and paratextual annotations. He carefully and methodically Christianized every text—a process ordered by the Van Tillian presuppositional philosophy that he used to determine the outcome of every thought, ensuring its accord with the mind of the Creator. Of course, this meant that Rushdoony's encounter with his dear books was circular, a closed loop structured from beginning to end by the Ur-book—the Bible. Thus, a kind of intertextuality governed Rushdoony's very being; the Bible governed his approach to information and determined the way he read every text he encountered. In turn, his drive to read and write about what he read was dictated by his calling to bring the hearts and minds of all into accord with Scripture.

In the cultural and political context of Woodland Hills and the greater Los Angeles area, Rushdoony found a particularly receptive audience that acceded to his vision of life bound by the Bible. Through a network of book clubs, bookstores, and family-centered civic organizations, Rushdoony sowed his unique vision of a biblically ordered, family-based form of conservatism. Although nameless and inchoate in 1964, by November 1965, Rushdoony called this project "reconstruction," and he singled out his followers as the "saved remnant" and "a dedicated minority" charged with undertaking this ambitious task.[8] But before anyone could be reconstructed according to Rushdoony's program, a pugnacious University of California, Riverside, history graduate student needed to go book shopping.

The Betsy Ross Book Shop

Just as Rushdoony's serendipitous encounter with Van Til's *The New Modernism* changed his perception of apologetics, the chance encounter between the son of an FBI agent and an employee in a "patriot bookstore" helped spark the birth of the Christian Reconstruction movement. In the fall of 1964, a college student named Gary Kilgore North walked into the Betsy Ross Book Shop and saw some of Rushdoony's books on the shelves. As he chatted with store employee Grayce Flanagan, North explained that he knew and corresponded with Rushdoony and might be able to put her in contact with him.

Two years earlier, in the winter of 1962, during the second semester of his junior year at UCLA, North had read Rushdoony's *Intellectual Schizophrenia*, which a friend in his Christian fraternity had lent him.[9] North had grown up in Southern California, the only child of FBI special agent Samuel W. North Jr. and Peggy North.[10] Samuel was so conservative that, as his son Gary later recalled, "when the U.S. Government suggested that employees drive with their lights on out of respect to the anniversary of Martin Luther King's assassination, dad drove home that evening with his lights off, risking a ticket and a collision."[11] Several years before the elder North's perilously dark drive home, his son was so excited by his exposure to Rushdoony's criticism of state-sponsored education—and Rushdoony's fleeting citation of Austrian economist Ludwig von Mises's *Human Action*—that he sent Rushdoony a letter in the spring of 1962. Soon, the two corresponded regularly about everything from libertarian economics to the Kingdom of God.[12]

North and Rushdoony first met in person during a series of summer lectures that Rushdoony delivered as part of an Intercollegiate Society of Individualists series at St. Mary's College, located near San Francisco, Cal-

R. J. Rushdoony's 1,300-square-foot library in Vallecito, California, houses approximately 40,000 volumes and would have served as the seed collection for Rushdoony's proposed Chalcedon College. Photo by author.

ifornia.[13] During a two-week session at St. Mary's, Rushdoony lectured to North and at least nineteen other students about the Calvinist foundation of the American political order. Other lecturers featured at the ISI conference included such right-wing luminaries as Hans F. Sennholz, Felix Morley, Francis Graham Wilson, Stefan T. Possony, and Ivan R. Bierly.[14] Of the lectures, North recalled: "I listened to Hans Sennholz on economics, and I slept through Francis Graham Wilson's Socratic monologues on political theory. . . . Rousas John Rushdoony lectured for two weeks on what became *This Independent Republic*. . . . I was so impressed that I married his daughter—a decade later."[15] After the ISI lectures, Rushdoony encouraged Bierly to hire North in 1963 as a summer intern at the Center for American Studies.[16] "I was paid $500 a month to read," North remembered, "which was the best job I have ever had."[17] At CAS, North and Rushdoony became part of the Calvinist alliance that helped destroy the center. But the partnership between the forty-seven-year-old reverend and the brash twenty-one-year-old North survived the end of the CAS to become a long-term friendship, as Rushdoony developed into North's spiritual and intellectual mentor.

During their earliest interactions, North was a political conservative by temperament and a recently converted dispensational evangelical.[18] After their work together at CAS, Rushdoony encouraged North's drift toward Reformed Calvinism by recommending him for entry into the Westminster Theological Seminary (WTS) in Philadelphia to study under Cornelius Van Til. North despised WTS, resented its rote curriculum, and hated Van Til's teaching style. He flunked out in epic fashion, testily abandoning the seminary in 1964. He eventually settled in as a graduate student in economic history at the University of California, Riverside.

After North dropped out of WTS to seek a secular graduate degree in California's public university system, he became a frequent shopper at the Betsy Ross Book Shop, located in a shopping center in L.A.'s Westwood Village district. North was impressed with the bookstore, praising it in a letter to Rushdoony: "The Betsy Ross shop has a good selection of books. The little lady who does the buying is apparently well informed, or at least she has some good people advising her. Much Rushdoony, little Possony."[19] If North's alliterative observation is accurate, it points to the niche regional market Rushdoony had developed in the 1960s.

It was during one such shopping trip to the Betsy Ross in 1964 that North suggested to Flanagan that she might want to get in touch with Rushdoony and passed along his contact information. Flanagan followed up on North's suggestion, and Rushdoony agreed to travel to Southern California to talk to Women for America, Inc., the organization that owned the Betsy Ross Book Shop.

Kitchen-Table Activists

Rushdoony's talk with the women at the Betsy Ross Book Shop indicated just how much midcentury conservatism had changed since he had begun his ministry on an Indian reservation in Nevada. The Right was moving farther and farther away from its rarified origins in the exclusive moneyed circles of white, anti–New Deal business leaders and college-educated intellectuals; it was transitioning into a self-consciously populist movement in which women—especially housewives and young professionals—played an important, if not quite dominant, role.[20] While much of California was awash in the welter of this new form of grassroots conservatism, Los Angeles and Orange County formed an especially volatile milieu of book clubs, patriotic stores, and civic groups dedicated to kick-starting a new, self-consciously "conservative" movement. Many of these "kitchen table activists," as historian Lisa McGirr has called them, were women who had the time and expertise required to create a confederation of dedicated activists committed to fighting foreign communism in the American heartland.[21]

As historian Michelle Nickerson has pointed out, many of these conservative women's organizations began as study groups organized by housewives in Southern California in the 1950s. The organizers designed these casual, informal "study groups" to turn members into "experts" on subjects ranging from grade-school textbooks to international communism.[22] These clubs spread rapidly, with 123 sprouting up in Southern California by the middle of the 1950s.[23] They had a "distinctly feminine style of political organizing," according to Nickerson, focusing on "luncheons and coffees, getting-out-the vote drives, and monthly newsletters."[24] "Over the 1950s," Nickerson continued, "right-wing activist women increasingly adopted the study group model as a way to foster a more militant conservatism that went beyond Eisenhower's 'Modern Republicanism.'"[25] This "housewife populism" shunned the perceived intellectual snobbery of liberal progressivism for a folksy, middle-class aesthetic of do-it-yourself education.[26]

The attention these groups paid to adult education both resonated with and helped create a demand for the John Birch Society (JBS), which similarly focused on small, local chapters involved in the self-directed study of anticommunist material. As the historian Jonathan Schoenwald has argued, the JBS was the crucible for forming the sensibilities and expertise of conservative citizen-activist housewives:

> Although most researchers agree that the majority of JBS members were men, women played critical roles in chapters across the country. Since many of these women were homemakers, they felt they could devote their time to the fight to roll back communism and liberalism. Knowing that women had not only the time, but also the energy and acumen to take on such responsibilities, coordinators often targeted them specifically. Consequently, women's confidence grew as their rosters filled, and their projects gained momentum. For these women, the society acted as a liberating agent, clarifying their political priorities, illustrating their potential as contributors to a cause, and helping women to enter the realm of political organizing in the early 1960s.[27]

The kind of activism and empowerment represented by the JBS and similar organizations tapped into the energies of restless housewives dealing with the new domestic challenges of postwar America. These female activists developed a political identity that was, in their minds, at once antifeminist and prowoman. Rejecting the dour vision of suburban lives depicted in Betty Friedan's 1963 *Feminine Mystique*, many women cultivated a sense of self-worth and political agency in their roles as submissive but politically active housewives. According to Nickerson, "By the 1960s, women had long been mixing domesticity and politics, mainly through political clubs," but "housewife activism" became increasingly public in the early 1960s, when "women began opening patriotic bookstores and libraries in the greater Los Angeles area."[28] These ideological entrepreneurs "developed a conservative political identity that drew upon collective understandings of their own marginality, as wives and mothers, in relation to state power."[29] As women's liberation and concomitant struggles over abortion and the Equal Rights Amendment would come to dominate politics in later years, many of these veteran JBS-affiliated housewife activists would lead the development of the antifeminist and "profamily" movements in the 1970s.[30]

In 1961 the nonprofit organization Women for America, Inc., joined this trend and opened the Betsy Ross Book Shop to distribute right-wing litera-ture in the Los Angeles area.[31] Women for America, according to Nickerson, "billed itself as 'an organization dedicated to the defeat of totalitarianism using education as a weapon.' In addition to running the book store, they also raised money for 'patriotic' libraries and sponsored 'Americanism' quiz-zes for college students in Los Angeles."[32] As an indication of the store's solid place within the mainstream of "fusionist" conservatism, William F. Buckley Jr. spoke at the shop's grand opening. On that occasion, a Betsy Ross associ-ate told a reporter that the store had no intention of "getting into the extreme right orbit."[33]

Four years after the bookshop's opening, Rushdoony made a brief presen-tation to Women for America. Although no record of the talk remains, the presentation impressed the target audience. In response, women associated with the Betsy Ross offered Rushdoony a deal. They would pay him a small but reasonable monthly salary if he would move to the Los Angeles area and run weekly Bible studies for the women associated with the shop as well as for anyone else who might be interested. The money was just enough to enable Rushdoony to support his family without needing to seek outside employment. He would therefore be free to research, write, and lecture full-time. Rushdoony recognized the potential in this agreement and accepted it. In order to maximize the arrangement, he immediately moved to establish a tax-exempt educational foundation, Chalcedon, Inc.

The Chalcedon Foundation

The mission of Chalcedon, Inc., better known today as the Chalcedon Foundation, was primarily education. For midcentury antistatists, it was not enough to outline the failures of the state and affirm its alternative. Whether in the form of Albert Jay Nock's Remnant, the John Galt–led individualist utopia envisioned by Ayn Rand, Richard Weaver's neoagrarianism, or the fusionist project of the *National Review* clique, the antistatist projects of midcentury conservatism rested not only on resistance but also on the cultivation of epistemological self-consciousness. Rushdoony similarly took up this mission. He hoped to shift humanity's epistemological framework away from autonomous reasoning and toward a God-centered mode of thought restricted by Scripture and predicated on thinking God's thoughts after Him. This mode of presuppositional reasoning means that facts only have meaning in relationship to God. Consequently, the first action any individual must take is bringing her or his thoughts in line with God's. The result of this reasoning is that all aspects of learning and scholarship, especially in terms of historical study, must be interpreted through God's plan for humanity. It is in this nexus between historical interpretation, human agency, and divine will that Rushdoony sought to intervene in human history in order to create an explicitly Christian mode of being in the world. The foundation for this action came from an unusual source: the creeds and councils of the Christian church.

The Council of Chalcedon

For Rushdoony, human social order rested on the proper understanding of the implications of the proceedings of all of the early ecumenical councils of the Christian church.[34] Of these councils, none was more important to Rushdoony's political project than the Ecumenical Council of Chalcedon. Held in A.D. 451 in the eponymous Byzantine city, the council produced the most comprehensive statement about the person of Jesus Christ. Based on the reasoning of Pope Leo I, the Confession of Chalcedon declared: "We confess that one and the same Christ, Lord, and only-begotten Son, is to be acknowledged in two natures without confusion, change, division, or separation. The distinction between natures was never abolished by their union, but rather the character proper to each of the two natures was preserved as they came together in one person and one hypostasis." Designed to definitively settle a host of long-festering Christological debates, the council provided the orthodox definition of the relationship between the human and divine natures of Jesus Christ.

From Rushdoony's Calvinist perspective, the vast arc of history displayed humankind's willful rebellion against the proceedings of Chalcedon. Fallen humans, according to Rushdoony, long to find in their own institutions the mechanisms for salvation, a possibility denied by the Council of Chalcedon. Before the council, Rushdoony argued that human beings typically attempted to understand salvation in terms of "self-deification."[35] In order to transcend human existence and the vicissitudes of nature, humans will opt for one of two primary means of sinful salvation. First, sinners might seek self-deification in terms of individual, mystical union with the divine. Second, and more relevant to Rushdoony's conservative audience, sinful humans might pursue corporate deification through the union of the individual with a body politic that is itself believed to be divine. Within the ancient Roman context, in which imperial officials tolerated and eventually embraced Christianity, some in the empire moved to conflate church and state because of the long-standing "Roman statist theology," which held that the empire "was the voice of God."[36] This suggested that Christ's divinity could be conflated with His humanness: "If the two natures of Christ were confused, it meant that the door was opened to the divinizing of human nature; man and the state were then potentially divine."[37] Any attempt to deify the state had massive implications, not only for Christians but for all of humanity.

Rushdoony interpreted Chalcedon as not only a statement on Christ's nature but also a definition of the proper relationship between divine and human governance. He filtered his understanding of Chalcedon through the prism of twentieth-century issues, focusing on the rise of seemingly omnipresent and increasingly omnipotent modes of human governance. Such structures of modern governance, Rushdoony warned, claimed to free human beings from the earthly constraints of their created, fallen nature. Modern nation-states offered security without responsibility, salvation without transcendence.

In Rushdoony's reading, the bishops gathered at Chalcedon offered a stark alternative to the modern soterial effects of the state. If the "two natures"— divine and human—of Christ came together "without confusion, change, division, or separation" exclusively in His unique being, no other institution, person, or form could save human beings from their innately sinful nature. The church could not save Christians because a salvific function would muddle the distinction between the transcendent and the profane. Similarly, the state could make no transcendent claims over human beings. The state could not offer collective salvation for humanity's fallen nature through income redistribution, welfare, democracy, or any other legislative or regulatory means. "Chalcedon," Rushdoony concluded, "handed statism its major defeat in man's history."[38] Only the millennial Kingdom, ruled by the all-sovereign god-man Jesus Christ, could both save and rule humanity.

The Definition of Chalcedon refused to accept self or corporate deification as an orthodox solution to the problem of Christ and humanity's relationship with Him. For Rushdoony, the council represented a great fissure in human history. On one side of Chalcedon lay all pagan institutions that confused the divine and the human; on the other side lay the possibility for founding a limited, truly Christian state constrained by the ultimate transcendence of Jesus Christ. Thus, Chalcedon separated "Christian faith from the Greek and pagan concepts of nature and being. It made clear that Christianity and all other religions and philosophies could not be brought together."[39] This theological antithesis had political implications: "Chalcedon prevented human institutions from professing to be incarnations of the deity and able to unite two worlds in their existence. The state was reduced to a human order, under God, and it was denied its age-old claim to divinity for the body-politic, the ruler, or the offices."[40]

Religious historian Molly Worthen has noted that Rushdoony's view is not quite as "eccentric" as a superficial reading might suggest.[41] In the fourth and fifth centuries, according to Worthen, "Christology was not an abstruse debate among churchmen, but a matter of immediate political concern. One's view of Christ shaped one's view of Caesar."[42] Regardless of the accuracy of Rushdoony's assessment of the Council of Chalcedon, he successfully inserted his interpretation into mid-twentieth-century controversies associated with the nature and meaning of the modern state. In Rushdoony's imagination—and in the imaginations of many American conservatives—the modern state represented the most perverse manifestation of humanity's desire for autosalvation. The biopolitical prerogatives of the modern state—those concerned with population management, production, consumption, debt, risk, and economic redistribution via taxation and inflation—created the context for social-engineering projects designed to save humans from their own fallen nature. Rushdoony viewed such developments as a hubristic open rebellion against the will of God.

Through his interpretation of the Definition of Chalcedon, Rushdoony enlisted King Jesus as his primary ally in the battle against the American federal government. But neither Christ nor Rushdoony could stand alone in this fight. They needed an organizational base to resist the state, and they needed resources to support their resistance. Although Rushdoony failed to convince the principals at the CAS of the viability of his project, his new Bible study program with Women for America provided him another opportunity to convince Christians that the "abstraction of doctrine and theology from life has been one of the great disasters in the life of the church."[43]

This perspective fit neatly within the midcentury efforts of so many conservative activists and thinkers to develop robust intellectual projects capable of resisting the liberal establishment's tyrannical statism. When Rushdoony intervened in this intellectual milieu, he brought his unique presuppositional message—that is, his insistence that conservatism needed a clearly formulated and rigorous *Christian* epistemology. The message appears to have resonated immediately with Women for America and some of the shoppers at the Betsy Ross Book Shop. At once elitist and populist, intellectually sophisticated and readily comprehendible to any literate Protestant, Rushdoony's message found a receptive audience in Southern California. He had pitched this message for nearly fifteen years to intellectuals and movement insiders. Only a few of them got it, and fewer still were willing to finance his project. Suddenly, however, in Southern California's populist conservative renaissance, Rushdoony found a small, dedicated minority of women and men who not only were willing to listen to him but also were willing to fund him *and* put his ideas into practice.

Rushdoony had found the Remnant.

This dedicated minority was inspired by an intense desire to save the United States from the threat of statist liberalism, moral decay, secularism, communism, and global governance. Their battle was ultimately bound up in an amorphously conceptualized but nonetheless real concern for the loss of individual freedom to an increasingly centralized federal government and a globalizing post–World War II world. For the women and men associated with the Betsy Ross Book Shop, this fight was not some abstract struggle of the forces of freedom against those of tyranny. Rather, it was a visceral, embodied fight located not simply in the individual citizen-subject but more concretely in the familialized citizen-subject who found meaning and purpose in the domestic sphere first and in the discrete, autonomous sphere of individuality second.

Although the values permeating American conservatism in the 1950s and 1960s emphasized "family" in the abstract, few of the major thinkers developed a practical model for placing the family at the center of the emerging conservative consensus. Traditionalists such as the Southern Agrarians had paid lip service to family as one of the "amenities" of life.[44] Likewise, in outlining his "six canons of conservative thought" and four "chief problems" facing "intelligent conservatives" in the twentieth century, conservative political theorist Russell Kirk barely mentioned the problems facing the modern family.[45] The ever-popular historian and political philosopher Richard Weaver elliptically connected the loss of familial sentiment to modern man's immersion "in time and material gratifications," but he said little else of practical value.[46] Meanwhile, the moneyed social reformers of the Right—from William Volker and Christian entrepreneur and philanthropist George Pepperdine to philanthropist and Sunoco president J. Howard Pew and Wal-Mart founder Sam Walton—certainly favored a romanticized concept of a nuclear familial unit under a patriarchal head, but they correlated this unit's success or failure directly to market instruments and efficient economic activity.[47] These broad intellectual and economic sentiments contributed to the familial bent of Southern Californian conservatism, but the latter was hardly reducible to them. The real push toward the family came from the activists themselves as they inhabited a rapidly changing world and worked to develop a conservative vision of America's future.

Since his work on the Duck Valley Indian Reservation in Nevada, Rushdoony had been at the forefront of insisting that the federal government should be the primary target of conservative concern because it undermined the family. There, he had come to believe that systems managed by a centralized bureaucracy stripped citizens of their humanity and deadened the God-given need to work for the glory of Christ. Rushdoony called for a revolution in the American constitutional system in which the country would resuscitate its moribund Christian heritage. His proposal for this renaissance fit perfectly with the sentiments of activists seeking to save the republic in living rooms throughout Southern California. He advocated a form of familialized conservatism, a religious and political project that joined family with ill-defined but oft-invoked concepts such as *liberty* and *freedom* as "formulas for resistance" against a monolithic federal government.[48] Through the cultivation of a familial structure with a strong patriarchal head and a submissive but powerful matriarchal heart, Rushdoony hoped to relocate the governance of the individual from the public sphere into a domestic one. He presented a familialized version of conservatism as an alternative to the individualist, economic, and traditionalist visions offered by other conservative thinkers.

At the grassroots level, Rushdoony found a receptive audience as a host of national and local groups drew attention to the domestic nature of this structuring familial sentiment. The John Birch Society, for instance, neatly encapsulated this domestic focus when it warned its members that "the battle for saving our Republic could well be won or lost in our living rooms."[49] Activism centered in the home transformed conservatism into a familial movement that found its motivating impetus more and more in the domestic sphere and less and less in the broader expanses of laissez-faire economic agitation, international intrigue, or even national political action.[50] In the postwar years, women and men rallying to the banner of conservatism tended to invest in the family a sense of "sacred intimacy" that had to be protected from the encroachment of the modern state and the unnatural efficiencies foisted on it by the marketplace.[51]

Agents foreign and domestic had *nurturance*, typically imagined as the emotional sine qua non of the nuclear family, in their crosshairs.[52] The state threatened to collectivize the "emotional infrastructure" of the family, while market forces and the international communist conspiracy would obliterate the family form by sending all women into the workplace or by abolishing marriage altogether.[53] Regardless of one's economic, political, or religious proclivities, the intensification of familial bounds in the postwar era created a sense that the family was under attack, and that women, its primary guardians, needed to mobilize to protect it. Much of this new activism focused on education—whether in the form of the reeducation of adults or the proper education of children—designed to inoculate students against the virus of social collectivism. But as fears of an international communist conspiracy waned in the face of growing domestic turmoil in the 1960s and 1970s, conservatives increasingly focused on family as the microcosm of America's angst and as the potential check against social and moral disintegration.[54]

The arrangement between Rushdoony and Women for America emerged at the vanguard of this broader trend in conservative circles to relocate political action and social reform into the domestic sphere. For Rushdoony, political activism and social change could happen in all spheres of life, but the farther these changes were removed from the family, the less effective they became. As a result, he worked to convince Christians—especially theologically conservative, fundamentalist, and evangelical Protestants—that they needed to rethink their political activism and refocus it on creating a proper Christian family.

The Origins of the Familial Crisis

As a number of recent historical studies have noted, the reasons for the increased interest in the family and its reproduction in the domestic sphere were myriad. In the postwar era, the Baby Boom was a national project. "Virtually everyone of childbearing age participated in the production of the Baby Boom," historian Elaine Tyler May has observed. "Americans of all racial, ethnic, and religious groups, of all socio-economic classes and educational levels, married younger and had more children than at any other time in the twentieth century."[55] Across all components of American society, behavior related to marriage and reproduction—and the ideas associated with them—changed dramatically from 1940 to 1960. The median age for first marriages fell from highs well above twenty-two for women and twenty-six for men in the late 1800s to below twenty-one and twenty-three, respectively. By 1960, fully 68 percent of the adult population was married; additionally, women not only had more children but, as one survey reported, craved larger families with the new "ideal" number of children increasing from two to four.[56]

With nearly every aspect of society participating in these trends, valorization of the family was not controversial. As historian Robert O. Self has noted, by the 1960s, "few Americans questioned the naturalness of the nuclear family." As a result of this consensus, "what divided Great Society liberals from their opponents [on the Left and the Right] was the nature of government assistance" for strengthening and intervening in the maintenance of families.[57] Questions abounded for Americans: Should government intervene in family life through redistribution of economic resources, educational reform, and other intimate matters? What sort of families would benefit from these state projects? Would state intervention in the American familial form fundamentally alter domestic structures for the better or for the worse?

As politicians and technocrats debated these questions, ad hoc structural changes related to suburbanization and economic policy in the wake of World War II favored the romanticization of the nuclear family structure. Returning soldiers found a country unprepared to house them. The Great Depression had strangled the housing market, leading to a dearth of new home construction.[58] In response to the postwar housing demand and shifts in federal industrial policy, enterprising developers and planners eschewed centralized urban planning. Investors threw up new suburban communities across the country.[59] In the greater Los Angeles area, as McGirr has recounted, this built environment of rambling ranch-style homes "reinforced privacy, individual property rights, home ownership, and isolation at the expense of public space."[60] The resulting landscape was, in the words of historian Darren Dochuk, a "fragmented frontier" in which communities fused and fractured along ethnic and religious fault lines.[61]

Government subsidies made this new familial environment possible. Low-interest loans to returning veterans through the GI Bill and Federal Housing Administration programs for nonveterans discouraged investment in inner-city neighborhoods in favor of the suburbs. Meanwhile, mortgage interest deductions on federal income taxes ceased to benefit only the rich and became a coveted form of income redistribution for middle-class homeowners.[62] Further, especially in Southern California, federal defense spending assured that many workers could pay their mortgages.[63] Developments such as Westside Village, Toluca Woods, and Westchester sprang up on the periphery of Los Angeles to house employees working for aerospace giants like Douglas, Lockheed, and Northrop.[64]

In the specific context of the greater Los Angeles area, the convergence of the postwar housing boom and shifting patterns of reproduction and marriage produced a new sense of familial intimacy organized around the valorization of an imagined "natural" order. This family centered on the male breadwinner who labored in the public sphere and the female domestic laborer who tended to home and children.[65] These new communities simultaneously allowed family members to imagine themselves as elements of discrete, autonomous units and provided new opportunities for families living in close proximity to one another to create tighter-knit communities around a shared sense of identity.[66]

Families and Conspiracy

Rushdoony intuited these powerful demographic and structural changes to the American family. His Chalcedon Foundation reached out to a nurturing remnant of family-centered, grassroots, housewife activists and their husbands who were seeking a strategic vision for cultivating and perpetuating their families in the face of rapid social and cultural change. Chalcedon's founding in 1965 meant Rushdoony could exploit the intense loyalties of frustrated activists who had energetically mobilized to support the John Birch Society during the first half of the 1960s only to have their political ambitions thwarted by Barry Goldwater's disastrous 1964 presidential campaign.[67] The JBS served a particularly important role in Rushdoony's early organizational efforts for Chalcedon because it had laid an infrastructural framework he could exploit.[68] Further, in Rushdoony's view, the JBS had correctly recognized the need for public (re)education of Americans, thus preparing many Southern Californians for his vision of Christian regeneration through education. Finally, the failure of political deliverance at the national level offered Rushdoony the opportunity to encourage activists to turn their attention away from reforming the state and toward a localized, familial vision. Rushdoony developed his new familial organizational strategy through dialogue with and criticism of the John Birch Society and its top-down, hierarchical political organization based on corporate models.

Founded by candy-maker Robert Welch—manufacturer of the "Papa Sucker," now known as the "Sugar Daddy"—the JBS was named for a Baptist missionary and air-combat intelligence officer who survived World War II but was killed by Chinese communists ten days after the war ended. Welch believed Birch was the first victim of World War III.[69] In the *Blue Book*, a collection of speeches Welch gave over two days in December 1958 that "set forth the background, methods, and purposes of the JBS,"[70] Welch clarified the nature of this struggle. "Communism," he explained, "is wholly a conspiracy, a gigantic conspiracy to enslave mankind; an increasingly successful conspiracy controlled by determined cunning, and utterly ruthless gangsters, willing to use any means to achieve its end."[71] To fight this conspiracy, the JBS focused the vast majority of its attention on public education.[72] JBS material focused tightly on the theme of self-education, so that works such as the society's *Blue Book* and its annual *White Books* were filled with impassioned pleas for Birchers to engage in "intensive study" so as to be "better informed" than most Americans and thus become leaders in a nationwide resistance movement against the communist conspiracy.[73] Welch's appeal to autodidacticism encouraged Birchers to decontextualize everything that they knew and recode it in terms of the guiding metanarrative of an insidious communist plot. Any sign, from the launch of the Soviet satellite Sputnik to municipal water fluoridation and the presence of John Steinbeck's *The Grapes of Wrath* in a high school library, could be enrolled in a chain of signifiers and recoded in terms of a vast communist conspiracy.[74]

Rushdoony found much to admire in the JBS educational mission. In a letter to Welch, he stated his profound admiration for him, writing: "Let me express my very great respect for your work, and for you personally. I regard you as the clearest and most courageous public figure of our day.

I have read your publications for years with essential agreement."[75] Welch returned Rushdoony's respect by commissioning articles from Rushdoony to appear in *American Opinion*, the official publication of the society.[76] At the same time, many in the society's Belmont, Massachusetts, headquarters were reading and circulating Rushdoony's writings.[77] Even as Rushdoony cultivated these connections, he also carefully distanced himself from the society, telling Welch that he needed to remain "unaffiliated" from the JBS because it "is necessary for a time yet to circulate as an independent in order to gain access to many of the clergy" who were not sympathetic to the JBS. This did not mean that Rushdoony needed to remain "independent as far as my allegiances."[78] To make the point, Rushdoony made a "contribution equal to that of home members"—a $24 annual fee.[79] Welch agreed, and Rushdoony became unofficially affiliated with the JBS.[80]

Rushdoony's complicated give-and-take with the JBS was both intellectual and organizational. Intellectually, he believed Welch addressed the right issues, but the society did not have a proper epistemological framework in place for interpreting political facts. "There is no such thing as brute factuality," Rushdoony wrote, "but rather only interpreted factuality."[81] Since facts cannot speak for themselves, it was not enough for Welch to simply put his painstaking research in front of good Americans; he also needed to provide the necessary framework for interpreting those facts. In terms of history, Welch was right to see a conspiracy at work driving forward a communistic agenda on the world stage, but he was wrong to see human agency behind the conspiracy: "The Bible as a whole presents a view of history as conspiracy, with Satan and man determined to assert their right to be gods, knowing, or determining, good and evil for themselves."[82] But this conspiracy of Satan and man is doomed to failure because of "the certainty of the Son's victory."[83] The JBS emphasized conspiracy but deemphasized Christ's preordained victory.

Organizationally, Rushdoony's private correspondence indicates that he believed that the weakest aspect of the JBS was Robert Welch himself and the tight corporate-style control he maintained over the organization: "One of the strong points of the JBS is the centralized authority. It is also one of its weakest points. It makes for strong concerted action, but it also makes the limitations of one man, Robert Welch, decisive."[84] In fairness to Welch, Rushdoony added, "We can expect Welch . . . and Rushdoony, and every other man, to have their shortcomings and limitations"; but on balance, in his private letters, Rushdoony was heavily critical of Welch and his management of the JBS.[85] To a potential Chalcedon backer weighing the possibility of sending significant support to Rushdoony, Rushdoony wrote: "I am not a member of the John Birch Society, nor have I ever been a member. . . . I have high regard for these organizations, which is not always to imply agreement, but I believe that as a clergyman and writer it is necessary to maintain my independence."[86] Ultimately, Rushdoony did agree with aspects of the JBS agenda, but he also worked at odds with the organization. Rushdoony's son, Mark Rousas, later said of his father's ties to the JBS: "Many of his early supporters were in the John Birch Society and the Goldwater movement, and they were disillusioned with the loss of Goldwater. . . . My father was trying to turn their attention to a different focus, to a more theological view, a moral view of culture, civilization."[87] In short, Rushdoony's problem with the JBS went beyond Welch's management of the organization and was ultimately tied to its lack of a clear theological underpinning. The JBS was "anti-Christianity" in Rushdoony's assessment since it did not explicitly recognize the presuppositional assumptions that Rushdoony believed must undergird an educational organization.[88] Consequently, he could cooperate with Welch, and even agree with the candy man's assessment of communism, but Rushdoony believed that the JBS was ultimately doomed to failure if it did not address the souls of men.

The Task of Reconstruction

Although the national visibility of the John Birch Society dominated the Southern California conservative milieu, all manner of overlapping and competing organizations sought to respond to the crisis facing the American family. When Rushdoony launched Chalcedon, Inc., into this already-crowded field of actors, he not only exploited his connections with the JBS but also used the lessons he learned from the failures of the CAS and the successes of the Volker Fund. Legally, he was determined to insulate Chalcedon from some of the powers of the state by securing tax-exempt status for the organization—a noted failure of CAS leaders. Immediately after incorporating Chalcedon, Inc., in early 1965, Rushdoony sought 501(c)(3) status for it as an educational institution.[89] He planned to develop Chalcedon into a Christian college with a full-time staff of lecturers and researchers who would be dedicated "to the orthodox Christian faith . . . within the tradition of the Council of Chalcedon."[90]

In a letter to the Internal Revenue Service (IRS) filed by Gaston, Keltner, and Adair Attorneys at Law, Rushdoony developed his plans at length, taking broad swipes at prominent Christian colleges. He reported that most

Christian colleges simply give their students "warmed-over Harvard and Chicago lectures."[91] These institutions failed to prepare young Christians to engage the real problems facing the modern world—namely, in terms of individual freedom, law, and civic engagement. "Basic to Christian freedom in the modern world," Rushdoony explained, "is an understanding of *law* from a Christian perspective."[92] Chalcedon College would "revise" the liberal-arts curriculum into an explicitly "Christian liberal-arts curriculum" founded on the presupposition that "man cannot usurp the role of God in relationship to the world."[93] The college would be staffed by research faculty who would not only teach but also be required "to develop orthodox Christian scholarship of a commanding character."[94]

Rushdoony developed his vision of a Christian college in an era inundated with faith-based schools. Large, well-established liberal-arts institutions such as Wheaton College in Illinois, Calvin College in Michigan, and Gordon College in Massachusetts claimed a uniquely Christian mission. Since the 1930s, these liberal-arts colleges had been supplemented by a growing network of private business and technical colleges built with a Christian mission in mind. Dochuk has outlined how religious leaders struck bargains (sometimes formally, sometimes not) with business interests throughout the South and the West to finance these schools. These newer colleges provided students with "spiritual and economic advancement while corporate leaders were supplied with a devout, well-trained, compliant workforce."[95] By bringing underdeveloped regions of the country into the national economy and mobilizing an underutilized and previously inefficient workforce, these colleges helped modernize the Sunbelt.[96] Heavily subsidized in the postwar era by the GI Bill, these liberal-arts and technical colleges mixed a bland probusiness Christianity with typical evangelical doctrines related to individual salvation, born-again theology, and premillennial dispensationalism.[97] In spite of—or, more precisely, because of—the liberal-arts education and managerial training provided by these institutions' curricula, they were, in Rushdoony's eyes, neither aggressively nor self-consciously Christian. Rushdoony believed he could offer something new in the already crowded midcentury Christian educational marketplace: a rigorous brand of Christian education built around biblical law.

Before he could secure the funding necessary to buy the land and hire a staff for his proposed college, Rushdoony relied on his connections to a network of conservative organizations to insulate his activities from taxation. He was a crafty bootstrapper who combined revenue from a host of sources to finance his project. To pay for his move to Woodland Hills in August 1965,

Rushdoony secured $3,600 in combined contributions from businessmen Phil Virtue and Walter Knott of Knott's Berry Farm fame.[98] As he waited for the IRS decision on tax exemption for Chalcedon, Rushdoony channeled contributions through his congregation at the Westminster Orthodox Presbyterian Church and through Knott's Americanism Educational League (AEL).[99] Formed in 1927, the league was one of the oldest right-wing organizations in California. Knott invested heavily in the AEL in the mid-1960s and used it to fund all manner of organizations, book-distribution efforts, and outreach to high school students, undergraduates, and community activists. Although only a tiny component of AEL's much larger educational project, Chalcedon reflected Knott's wider commitment to reforming education according to his probusiness, Christian commitments.

The Chalcedon Report

In October 1965, Rushdoony began self-publishing a mimeographed newsletter, which he sent to his small circle of supporters.[100] He believed that his supporters were entitled to regular updates on his activities since they were ultimately supporting not just a weekly Bible study but also a far wider and more ambitious movement to change the very nature of American society. Originally known simply as the *Newsletter*, Rushdoony's son, Mark Rousas, recalled that the report began as a simple, single-page letter: "It included an essay and a report on his [Rushdoony's] activities, so that the end of each *Newsletter* reported on the number of talks given, chapters written, and his travels."[101] For his first report, Rushdoony sat down and wrote a precise count of his activities for the previous two months: "I spoke 15 times, wrote 3 chapters, and also wrote 2 short articles. Sunday activities were established: Sunday morning 11 A.M., preaching at the Orthodox Anglican Church of the Holy Spirit in Santa Ana, a 2:30 study class in Westwood Village, a 7:30 class in San Marino, with a total of 226 miles of driving."[102] His supporters knew exactly what they were paying for, down to the mile.

This first newsletter also included a statement of purpose outlining the ideas underlying Chalcedon. Though his report was brief—filling barely a page—Rushdoony told his supporters that they were witnessing a major transition in human history in which a Christian order has "been extensively captured by the forces of humanism and statism, and a new age of terror is developing all around us."[103] In the face of this onslaught, the supporters of Chalcedon were at the vanguard of a "renewal" of "our historic Christian liberty." They were standing up against statism for the "*basic government*" of the "Christian man." Rushdoony connected this binary opposition between

Christian self-government and statism with his interpretation of the Definition of Chalcedon: "Our choice today is between two claimants to the throne of godhood and universal government: the state, which claims to be our shepherd, and savior, and the Holy Trinity, our only God and Savior."[104] With no lack of ambition or sense of historical import, Rushdoony concluded: "What you are doing, in your support of me, is to sponsor a counter-measure to the prevailing trend, to promote by your support, interest, *and* study, a Christian Renaissance, to declare by these measures your belief that the answer to humanism and statism is Christian faith and liberty."[105]

In his November 1965 newsletter, Rushdoony set out the themes that would dominate the rest of his life's ministry. He explained to his readers that the current humanist age, with its statist proclivities, posits the basic premise that there is no God.[106] "No God means no law," he wrote, "and no law means that nothing can be a crime." In this Nietzschean moment of the transvaluation of all values, the only seemingly valid response to humanity's problems is science. But such scientism rendered a human being into little more than a "laboratory test animal," warned Rushdoony. The monolithic state runs its experiments on a pliant, cowed populace willing to abandon the freedom of self-governance for the comforts of a totalitarian nanny state. But the state, ruled by its arrogant "scientific planners," will be judged by God for its sins and punished, leaving all men a simple choice between "whether we will be among those judged, or among those, the saved Remnant, who undertake even now *the task of reconstruction*."[107]

And there, suddenly crystalized for a small group of housewives and their middle-class, professional husbands, was the project: *reconstruction*. Chalcedon, its founder, and his supporters had birthed a movement. *Christian Reconstruction* through biblical discipline was the duty of every Christian.

For all of the world-historical grandeur implied in the task of Christian Reconstruction, the movement had humble, parochial origins. As Mark Rushdoony's recollections illustrate, the newsletter, and Chalcedon's activities more generally, were largely a family affair. According to the younger Rushdoony, the Chalcedon Foundation needed volunteer labor to produce the monthly newsletter and stuff the requisite envelopes. This shoestring venture operated out of the Rushdoony living room and kitchen, with Rushdoony's family providing much of the labor, along with the work of many others, especially the female supporters of Chalcedon.[108]

Rushdoony's personal journals recorded the familial network behind Chalcedon. Rushdoony regularly recorded notes related to the monthly editing, printing, and mailing of the letter, which now went by the name of *The Chalcedon Report*. This process normally took several days and was a team effort among the Rushdoony family and, until the early 1980s, women associated with Women for America and their Bible study group. Rushdoony recorded the clearest account of this process in his notes related to the production of *The Chalcedon Report* no. 55. On February 24, 1970, Rushdoony drafted a report chastising many Christians for their lack of a real, positive faith. He accused most Christians of practicing a faith that "is essentially negative" with its "main impetus in disgust."[109] The report opened with a reference to British cartoonist Paul Sellers's *Eb and Flo* comic strip and closed with a searing condemnation of modern Christian "Pharisees" who denounce evil but who have never "exercised dominion under God" and advanced the Kingdom of Christ.[110]

Since Rushdoony wrote longhand with pen and inkwell, the responsibility fell to his wife, Dorothy, to proofread and type the monthly letter.[111] On March 2, after the letter had been typed, Dorothy and Rushdoony went to the Flanagan's house to run off mimeograph copies. Finally, on March 4, Dorothy took the copies to Peggy North's, where the two stuffed envelopes, completing the monthly cycle. This is only one instance of a monthly ritual that did not change significantly until Chalcedon began using a mailing service in the mid-1980s.[112] Until the process was mechanized and professionalized for the purpose of efficiency, Rushdoony relied on his family and network of supporters such as Peggy North, Grayce Flanagan, and others to provide material and logistical help to keep the Chalcedon Foundation running. As Mark Rushdoony's recollections suggest, this process contributed to the cultivation of a sense of shared purpose between the Rushdoony family and its supporters. Chalcedon was developing into something of an extended kinship network organized around the nucleus of the Rushdoony family and spreading out through a network of supporters, many of whom were themselves tightly bound families seeking to cultivate a uniquely Christ-centered vision of civic and private life.

Lecturing the Remnant

Along with the launch of Chalcedon and the *Newsletter*, Rushdoony also began an intensive series of public lectures to organizations not directly connected to churches or parachurch organizations. Although he spent most of his time lecturing in California, he also accepted invitations to speak to organizations around the United States. Rushdoony took his message of resisting the state through individual spiritual reconstruction to four primary audiences: ministers, Bible study groups, business leaders, and college students.[113] His correspondence offers only a few concrete glimpses of the extensive travels that laid the foundation for Chalcedon. It says almost nothing of his outreach to other ministers, but it offers some details on his work with Bible study groups, business leaders, and college students.

Rushdoony aimed his Bible studies at women and their practical concerns related to education, economics, and patriotism. Unlike many of the more elitist intellectual and economic reform projects on the Right, Rushdoony took an open and inclusive approach to bringing women into his movement. This may have been due partly to his early cooperation with the John Birch Society, which so obviously had reaped the benefits of the dedicated activist housewife. His records of these events conspicuously note that many of the meetings took place on weekdays in private homes in the late morning or early afternoon—indications that his audiences were primarily homemakers. The frequency of these sorts of meetings suggests that Rushdoony clearly targeted women's groups, while the topics—education, family issues in a global context, student unrest on college campuses—highlight his audiences' concerns. As Chalcedon grew, he used such meetings to recruit women to provide volunteer labor for the organization in the form of common secretarial and office duties in order to help him manage his voluminous correspondence and to maintain his prolific writing schedule. He also knew wives were conduits to their husbands' wallets.

Rushdoony's willingness to target conservative women and make them agents in the project of Christian Reconstruction meant that many of his early audiences were not only businessmen and male college students but also conservative women's groups and home Bible study meetings organized by women in the living rooms of his supporters. Between 1964 and 1970, Rushdoony spoke on religious issues at least 115 times to small groups and Bible studies.[114] He led studies at a regular circuit of homes, with most participants numbering fewer than thirty. Although it is not clear from his records who attended, these home Bible studies were likely made up of women and men who shared components of his theological position or his conservatism. The subjects of the talks suggest that they were aimed at well-educated audiences interested in Christian perspectives on popular culture, education, anticommunism, hard money economics, JBS-style conspiracy theorizing, and revisionist history.[115] It is difficult to assess what sort of influence these home Bible study meetings had on their audiences, but their frequency and their small but stable attendance numbers indicate that most of the regular attendees formed the bedrock of Rushdoony's economic and social support.

When Rushdoony reached outside of the domestic sphere, he exploited his connections to organizations like FEE and the defunct Volker Fund to tap into chambers of commerce and other probusiness organizations around California. For example, in the early months of 1965, Rushdoony was an active lecturer in libertarian philosopher and Congregational minister Ed Opitz's Remnant group.[116] This brought Rushdoony to the attention of Robert D. Norton, vice president of Coast Federal Savings and Loan Association, a business that invested heavily in conservative causes.[117] Norton invited Rushdoony to participate in Coast Federal's Guest Speaker Program, which had previously included such conservatives as Ludwig von Mises and Opitz. Rushdoony accepted the opportunity and spoke on the relationship between business and Christian ethics, titling his lecture "Christian Social Ethics: Love, Justice, and Coercion."[118] For his troubles, Coast Federal paid his travel expenses and gave him a $150 honorarium.[119] The talk put him in front of about "60 managers" at the savings and loan.[120]

The same year, Rushdoony also spent a significant amount of time lecturing to student groups, including the Yuba County Young Republicans.[121] Just as he tailored his talks to the practical concerns of mothers or bankers, Rushdoony typically spoke to Young Republicans about radical elements on California's university campuses. In April 1965, Antonia Fiske of the Yuba County Young Republicans asked Rushdoony to lecture on "The Religion of Revolution" and its relationship to the "negro movement" and Free Speech Movement at the University of California, Berkeley. Rushdoony lectured to "20 or 30" likeminded Republicans, and Fiske distributed his pamphlets and encouraged students to buy his books.[122] Members of the chapter praised Rushdoony's talk and thanked him for the intellectual "ammunition" he gave them.[123]

Individually, such meetings in front of a handful of housewives here, sixty businessmen there, and twenty Young Republicans elsewhere meant little. In the aggregate, however, these speaking engagements put Rushdoony in front of hundreds, perhaps thousands, of people a year. Between January 1965 and May 1966, Rushdoony lectured in Seattle, Washington; in Houston, Texas; in Redding, California; in Anderson, California; and at Jackson Theological Seminary in Jackson, Mississippi, and he participated in "various seminars held in different parts of the country." In January 1966, Rushdoony recorded that he had spoken 212 times during the previous year to diverse audiences, many of whom "were neither Christian nor conservative."[124]

Since Rushdoony was in such close contact with his supporters through his familial and friendship networks, he moved away from recounting his speaking and writing in his *Newsletter* and instead offered his readers a monthly essay on a range of topics.[125] After winning tax-exempt status for Chalcedon in December 1968, Rushdoony solicited suggestions for a new title for the publication, and in April 1969, the *Newsletter* officially became *The Chalcedon Report*.[126] Before he changed the name of the publication and stopped reporting his exact activities, his newsletters recorded that between 1965 and 1968, Rushdoony lectured 886 times and wrote 4,550 pieces of correspondence following up on these appearances.[127] This sort of tireless work and his follow-up on all of his lecturing ensured that Rushdoony was always on the minds of those with whom he came into contact. These connections with women, ministers, businessmen, and political activists put Rushdoony in front of a wide variety of people with the resources necessary to support the establishment of the Chalcedon Foundation.

Conclusion: Biblical Law

It is in Rushdoony's specific interpretation of God's plan for victory that the true novelty of Chalcedon emerged. By the time Rushdoony had produced six of his monthly *Newsletters*, a latent theme in his thinking had become the animating force behind the publication: biblical law as the condition for Christian victory. Biblical law had been a theme in Rushdoony's writing starting with his first book on Van Til, and it remained so in every book thereafter. By the time he founded Chalcedon, Inc., in 1965, Rushdoony had begun an encyclopedic study of Old Testament legal standards as examples of precedent for interpreting contemporary social and political issues. His progressively tighter focus on biblical law grew from the lawlessness he perceived all around him. Month after month, Rushdoony's *Newsletters* read like dispatches from some postapocalyptic dystopian future—riots; mass killings; government-sponsored torture; food shortages; scientific planners run amok.[128] Rushdoony's moral, of course, was that the future was now. The terrors of the present age, he concluded, were a consequence of Christians abandoning the "law-spheres" of God—politics, economics, the family, the state—to retreat toward the pietistic conversion of souls. Every month, he outlined clear connections between ancient biblical legal precedents and the crises of the current age. "One of the most important things for us to know, in understanding our world," he soothed readers, "is that it is a world under God's law."[129]

Through his reading of biblical law, Rushdoony analyzed myriad modern problems ranging from debt, war, civil unrest, torture, love, overpopulation, the state, and patriotism. In 1966, in a small pamphlet titled *Preparation for the Future*, Rushdoony outlined the potential power of his new vision of biblical law. The short tract prophesied the coming collapse of the American economic system.[130] Rushdoony advised readers to buy silver and gold, carefully selected parcels of land capable of supporting crops and livestock, and other goods with inherent value, such as guns, alcohol, and tobacco. Although the vast majority of the pamphlet focused on Rushdoony's theological interpretation of inflation and the value of hard money, it closed with this vivid depiction of the coming collapse: "Eight major dams provide most of America's electricity: these will be targets of action. Gasoline will be poured into the sewer systems and ignited to burn out a city's communication lines. Meanwhile, it is expected that most Americans will be 'cream puffs,' mere victims who will 'sit and wait for television to come on.'"[131]

For Rushdoony, this nightmare urbanscape was the inevitable outcome of a society governed by lawless men—men who opted to follow their own wills rather than the law of God.[132] He challenged his audience to prepare for "increasing racial and leftist revolutionary violence" by committing to a new vision of future-oriented Christianity that focuses not on mere survival, but victory.[133] "Basic then to preparation for the future," he wrote, "is to believe it is absolutely in God's hands, not in the hands of the enemy, and that God shall triumph mightily. We shall share in that victory. We must prepare, therefore, not for survival but for victory. We must begin now to build the institutions for Christian liberty, to establish new and true churches, to teach children in the fundamentals of Scripture, and to instruct them in Christian American Constitutionalism. We must begin to believe in and understand the Scriptures."[134]

The nihilistic self-destruction Rushdoony foresaw in *Preparation for the Future* was grounded in his belief that American culture was in a state of inexorable decline. But this decline did not mean that Christians were doomed with it. Through the proper understanding of law and its implications for the future, Christians would triumph. God's law, as revealed to the ancient Hebrew prophet Moses, remained relevant and binding for modern Christians. Through the 1960s and 1970s, Rushdoony tried to impress this insight on the supporters of Chalcedon by outlining what a social order structured by the normative standards of biblical law would look like, and how the law could work on the lives and bodies of the remnant of Christian women and men. They could raise up a new generation of law-abiding Christians. In biblical law, Rushdoony had found the mechanism for organizing his dedicated minority of self-governing Christians.

CHAPTER FOUR

Lex Rex

Neoevangelicalism,
Biblical Law, Dominion

*Every law-order is a state of war against the enemies
of that order,* and all law is a form of warfare.
—R. J. RUSHDOONY, *The Institutes of
Biblical Law*, 1:93 (emphasis in the original)

*Love worketh no ill to his neighbour:
therefore love is the fulfilling of the law.*
—Romans 13:10 (King James Version)

In the spring of 1967, as he built the infrastructure for the Chalcedon Foundation, R. J. Rushdoony had a conversation with an incarcerated gang leader. An early *Newsletter* recorded Rushdoony's characterization of the criminal as a "very brilliant young college student" who drank deeply from the fetid springs of modern, humanistic education. In college, the student learned evolutionary theory and theoretical physics. He read existential philosophy. After some reflection, the young man, having "more epistemological self-consciousness" than his wealthy, prominent parents, concluded that the universe is the product of random contingency and, therefore, bound by "no absolute law."[1] Further, philosophical existentialism suggested that all value and meaning are the products of human agency. If nature is random and all social constraints on human behavior are equally capricious, then human law, the student reckoned, was similarly arbitrary. After having this epiphany, the young Übermensch told Rushdoony how he started a gang, committed all manner of horrible crimes, got rich, "and enjoyed more of the 'best' pleasures of life."[2]

Rushdoony never identified this young man who turned to crime as the logical response to humanistic education. Maybe he was a real person Rushdoony interviewed; perhaps he was a pastiche of many of the lawless youths Rushdoony regularly encountered during his frequent speaking tours at colleges and universities across the country. Regardless, one thing is clear: Rushdoony respected this gangster-philosopher because he saw the world more clearly and acted more consistently than his parents and most average Americans. This young man, Rushdoony believed, was undone by a network of interwoven cultural changes that undermined his faith in a created world ruled by the law of a sovereign God. On God's law rested peace, prosperity, and moral order. Without it, there was only chaos.

Ugly America

In the mid-1960s, Rushdoony was hardly alone in perceiving the broader cultural implications of a general breakdown in law and order in the United States. In the lived experience of so many Americans, the sixties were a decade of delinquency, crime, and the fraying of a once tightly woven social fabric. The broad postwar consensus revolving around the fantasy of the nuclear family with its breadwinner father and stay-at-home mother seemed an unattainable ideal to so many.[3] Racial tensions and the civil rights movement threatened to upend the *herrenvolk* status quo of America's de facto apartheid state. Violent crime rates skyrocketed. The number of rapes and murders grew exponentially; property crime—whether in the form of petty theft, inner-city riots, or destructive student demonstrations—unnerved many middle-class Americans. Public and private college campuses across the country became incubators for all manner of radicalism: sexual liberation, recreational drug use, antiwar agitation, and contempt for traditional social values. Decolonization in the Global South, the spread of communism, and the escalating war in Vietnam all pointed to the emergence of a dangerous new global order that refused to respect American hegemony.

In response to the turmoil—especially domestic issues related to crime and poverty—doctrinaire liberals doubled down on monumental welfare schemes harkening back to the perceived successes of the New Deal. In 1964 President Lyndon Baines Johnson called on the graduating class of the University of Michigan to guarantee "abundance and liberty for all" and to fight to end "poverty and racial injustice." He challenged them to "prevent an ugly America" founded on a greedy, "rich," and "powerful society" and urged them to instead build a "Great Society" that would use America's abundant "wealth to enrich and elevate our national life."[4] Conservative Republicans retorted that this "great" society simply subsidized social breakdown by offering federal handouts to the agents of America's social disintegration: blacks, student radicals, and the willfully impoverished.

In the shadow of political battles over Great Society federal programs, social conservatives mobilized a new rhetoric of "law and order" to address the problems of crime, poverty, and student radicalism. According to historian Michael W. Flamm, "law and order" was a "mutation" of the previous decade's "peace through strength" anticommunist rhetoric[5]. Hard-nosed tactics of crime prevention and prosecution mingled easily with tough-love prescriptions for the poor, disenfranchised youths, and the racially oppressed. By emphasizing the visceral fear felt by many Americans concerned with the very real rise in crime, many social conservatives sought to challenge the liberal bureaucratic establishment with a decentralized, localized, and aggressive strategy of law enforcement designed to punish, not reward, the agents of social decay.

While the nation's great cities burned, criminals terrorized law-abiding citizens, and war raged abroad, America's churches quarreled over the Christian-ness of civil disobedience and "law and order." Mirroring the left/right split in the larger political debates of the era, religious organizations approached the problems of crime, violence, and social disorder in a similarly polarized manner. Mainline Protestant institutions by and large stuck to their progressive message, emphasizing ecumenism across religious bodies and social justice for the poor and minorities. Members of prominent parachurch institutions such as the National Council of the Churches of Christ (NCC) went so far as to appropriate some of the tactics of civil disobedience pioneered by civil rights activists resisting Jim Crow in the South and critics of the war in Vietnam.[6] In 1967 a working group at the NCC's General Assembly unnerved many of its more-moderate members and enraged conservatives when it proposed a "general strike" and urged members to aid draft dodgers to resist escalation in the Vietnam conflict.[7]

More theologically and socially conservative Protestant congregations rejected public activism. Instead, they turned to their own set of time-honored themes of personal regeneration through Christ and loyalty to established authority. Disturbed by the drift toward civil disobedience in mainline churches and the general public, the National Association of Evangelicals (NAE) issued a resolution reaffirming their "high regard for law and order."[8] It condemned the "un-American mood which has invaded our society which demonstrates itself as godless, revolutionary and disloyal to the government."[9] The resolution went on to censure Americans who critique "our law enforcement agencies[,] who seek to fulfill their divinely endowed function of maintaining peace and safety."[10] Billy Graham, the most prominent evangelist of the era, echoed these themes in a sermon responding to the Watts riots: "There is no doubt that the rioting, looting, and crime in America have reached the point of anarchy."[11] Further, he insisted in the pages of *Christianity Today* that mainline "liberal" Protestant churches that protested the war in Vietnam or offered a Social Gospel response to poverty were, in fact, "deeply penetrated" with "secularism, materialism, and even Marxism."[12] Law and order would only be restored as Americans returned, one by one, to the loving bosom of Christ.

Against this tumultuous backdrop, Rushdoony preached his own concept of "law and order" that simultaneously embraced the uneasy spirit of the period and pushed against the central assumptions of reformers on the left and right. Neither bound to the political vision of Republican antiliberalism nor accepting of the pieties of traditional American evangelicalism, Rushdoony advocated a *revolution* in Christian concepts of law and justice. In the literal sense of the term, Rushdoony argued that Christians must *return* to the ancient legal codes revealed to Moses amid thunder, lightning, and angelic trumpet blasts at Mount Sinai. There, shrouded in a thick black cloud, the Lord God gave Moses an eternally binding covenant that, according to Rushdoony, modern American Christians had wrongly abandoned. America—God's covenant nation—was in crisis. The answers to this problem could not be found in more police officers, more-conservative politicians, a more-aggressive foreign policy, or a slick evangelical outreach to the souls of a broken nation. Civic salvation would not come through public protest and civil disobedience.

Instead, Rushdoony argued that American Protestants must demolish three areas of conventional evangelical thinking. First, he made it his mission to destroy the hard-won gains made by a generation of wrongheaded evangelical theologians and preachers who mistakenly emphasized pietism and conversion as the answer to all of humanity's problems. Second, conservative Christians must overcome their aversion to taking social responsibility for the nation and instead assert Christ's sovereignty in all spheres of human existence through the application of Mosaic law. Third, fundamentalist and evangelical Christians needed to abandon their all-too-recent infatuation with premillennial rapture theology and return to the aggressive postmillennial vision of the ultimate triumph of Christ's Kingdom on earth.

None of this, of course, would be easy. In fact, the great bulk of contemporary evangelicals could respond that each of these three changes was nothing short of heresy. Taken together, they were especially hard to swallow.

Initially, Rushdoony agitated for these changes within the converging tributaries of the neoevangelical consensus. Even as he worked to turn the Chalcedon Foundation into Chalcedon College, Rushdoony made a doomed bid to be a power player at the neoevangelical journal *Christianity Today*. Seeking the patronage of Sun Oil Company chairman J. Howard Pew, Rushdoony waged a one-man war against Carl F. H. Henry, the journal's executive editor. After losing his fight to drag the editorial policies of this already-conservative publication farther to the right, Rushdoony focused his efforts on the no-less-ambitious project of persuading conservative Protestants to rethink their entire theology of political and social engagement by adopting the strictures of Old Testament law. In this vision of "law and order," they would find the peace of Christ's law-word.

Rushdoony versus the Neoevangelical Coalition

For Rushdoony, the problem of lawlessness in American society was in its essence a theological problem. He had spent the previous two decades attacking fundamentalists and more-moderate evangelical Protestants for failing to provide a clear synthesis between conservative theology, church discipline, and the daily life of committed Christians. In one of his numerous newsletters on the "law and order" problem, Rushdoony laid the blame for social disintegration at the feet of America's evangelical Christians. "We have anarchy because we do not have godly authority," he told his readers. "To re-establish law and order," he insisted, "we must again have godly authority. . . . The weakness of much of evangelical Christianity is a moralistic reduction of the faith to a few 'thou shalt not's,' but the alternative is not license, but, as Christian athletes . . . to commit our entire being to the cause of Christ and His sovereign authority."[13] Rushdoony blamed America's religious leaders for failing to emphasize the Bible as the ultimate source of social stability.

Determined to bring the fight for social reform directly to the church, Rushdoony reached out to the Billy Graham wing of American evangelicalism. In the mid-1960s, as he struggled to raise funds for the Chalcedon Foundation, he approached the emerging neoevangelical movement as a site of potential cooperation and reform. As this became more and more unlikely, he turned his attention to directly condemning its principal representatives and even made a foolhardy attempt to attack *Christianity Today* in its own pages.

Christianity Today

No single national Christian publication was more prominent in the mid-twentieth-century struggle to create a coalition of theologically conservative, socially aware Protestants than *Christianity Today*.[14] As one historian has observed, *Christianity Today* was, at midcentury, "the flagship publication of mainstream evangelicalism."[15] Billy Graham and a group of financial supporters founded the magazine in 1956 to "plant the evangelical flag in the middle of the road, taking a conservative theological position but a definite liberal approach to social problems. It would combine the best in liberalism and the best in fundamentalism without compromising theologically."[16] The journal relied on subsidies from numerous sources, including Billy Graham's public ministry, the William Volker Fund, W. Maxey Jarman (who developed Genesco into one of America's largest apparel companies and was a major supporter of Graham's ministry), and J. Howard Pew.[17] With this kind of financial support, Graham hoped the magazine could become "nothing less than the finest journal in the Western world, comparable to what *Time* is in current events."[18]

Hoping to cultivate intellectual authority in conservative Protestant circles, Graham and his supporters recruited Harold John Ockenga—a graduate of Westminster Theological Seminary, the first president of the National Association of Evangelicals, and a cofounder of Fuller Theological Seminary—to sit on *Christianity Today*'s board. Ockenga called on socially and theologically conservative Protestants to directly engage American culture. Although he noted that evangelicals had "suffered nothing but a series of defeats for decades," he insisted that fundamentalists not remain incarcerated in a dispensationalist prison of their own creation.[19] Eschatological hopes for the immediate return of Christ should not force fundamentalists to "abdicate" their responsibility as leaders in the world.[20] Their conservative brand of Christianity, Ockenga argued, "will be the mainspring in many of the reforms of the societal order."[21]

Taking Ockenga's bid for social relevance as their guide, Graham and the other interests backing *Christianity Today* tapped Fuller professor Carl F. H. Henry to edit the new publication. Henry gained notoriety with *The Uneasy Conscience of Modern Fundamentalism*, a 1947 tract that, in the assessment of historian David Swartz, offered a "radical" indictment of fundamentalist separatism.[22] Henry attacked the pietistic tendency in fundamentalism and urged theologically conservative Protestants to rethink dispensational premillennial eschatology because, according to Swartz, he felt it "inhibited social action among many fundamentalists."[23] Henry believed he offered an alternative to the lack of humanitarian outreach by fundamentalists while simultaneously rejecting theological modernism's failure to address personal salvation.[24]

Together, Graham, Ockenga, and Henry formed the public, organizational, and intellectual trinity behind "neoevangelicalism," or "new evangelism."[25] According to Ockenga, neoevangelicalism could be distinguished from fundamentalism because, although it reaffirmed "the theological view of fundamentalism," it was a "ringing call of repudiation" of fundamentalist separatism "and [a] summons to social involvement."[26] This midcentury movement envisioned a socially relevant brand of theologically conservative Protestantism. The movement has since been described as the "third force" of American Protestantism, occupying a sort of organizational, political, and theological middle path between fundamentalism and theological liberalism.[27] Through the skillful means of deft media outreach—such as Graham's highly popular crusades, print publications like *Christianity Today*, and the NAE's lobbying to protect religious radio broadcasters—neoevangelicals hoped to displace the shriller voices of what they regarded as insular, separatist fundamentalism while simultaneously challenging the cultural hegemony of the liberal Protestant establishment.[28]

As Graham emerged as the public face of the new evangelicalism, *Christianity Today* developed into its intellectual and journalistic voice. During the publication's first decade, Henry attempted to produce a magazine that "spoke for evangelicals," a sophisticated journal that was "published across the street from the White House"[29] and reached a broad audience of laypeople, clergy, policy makers, and business leaders. He wanted a magazine and staff that, according to historian Stephen Board, "valued journalistic reporting, scholarly credentials, and, most of all, serious debate."[30] With this focus on journalism and scholarly debate, Henry hoped the publication would combine "an irenic spirit with theological integrity" so that evangelicals might move beyond factional theological concerns to address social issues.[31]

With its mission to cultivate a new form of socially engaged and culturally aware conservative evangelicalism, *Christianity Today*'s editors sought out authors capable of writing articles on a wide range of contemporary issues facing socially and theologically conservative Protestants. They were particularly interested in critics of theological modernism who could communicate complex theological issues to a generalist audience. They reached out to clergy, laity, and academics at churches and Christian liberal-arts colleges around the United States.

In 1957 *Christianity Today* associate editor Dr. J. Marcellus Kik sent R. J. Rushdoony, then known primarily as a promising young critic of modernism and secular education, a letter announcing the launch of the new venture. At the time, Rushdoony had not yet abandoned the mainline Presbyterian Church (U.S.A.) for J. Gresham Machen's separatist Orthodox Presbyterian Church. If Rushdoony had done so, Kik would likely never have reached out to him because, as Henry later recalled of his editorial strategy, "We solicited articles from evangelicals in mainline denominations, not because we were precommitted to ecumenism but because writers in the independent churches might give the magazine an anti-ecumenical cast that would hinder our outreach."[32] Rushdoony's combination of mainline affiliation and growing stature as a capable critic of theological modernism prompted Kik to solicit his submissions: "I would like to have you suggest articles which you might like to contribute to our new magazine. . . . It is my hope that you will accede to our requests."[33] Rushdoony jumped at the opportunity.

Rushdoony accepted Kik's invitation because, like many theologically conservative clergy of his day, he perceived that this new publication might serve as a response to the dangerous liberalism embodied in other national Protestant publications such as *Christianity and Crisis* and *Christian Century*. Just as Rushdoony had criticized Spiritual Mobilization's *Faith and Freedom* a decade earlier, he similarly recognized that the proposed magazine was not "as Calvinist as I would like it."[34] Nonetheless, he was clearly a model author and reader of the new venture: he was a self-identified fundamentalist who rejected the cultural isolationism of many of his peers and longed for a more robust Christian engagement with contemporary culture.[35]

In spite of his sectarian misgivings, Rushdoony supported the publication with short articles, book reviews, and freelance editorial work.[36] In the first volume (1956) of *Christianity Today*, he published one of his first articles authored for a wide, non-Calvinist Protestant audience, and with it, he began a long, restive relationship with the neoevangelical publication.[37] In turn, the editors ran favorable reviews of some of Rushdoony's early books, including *By What Standard?* and *Van Til*.[38] Rushdoony's relationship with *Christianity Today* deepened when the editors realized that he had a particular strength for clarifying complex theological ideas for general readers. As a capable popularizer of the difficult ideas of Cornelius Van Til, *Christianity Today*'s editors specifically sought out Rushdoony to help edit and clarify the Westminster theologian's submissions. In one note soliciting Rushdoony's aid, Kik conceded: "Both Carl Henry and myself have struggled with [Van Til's manuscript] in order to clarify it. Since you have clarified the writing of Van Til previously, I thought the best thing we could do is to send it to you to work over. Please remember 95% of our readers have no knowledge what *geschichte* is. Anything you can do to clarify will be helpful."[39] Rushdoony fulfilled this request and occasionally worked as a freelancer for the magazine.

A Definite Strain of Heresy

Even as he worked to further the general mission of *Christianity Today*, Rushdoony also regularly criticized the editors. In 1959 Rushdoony attacked Henry and Kik's decision to publish a favorable review of the writings of William Faulkner.[40] Believing the editors must be unfamiliar with Faulkner's oeuvre, Rushdoony informed the editors that the southern author "specializes in inventing fantastic and twisted versions of violence."[41] He then offered a litany of vulgar anecdotes culled from Faulkner's writing: Popeye's corn-cob rape of Temple Drake in *Sanctuary*; Vardaman Bundren, from *As I Lay Dying,* accidentally auguring holes into his dead mother's face; and, in "A Rose for Emily," the poisoned, rotting corpse of Homer Barron in the titular character's bedchamber. After citing this vivid inventory of the evils in Faulkner's work, Rushdoony concluded: "I maintain that the defense of or liking for Faulkner is a sign of moral and spiritual degeneracy . . . and that *Christianity Today* has no moral right to protest filth on the newsstands and then give such prominence to Faulkner. I realize that the editors have probably not themselves read Faulkner or they would not have accepted the article."[42]

If Rushdoony meant this final sentence as a rebuke of the intellectual vapidity of the magazine's editors, they hardly noticed. Instead, Kik admitted that he and others at the magazine had never read Faulkner. "If the editors had read William Faulkner's works," Kik began, "and they are as you described them, you may be assured this article never would have appeared in our magazine."[43] Kik's statement underscores how far the editors of the "flagship" journalistic and intellectual endeavor of neoevangelicalism had to come in order to effectively banish any lingering residue of fundamentalist cultural isolationism. Rushdoony's warnings about Faulkner would have hardly been unusual coming from a socially and theologically conservative clergy member, but the difference was that Rushdoony had actually read Faulkner as part of his undergraduate education at Berkeley. And he continued to read modern fiction as a minister, weaving its degenerate imagery into his sermons and writings. Further, the heavy-handedness with which he addressed Kik and the other editors—all learned and highly respected clergymen—indicated that Rushdoony was more than willing to bruise a budding professional relationship in order to play the role of informed Christian culture warrior.

By the mid-1960s, Rushdoony's willingness to cooperate with the editors of *Christianity Today* evaporated. The "irenic" spirit envisioned by Henry was giving way to something new: once-curious fundamentalists who had suspended their critical judgment of neoevangelicalism turned their anger from perceived enemies in modern culture toward the neoevangelical project itself.[44] Rev. Carl McIntire—"God's angriest man," as media scholar Heather Hendershot has described him—had already spent much of the late 1950s and early 1960s attacking neoevangelicalism on his popular religious radio program.[45] Graham's "ecumenical evangelicalism," which shockingly suggested that there might be a range of acceptable positions on theological and doctrinal matters, made many fundamentalists suspicious of neoevangelicalism. These concerns came to a head in the mid-1960s as the socially and politically active conservative religious pressure groups emerging across the country suddenly had the resources necessary to offer an alternative to neoevangelicalism.

Rushdoony joined a growing chorus of neoevangelical critics, and he took his attack directly to the top. No longer content to protest the filth in Faulkner to some associate editor, Rushdoony directly confronted Dr. L. Nelson Bell, the journal's executive editor and Billy Graham's father-in-law. In a 1961 letter to Bell, Rushdoony cut to the heart of the matter: "I am writing to you, as executive editor, to express my concern over certain very pronounced tendencies in *Christianity Today*. I have reference to the very marked hostility being displayed towards the orthodox view of Genesis."[46] Rushdoony was particularly concerned with a handful of book reviews that he believed did not line up with fundamentalist interpretations of the historical factuality of the events recorded in Genesis 1:11. Rushdoony concluded his critical essay by suggesting that he was part of a larger community of clergy concerned "over this tendency" at the magazine. "It does indicate," he asserted, "a definite strain of heresy as the official stance of what professes to be an orthodox publication. And, unless radical changes are made, we can only assume that the publication intends to go further along these lines."[47]

Rushdoony's note suggests that he was either unaware of or unconcerned with the fact that Henry and Graham intended the publication to include a spectrum of opinions popular among evangelical thinkers. While it is true that *Christianity Today* was generally fundamentalist in its stance on the Genesis creation narrative, it is also true that even among fundamentalists, there was some nuance and sophistication in interpreting the literal historicity of Genesis. That Rushdoony so aggressively moved to foreclose this range of opinion suggests that any cooperation with the big-tent mission of the Henry/Graham neoevangelical coalition was impossible.

In a strongly worded letter to Dr. C. Gregg Singer, a history professor at Catawba College in North Carolina, Rushdoony spelled out his concerns about *Christianity Today*'s breed of neoevangelicalism. "*Christianity Today*," he explained,

> rejected the position the Reformers stood for. It holds to the position known as "neoevangelicalism," or the "new evangelicalism." This position . . . plays down [Kuyper's concept] of the antithesis, holds that doctrines which divide "Christians," such as infallibility, the atonement, etc., should not be sharply stated but only generally so, and that "love" must be emphasized ad nauseam. . . . But, most of all, there is a determined hostility to Calvinistic thinking, because it represents an uncompromising stand on the Biblical faith. *Christianity Today* wants to further "dialogue" with the opposition. And "dialogue" today is really a technical word in the vocabulary of the left, and it means surrender in order to have common ground.[48]

This sort of rhetoric hardly would have endeared Rushdoony to Henry and others at *Christianity Today*, and it also made clear his now-unequivocal hostility to a magazine he had initially approached with such high hopes. More important, however, Rushdoony's statement to Singer highlights the fact that Rushdoony believed that neoevangelicalism was a closed coalition that was "capturing old Fundamentalism, and old orthodoxy."[49] That Rushdoony feared a movement that shared most of his core theological values but did so in an insufficiently rigorous manner suggests a form of theological purism that had drastic sociological implications; he was rapidly moving toward a theological position that precluded any ability to cooperate with anyone who disagreed with his interpretation of Scripture, no matter how minor or insignificant the distinction. And he was moving to this position just as J. Howard Pew offered him the chance to replace Kik and become a regular contributor to *Christianity Today*, a position that could possibly entail considerable influence in the neoevangelical coalition.

J. Howard Pew

Oilman J. Howard Pew, perhaps most famous today as one of the cofounders of the Pew Charitable Trusts, was a prominent Presbyterian layman and major financial backer of *Christianity Today*. Pew's massive oil fortune, according to historian Darren Dochuk, was "instrumental" in shaping America's conservative drift in politics and theology.[50] His money influenced the political careers of Barry Goldwater, Richard Nixon, and Ronald Reagan, helped bankroll Billy Graham's ministries, reshaped mainline Presbyterianism, and molded popular conceptions of evangelical theology.[51]

As a noted and wealthy layman in the Presbyterian Church (U.S.A.), Pew had long been an outspoken critic of theological modernism and socially "liberal" movements such as the Social Gospel. He believed it was his duty, as historian E. V. Toy has noted, to "counteract the misconceptions that many ministers had about businessmen."[52] Like many midcentury figures influenced by Protestant fundamentalism, Pew feared that theological liberalism went hand in hand with social liberalism in a way that undermined the possibility for the individual redemption of human beings in favor of a collectivist form of social redemption that he believed to be utopian and unbiblical. Further, he was part of a generation of socially conservative business leaders who used their economic influence to counteract what they interpreted as liberalism among American clergy.[53] Pew was a significant financial backer of such right-wing, religiously affiliated organizations as Spiritual Mobilization, the Foundation for Economic Education, and the Christian Freedom Foundation. He was particularly interested in saving American Presbyterianism from what he saw as a dangerous leftward drift in terms of both theology and politics. Pew's concern for the general "liberalization" of American Protestantism led to his heavy emotional and financial investment in *Christianity Today*. It also prompted him to flirt with hiring Rushdoony as a key ally in his struggle against the liberal Protestant establishment.

Rushdoony and Pew's budding relationship was directly linked to Pew's wider fight against theological and social liberalism. Rushdoony admired Pew's doggish struggle in the late 1940s and early 1950s as chairman of the National Lay Committee of the NCC. When his Lay Committee failed to check the power of the clergy, Pew angrily declared that the NCC and its various organs "constitute the most powerful subversive force in the United States."[54] After angrily disbanding the Lay Committee, Pew continued his quest to resist theological and social liberalism in the church via a host of other initiatives, such as Spiritual Mobilization and the Christian Freedom

Foundation, which eventually brought him into contact with R. J. Rushdoony. Their cooperation in these organizations was not accidental. They shared many sympathies: staunch support of a Reformed worldview; distrust of the NCC and other "socialistic" parachurch organizations; support for the John Birch Society; and respect for Westminster Theological Seminary.[55]

Pew and Rushdoony crossed paths because of Pew's support for *Christianity Today* and another important midcentury right-wing journal, *Christian Economics*. Rushdoony had been a longtime reader and contributor to the latter publication when its editor and the CFF president, Howard E. Kershner, recommended that Pew enlist Rushdoony as an ally in the fight against liberal Protestantism. When Marcellus Kik died suddenly in the fall of 1965, Kershner recommended the "very scholarly and sound" Rushdoony as a possible replacement.[56] Following Kershner's suggestion, Pew quickly settled on Rushdoony as a possible contributor to *Christianity Today* and, eventually, as a potential replacement for Kik.

"Knowing how interested you have been in the history and development of our Church down through the ages," Pew wrote to Rushdoony shortly after Kik's death, "I was wondering if you would like to continue Dr. Kik's work."[57] Rushdoony eagerly responded, "I am honored that you are considering me to continue Dr. Kik's work, and am greatly interested."[58] Pew carefully vetted Rushdoony for the position, going so far as to investigate his divorce from Arda Gent and remarriage to Dorothy Kirkwood. In response to one such inquiry, C. Gregg Singer wrote to Pew assuring him that the ultraconservative Orthodox Presbyterian Church (OPC) had accepted Rushdoony's divorce. Singer reported on the facts of the divorce and explained that "the OPC committee and presbytery accepted Rushdoony and found his grounds valid. In its 30 year history, the OPC has only accepted two divorced men, and, in the other case, it was an annulment rather than a divorce."[59]

Satisfied with Rushdoony's personal character, Pew moved to give him a prominent national platform in the pages of *Christianity Today*. On Monday, February 14, 1966, Pew flew Rushdoony from Los Angeles to Phoenix for a private audience. There, the two men discussed Rushdoony's desire to start a Christian college under the auspices of the Chalcedon Foundation, and Pew proposed his hope that Rushdoony might replace Kik.[60] During the meeting, Pew also solicited a series of four articles on the topic of "The Mediator: Christ or the Church?" The articles would, in Pew's words, address "the need of the church to keep out of economic, social and political affairs."[61]

This offer set Rushdoony on a collision course with Henry and the other editors at *Christianity Today* who, though largely in agreement with Pew and Rushdoony's criticism of clerical politicking, were trying to avoid showy theological arguments that might alienate socially moderate members of the evangelical coalition. The resulting conflict among Pew, Henry, and Rushdoony provides a clear illustration of the tensions surrounding the creation of the institutional, symbolic, and theological boundaries emerging at the edges of the neoevangelical coalition.

Failed Mediations

Pew maintained tight financial control over *Christianity Today* during its early years of operation. As historian Kim Phillips-Fein has noted, Pew previously had focused his attention on denominational publications with limited appeal and on such polemical interdenominational publications as *Faith and Freedom* and *Christian Economics*, which warned of the dangers of liberal politics and the threat of socialism to American religion. Unlike these previous efforts, which Phillips-Fein pointed out had small readerships and little popular support, "*Christianity Today* was a project genuinely rooted in the network of revivalism and evangelicalism, and it was far more successful than fringe groups [such as Spiritual Mobilization, the Christian Freedom Foundation, and the Foundation for Economic Education] that had wanted to bring capitalism to Christianity and businessmen into the church. But its very independence—its determination to be a 'forum' rather than an 'organ'—at times frustrated the oilman, and in 1964 he offered his resignation from the board of the magazine."[62]

Even though Pew resigned from *Christianity Today*'s board, he continued to subsidize the financially troubled journal and used his fiscal commitment to justify supervision of its production. Pew worried that Carl Henry was a socialist who might use *Christianity Today* to covertly spread a collectivist Christian agenda.[63] With his cash on the line, Pew insisted that he had a right to review advanced proofs of each edition of the publication. Fortunately for Henry, Bell and Kik believed such arrangements reduced the editorial staff's "professional dignity" to the level of "salaried propagandists," and they worked to insulate Henry from some of Pew's meddling.[64]

L. Nelson Bell's attempt to conceal Pew's micromanaging did not stop the oilman from using his influence to hand-select authors and articles he wanted published. Pew intended Rushdoony's "Mediator" series to be a clarion conservative voice in what he perceived to be a mealymouthed, perhaps even crypto-socialist, publication. The series would highlight the theologian's and the businessman's shared skepticism of clerical activism.

In an unpublished draft of the first essay in the series, Rushdoony did not disappoint. "The modern attempt to reduce Jesus to the level of political reformer, and the church to the same level," he wrote, "is a denial of Christ's true Kingship."[65] When Rushdoony submitted the first article for consideration, Pew declared, "I am entirely in agreement with it," and he encouraged the editors of *Christianity Today* to publish it immediately.[66] In a letter to Bell, Pew gushed: "Mr. Rushdoony is a scholar and I believe as well equipped to write on this subject as anybody I know. . . . Time is running out and we should get these articles in *Christianity Today* very quickly."[67] Pew pushed the issue so aggressively that Rushdoony believed that it was a foregone conclusion that his essays would eventually appear in the magazine. To C. Gregg Singer, Rushdoony explained: "I have at least one article soon to appear in *Christianity Today*, but not because the staff wants it there, but because Mr. Pew does."[68]

Given Rushdoony's certainty about Pew's support, what happened next likely came as a shock. Henry accepted the first article in the series, but he rejected the second. Henry and his editors focused on a key passage in which Rushdoony interpreted Satan's Temptation of Jesus in the wilderness as a rejection of socialism. "In the Temptation," Rushdoony argued, "Jesus has maintained the integrity of his vocation. The First Temptation was to turn the stones of the wilderness into bread. The world was full of hungry men, starving babies, economic problems and Satan demanded in effect that Jesus prove Himself a savior, a compassionate redeemer, by dealing with the politico-economic crises of man."[69] Rushdoony interpreted Jesus's rejoinder—"Man shall not live on bread alone"—as a categorical rejection of socialism: "Salvation is not in the manipulation of man's environment: it is the regeneration of man's heart, and hence . . . the apostles were clearly forewarned against proclaiming a social (or socialist) gospel in place of the atoning, redemptive work of the crucified and risen Jesus Christ."[70]

Henry, citing both his reading of the article and the authority of his reviewers, declared Rushdoony's interpretation of the Temptation "highly fanciful."[71] To add insult to injury, Henry's anonymous reviewers offered bitingly personal negative comments about the argument and its author. They deemed the essay "bizarre" and "laughable."[72] One reviewer asserted that Rushdoony knowingly "twisted" the passage and was therefore trying to "pervert" Scripture.[73] Enraged, Rushdoony curtly demanded the return of both essays: "Kindly return my first essay to me. It is one of a series of four, and I have no desire to break up the series. Moreover, it is for me more a liability than an asset to be published in *Christianity Today*."[74] Henry returned both essays but insisted that he and his editors had found the first essay adequate after making "some factual corrections."[75]

Henry gave a carbon copy of his reviewers' insulting comments to Pew. His willingness to share these attacks on Rushdoony's second "Mediator" essay suggests that Henry wanted to let the meddlesome Pew glimpse the editorial process. Given Pew's initial support for Rushdoony as Kik's successor, it is likely that Henry was concerned about the possibility of a vocal critic of *Christianity Today* becoming a patron of one of the magazine's major financial supporters. Although Henry usually struggled to keep Pew out of the editorial loop, by sharing the consensus opinion of the reviewers that Rushdoony was a theological crackpot, he likely served his own strategic interests of maintaining editorial control over the publication.

Regardless of whether Henry rejected the essay for theological or political reasons, Rushdoony abruptly ended any hopes of developing a potentially lucrative patronage arrangement with Pew. In an angry letter to Pew, Rushdoony briefly summarized his reluctance to work further with *Christianity Today*, concluding: "I cannot work with pygmies; you are in a position where you can command them, and I am not. . . . I am sorry that this terminates our association, because I do have a very great respect for you and your faith."[76] There is no evidence that Rushdoony wanted Pew to intervene on his behalf or that Rushdoony tried to save their relationship by editing the essay. In fact, as Gary North later recalled, just as this publishing deal with Henry collapsed, Pew had said to Rushdoony, "I want you to help me win back the Presbyterian Church" from theological and social liberals. According to North, Rushdoony responded, "I am not interested in winning back the Presbyterian Church. It's too late." This reaction, North remembered, "cost him a well-funded career, at least until Pew's death in 1973. Pew ended the meeting and never called him again."[77]

Rushdoony's failure to navigate the editorial process at *Christianity Today* and his contempt for mainline Presbyterianism was significant on multiple levels. First, it effectively ended his chances of ever playing in the neo-evangelical court. While others from the neo-Calvinist and conservative Reformed worlds joined the neoevangelical coalition, Rushdoony refined the concept of Christian Reconstructionism—in part, as a reaction to neo-evangelicalism. Second, Rushdoony would have to wait another two decades before he would find a benefactor with pockets even a fraction as deep as Pew's. While it is clear that Rushdoony mishandled his relationship with Harold Luhnow and the Volker Fund, it appears that Rushdoony learned something from this earlier failure and concluded that any relationship with

Pew would be on the oilman's terms, not his. As a result, the reverend was far less aggressive in asserting his position with Pew, and for his part, Pew was willing to flirt with Rushdoony but reluctant to go to the mat to protect him.

Finally, and perhaps most importantly, Rushdoony's fight with *Christianity Today* helped establish the way that the wider community of America's theologically and socially conservative Protestants would receive Rushdoony's ideas. Rushdoony's decision to first criticize and then actively attack the neoevangelical mainstream became a point of identificatory distinction not only for Christian Reconstructionism but also for neoevangelicals. Although many within the neoevangelical coalition adhered to a vaguely conservative social and economic political philosophy, few cleaved to anything as systematic or totalizing as Christian Reconstruction.[78] Consequently, over the next two decades, Christian Reconstruction emerged as a limit for neoevangelicalism; it was at once irreducibly interwoven into the textual, institutional, and theological milieu of conservative neoevangelical Protestantism and perceived as a threat to traditional orthodoxy.

Sanctified by Grace, Regenerated by Law

While Rushdoony's Mediator series ostensibly served Pew's purpose of criticizing the intervention of the NCC and other Christian organizations into contemporary economic and political controversies, it rested on ideas that Rushdoony had been developing since his time in Owyhee. Specifically, Rushdoony structured the essay around the basic ideas he had developed to explain the contemporary political implications of the Definition of Chalcedon. In the first essay of the Mediator series, Rushdoony argued that when Jesus told Pilate "my Kingdom is not of this world," the godman "thus had separated His divine kingship from human kingship."[79] This meant that God's "universal law" limited all human kingdoms.[80] God's law emerged as a central category in the essays and revealed the true impetus behind the series. Rushdoony did not intend to provide a theological rubber stamp for Pew's ecclesiastical ambitions, nor did he simply hope to challenge neoevangelicalism. Instead, the series embodied one of Rushdoony's earliest attempts to argue that Christians must turn their attention to the legal foundations of their religion. This insight—however controversial, loved, or loathed it would become eventually—grew out of Rushdoony's perception that lawlessness and rebellion were creeping into all spheres of society. If social breakdown was total, it required a totalizing solution. The logical response, then, was to turn back to God's law and away from the failed forms of modern Christianity and humanism that had led to the current crisis.

Evangelical Universalism

In his political biography of Billy Graham, historian Steven P. Miller summarized neoevangelical political theology as an expression of a long-standing American tradition of "evangelical universalism." According to Miller, evangelical universalism "viewed the individual soul as the primary theological political unit of society, prioritized relational over legislative solutions to social problems, and it tended to acquiesce to the ultimate inscrutable realm of ordained legal authority."[81] Graham embodied these concerns in his very personal attempts to minister to public figures he hoped might be paragons of Christian statesmanship and custodians of America's Christian civilization.[82]

Carl F. H. Henry had offered an early expression of these ideas for intellectuals, students, and pastors in *The Uneasy Conscience of Modern Fundamentalism*. There, Henry attacked fundamentalists for their social and political retreat, but he also warned against the politically liberal position, embodied in the Social Gospel, of viewing the state as the primary mechanism for social reform.[83] Keeping with well-trodden evangelical themes, as David Swartz has highlighted, "Henry's clearest suggestion for social change had less to do with party politics than with personal transformation."[84] When he came to *Christianity Today* in 1956, Henry emphasized the distinction between divine salvation and civil law. For Henry, and for many of the self-identifying neoevangelicals influenced by his vision of social engagement, law was largely "negative" or "preservational."[85] According to Miller, "in contrast to the regenerative, transformational effects of individual conversions, the state did possess a legitimate role to play in upholding and implementing justice. That role, though, was more corrective and constructive—mere justice, in contrast to regeneration and its by-product of human reconciliation."[86]

This negative view of the law and its operation in the lives of humans may have dominated the sensibilities of many evangelicals, but it hardly exhausted the perspectives available to theologically and socially conservative Protestants. By the mid-1960s, abstract theological concepts of the law took on a new salience as concerns about the breakdown of moral and legal order became central themes in American national politics. Barry Goldwater, that most Pyrrhic of conservative crusaders, emphasized crime and domestic social decay in his combative 1964 acceptance speech at the Republican National Convention. "Tonight there is violence in our streets," Goldwater declared, "corruption in our highest offices, aimlessness among our youth, anxiety among our elders and there is a virtual despair among the many who look beyond material success for the inner meaning of their lives."[87] Goldwater made "enforcing law and order" a central component of his campaign. By 1965, his words seemed prescient for many Americans. The Watts Riots, uprising on college campuses, and nationwide resistance to the military draft made "law and order" a national concern.[88] Following the trail blazed by Goldwater, conservative politicians ranging from George Wallace to Richard Nixon and Ronald Reagan effortlessly conflated disparate forms of social protest with base criminality. Popular political discourse linked the civil rights movement, anti–Vietnam War protests, and libertine sexual experimentation and illicit drug use with the real and perceived rise in violent crime.

This volatile environment led some socially and theologically conservative Protestants to conclude that neoevangelicalism's negative view of the law was insufficient for the dark realities of the time. Discontent with the "law-and-order" question convinced many conservative Protestants that it was time to rethink the relationship between Christianity and civil order. Fortunately for a small number of Southern Californians, R. J. Rushdoony had been thinking about God's law for almost two decades and was ready to publish a series of books and articles that would prod a generation of evangelicals to rethink their basic assumptions about the relationship between Christianity, civil law, and democracy.

Anti-Babel

The contours of Rushdoony's system of legal reasoning had their roots in the 1940s and his seminary training at the Pacific School of Religion. There, Rushdoony remembered, he "got clobbered . . . for opening my mouth once or twice about Biblical law. So I pulled in my horns and said nothing for almost a generation until I felt I was almost ready."[89] During this generation of preparation, Rushdoony began hinting at the implications of biblical law in his writings of the late 1950s, extending across an array of articles, books, and public lectures. As early as 1958, in *By What Standard?*, Rushdoony indicated that God's law played a significant role in setting the normative limits for human behavior.[90] As he lectured, preached, and wrote, this basic insight about the importance of law gave way to a broader agenda of Christian governance. In this system, Rushdoony argued, the Bible prescribed a social order in which male patriarchs exercised God's dominion mandate over the earth through an extended network of Christian families under the authority of God's law.

By the early 1960s, in a series of historical studies, Rushdoony began working through the trine concepts of Christian dominion, biblical law, and postmillennial eschatology that would form the bedrock of his most-mature and influential theological writings. Beginning with 1961's *Intellectual Schizophrenia*, a critical study of humanistic pedagogy in state-funded public schools, Rushdoony began fleshing out the relationship between dominion and law. "Man is called to exercise his image mandate in knowledge, righteousness, holiness and dominion," he wrote, "subduing the earth agriculturally, scientifically, culturally, artistically, in every way possible asserting the crown rights of King Jesus in every realm of life, claiming the kingdoms of this world as the Kingdoms of our Lord and his Christ."[91] Education and its product—knowledge—were merely components of this wider project of dominion, which, in Rushdoony's early work, rested on a still nebulous concept of biblical law.

Rushdoony further refined the relationship between law and dominion in his twin studies of American history, *This Independent Republic* (1964) and *The Nature of the American System* (1965). In these thematically and theologically linked studies, Rushdoony argued that the American concept of liberty as it developed from colonization, through the Revolutionary era, and beyond rested on a Calvinist-derived theocratic "Christian commonwealth" that thrived in the northern colonies and parts of the South. Rushdoony believed he found evidence that significant portions of the civil structure of the early New England and southern colonies were, "almost from [their] inception, *a Protestant restoration of feudalism.*"[92] His reading of colonial history emphasized a decentralized feudal order with no kingly head. Instead, the Protestant form of feudalism found in the colonies made every man a priest and king of his own dominion. As such, Rushdoony argued that this "American feudal system" undermined the "Babel-like unity" of the centralized nation-state emerging contemporaneously in Europe. The American feudal order assured that the "*state was thus placed under God, not in the being of God as in paganism.*"[93] In this idiosyncratic reading of American history, the Revolution became an antistatist "counter-revolution" that denied the concept of *human* sovereignty and distrusted the "people." Democracy, Rushdoony asserted, like many of his conservative contemporaries, was never the intent of early Americans.[94]

America's early colonial environment was made up of decentralized, independent, but interconnected Christian theocracies organized by the "sovereignty of God and His kingship."[95] With Christian liberty under God's law (and not humanity's), colonial men were free to serve the threefold office of king, prophet, and priest under God's law. "As king," Rushdoony explained, each Christian male is called "to exercise dominion in the name of God over all creation; as prophet, he is to interpret all things in terms of his sovereign God; as priest, he is to dedicate all things to his sovereign, God."[96] Men are called by God to exercise these offices of dominion in every sphere of life. The spheres radiate out from the reconstructed Christian self to form the family, the church, and the state. Faith in and dedication to God's final sovereignty dictated that no sphere can be made subservient to another. Therefore, every sphere provides a check to the potential tyranny of the others. It is in this sense that Rushdoony later wrote of the church and family as the primary instruments of "anti-Babel"; that is, at every turn, true Christian families and churches provide a check against the totalitarian claims of the state on the lives of humans.[97]

Demolition and Reconstruction

Rushdoony founded the Chalcedon Foundation in 1965 to embody the anti-Babel forces of Christian liberty. The purpose of the new organization was neither to save America through political action nor to call the country back to its historically Christian roots. In Rushdoony's view, the first goal (which was synonymous with the resurgent midcentury conservative movement embodied in the likes of Goldwater, the JBS, and *National Review*) is myopic and present-focused, while the latter (a mission often associated with the Christian Right of the 1980s) is hopelessly nostalgic. On the fortieth anniversary of the foundation of Chalcedon, Mark Rushdoony succinctly summarized the "future-oriented" purpose of his father's organization: "Its purpose was not to convert non-believers, but to teach believers. Its purpose was always to train Christians to be faithful to the law-word of God. Chalcedon was self-consciously established to fill a large void in Christianity. The church was so busy focusing on the 'fundamentals' and the 'simple gospel' that it tended not to go beyond preaching the gospel and baptizing. Chalcedon was to be a ministry about faithful obedience, about the other half of the Great Commission: teaching men to observe all things Christ commanded."[98] It was this focus on the future that led Rushdoony to some of his most profound and innovative ideas of the late 1960s. Specifically, following the publication of *This Independent Republic* and *The Nature of the American System*, Rushdoony began expounding upon the latent theme of biblical, or

Mosaic, law that ran throughout his writings but that, up to this point, had remained largely undeveloped.

Rushdoony's interest in law grew from the twin failures of neoevangelicalism and Van Til's presuppositional theology to provide clear, systemic responses to the chaotic social environment of the late 1960s and early 1970s. First, Rushdoony denounced the evangelical universalism represented in the popular message of Billy Graham as "pious irrelevance, anti-nomianism, phariseeism, and a general immoralism."[99] Neoevangelicalism offered Christians an ad hoc mishmash of feel-good pieties and moral tsk-tsking, but not a systematic plan of obedience and action in the world. "The strength of the Christian," Rushdoony wrote, "can only be a 'system,' i.e., systematic theology, a knowing, intelligent, and systematic obedience to the triune God, and faithful application of God's law order to every sphere of life. If the Christian operates without this system, he is a humanist without knowing it. And this is the reason for the great impotence of conservative, evangelical Christianity."[100]

This failure of conservative evangelical leaders to provide a systemic form of Christianity was, in Rushdoony's assessment, "the central failure of the modern age." "In the United States," he continued,

> as nowhere else in the world, the culture should be dominated by
> the churches. The majority of Americans are church members. If
> we eliminate those who are modernists, we must still recognize that
> thirty to forty million Protestants claim to be evangelicals. No other
> group in America, however, has less impact on national life. . . . The
> more this Protestant evangelicalism is "revived," the more irrelevant
> it becomes. The deeply rooted antinomianism of its pietism . . . has
> made it unable to work effectively in society. It has become present
> oriented and experiential. Its answer to problems is not the applica
> tion of god's law-word to man and society but instead a yearning
> for more emotional experiences.[101]

Contemporary evangelicalism might revive the spirit, but it provided none of the necessary tools to reconstruct a sick society.

Next, Rushdoony also recognized the *positive* limitations of the presuppositional apologetics of Cornelius Van Til. That is, up until the mid-1960s, Rushdoony viewed Van Til's system as purely *negative*; it demolished modern philosophy and its anthropocentric image of man, but it did not build anything to replace the humanistic system it destroyed. Gary North, in his typically vivid prose, made this point:

Van Til was analogous to a demolitions expert. He placed explosive charges at the base of every modern edifice he could locate, and book by book, syllabus by syllabus, he detonated them. One by one, the buildings came down. But he left no blueprints for the reconstruction of society. He saw his job as narrowly negative: blowing up dangerous buildings with their weak (schizophrenic) foundations. This narrowly defined task was not good enough for Rushdoony. He recognized early that there has to be an alternative to the collapsed buildings. There have to be blueprints. But where are they to be found? Step by step in the 1960's, he concluded that the source of the missing blueprints is Old Testament law.[102]

This conclusion, as North noted, grew from Rushdoony's interpretation of Van Til's antithesis between autonomous and theonomous reasoning. In this binary opposition, intellectual autonomy—self-rule of the mind—emerges as sinful pretense, whereas theonomy—God's rule of the mind—is the only source for legitimate knowledge.

Neoevangelicals could revive, presuppositionalists could destroy, but neither could reconstruct. This perception of the twin failures of neoevangelicalism and neo-Calvinism prompted Rushdoony to develop a systemic Protestant casuistry to respond to the "law-and-order" problem of the 1960s.[103] If Rushdoony had made multiple references to the importance of biblical law as the necessary foundation for Christian reasoning in his earliest works dating to the 1950s, then it was not until he moved to Woodland Hills in 1965 and founded the Chalcedon Foundation that he refined this focus and began offering an expansive rereading of modern American culture through the lens of biblical law.

Although the *Newsletter* made clear references to Rushdoony's research in biblical law in its first issues published in 1965, his earliest public lecture on the topic appears to have been in 1969 at Westmont College in Santa Barbara, California. There, he capped several days of lectures with a chapel discussion of "Biblical Law."[104] Sitting in on the lectures was nineteen-year-old Greg Bahnsen, a Westmont sophomore. Rushdoony's ideas about biblical law "amazed and intrigued" the ambitious young philosophy major, who would later study under Van Til at Westminster Theological Seminary and earn a Ph.D. from the University of Southern California.[105] He went on to write *Theonomy in Christian Ethics* (1977), widely regarded as the most intellectually rigorous argument for theonomic principles in Christian apologetics.

As 1969 ended, Rushdoony developed his chapel discussion into the first five chapters of what would eventually become the first volume of *The Institutes of Biblical Law* (1973). By 1970, biblical law and related topics, such as Christian Reconstruction and dominion, had become the central topics in his public lectures and Bible study meetings. At the end of 1970, he recorded that he had completed a staggering fifty-four chapters of the *Institutes*, the vast bulk of the tome.[106] The mission of Chalcedon and his calling by Women for America was coming into focus as Rushdoony developed a unique theology that identified biblical law as the primary structuring force in human life.

The Kingdom of God

In the earliest drafts of lectures and chapters of what ultimately became *The Institutes of Biblical Law*, Rushdoony argued that Old Testament law is still binding for modern Christians. Why biblical law? Because, as Rushdoony concluded after more than three decades of reading, researching, lecturing, and writing—eventually condensed into 1,791 pages and three volumes— "the law is always discriminatory."[107] The law constrains the ability of autonomous, rational humans to think apart from God by setting clear parameters on how one may interpret the world, and therefore on how one may act in the world. "The law," he elaborated, "cannot favor equality without ceasing to be the law: at all times, the law defines . . . those who constitute the legitimate and the illegitimate members of society. The fact of law introduces a fundamental and basic inequality in society."[108] In a nearly Durkheimian sociological idiom, Rushdoony insisted: "The true holiness of man is man's separation unto God in faith and in obedience to God's law. The law is thus the specified way to holiness."[109] Biblical law defines what is holy by drawing strict distinctions.

For Rushdoony, every jot and tittle of biblical law—from invocations of the death penalty to rules about the length of fringe on priestly garments— functioned as the structuring blueprint for all aspects of life.[110] He focused a considerable amount of his study of the law on explaining its relevance to the formation of families. In fact, his writings on family arguably make up the vast bulk of Rushdoony's literary output. The *Institutes*, however, are notorious not only for his discussion of family matters in terms of biblical law but also for his mind-bending conflation of ancient legal codes with contemporary cultural problems in the United States. Any given analysis might seamlessly join ancient Jewish precedents outlined in the Mishnah with the theology of John Calvin and the personal-advice columns of Ann Landers into a critical assessment of an important contemporary issue.[111]

Theonomy

The first volume of the *Institutes* achieved this synthesis of the ancient and modern through an exhaustive exposition of the Decalogue. The first ten chapters of the book treat each commandment individually by intertwining a singular commandment—such as "Thou shalt not kill" or "Thou shalt not commit adultery"—with complex readings of Scripture and contemporary scholarship related to the commandment.[112] After painting a composite image of the general concept behind the commandment, Rushdoony sought the prohibition's specific manifestations throughout the entire Bible. Moving from the general to the specific, he piled up example after example of scriptural precedents for God's reaction to violations of a given commandment. With this scriptural case law in hand, Rushdoony carried his analysis into different historical periods to illustrate how Christian communities in various times enforced (or failed to enforce) these rules. For every commandment, Rushdoony's exegesis of the law was mechanistic, precise, and encyclopedic.

For example, in Rushdoony's reading of the ninth commandment, "Thou shalt not bear false witness against thy neighbour," he not only found a prohibition against lying about one's neighbor but also found the roots of Western notions of privacy and personal security.[113] Rushdoony carefully parsed the commandment to note that it is not an absolute injunction against lying or strategically withholding the truth but rather an order to speak truthfully in all moral and legal matters related to others.[114] This meant that witnesses must be honest under penalty of death, but that no one can be forced to confess or testify against one's self. Here, Rushdoony found the biblical roots of the Fifth Amendment to the U.S. Constitution, which protects against self-incrimination. He also elaborated why every Christian must stand against any form of forced confession, whether derived from torture, ordeal, or modern means such as lie detectors and wire tapping.[115]

Ultimately, the end of biblical law is God's absolute sovereignty over all aspects of life on earth. This is most clearly illustrated in the various offenses requiring the death penalty. In total, Rushdoony outlined seventeen crimes that civil authorities in a biblical order would punish with execution.[116] Many of the offenses relate to violations of the first commandment, "Thou shalt have no other gods before me."[117] God decrees death in cases involving blasphemy, propagating false doctrines, sacrificing to foreign gods, and witchcraft. Another class of capital offenses included refusing to recognize a court ruling or failing to pay restitution for a crime. These violations marked rebellion against the community's law-order. Of all the crimes, however, Rushdoony spent most of the book outlining those that amounted to war against the family and therefore necessitated death. Murder, cursing a parent, kidnapping, adultery, incest, bestiality, homosexuality, rape, and habitual delinquency all struck out against the propagative, future-oriented nature of the family. Death was necessary in these cases because each crime asserted the sovereignty of humanity over God's law.

Death penalties for offenses against the family, Rushdoony told his readers, "seem severe and unnecessary" to a "humanistic mind," which values human life higher than God's law. Humanism, humanity's ultimate sin, uses "church, state, and school" to wage "religious war" against Christianity and God's law.[118] "The struggle is between God's absolute justice and His law-order and man's lawless self-assertion of autonomy."[119] In this sense, the death penalty—whether enacted by a civil magistrate or through the miraculous overflowing of God's divine wrath—is God's ultimate check against humanity's autonomy. The result, then, is "unceasing warfare" between humanistic law and biblical law.[120] Law sanctifies by separating and purifying. It mediates between man and God by granting life and by taking it.

With biblical law established as the mediatory category that codes and recodes all social meaning via a process of discrimination and differentiation, Rushdoony developed an alternative image of society that he referred to variously as Christian Reconstruction or theonomy. Restating themes that had already emerged in *Intellectual Schizophrenia*, *This Independent Republic*, and *The Nature of the American System*, Rushdoony pointed his readers to Genesis 1:26–28. This passage ordered humans to "be fruitful, and multiply, and replenish the earth, and subdue it: and have dominion over the fish of the sea, and over the fowl of the air, and over every living thing that moveth upon the earth."[121] In Rushdoony's exegesis, these words are a "creation mandate" or "dominion mandate" requiring humans to "subdue all things and all nations to Christ and His law-word."[122]

Rushdoony was hardly the first Protestant to focus on Genesis's discussion of Adam's "dominion" over the earth. The issue of Adam's sovereignty over the earth has been a central concern for various conceptions of covenant theology reaching back to its earliest expressions in Reformed Protestant theology. In order to tease out the complex relationship between predestination and free will in Calvinist tradition, sixteenth-century Reformed theologians developed the concept of covenants to explain the relationship between God and humans.[123] Specifically drawing on German reformers, early American Presbyterians used "covenant" or "federal theology" to distinguish between the "legal covenant" or "covenant of works" made between God and Adam and the "covenant of grace" established with Abraham.[124] The covenant of works required strict obedience to God's laws in exchange for salvation and Adam's total dominion over the earth. Adam failed in his obligation for obedience and therefore forfeited dominion, but he nonetheless remained bound by the moral and natural laws of the covenant. In response to the Fall, Reformed theologians argued, God, through divine revelation, established a covenant of grace with Abraham that required only faith as the necessary mechanism for salvation.[125] Dominion would then take on various meanings in subsequent forms of covenant theology that developed in the United States, with some theologians arguing that the Fall terminated the "dominion mandate" of Genesis and others retaining it in terms of environmental stewardship or godly labor.

Rushdoony followed this long tradition of covenant theology in the United States, but he insisted that most popular concepts of the covenant failed to acknowledge the relationship between biblical law and God's covenantal promises with humans.[126] He argued that in combination, the atoning sacrifice of Christ and the sanctifying power of biblical law provide the two necessary mechanisms that allow Christians to abrogate the curse of the Fall. Through the law, the reconstructed Christian male—or "dominion man," as Rushdoony called him—could "take dominion" over the planet and "reconstruct" all of life in Christ's image.[127]

The concept of "dominion man" became the foundation of Rushdoony's entire social and political project. Rushdoony insisted that "*basic government* is the self-government of the Christian man."[128] This statement is built on two fundamental presuppositions. First, God gave human beings a foundational form of governance. Second, this godly governance is located in the created minds and gendered bodies of Christian men.

In terms of governance, Rushdoony distinguished between those explicitly political forms of state power that one might casually refer to as "government" and a broader, more amorphous concept of government that orders and structures all aspects of human life. Rushdoony understood that historically, governance has not been the sole domain of the territorial nation-state. Governance, in terms of the conduct of behavior and the management of populations, happens in many social domains and across a wide array of actions, shaping human subjects in ways that a state-centered perspective either ignores or obscures.[129]

Rushdoony's concept of "dominion man" not only took this wider understanding of governance for granted but, following Abraham Kuyper, it also distributed governance into a decentralized, horizontally arranged set of mutually exhaustive spheres that emanate from discrete, individuated men.[130] As creatures created by God, human males are governed by the normative gender roles inscribed on their bodies and in their minds by the very fact of creation. "In the Biblical view," wrote Rushdoony, "man was created as Adam, alone, and allowed to remain alone for some time, to know his calling as God's vicegerent and image-bearer before he knew himself in marriage and society. . . . In a sense, 'privation' and isolation . . . was the first condition of man in Paradise and the ground of his status as man. As a consequence, marriage, the family, the church, state, and every other God-ordained institution, while God-given and necessary in their respective spheres, were under man and never prior to him as the creature and image-bearer of God."[131] Therefore, when Rushdoony wrote of the Christian *man*, he specifically meant *men* and not men and women. God's command that man exercise dominion over the earth required multiple forms of work—including "manual labor, agriculture, and science"—that culminated in Adam's classification of creation recorded in Genesis 2:19.[132] It is only after Adam "had a tested maturity in terms of his work" and had finished "subjugating and developing the earth and bringing it under the dominion of and into the service of man" that God provided Eve as a "helpmeet" in the project of dominion.[133]

With the creation of Eve, Adam entered into marriage and society simultaneously. The origin of society is therefore located in the union of male and female in the institutional form of the family. Biblical law, in Rushdoony's view, clearly establishes the nature of the family by fixing the relationship between male and female into an ethical hierarchy. God's law-word establishes marriage as a "covenantal instrument," which mediates the relationships between human beings by coding and recoding the limits and potentialities of male/female interaction.[134] First, Adam was the primary instrument of dominion, but his *individual* calling was extended into a *social* calling with the simultaneous creation of Eve and the form of the family when "it is unto 'them,' male and female, that God gives the order to exercise dominion."[135] Next, this logic led Rushdoony to regard woman as a derivative instrument of dominion. Her primary duty in marriage is submission to the authority of her husband. Woman, therefore, is the necessary partner in dominion but cannot exercise it alone.

The primary purpose of marriage is to govern a man's ability to exercise dominion, and, in this sense, Rushdoony argued that marriage cannot be reduced to the sentiment of love, to the function of procreation, or to economic subsistence. First, love is an insufficient ground for the government of marriage because love only has meaning within the context of biblical law. For a man, his duty is love, but here, love has a specific and unique meaning: "service."[136] This service emerges from the man's submission to Christ and His law.[137] Within the family, the evidence of the man's love can be seen in his "wise and loving government of his household." This led Rushdoony to conclude that "a man's life is his work, not his wife," and this work is dominion in the service of the Lord.[138] Second, the purpose of the family is not located in the act of procreation: "The primary purpose of marriage is not simply procreation, but that procreation is an aspect of subduing the earth and exercising dominion over it."[139] Woman, therefore, as man's partner in dominion, is much more than a mother—"she manages the farms and business, and is a queen exercising dominion."[140] Finally, one does not enter into the family form to ensure economic success; the family absorbs the economic sphere into the project of subduing the earth for King Jesus.[141]

The relationship between biblical law, dominion, and the family led Rushdoony to an important conclusion: the family is the "most powerful institution in society."[142] The law-order that controls the family controls the future. Christians must refuse to allow the state or the church or any other sphere of law to claim precedence over the family and its governance. They must insist on *theonomy* over *autonomy*. Theonomy grants the family control of three "key areas of society": children, property, and inheritance.[143] These three areas are granted to the family because "the law is not oriented to the past . . . but rather to the future and to progress away from primitivism."[144] In this sense, biblical law is a positive, dynamic mechanism for Christian expansion. It establishes the family as the productive institution responsible for ushering in the future Kingdom of God. In contrast, the state, when constrained by the positive limitations of God's law, serves only the negative function of enforcing justice, while the church acts as a preservative cultural force; neither is productive.

Postmillennialism

The productive and reproductive aspects of the family make it the primary instrument of dominion.[145] This point is essential to understanding Rushdoony's Christian social theory; it is based on postmillennial eschatological assumptions about the ultimate victory of Christ in terms of the future establishment of His Kingdom on this planet by reconstructed men. For Rushdoony, history not only has a teleological arrow, but that arrow also is determinative of an ever-increasing cultural complexity and the Christianization of *all* things—not simply of human beings, but of the cosmos itself.

Simplifying greatly, postmillennialists assert that Jesus Christ will only return to rule the earth after Christians have first established His Kingdom. In contrast, premillennialists hold that Jesus will return before the establishment of the millennial Kingdom. Postmillennialism once dominated the American eschatological imagination. Europeans brought various forms of this perspective with them in the imperial projects of Catholic Iberian colonialism and English Protestant Puritanism.[146] According to literary historian Frank Graziano, Catholic and Protestant postmillennialists imagined that "history is theophany": "the mood is constructive, and actions are decisive, with human efficacy guided by divine will as the cosmic plan unfolds."[147] Historians generally agree this constructive, postmillennial urge dominated the actions of nineteenth-century evangelicals in the United States, who spent so much time and effort addressing such momentous social issues as slavery, temperance, and public education in order to usher in the millennial moment.[148] As religious historian Paul Boyer has noted, since the seventeenth century, the Reformed Calvinist vision of the Puritans has played a singular role in imbuing the American eschatological imagination with a "reformist, perfectionist, and expansively nationalistic spirit."[149] This postmillennial historical perspective was, according to historian George Marsden, "by far the prevalent view among American evangelicals between the Revolution and the Civil War."[150] American evangelicals believed that "the prophecies in the book of Revelation concerning the defeat of the anti-Christ (interpreted as the Pope and other leaders of false religions) were being fulfilled in the present era, and were clearing the way for a golden age."[151]

In the late nineteenth and early twentieth centuries, the dominant cultural structure of Reformed Protestantism crumbled as a rapidly urbanizing, industrializing nation had to absorb waves of Catholic immigrants and other suspect populations. The optimistic spirit of postmillennialism had to reckon with the failures of Progressive legislation—such as anti-alcohol temperance laws and market regulations—to change human behavior and usher in God's Kingdom. Facing greater ethnic diversity, a rapidly changing socioeconomic structure, and the calamitous violence of World War I, evangelicals rethought the optimistic, reform-minded implications of postmillennialism.[152] Many of the evangelicals who would later form the backbone of American fundamentalism rejected postmillennialism for what historian Randall Balmer has called a "theology of despair" that "ceded the temporal world to Satan and his minions."[153] By the middle of the twentieth century, the vast majority of socially and theologically conservative evangelicals adhered to some popular form of dispensational premillennialism that awaited the immediate rapture of the church, followed by judgment and the destruction of a fallen world.

Although dispensational premillennialism dominated Dallas Theological Seminary, Wheaton College, Fuller Seminary, and many of the elite educational institutions of fundamentalism, a sizable number of conservative Protestants rejected the new eschatological consensus. Most notably, those influenced by Calvinist thinking at institutions such as Princeton, Westminster, and Calvin Theological Seminaries and smaller, regional institutions that served Reformed communities in the Midwest remained sympathetic to the postmillennial and amillennial eschatologies that had dominated nineteenth-century American Protestantism. In the views of many conservative Protestants influenced by these institutions, premillennialism tended to emphasize evangelization at the expense of political engagement and social reform. The result, claimed these critics, was a politically and socially impotent form of Christianity. Rushdoony, long disappointed with the social implications of premillennialism, encountered these other perspectives in the late 1940s and early 1950s and recognized their potential implications for building a more socially engaged form of Protestant Christianity.

Beginning in the 1940s, publishing houses with a conservative Calvinist bent released a wave of books that led to the revival of interest in non-premillennial eschatologies. Rushdoony first encountered this trend sometime in the mid-1940s in the form of William Hendriksen's *More than Conquerors* (1940). Published by Herman Baker's Baker Book House for the Reformed Dutch community near Grand Rapids, Michigan, the book offered a preterist interpretation of the biblical book of Revelation. Preterists argue that the prophecies in biblical books such as Daniel and Revelation describe events that have already happened. Hendriksen's book dismissed premillennial interpretations of John's Apocalypse that treated the book "as a kind of history written beforehand."[154] "What possible good," Hendriksen asked, would dispensational interpretations that discovered "in the last book of the Bible copious and detailed references to Napoleon, wars in the Balkans, and the great European War of 1914–1918" have been for the "suffering and severely persecuted Christians of John's day"?[155] Instead, Hendriksen insisted that John's Apocalypse described events taking place in the first century A.D. that were directly relevant to the persecuted church in that moment. For Reformed Christians like Rushdoony, Hendriksen's lively and clearly argued interpretation of the Apocalypse renewed interest in postmillennial and amillennial eschatological models that rejected the fanciful prophetic speculation of many popular dispensationalist interpreters.

Roderick Campbell's *Israel and the Covenant* (1954) followed close on the heels of Hendriksen's text to offer an eschatology of the triumph of the church in human history. Campbell's text fundamentally reoriented Rushdoony's perspective to focus on the church's role in Christianizing the entire world.[156] According to Campbell, the *telos* of history "is nothing less than a Christianized world."[157] In Campbell's model, the church is the "white robed army" that will ride with Christ into the final battle against Satan. Its purpose is to rule over a "new theocracy" of an ever-expanding Christian Kingdom.[158] This Christian world, Campbell explained, "does not mean that every living person will then be a Christian, or that every Christian will be a perfect Christian. It does surely mean that the righteous rule and authority of Christ the King will be recognized over all the earth. It will mean *liberty* in every land under the righteous Law of Christ, *equality* of every race as loyal citizens of the Messiah's Kingdom, and *fraternity* within the world-wide community of the new and better covenant."[159] The revolutionary implications of this millennial vision—*liberty*, *equality*, and *fraternity* under God's law— clarified Rushdoony's thinking on the relationship between eschatology and the purpose of the Christian church. By the end of the 1950s, these popular works convinced Rushdoony that the union of God's law with a triumphant, militant church had revived a postmillennial "*eschatology of victory*" that asserted the "Crown Rights of King Jesus" in the world.[160]

Dominion

Rushdoony combined these postmillennial themes into his own family-centered vision of Christian dominion. In Rushdoony's eschatology, Christian families will expand in time and space to bring all of creation under God's authority. In this sense, Rushdoony emphatically rejected the romanticization of the midcentury "nuclear" family as some "narrow, ingrown entity" geographically bound to the suburbs and prisoner to the soul-deadening parameters of the Cold War state.[161] Instead, he told his readers, "With each marriage, the relationships [are] extended outward" by the cultivation of covenant families under the authority of a reconstructed father.[162] "The family," concluded Rushdoony, "with each generation, moves outward by marriage, and the interlocking network of law units is thereby spread further. The family governs itself, and, in so doing, its government covers many spheres of life and its future orientation means that its functions are not present-bound. Over the centuries, families have most tenaciously preserved past and present while working to govern the future."[163] Here, Rushdoony envisioned the inexorable, postmillennial growth of the Kingdom of God from disparate, unconnected, reconstructed families into a unified imperium that one day would fill the whole earth. Rushdoony envisioned the millennial Kingdom as a world empire built from interconnected, self-governing family units, all bound together by their mutual adherence to biblical law and recognition of the ultimate sovereignty of Jesus Christ.

This view of imperial Christendom on its relentless march toward world domination had its roots in the Dutch Calvinism of Abraham Kuyper. In his highly influential *Lectures on Calvinism*, delivered at Princeton Theological Seminary in 1898, Kuyper told his American Presbyterian audience that had sin not entered the world, men would have united the earth under a single, global Kingdom organized around the patriarchal family unit.[164] While Kuyper believed that any longing for such a world empire was merely "a looking backward after a lost paradise" destroyed by sin, Rushdoony insisted that paradise was merely the beginning of man and not his end.[165] Rushdoony rejected Kuyper's pessimism to insist that the grace of Christ and the regenerative power of biblical law must serve as the mechanisms for the justification and sanctification, respectively, necessary for reestablishing mankind's mandate to build a single world empire. Although Rushdoony conceded that Eden "was free from sin," he insisted that it was not the ideal place that many Christians assume it to have been. Eden represented a "still primitive society, man's beginning, not the end. The goal is the developed Kingdom of God, the New Jerusalem, a world under God's law."[166]

The organic, aggressive expansion of the family marked Rushdoony's uniqueness from many of his contemporary political and intellectual conservatives and the neoevangelicals upon whom he had declared war. He focused exclusively on the teleological, progressive, and productive force of God's law as it hurtles men and their institutions forward toward the total victory of Jesus Christ in history. Rushdoony neither looked longingly to a lost Eden nor forward to the rapture of believers from this fallen planet. He exhibited unwavering faith in the coming of God's Kingdom on earth, a Kingdom in which mankind is justified through the grace of Christ and sanctified by His law. While grace is instant, sanctification is a progressive process that develops slowly over hundreds or thousands of generations as

Christian men take dominion over not only their own lives but also their families. They eventually will control all societal institutions, and the whole earth will recognize the sovereignty of Christ.

To illustrate this point, Rushdoony was fond of quoting Matthew 6:33: "But seek ye first the kingdom of God, and his righteousness; and all these things shall be added unto you."[167] The only route to the Kingdom comes through the righteousness of the law. By rejecting biblical law, humanists failed to recognize the transcendence of "terminal truths." This inevitably led to a "death of man philosophy" embodied by a generation of rebellious young Americans who were tearing the republic apart.[168] While humanists might be forgiven their antinomian suicidal foolishness, conservative evangelicals and fundamentalists had no excuse; they should know that God's Kingdom is their rightful inheritance. Yet they, too, had abandoned the law and the Kingdom for their retreat into premillennial fantasy.

In his aggressive rejection of the neoevangelical coalition that formed in the 1960s, Rushdoony tried to point socially and theologically conservative Protestants back to a tradition he believed they had abandoned during the first half of the twentieth century. His emphasis on the Old Testament over the New Testament and his postmillennial eschatology were, in his mind, a return to America's Calvinist heritage, not an aberration or break with tradition. Yet this imagined continuity was more than a throwback to the past; it was a strategy for the cultural, social, and political conquest of the future. Beginning with Christian self-government, the process of Christian Reconstruction functions as an epistemological and self-reconstruction that works through techniques of discipline and conduct manifested primarily in the form of the family.[169] The self Rushdoony envisioned is reconstructed through theonomy—a form of counter-governance designed to resist modern forms of state-centered discipline and control—and cultivated via a network of family-oriented organizational structures such as the Chalcedon Foundation, homeschools, seminaries, and alternative civic organizations.[170]

Conclusion: Law, Order, and the Problem with Theonomy

In 1970 Hal Lindsey started the Jesus Christ Light and Power Company, an experimental communal ministry aimed at students enrolled at the University of California's Los Angeles campus.[171] The ministry's name referred to the notion that the heavenly glow of the body of King Jesus would light the nighttime streets of a postapocalyptic New Jerusalem.[172] Lindsey had worked for Bill Bright's Campus Crusade for Christ, but he left to develop his own ministry focused on prophetic interpretation in a premillennial dispensationalist mode.[173] Through connections with the Jesus People movement and other Southern Californian Christians, Lindsey opened a dormitory in Westwood, California, in an old UCLA frat house for about forty students.[174] The JC Light and Power House embodied the swirling milieu of evangelical activism, countercultural sentiment, and the search for meaning in terms of Christ's word. It offered hippies and druggies a place to crash.[175] Students signed up and paid a small fee to take classes in which Lindsey expounded on the narrative of geopolitical apocalypse outlined in his 1970 best seller *The Late Great Planet Earth*. His students grew their hair long, wore tie-dye, and spoke the language of the counterculture.

Unlike the violent, antinomian student-criminal who opened this chapter, the young men and women attending the JC Light and Power House's meetings were hungry for a durable, permanent vision of law and order. They longed for ideas—Christian or otherwise—that bucked the conventional wisdom of their suburban upbringing and challenged the curriculum taught at nearby UCLA. When R. J. Rushdoony came to speak at the Light and Power House in the 1970s, he preached a new form of "law and order" that excited some of Lindsey's students: *theonomy*. To one young man in the audience, the stocky, bearded, well-dressed Rushdoony looked and sounded like some postmodern American Moses.[176]

After Rushdoony's talk, some students from the JC Light and Power House started attending his Sunday Bible studies held in the mortuary chapel of the nearby Westwood Village Memorial Park Cemetery. There, near Marilyn Monroe's cremated remains, Rushdoony led a handful of interested Christians—ranging from the buttoned-down supporters of Women for America, Inc., to the Jesus Freak posthippies of the Light and Power Company—through his studies of biblical law and Christ's inevitable victory in a fallen world. On a Sunday afternoon in 1976, during one of these intimate, low-key meetings at the Westwood chapel, a member from the Light and Power House quizzed Rushdoony on his theonomic vision. Ever the doting, grandfatherly patriarch, Rushdoony fielded the questions while holding two young children on his lap. The Light and Power House student wondered, *What would happen to a Hindu in a reconstructed America?* "As long as he didn't practice his faith, the Hindu would be fine," Rushdoony responded as he absentmindedly bounced the children on his knee. *And what if said Hindu did practice his faith?* "Then he'd be guilty of violating the laws of the state." *And?* "And," still fawning over the tots, Rushdoony concluded, he would "be subject to capital punishment." Silence. The meeting broke up soon afterward.[177]

As the uneasy interest in theonomy among the Jesus People at the Light and Power Company illustrates, the 1970s marked a turning point in Rushdoony's ministry. Legal concerns dominated a corner of the evangelical imagination. Crime undoubtedly was a visible problem; but, more subtly, a series of court rulings at the local, state, and federal levels had just ended Bible reading and prayer in public schools, while pressure to integrate racially divided school districts led to forced busing and federal attempts to regulate private Christian schools through tax policy. Not only did criminals ignore "law and order" but, suddenly, America's courts also seemed willing to arbitrarily overturn centuries of tradition and throw out decades of legal precedent. Many socially conservative Christians regarded these legal mutations as a direct threat to their ability to raise and educate their children as their conscience dictated.

To the parents of the two children Rushdoony bounced on his knee during his discussion at Westwood chapel, theonomy and the execution of crypto-Hindus likely seemed much less dangerous than public lawlessness and the iconoclastic judicial decisions of the previous decade. Theologically conservative fundamentalists and evangelicals on the political left and right were fed up with an overweening federal bureaucracy that drafted young men to kill and be killed in Vietnam, regulated parents' ability to school their children as they saw fit, and generally reached deeper and deeper into the intimate structure of the American family.[178] Whether it was Christian leftist Jim Wallis declaring himself a "post-American" or R. J. Rushdoony proclaiming American democracy a "heresy" that ignored God's law, an aggressive "Christian antiliberalism" was coalescing in evangelical and fundamentalist circles.[179] This appetite for clear articulations of Christian resistance fed all manner of rogue ministries. Rushdoony's call to "take dominion" from America's secularizing political forces appealed to pre- and postmillennial Christians alike: they might not agree on the Rapture, but they all agreed that pietistic inaction was not an option. As the 1970s ended, a small number of evangelicals and fundamentalists were ready to take up Rushdoony's challenge. It was time to press Christ's dominion mandate into the heart of America's political, educational, and legal systems.

CHAPTER FIVE

Dominion Men

The New Christian Right, Christian Activism, Theology, and the Law

But it is dominion that we are after. Not just a voice.
It is dominion we are after. Not just influence.
It is dominion we are after. Not just equal time.
It is dominion we are after.
World conquest.
—GEORGE GRANT, *The Changing of the Guard*, 50–51

And there was given him dominion, and glory, and a kingdom,
that all people, nations, and languages, should serve him: his
dominion is an everlasting dominion, which shall not pass away,
and his kingdom that which shall not be destroyed.
—Daniel 7:14 (King James Version)

With the publication of *The Institutes of Biblical Law* in 1973, R. J. Rushdoony emerged as a national figure among theologically and socially conservative evangelicals and fundamentalists. In a March 1974 *Christianity Today* review, theologian Harold O. J. Brown declared, "Without a doubt, the most impressive theological work of 1973 is Rousas J. Rushdoony's *Institutes of Biblical Law*, a compendious treatment of a whole gamut of questions in governmental, social, and personal ethics from the perspective of the principle of law and the purpose of restoration of divine order in a fallen world."[1] This acknowledgement of Rushdoony's mammoth theological work totaled only one sentence, but it pointed to the ever-wider reception his work was receiving outside the narrow religious and political circles in which he had worked for much of his life.

With the *Institutes*, Rushdoony inaugurated a movement that would reach its full potential only when his ideas seeped out of the narrow Reformed world and into the wider institutions of American fundamentalism and evangelicalism. Rushdoony did not achieve this transition alone. He cultivated a small but sophisticated cadre of young activists—economists, theologians, and lawyers—to reconstruct America. Steeped in this ethic of dominion, aided by their wifely helpmeets, and committed to conquering the world for Christ, Rushdoony's dominion men pushed the agenda of Christian Reconstruction into three interconnected spheres of conservative evangelicalism: political organization, education reform, and judicial activism.

The New Christian Right

When Rushdoony formed Chalcedon, Inc., in 1965, he initially hoped to build a Chalcedon College that might provide an institutional foundation for reconstructing the United States into a confederation of Christian states governed by biblical law. As he struggled and failed to raise enough capital to support the establishment of such an institution, he shifted his focus toward building something more unique and, in retrospect, quite effective: a decentralized network of loosely affiliated scholars, activists, politicians, lawyers, and families all dedicated to Christian Reconstruction.

Rushdoony envisioned that Chalcedon would "establish, conduct and maintain an educational institution, offering courses of instruction beyond high school."[2] The faculty teaching these courses would "promote orthodox Christian scholarship"[3] and instill in the students a basic "understanding of *law* from a Christian perspective."[4] When Chalcedon secured tax-exempt status from the Internal Revenue Service in 1968, it began drawing regular contributions from supporters. Tax exemption allowed Chalcedon to hire staffers who would write books, fund lectures across the United States, and start a small but popular audiotape ministry.[5] The foundation grew slowly but steadily with support from a host of right-wing public figures and numerous smaller supporters involved in grassroots conservative organizing.

This limited success did not add up to the funds necessary to buy and develop a campus for the college. Rushdoony did manage to persuade a small number of his early backers in the Los Angeles area to support the purchase of a large ranch property in San Luis Obispo County, California, that could eventually serve as the proposed campus. Ultimately, however, the deal became mired in competing interests among his various supporters. The subsequent real estate boondoggle spoiled Rushdoony's relationships with some of his earliest financial backers and set Chalcedon back years because of the legal issues related to the failed venture. Eventually, in 1977, Rushdoony raised the necessary capital to purchase a thirty-acre site in Northern California near Vallecito, a tiny town in Mother Lode country.[6] Rushdoony picked Vallecito for two reasons. One was its rural location and the cheap real estate; the other was his belief that prevailing winds might reduce the threat of fallout in the event of a nuclear attack on nearby San Francisco or Sacramento.[7]

In Vallecito, Rushdoony never realized the dream of Chalcedon College. Instead, he established his own little fiefdom, complete with regal peacocks to patrol the frontiers of his dominion. He built a library to house his precious, ever-expanding collection of books. His hilltop Sierra Nevada ranch house became a pilgrimage site for like-minded Christian conservatives. Lobbyists and legislators from Sacramento came calling. College students and young evangelists visited his library to buttress their presuppositional worldview. For those unable to find their way to Rushdoony's isolated domain, thousands of letters poured into Vallecito. Rushdoony spent hours on the phone every week providing counsel to homeschooling parents under assault by prosecutors. The foundation's telefax machine chirped and blinked, receiving messages from supportive homeschoolers, questions from reporters across the country, and brief handwritten notes from Washington insiders.

The whole enterprise pulsed with an energy unseen since the Goldwater fever of the 1960s. Something was coalescing at the intersection of conservative Protestant theology and the emerging infrastructure of a new political and social movement—the so-called New Christian Right or, more simply, the Religious Right. Rushdoony's Chalcedon Foundation was a tiny, underfunded node in the network of this much larger infrastructural realignment in American religious and political culture.

"You Are Trying to Repeal 20 Centuries of Christian History"

In Dallas, Texas, in August 1980, the Religious Roundtable, a Christian organization that included prominent national Protestant leaders from Campus Crusade for Christ and the National Association of Evangelicals, organized the National Affairs Briefing Conference. The conference organizers invited President Jimmy Carter and his Republican rival, former California governor Ronald Reagan, to address a group of politically and socially conservative clergy. Carter declined; Reagan accepted. When Reagan stepped to the podium at the 17,000-seat Reunion Arena, he told the nonpartisan group of conservative pastors and clergy, "I know you can't endorse me, but I endorse you and what you are doing."[8] The arena went wild.

During one backroom meeting at the conference, Gary North turned to Christian education activist Robert Billings and lamented the fact that his father-in-law, R. J. Rushdoony, was not among the speakers leading up to Reagan's daring endorsement. Billings, who would later help lead Jerry Falwell's Moral Majority and serve in the Reagan administration's Department of Education, responded: "If it weren't for his books, none of us would be here." North replied, "Nobody in the audience understands that." Billings countered, "True, but we do."[9] Insiders knew about Rushdoony's influence, even if the rank-and-file did not.

Five months later, the man whose ideas helped make a candidacy possible also helped make a president cry. In January 1981 Rushdoony attended a Council for National Policy (CNP) meeting in Dallas. Those present at the Dallas meeting formed a who's who of the leaders of the newly insurgent Christian Right—Howard Phillips, founder of the Conservative Caucus, a powerful conservative lobbying organization; Jerry Falwell, pastor of the Thomas Road Baptist Church and head of the Moral Majority; Connie Marshner, a veteran conservative activist generally counted as a pioneering leader in the "pro-family" movement; and Paul Weyrich, cofounder of the Heritage Foundation and a highly successful political fund-raiser, whom historian Randall Balmer eulogized as the "evil genius" of the American conservative movement.[10]

Around 5:00 P.M. on January 18, Phillips learned of a proposed bill that would allow federal regulators an inordinate amount of control over private Christian schools and colleges. During the presidential campaign, Reagan had railed against a three-judge D.C. district court's ruling in *Green v. Connally* (1971). The *Green* ruling upheld an IRS decision to revoke the tax-exempt status of any organization that engaged in racial discrimination because, the court held, such a group could not be a "charitable" organization. The facts in *Green* dealt with a private segregated school in Mississippi, but the ruling had implications for churches, clubs, and religious schools across the United States. Using this precedent, the IRS set more rigorous tax-exemption guidelines and enraged religious conservatives when it applied them to Bob Jones University (BJU) because of its policies banning interracial dating. In 1978 the tax agency used the *Green* ruling to issue new guidelines that led to the successful revocation of BJU's tax-exempt status.

During his presidential campaign, Reagan had pleased conservatives by condemning *Green* for allowing bureaucratic impunity in education and desegregation policy. After the election, when representatives of the National Association for the Advancement of Colored People and some Republicans attacked Reagan for supporting "tax-exempt hate," he shocked his conservative supporters by proposing a bill to codify the *Green* decision.[11] Reagan insisted his disagreement had not been with the logic behind *Green* but, as historian Joseph Crespino has documented, "with bureaucrats usurping the rights of Congress."[12] The administration fast-tracked the bill in an attempt to move beyond the embarrassing issue.

The news of the bill sent attendees at the CNP meeting into a fury. Phillips phoned the White House and asked to speak to Reagan's chief of staff Ed Meese about the bill. Meese immediately returned the call to the influential Phillips, but rather than berate Meese, Phillips promptly handed the receiver to Rushdoony. Rushdoony calmly outlined the legal and philosophical dangers of the bill. He questioned how the "conservative" Reagan administration could launch such a direct assault on its key constituents—religiously conservative Christians who wanted to educate their children outside of the boundaries of state-funded public schools. In response, wrote Rushdoony in his journal, "Meese claimed tax exemption is a subsidy which gives the state the right of control. I said, [']You are trying to repeal 20 centuries of Christian history.['] I then asked for [a] meeting before [the] measure went to Congress; he said it was on its way. I asked for [a] meeting anyway, and he said yes. Then Howard, Jerry Falwell, Connie Marshner, Paul Weyrich, Father Charles Fiore, and Dr. E. V. Hill also spoke."[13]

Rushdoony got his meeting eight days later. Phillips, Marshner, Weyrich, Rushdoony, and several other conservative leaders gathered in the White House to discuss the implications of the new regulations. For his part, Meese assembled a team of Justice Department lawyers to defend the legislation. The lawyers argued that some Christian institutions hid behind their private, religious status to racially segregate their classrooms by denying admission to various minority groups. The suggestion that the Justice Department might leverage a school's tax-exempt status as a means of combating racism angered Rushdoony and the other activists present. One Christian lawyer argued that the administration was using tax policy to trump a religious institution's First Amendment right to practice religion freely and peaceably assemble. During his time to speak, Rushdoony insisted that the law would allow the "federal gov[ernment to] require women priests, pastors, and homosexual ones, as public policy."[14] Meese's lawyers conceded Rushdoony's point but insisted that "it is within the legitimate power of the federal [government] if it so chooses. This administration will not so choose."[15] Meese agreed to consider some amendments to the bill, but he made it clear the bill was a top priority for the Reagan administration and was on its way to passage through Congress. Phillips and Richard Viguerie, a prominent conservative activist and fund-raiser, responded angrily to Meese's unwillingness to compromise and the pair made a public statement on the nightly news attacking the bill and insinuating that President Reagan had betrayed his most important political supporters.

That evening, following the meeting and the media hoopla, Rushdoony dined with conservative pundit Patrick J. Buchanan and his wife, Howard Phillips and his wife, and John Lofton, a conservative cable-news personality and syndicated columnist for the *Washington Times*. During dinner, news arrived "that Reagan had tears in his eyes watching Howard Phillips [and] Richard Viguerie's TV comments."[16] Rushdoony pitilessly summed up the entire event in his personal journal with a harsh assessment of Reagan's political trustworthiness: "As in California, he expects loyalty while giving none, and he works to please his critics."[17]

The Think Tank of the Religious Right

The controversy over the bill to codify the *Green* decision grew out of a series of federal policies and court decisions from the civil rights era. These legal changes granted the federal government extensive power to use forced busing to integrate racially divided public school districts. They also allowed the IRS to use federal tax policy to pressure segregated private Christian schools to integrate by threatening to revoke a school's tax-exempt status. The loss of local control embodied in these changes compounded the effects of a series of court rulings at the local, state, and federal levels that ended Bible reading and prayer in public schools. Some Christians tried to escape such meddling in public schools only to learn that the long arm of the federal government threatened to regulate private institutions as well. To so many socially and theologically conservative Christians, these changes cut to the very heart of their ability to raise and educate their children as their religion required.

Three U.S. Supreme Court rulings that allowed both the federal and state governments to regulate education more tightly proved particularly distressing to Rushdoony and many other conservative Christians. First, the combined weight of *Engel v. Vitale* (1962), *Murray v. Curlett* (1963), and *Abington School District v. Schempp* (1963) effectively ended the practice of prayer and Bible reading in public schools.[18] *Engel v. Vitale* determined that public schools could not compose and encourage the recitation of an official, nondenominational school prayer even if the prayer was voluntary and students were allowed to recuse themselves from its recitation. Meanwhile, the consolidated 8-to-1 ruling of *Murray v. Curlett* and *Abington School District v. Schempp* prohibited the recitation of the Lord's Prayer and the reading of the Bible in public schools. Atheist activist Madelyn Murray brought the former case challenging a Baltimore Board of School Commissioners ruling that required "reading, without comment, of a chapter of the Holy Bible and/or of the Lord's Prayer."[19] In *Abington*, the court similarly ruled against a Pennsylvania statute that required that ten verses from the Bible be read each school day.

These court rulings and the IRS's subsequent pursuit of BJU worried conservative Christian leaders, prompting them to create a loose coalition of organizations determined to resist what they perceived as an orchestrated secular-humanist attack on religious establishments. The outcry was so vocal and fierce that historian Randall Balmer has argued that the desegregation enacted by the *Green* ruling led directly to the creation of the political machinery of the Religious Right. According to Balmer, *Green* "galvanized evangelical leaders who, at the behest of the conservative activist Paul Weyrich, united in defense of Bob Jones University—and in defense, they insisted, of the sanctity of evangelical institutions. Leaders of the Religious Right decided later to add other issues—prayer in schools, pornography, abortion—to their political agenda in preparation for the 1980 presidential campaign."[20]

Setting aside the racist implications of Balmer's charge, it is clear that beginning with *Engel* and accelerating forward through *Green*, some evangelicals saw in the combined weight of these rulings a direct threat to their ability to practice their faith, educate their children, and govern their own lives.[21] Similarly, education historian Gaither has noted, "For the first time a pan-denominational coalition of Christian conservatives united in vocal opposition to the Federal Government's attempt to regulate them. Tens of thousands, many of whom had never done so before, wrote letters to congress protesting the IRS initiative" enabled by *Green*.[22] These legal decisions contributed to a series of high-profile battles over public education policy, such as the Kanawha County, West Virginia, textbook controversy, which illustrated to many evangelicals how political, judicial, educational, and cultural issues were intimately interrelated.[23] While some evangelicals opted to fight for direct political control of local public school boards, these controversies, according to sociologist William Martin, also "spurred . . . the growth of private Christian day schools and an increase in home schooling."[24] It was in this broad-based, national struggle to define the limits of the "Christian" classroom and its relationship to the "secular" courtroom that Rushdoony's Chalcedon Foundation found its new calling in the 1970s.

In response to these legal changes, Rushdoony and many other conservatives began their aggressive rhetorical condemnation of "activist judges" who "legislate from the bench" because liberal values could not win at the ballot box. This rhetoric pointed to a real trend during the 1960s and early 1970s, when a network of public interest law firms began to seek reforms through legal rather than political mechanisms.[25] It was through the effort of a painstakingly built and well-funded network of advocacy groups, legal historian Steven M. Teles has argued, that "liberals" secured a series of major judicial victories related to civil rights, women's rights, environmental protection, church/state separation, and so on that eventually became controversial cornerstones of contemporary American culture.

Conservatives, who regarded many of the rulings with suspicion and even hostility, found themselves generally unprepared and unable to resist the judicial shifts. The result, according to Teles, was a slow process of trial and error, failure and mixed success, whereby conservatives built a counternetwork of public interest law firms. These firms were staffed by "authentic members of a conservative 'new class'" who were "products of a new constellation of conservative institutions committed to a set of ideological principles rather than corporate interests."[26] Rushdoony's Chalcedon Foundation was itself a small but sparkling member of this new firmament of conservative legal institutions. Rushdoony pressed theologically and socially conservative Protestants to realize the importance of public interest law, not only for defending what remained of America's "Christian" heritage but also for creating new social, political, and cultural potentialities for conservative Christians.

Concomitant with this legal renaissance, a small network of political strategists who cut their partisan eyeteeth on Barry Goldwater's failed 1964 presidential bid recognized that something new was in the offing in American party politics. Sophisticated polling techniques revealed socially and theologically conservative Protestants' discontent with moderate Republicans and President Jimmy Carter. In turn, by harnessing the power of massive computer databases, direct mailing, cable TV programming, and restructured campaign financing laws, a new generation of GOP activists built the infrastructure of institutions designed to channel conservative anger into electoral results. A durable weave of AstroTurf organizations and grassroots activism, the ad hoc infrastructure of the Religious Right that coalesced in the late 1970s promised to remake American culture and politics in novel ways.

With its direct engagement with the grassroots activism of the era, the Chalcedon Foundation played an underappreciated role in the rightward list of American culture. By the late 1970s, books by Rushdoony and a growing cohort of young Reconstructionists—including his son-in-law Gary North and other disciples, such as Reformed theologian Greg Bahnsen— appeared on numerous seminary and Christian college syllabuses. Hundreds of libraries—secular and religious—collected books by Reconstructionists. Faculty and students in conservative Protestant seminaries across the country debated these texts. Graduate students wrote theses and dissertations rejecting, contesting, or supporting the Chalcedonian agenda.[27] Law-review articles in journals from major law schools and judges deciding cases cited Rushdoony as an expert on religious issues.[28] The innovative, television-based ministries of Pat Robertson and D. James Kennedy wrangled with the implications of Christian Reconstruction for resisting the secular culture they feared. In 1981, when *Newsweek* ran an electoral postmortem designed to help readers understand the Reagan Revolution, it listed only one "think tank" on the Religious Right: the Chalcedon Foundation.[29]

By the early 1980s, the Chalcedon Foundation had achieved a remarkable feat: by leveraging limited resources, Rushdoony had cultivated a small group of like-minded young men with a prodigious literary output. Gary North extended the reach of Rushdoony's ideas into grassroots political activism and the farthest-flung edges of the American Right, ranging from the militia movement to the Ron Paul wing of the Libertarian and Republican Parties. Meanwhile, Gregory L. Bahnsen took Rushdoony's ideas into the educational institutions of America's most conservative Reformed polities to influence the Orthodox Presbyterian Church. Finally, although he would eventually distance himself from the movement, the activist lawyer John W. Whitehead initially owed a significant intellectual debt to Rushdoony's legal ideas. Dominion men all, they played pivotal roles in establishing the significance of the Chalcedon Foundation in the 1980s.

Gary North and Grassroots Politics

After Gary Kilgore North first wrote to Rushdoony in 1962, the two began a long and incredibly complex relationship. Rushdoony immediately recognized North's potential in their first exchange of letters. He helped North gain a foothold inside the institutions of postwar libertarianism and conservatism—especially within the network of organizations supported by the Volker Fund—and pushed him to his ill-fated tenure at Westminster Theological Seminary, one of the most prestigious educational institutions in conservative theological circles. Rushdoony also helped North pursue the study of "Christian economics" within the context of the secular academy.

Although the two men became close friends and confidants, their relationship was strained by their intense, combative personalities. North would eventually marry Rushdoony's second-youngest daughter, Sharon, and enter into Rushdoony's tightly knit family. Through the 1970s, the two men managed to build a strong working relationship that shaped both the Chalcedon Foundation and North's own think tank that took shape in the form of the Institute for Christian Economics. In time, however, their strong personalities and conflicting ambitions led to familial tensions paralleled by a theological and organizational schism within the Reconstructionist movement, with one side located in California and centered on Rushdoony in Vallecito and another concentrated in Tyler, Texas, around North. But before all of that, Rushdoony apprenticed his future son-in-law and rival in the complex world of conservative religious activism.

"Romanticism Isn't a Part of My Makeup"

After departing Westminster Theological Seminary, North enrolled at the University of California, Los Angeles, in the fall of 1964, dropped out, and transferred to the University of California, Riverside, in the spring of 1965. At UC Riverside, North completed his dissertation on Puritan economic concepts in early American history.[30] He supported the project with teaching and research fellowships until 1969. This support included the prestigious Weaver Fellowship (named in honor of Richard M. Weaver, author of *Ideas Have Consequences*) from the Intercollegiate Studies Institute and another grant from the conservative Earhart Foundation. Significantly, both fellowships came from organizations firmly established within the mainstream of "fusionist" conservatism.

North also applied for and received scholarship assistance from Rushdoony's Chalcedon Foundation. North's application for Chalcedon is particularly interesting for the recommenders he assembled to attest to his scholarly acumen. Influential conservative intellectual and sociologist Robert A. Nisbet recommended North highly: "He is an outstanding mind in all respects and has a personality and bearing to match. I regard him as a natural teacher and scholar, and it is inconceivable that he will not in time become an influential member of the academic profession."[31] Edwin S. Gaustad, then a young scholar who would eventually become one of the most prominent historians of American religion, declared North to be "widely read and highly motivated" and offered unqualified support for this "exceedingly diligent, capable student."[32] Finally, Warren I. Cohen, a respected historian of U.S. foreign policy, estimated "that North was the brightest student at the University that year [1963] and he is undoubtedly the most stimulating student with whom I have ever worked."[33] But Cohen's recommendation was bluntly honest about North's political views: "Mr. North's views are by no means acceptable to me—in fact I find them most distasteful—but rarely have I heard so-called 'conservative' positions argued more persuasively or with such marvelous wit."[34] Caveats aside, Cohen's recommendation was ultimately as positive as those of Nisbet and Gaustad, if not more so. In each case, these scholars—one well-respected and tenured faculty member and two junior faculty who would become major figures in their respective fields—gave North the highest marks and glowing assessments of his potential for future work in academia. Rushdoony, accordingly, gave him the scholarship.

As his scholarship support from the Intercollegiate Society of Individualists, Earhart, and Chalcedon wound down, North became a frequent contributor to the Foundation for Economic Education's *The Freeman* and in 1970 became a part-time employee of Rushdoony's Chalcedon Foundation.[35] In 1972 North went to work for FEE full-time in New York, but the following year he left to work for Rushdoony at Chalcedon. By the time North came to Chalcedon as a full-time employee, he was a bona fide veteran of the American conservative and libertarian intellectual establishment. He had worked for two of its most important think tanks, benefited from the financial support of two other prominent organizations, and maintained friendly relationships with such important movement insiders as Leonard Read, Ed Opitz, and Murray Rothbard, among many, many others.

North further strengthened his ties with Rushdoony and the Chalcedon Foundation when he married Rushdoony's daughter Sharon on February 23, 1972, in a small ceremony followed by a reception dinner. North's courtship of Sharon reveals how his personal feelings for his soon-to-be wife mingled with his broader religio-political concerns about the threats of socialism and the necessity for a female helpmeet in the fight for dominion. In a letter declaring his interest in Sharon, North explained to Rushdoony: "I settled on her, in principle, years ago." But Sharon Rushdoony initially rejected him.[36] Then, in 1971, something suddenly changed her mind, and she approached North about a relationship. "I think it was prayer" that changed her mind, North explained to Rushdoony.[37] In response to Sharon's sudden interest, Gary arranged for her to travel from California to Upstate New York, where he was working for FEE. In order to "watch out very carefully for our reputations," a local preacher agreed to oversee the courtship and ensure that Sharon was never "unescorted."[38] Rushdoony agreed to this arrangement and sent Sharon to visit North, drily noting in his journal: "marriage to Gary contemplated."[39]

North indicated that their courtship and possible marriage would be rocky, not because of personal issues but because of the threat of international socialism and North's need for a steady helpmeet in his dominion work as a Christian writer and political dissident. He promised that he would protect Rushdoony's daughter as best he could "from the mess that's in the works."[40] Although North did not specify what this "mess" entailed, it seems to have been related to the threat of socialism and impending economic collapse. "It's my brains," he wrote to Rushdoony, "against the insanity of socialist controls."[41] Gary's mature clarity regarding the threats working against his union to Sharon did not end with his awareness that he must protect his soon-to-be wife from the socialist menace. It also extended to his awareness that their relationship could not be based on something as trifling as romantic love. "I'm going into this with my eyes open," explained North. "Romanticism isn't a part of my make-up. I asked [to court] her years ago, not because I was in love with her, but because I respected her. I still respect her, and I'm growing to love her."[42] Ultimately, North concluded that his respect grew from Sharon's best qualities: "She is everything I could ask for from a wife of my youth. She is quiet, theologically aware, not a red-hot, steady, and careful with her money. That is what I need, if I need anyone. . . . I think we can get more accomplished together than individually."[43] Rushdoony apparently agreed that Sharon and North might form a dominion family, and he blessed the union.

"Scary" Gary

As a son-in-law, North proved to be a prolific popularizer of Rushdoony's theological ideas as well as a capable political organizer. Rushdoony specifically brought North to Chalcedon to research the relationship between biblical law and laissez-faire economics. North rewarded Rushdoony's confidence with the publication of *An Introduction to Christian Economics* (1973), an economic companion volume to Rushdoony's *Institutes*.

During his time at Chalcedon, North began engaging in political projects that differed from those favored by Rushdoony. Where Rushdoony tended to lean toward avoiding the immediate gains of electoral politics by favoring the patient creation of institutions focused on education and family building, North preferred more direct, confrontational action. North reached out across sectarian and political boundaries in order to engage all manner of allies, including secular libertarians, Latter-day Saints, and Pentecostals.

This meant that North brought Rushdoony-style Reconstruction out of the family and the homeschool by injecting it into political environments that proved oddly receptive to Rushdoony's ideas.

In his political endeavors, North initially flirted with national politics before turning exclusively to grassroots organizing. In 1976 he worked in Washington, D.C., as a staffer for Texas representative Ron Paul. Paul won a special election in the spring to fill a vacant seat and then lost in the regular election in November, making him, in North's words, "America's only Bicentennial Congressman: elected and defeated in 1976."[44] Paul's legislative assistant, John W. Robbins, hired North as his research assistant in the summer of 1976. "We were truly the odd couple," North wrote of his time working with Robbins on Paul's staff. "Robbins, as a defender of [theologian] Gordon Clark, was completely hostile to Clark's chief rival, Cornelius Van Til. I am a disciple of Van Til's apologetic method.... Dr. Paul had no knowledge about the rival positions that Robbins and I represented. I am not sure that he understood fully the extent of our Calvinism. He surely did not know about our rival views of epistemology."[45]

Despite their rivalry and Paul's ignorance of the religious basis for their political activity, North and Robbins cooperated well enough, although North appears to have had very little influence on either Robbins or Paul's activities on the Hill: "I stuck to my knitting; Robbins stuck to his. I did research on various economic issues; Robbins did research on specific pieces of legislation that were being considered by Congress.... I never got involved with the specifics of most of the legislation, unless it had something to do specifically with banking."[46] North wrote statements here and there on the dangers of the International Monetary Fund and the significance of other economic issues, but, because of Paul's midterm defeat, he was not in Washington long enough to have had any appreciable effect on policy or legislation.

After Paul left office in January 1977, North wrote a testy screed warning Christians that national politics could do nothing to address America's problems.[47] "I am a believer in local politics," he wrote. "Those who believe in political salvation at the national level are certain to be disappointed."[48] In typical North fashion, he concluded the essay with the kind of soul-crushing pessimism reserved for only the most-committed true believers and fellow travelers: "Things are going to get a lot worse before they get worse."[49]

North roamed in search of a new employer and institutional home. He briefly flirted with becoming a member of Dan Quayle's congressional staff but was eventually denied the job.[50] Turning his attention away from Capitol Hill, he turned first to journalism, writing for financial adviser Howard Ruff's *Ruff Times* until 1979, and then tried academia again by serving briefly on the economics faculty of Campbell University in North Carolina, a Baptist-affiliated school.[51] In December 1979, North and his family finally settled in Tyler, Texas, for a simple reason: "no state income tax."[52] After settling in Tyler, North developed his own nonprofit think tank called the Institute for Christian Economics (ICE). He modeled ICE on the Chalcedon Foundation but also looked to FEE and the ISI for inspiration. The result was an organization dedicated equally to the concept of biblical law and its application to economic issues.

North's unrelenting pessimism, his prolific literary output following his departure from Washington, and his hard-boiled rhetoric eventually earned him the nickname "Scary" Gary. His post-Paul pessimistic turn away from national politics was particularly significant for Christian Reconstruction because, after settling in Tyler, North developed practical strategies and tactics for Christians to deploy at the grassroots political level.[53] While Rushdoony had always been engaged at the local political level, the older theologian's writings and lectures on the subject were hardly practical in a way that activists might distill lessons from them. It is one thing to *assert* that politics and epistemology are intrinsically linked; it is another thing to *demonstrate* how one might translate this assertion into a set of carefully formulated political tactics framed within the overarching strategies of Van Tillian epistemology and Christian Reconstruction. North worked to develop the latter approach through his careful study of the economic theory that he believed he had uncovered in the Old and New Testaments. This new social and economic theory would ultimately lead to a theological rift between him and Rushdoony that eventually would destroy their personal relationship.

Greg L. Bahnsen and Reformed Theology

While Gary North toiled away in the trenches to further Christian Reconstruction at the political grassroots, the movement was also making slow inroads into theological seminaries, small Christian colleges, and diffuse networks of audiotape ministries and Bible study programs. While Rushdoony built much of this influence from the ground up, he had a significant amount of help from his small, nationwide network of supporters and from a new generation of young Presbyterians who encountered his ideas in their highly conservative local churches. None of these young men proved more significant than Greg L. Bahnsen.

As a child, Bahnsen was often ill. "Asthma, tonsillitis, ear infections, and severe blood platelet problems" plagued him from birth, recalled Bahnsen's son, Greg L. Bahnsen Jr.[54] The elder Bahnsen's thin blood left him prone to bleeding from the slightest bump or scratch, while an undiagnosed heart condition later exempted him from the draft at the height of the Vietnam War. At the age of five, an accident with a water can crushed his right hand, leaving it permanently mangled. Health problems of all sorts haunted him throughout his life, but he refused to allow them to prevent him from participating in all manner of sports and extracurricular activities when he was a child and an adolescent, eventually becoming senior president of his 2,500-strong high school class.

Early in life, Bahnsen had the good fortune to move from Auburn, Washington, to the Los Angeles, California, suburb of Pico Rivera, where he found himself near the epicenter of the Christian Reconstruction movement. In Pico Rivera, the Bahnsens joined the Beverly Orthodox Presbyterian Church in 1959.[55] They joined a Reformed congregation pulsing with ideas that ranged from the old-line antiliberal theology of J. Gresham Machen to the modish theonomic postmillennialism of R. J. Rushdoony. In 1963 Bahnsen met Rushdoony at an OPC youth camp. The meeting deeply affected the young man, and he decided to join the ministry.[56]

Like Gary North, Bahnsen's postsecondary preparation for the ministry wound through secular and religious institutions. In 1966 he enrolled in Westmont College, a small Christian liberal-arts institution founded by Ruth Kerr, the head of the Kerr Glass Manufacturing Corporation, the company that sells the ever-popular mason jar home-canning system. While at Westmont, Bahnsen majored in philosophy, and in 1969 he married his high school sweetheart, Cathie Wade. The couple would have two sons and adopt a daughter from South Korea before their eventual divorce in 1990.[57] But in 1970, long before their marriage fell apart, Greg graduated magna cum laude from Westmont, and he and Cathie moved to Flourtown, Pennsylvania, so he could study at Westminster Theological Seminary under Cornelius Van Til.

Unlike North, Bahnsen thrived at WTS. He completed the coursework for his master's of divinity and theology simultaneously in 1973. Faculty at WTS regarded him highly. Professor John Frame declared Bahnsen "absolutely the very most prepared student I have ever had."[58] Van Til reportedly allowed Bahnsen to teach his classes, and he wanted Bahnsen to replace him when he retired.[59] After graduating from WTS, Bahnsen enrolled as a Ph.D. student in philosophy at the University of Southern California. He supported his work with a fellowship from WTS and, as North had done, with an ISI Weaver Fellowship.[60]

The Theonomy Saga

When Bahnsen returned to California for graduate work in 1973, he reconnected with the vibrant OPC community in which he had grown up. He served as youth director at the Manhattan Beach OPC and joined Gary North and Rushdoony as part of the tiny staff of scholars at the Chalcedon Foundation.[61] While on the Chalcedon staff, North began writing his regular *Chalcedon Report* column, "An Economic Commentary on the Bible," and Bahnsen commenced a series of columns titled "Christ in the World of Thought."[62] Chalcedon provided Bahnsen the opportunity to revise his WTS master's thesis into his first and most influential book, *Theonomy in Christian Ethics* (1977).

In 1975 Reformed Theological Seminary (RTS) in Jackson, Mississippi, hired Bahnsen as a professor of apologetics, and he began teaching theonomy and presuppositionalism. He immediately attracted a small group of students who shared his sensibilities. This clique would eventually play prominent but controversial roles in the various strains of Christian Reconstructionism that developed in the 1980s.

Even within a conservative institution such as RTS, theonomy proved a highly controversial subject, and Bahnsen eventually alienated much of the faculty with his combative defense of the concept. Although the details related to his RTS tenure are difficult to parse because of the layers of self-serving memories related to the controversy, it appears that Bahnsen's personality created as much ill will as his theology. In terms of the latter, Bahnsen's positions on theonomy and the implications of applying biblical law for contemporary Reformed Christians immediately solidified into distinct fault lines between faculty members and factions among students. Many faculty and students also rejected other aspects of the Reconstructionist platform, including its postmillennial eschatology and its presuppositional apologetic strategy. Further compounding these theological tensions was Bahnsen's youth and zeal. He was the youngest member of the faculty. He was smart, and he knew it. One critic observed that he had a tendency to speak "first, third, and last on all issues" in faculty meetings.[63] He also, some charged, encouraged his supportive students to attack the positions of other faculty members.

When the Presbyterian and Reformed Publishing Company released Bahnsen's mammoth *Theonomy in Christian Ethics* in 1977, RTS's anti-Bahnsen faculty immediately called an emergency meeting to interrogate Bahnsen on the book's content. The book presented a highly technical defense of Rushdoonian theonomy and Van Tillian presuppositionalism through a close examination of the Gospel of Matthew's record of the Sermon on the Mount. According to Bahnsen, when Jesus declared, "Till heaven and earth pass, one jot or one tittle shall in no wise pass from the law, till all be fulfilled," He attested to the "abiding validity of the law in exhausting detail."[64] In his own exhausting detail, Bahnsen led readers through a dense study of ancient Greek sources, modern philosophy, and the errors of contemporary American dispensationalists and Pentecostals.[65] At its heart, the book developed Rushdoony's thesis that biblical law sanctifies obedient Christians.[66] For Reconstructionists, *Theonomy* stands alongside Rushdoony's *Institutes of Biblical Law* (1973) and North's *An Introduction to Christian Economics* (1973) as an intellectual monument to the movement's significance. For critics of Reconstruction, Bahnsen's *Theonomy* proved singularly controversial in Reformed circles. It inspired myriad critical seminary theses and dissertations, popular assaults in denominational publications, and fractured church polities.

When the RTS faculty called on Bahnsen to defend his controversial reading of Matthew 5, few of them had actually read the dense, 600-page work in its entirety, but that did not stop them from leaping to attack the text.[67] Incredulous, Bahnsen aggressively defended himself and insulted several of the faculty during the impromptu meeting. Afterwards, faculty members hostile to Bahnsen cracked down on his disruptive students. Officials in the wider RTS system delayed the implementation of curriculum changes that Bahnsen had developed for the Atlanta branch of the seminary. Bahnsen's job was on the line.

In response, Rushdoony offered frank counsel to Bahnsen and his students. Rushdoony advised the students that Bahnsen had led them poorly and encouraged them to act lawlessly. Rushdoony explained that their duty as students was to complete their training, not defend a specific faculty member. He admonished them to take postmillennialism seriously: "One of the great weaknesses of our time is a humanistic perfectionism. We want all problems resolved overnight, if not sooner. The church has been settling into a hardened antinomianism for some centuries, especially since the Enlightenment and the rise of pietism. I think that we can rejoice at the progress being made."[68] Bahnsen and his students were not under the authority of Chalcedon or a church that supported their position, and this made them vulnerable if they were not careful. "I am under attack," Rushdoony warned, "as are all the Chalcedon men and especially Greg Bahnsen at this point, because he is the most vulnerable, since he is under a non-Chalcedon authority."[69] In short, Rushdoony offered the students the advice that had gotten him through the liberal bastions of UC Berkeley and PSR: work hard, keep your mouth shut, and remain conservative at all costs.

To Bahnsen, Rushdoony offered tough love. He told Bahnsen that the real issues were personal and cultural, not theological. He insisted that Bahnsen's manners were too "northern" for his audience, and he had, perhaps inadvertently, rubbed the largely southern faculty the wrong way. Further, and more pointedly, Rushdoony insisted Bahnsen was so disorderly that he was actually resisting the legitimate authority of the senior faculty members, a grave sin. "Greg," Rushdoony wrote, "you must place yourself under authority."[70] In particularly harsh words, Rushdoony called Bahnsen a "big baby, determined to get your own way."[71] Bahnsen had attempted to combat the faculty by writing to faculty members at RTS Atlanta and to OPC churchmen seeking support. Rushdoony had heard of these letters and recognized their impropriety in the small, insular world of conservative Presbyterianism. He warned Bahnsen, "Please, stop writing letters. Leave it to the Lord. He is better able to handle this than any of us. You have a very great future. Don't get in your own way!"[72]

As the faculty squabbled over Bahnsen's future at RTS, his students, taking Rushdoony's advice to heart, tried to restrain him. Nearly a decade later, James B. Jordan, one of Bahnsen's most supportive and influential students, wrote an open letter to the RTS Jackson faculty to illuminate the controversy. Jordan apologized for siding with Bahnsen, who he now recognized as being "vocal and belligerent" during the controversy.[73] Jordan insisted that he and other students tried to restrain Bahnsen in his dealings with faculty and students, many of whom Bahnsen apparently regularly abused in class. The problem came when the faculty decided to approach Bahnsen about his theology rather than forcing him to rein in his bad behavior. "Had the faculty addressed Bahnsen primarily on the question of his personal deportment," wrote Jordan, "who could have defended him? Unfortunately, the faculty chose to debate the theological question of 'theonomy,' and this put me (and others) in the position of standing with Bahnsen in that respect. As the debate heated up, I confess that I wound up involved in the theological debate."[74] Jordan's letter—especially when considered alongside Rushdoony's—suggests that Bahnsen's personal behavior was at least as disconcerting to RTS faculty as his theology.

Whatever Bahnsen thought of Rushdoony's advice and efforts by his students to restrain his behavior, it was too little too late: RTS Jackson refused to renew Bahnsen's contract in 1978. He and his family found themselves heading back to Southern California. After his disastrous tenure at RTS Jackson, Bahnsen struggled to find work teaching at seminaries or Christian colleges. Eventually, he accepted a pastorate at Covenant Community Church and landed a teaching job at Newport Christian High School, a private Christian academy in Newport Beach, where he taught hundreds of young women and men.[75] He continued his ministry as a writer, debater, and lecturer but never again had the sort of direct influence on the cultivation of seminary graduates and ministers that his position at RTS had allowed.[76]

Bahnsen's firing from RTS was disastrous for Reconstructionism as an institutional movement. In his brief time at RTS, he had taught a group of students who formed the hard core of the second and third generation of Reconstructionists. His students, including Kenneth Gentry, James B. Jordan, David Chilton, and Gary DeMar, became authors, activists, and think-tank organizers who circulated between Rushdoony's Chalcedon Foundation and Gary North's Institute for Christian Economics. Between them, Gentry, Jordan, Chilton, and DeMar alone authored, coauthored, or edited no fewer than sixty-seven books and hundreds of newsletter and journal articles and essays.[77] DeMar also became the leader of American Vision, a prominent Atlanta-based think tank that publishes books and supports the Reconstructionist agenda. Had Bahnsen maintained his professorship until his sudden death in 1995, it is likely he would have cultivated a massive body of similarly prolific students committed to theonomic Reconstruction.

Beyond Bahnsen's mentorship of a new generation of Reconstructionists, his most notorious RTS student was Paul Jennings Hill.[78] After studying under Bahnsen, Hill became a Presbyterian minister in the conservative polities of the PCA and OPC. During the 1980s, Hill became active in the antiabortion movement. Bahnsen's theonomic perspective convinced Hill that murdering abortionists was a revolutionary act justified under biblical law. He advocated "defensive action," or direct violence, to disrupt the activities of abortion clinics. Hill joined the ranks of an increasingly radical antiabortion movement embodied in the loose network of activists known as the Army of God. Through his connections with abortion clinic bomber Michael Bray, Hill used Bahnsen's articulation of theonomy and the writings of other Reconstructionists—including R. J. Rushdoony and Gary North—

to develop an intellectual justification for their brand of theocratic vigilantism.[79] The PCA and OPC excommunicated Hill after he refused to stop speaking publicly about his views regarding violent resistance to abortion.

Hill's embrace of vigilante violence exposed a deep tension in the Reconstructionist movement. Although none of the prominent intellectual leaders of Reconstructionism—including Bahnsen, Rushdoony, and North—advocated violence, many in the radical antiabortion movement were inspired by theonomy to develop a biblical defense for their actions. While Rushdoony had long condemned any form of antiabortion civil disobedience as antinomian sin, North and John W. Whitehead had supported figures such as Randall Terry and his antiabortion ministry Operation Rescue. Rushdoony eventually left the Rutherford Institute's board because of a disagreement with John Whitehead over support for Terry and Operation Rescue.[80]

On July 29, 1994, outside a women's clinic in Pensacola, Florida, Hill shot surgeon Dr. John Britton in the head with a shotgun. Britton performed abortions at the clinic, and Hill had been observing the clinic's staff and their security procedures for months. Hill's point-blank blast also killed Britton's escort, James H. Barrett, and wounded Barrett's wife, June. North, who had previously ignored several letters from Hill, responded to Hill's violent actions with a vicious tract, *Lone Gunners for Jesus: Letters to Paul J. Hill* (1994). In *Lone Gunners*, North vigorously condemned Hill and insisted that Reconstructionism does not support revolutionary violent action of any kind. Not one to mince words, North argued that Hill would burn in Hell for his actions.[81] Regardless of Hill's final destination, the state of Florida expedited his journey when it executed him via lethal injection on September 3, 2003.

Even without a steady stream of graduate students to maintain the momentum of his first class of controversial advisees at RTS, Bahnsen nonetheless managed to have an outsized influence on Reformed, evangelical, and fundamentalist Christians. Over the years at Chalcedon and then RTS, Bahnsen developed a reputation as a smart, driven young theologian determined to challenge all Protestants—not just Presbyterians and Reformed Christians—to take Van Tillian presuppositionalism and Rushdoonian Reconstructionism seriously. This meant that he eagerly reached beyond the boundaries of conservative Calvinism into secular and evangelical institutions. By the mid-1990s he had started an audiotape ministry that was mailing out more than 50,000 recordings a year.[82]

For secular audiences, Bahnsen gained some notoriety for his public debates with a host of critical panelists, including Catholics and non-

Greg L. Bahnsen, ca. 1990. Following his termination from Reformed Theological Seminary in Jackson, Mississippi, Bahnsen struggled to find his professional calling. By the late 1980s, he regrouped to build a popular lecturing ministry. He traveled throughout the United States, teaching presuppositional apologetics to small church groups and engaging in high-profile public debates with atheists and critics of theonomy. At the height of his popularity, before his sudden death in 1995, his Covenant tape ministry was selling more than 50,000 recordings a year. Courtesy of Covenant Media, http://www.CMFnow.com.

Reconstructionist Reformed Christians. He also especially enjoyed debating atheists in college forums, eventually taking on noted skeptics and secular humanists such as Gordon Stein and Edward Tabash during the 1980s. In these forums, Bahnsen used Van Til's presuppositional approach to show that his opponents relied on a Christian model of an orderly universe while simultaneously and schizophrenically appealing to naturalistic arguments when it suited them. With numerous edited versions of the debates uploaded to video and MP3 sharing sites, the Internet has provided them a second life.[83]

In evangelical circles, much of Bahnsen's influence came negatively from critical engagement with his *Theonomy*. Through the 1970s and 1980s, students from Dallas Theological Seminary, Westminster Theological Seminary, Gordon-Conwell Theological Seminary, and dozens of smaller, less-well-known colleges and seminaries addressed Bahnsen's writings in their theses and dissertations. Dozens of students defended theses critiquing Christian Reconstructionism, with most focusing their attention on Bahnsen's and Rushdoony's voluminous writings.[84] These works ranged widely, with some taking up the issue of theonomy and others considering post-millennialism. Other works treated Bahnsen and Rushdoony as standard citations or points of departure for launching their projects. Regardless of the disagreements and theological nitpicking, even Bahnsen's most vocal evangelical critics regard him "as one God singularly gifted for the spiritual warfare of our time" with a penchant for "confrontation and for the intellectual exposure of Satan's lies. In those respects, Bahnsen still has no peer."[85]

John Wayne Whitehead and Christian Legal Activism

When North and Bahnsen left the Chalcedon Foundation to develop their respective political and theological projects, Rushdoony shifted his attention to advocacy in church/state legal disputes specifically related to matters of homeschooling and private education at the elementary and secondary levels. This focus on practical legal issues marked a significant departure from his early activities, as Rushdoony now spent a considerable amount of time convincing able young Christian men to attend law schools instead of seminary. Of the many bright and determined young lawyers who Rushdoony encouraged to litigate in the interest of Christian liberty, his support of John W. Whitehead, a recently converted Christian, was especially crucial for Christian Reconstruction.

Born in 1946 and named after the all-American actor, John Wayne Whitehead served as a lieutenant in the U.S. Army from 1969 to 1971, but a back condition kept him stationed at Fort Hood in Killeen, Texas, far from the fighting in Vietnam. After mustering out of the military, Whitehead graduated from the University of Arkansas Law School in 1974. In the wild early days of his legal practice, Whitehead was a dope-smoking, acid-dropping, aspiring civil rights attorney working in Fayetteville, Arkansas, who accepted

bags of weed as payment for his services.[86] Then, in November 1974, Whitehead stumbled across a copy of Hal Lindsey's *The Late Great Planet Earth*
in a J. C. Penney department store.[87] Thinking that the improbably named
book had to be science fiction, he bought it and read it in twenty-four hours.
While his wife, Carol, and young son Jayson were away visiting family over
the long Thanksgiving weekend, Whitehead read the Gospels. He thought
about the life of Christ.

Not yet converted, Whitehead spent the Friday after Thanksgiving par-
tying with friends. After a hard evening of drinking and smoking pot, two
of Whitehead's friends tried to coerce him into having gay sex. Through
a parasensory "mind voice," one of his friends told Whitehead that Satan
could "*help him in many ways*" if he gave into their sexual demands.[88] Horrified, Whitehead resisted their telepathic homosexual assault by repeatedly
declaring, "Jesus Christ, You are my Savior." His stoned, drunken friends
"began to moan audibly" and relented in their perverse demands.[89]

Following his Thanksgiving encounter with Satan's power, Whitehead
confessed his conversion to his wife, and the family decided to move to California to join Hal Lindsey's Jesus Christ Light and Power Company ministry.
While bunking at the JC Light and Power House, Whitehead found himself
in the heady new world of evangelical countercultural activism. In January
1976, he met R. J. Rushdoony during one of the theologian's lectures at the
Light and Power House. When Rushdoony realized Whitehead was a lawyer, he immediately invited Whitehead to attend his weekly Bible studies
held in the chapel at Westwood Village Memorial Park Cemetery. Unconcerned with Rushdoony's eschatological distance from Lindsey, Whitehead
recognized Rushdoony's intellectual rigor. He also realized that Rushdoony
commanded vast bodies of scholarly literature. In a single conversation,
Whitehead was stunned to realize that Rushdoony was equally as capable
of talking about farming practices in Vietnam as about the arcane aspects of
the National Basketball Association's league rules.[90]

Touched by Rushdoony's kindness, entranced by his intellect, and fascinated by his vision of biblical law, Whitehead built a strong relationship
with the theologian. Rushdoony encouraged Whitehead to develop his budding interest in Christian legal advocacy by inviting the lawyer to write a
manuscript based on research he was developing to support evangelicals
resisting state intervention in private education. During the late spring of
1976, Whitehead researched the project in law libraries in Los Angeles and
Rushdoony's massive private library in Vallecito.[91] As the draft neared com-
pletion, Rushdoony provided comments and helped secure a contract with

Mott Media, a small Christian publisher, to distribute the book. The following year, Whitehead published *The Separation Illusion: A Lawyer Examines
the First Amendment* (1977). Rushdoony provided the book's foreword, and
TV megapreacher D. James Kennedy offered a glowing endorsement.

Homeschools

Rushdoony's support for Whitehead's book grew from his mounting concern that secular educational reforms were rolling back the last vestiges of
America's Christian civilization. Through word of mouth and his lecture
tours, Rushdoony's notoriety spread in Christian homeschooling and day-
schooling circles. Since the publication of *Intellectual Schizophrenia* in 1961,
Rushdoony had been at the forefront of a movement to encourage theologically and culturally conservative Christian parents to remove their children
from publicly financed, secular schools. *Intellectual Schizophrenia* collected
a series of lectures Rushdoony delivered to a group of Christian educators,
jumpstarting his career as a public defender of homeschooling and making him a minor celebrity in the small but growing subculture of homeschooling Christians.[92] The book honed in on the secularization of American public education and, like many theologically conservative critics of
public education, argued that the de-Christianization of education would
lead to moral degeneration and cultural collapse. Unlike many homeschooling proponents, however, Rushdoony's criticism of public education did not
begin with an assessment of its failed pedagogy. Instead, Rushdoony's attack
on public education was initially quite unique in theologically conservative
circles. He focused on the *epistemological* foundation of what he variously
labeled "secular," "humanistic," or "statist" education and developed the
oppositional category of "Christian scholarship." Rushdoony's radical critique dug straight to the roots of public education and exposed the political consequences of its epistemological foundation. Specifically, Rushdoony
traced public education to what he saw as its ultimate source: *sovereignty*.

The Christians to whom Rushdoony spoke and wrote in the 1960s and
1970s sought to reverse a century-long trend of ceding family governance
to other institutions.[93] Rushdoony identified this historical tendency as a
disease and sought to diagnose it as a specific symptom of man's rebellion
against the sovereign power of God's law. His prognosis was that humans
could treat the illness through the steady refamilialization of life. Public
education was, in Rushdoony's eyes, a first step in the process of the defamilialization—and therefore of de-Christianization—of U.S. culture. For
Christian parents to "surrender children to the state is to turn them over

to the enemy," Rushdoony insisted.[94] Such an action invites God's collective judgment on a generation of parents and their children.

The solution to this rebellion, according to Rushdoony, is to reestablish the family as humanity's educational womb. The family, in this framework, is God's primary instrument for reconstructing the forces of antinomianism and reasserting God's sovereignty over the lives of men. The family's role in educating the next generation transcends all other institutions or social spheres and, as such, is the only legally legitimate space for educating children. In *Institutes of Biblical Law*, Rushdoony proclaimed that "the best and truest educators are parents under God. . . . The moral training of the child, the discipline of good habits, is an inheritance from the parents to the child which surpasses all other. The family is the first and basic school of man."[95] The consequence of this logic is that Christians not only have an obligation to educate their children, but they also must free their children from public, state-funded education of *any* sort.

Rushdoony's analysis of education—most consistently expanded in *Intellectual Schizophrenia* and its companion volumes, *The Messianic Nature of American Education* (1963) and *The Philosophy of the Christian Curriculum* (1967)—has since become a cornerstone of a vast movement of Christian educators, some of whom know of his work but many of whom do not.[96] This work put Rushdoony at the forefront of a movement that, as Milton Gaither argued in his history of American homeschooling, has steadily reversed the trend of defamilialization: "Some of the fuss over homeschooling may be due to the fact that it has been on the cutting edge of a larger renegotiation of the accepted boundaries between public and private, personal and institutional."[97] Rushdoony's early leadership in this battle to redraw the lines between family and the public sphere helped other activists see that the personal—and the familial—is always political.

Beyond the frequent citation and use of Rushdoony's philosophical studies of American education cited above, two of his public-lecture series—*A Christian Survey of World History* (1972) and *American History to 1865* (1973)—have become fixtures in Christian homeschooling curriculums. These works circulate freely in certain circles of homeschoolers that may or may not be fully aware of Rushdoony's larger project of Christian Reconstruction. Both lecture series, complete with the requisite study guides and parental material, are available in numerous homeschooling supply catalogs and on many websites.[98] As a result of the wide use of these texts, Rushdoony's impact on the pedagogical and epistemological presuppositions of homeschooling parents is inestimable.[99] As Gaither has argued,

In the homeschooling movement Rushdoony's influence has been direct and powerful. His writings have bequeathed to the conservative wing of the homeschooling movement both a strong sense of opposition between God's law and human laws and a tendency to think of itself as a divinely guided instrument in restoring a Christian America. Many homeschooling families and organizations are every bit as serious about integrating the Bible into public and private life as was Rushdoony, and they see the homeschooling of their children as the first step in the process.[100]

Yet limiting Rushdoony's influence to the integration of "the Bible into public and private life" is far too simplistic. Even as he was writing and lecturing to parents who wanted to teach their children to become self-conscious Christians, he began lobbying for and building the legal and institutional mechanisms necessary to protect the rights of those parents and their children. It is in this sense that Rushdoony used the public space of America's courtrooms to carve out the private, domestic spaces necessary for the familializing process of Christian Reconstruction to thrive.

Courtrooms

While lecturing on the Christian education circuit to promote his interpretation of a Christ-centered elementary- and secondary-school curriculum, Rushdoony became increasingly aware of a distressing trend: parents and church leaders who had sought refuge from public education by establishing homeschools and church schools found themselves the targets of prosecution by state and federal regulators. In many cases, local authorities prosecuted parents for refusing to meet this or that standard of the state-established curriculum or for failing to fully disclose some aspect of their private school's bureaucratic operations. As Rushdoony encountered parents and attorneys involved in these cases, he began putting them in contact with one another. As a result, he helped to slowly stitch together a patchwork of Christians united by their hitherto unknown common goal of abandoning public schools.

By the middle of the 1970s, Rushdoony spent more and more time weaving this network together. Phone calls came daily from parents and pastors engaged in these cases, and Rushdoony counseled them on how to handle their legal problems. "One of the growing, time-consuming, but necessary activities," he wrote to someone seeking Chalcedon literature on independent schooling, "is answering telephone calls from groups facing state and federal pressures to give them counsel."[101] Rushdoony blamed this necessary work on the failure of a previous generation of evangelicals and fundamentalists to stand up and resist a half century's worth of court rulings: "It has been the dereliction and withdrawal from social relevancy of conservative Christianity which has led to our present plight. It is a happy irony of history that they are now being compelled to make the key resistance."[102] Pastors and attorneys across the country sought the counsel of Rushdoony, a leader in the burgeoning resistance.

Rushdoony's expert status crystalized in the mid-1970s during the highly controversial fight over the Ohio State Board of Education's ability to license schools that failed to meet its new "Millennium Standards." Rushdoony traveled to Cleveland, Ohio, to speak with the lawyers involved. There, he met David C. Gibbs, an attorney defending Christian clients against the Ohio Department of Education. Gibbs was appealing the case of Rev. Levi W. Whisner and twelve codefendants who had been charged, tried, and convicted of sending their children to Tabernacle School, a private Christian school not licensed by the state. The state charged that Whisner and his codefendants failed to comply with compulsory education standards, while Whisner and his supporters—directly appealing to decades' worth of Rushdoony's writings—countered that the state standards forced them to teach "secular humanism," a violation of their religious freedom.[103]

The Ohio State Supreme Court eventually overturned Whisner's conviction in *Ohio v. Whisner, et al.* (1976), helping to galvanize Rushdoony's commitment to legal activism. He believed the state was "requiring all Christian schools to teach humanism,"[104] but he thought his *Messianic Character of American Education* has sparked resistance in Ohio to the state educational code's requirement that all schools teach humanism. Parents this fall will be charged and their children taken from them for having their children in Christian schools."[105] If the Christian schools refused to teach humanism, Rushdoony believed that the state would shut them down and prosecute the parents as it had done to Whisner. Gibbs and others associated with the Whisner case appropriated many of Rushdoony's ideas, especially his emphasis on secular humanism as a religious establishment and the argument that state education amounted to nothing less than Moloch worship.[106]

Rushdoony threw his support behind Gibbs by encouraging readers of the *Chalcedon Report* to contribute to Gibbs's work.[107] He also tried to connect Gibbs to some of his associates on the far edges of the Right. Rushdoony pointed Gibbs to Lawrence D. Pratt, a Rushdoony confidant who later served as president of Gun Owners of America, a gun owners' rights group that believed the National Rifle Association was too moderate. Pratt was setting up a legal organization called the Foundation for Law and Society. Rushdoony pressed billionaire Texas oilman Nelson Bunker Hunt to support Gibbs and Pratt, writing: "Their work will be of central importance in the legal defense of Christian Liberty for Christian schools, for business enterprise, etc. . . . Any assistance you can give them will help us establish a very important agency in the defense of our Christian freedom."[108]

As Rushdoony's commitments to these cases intensified, legal activism began dominating the other activities of Chalcedon. In the wake of the *Whisner* decision, Rushdoony became a much-sought-after expert witness in court trials related to independent Christian education. As a highly polished public speaker equipped with a seemingly encyclopedic knowledge of U.S. history, educational policy, and Christian theology, his testimony won the affection of conservative Christians while baffling state attorneys. Between 1980 and 1988, Rushdoony testified twenty-three times in court cases all over the United States.[109] These cases were related to Christian schooling, the establishment of religion by the state, and the independence of Christian churches from state licensing requirements.

During a trial of homeschooling parents in Macon, Georgia, Rushdoony testified that the proceedings were "evil because such trials have America's finest on trial, while hoodlums are free in the streets."[110] In another case in Nebraska, as Rushdoony approached the witness stand, a women associated with the Christian defendant leaned toward another in her group and whispered, "Whose side is he on? Our side or theirs?"[111] During the course of Rushdoony's testimony, the woman audibly concluded: "He's not on our side. He's on the Lord's side."[112] Rushdoony's intelligence and ferocity on the stand prompted prosecutors to take him seriously as a threat to their cases. They made efforts in some cases to suppress his testimonies, and in a federal case in Maine, the government attorney produced carefully annotated copies of Chalcedon publications and used them during Rushdoony's cross-examination.[113]

In these trials, lawyers called on Rushdoony as an expert who could establish that compulsory public school attendance policies and state-licensing procedures for private schools and homeschools put an undue religious burden on conservative Protestants. Rushdoony's expert testimony served to establish two basic facts in many of the cases. First, building on the Kuyperian notion of the antithesis and Van Til's presuppositionalism, he argued that for many evangelicals and fundamentalists, education is an inherently religious matter. Second, if all education is, at its essence, religious, then submitting to any educational standards other than explicitly Christian ones is inherently sinful for conservative Protestants. For example, in *State ex rel. Nagle v. Olin* (1980), the Ohio State Supreme Court explicitly relied on Rushdoony's testimony to overturn the conviction of James Olin for violating the state's compulsory attendance law.[114] Rushdoony told the court that "all education is inherently religious, in that it transmits the ultimate values and standards of a culture or community."[115] Since the state's minimum standards require "a school to transmit the religion of humanism," compulsory attendance shifts "a child's priorities and values away from God as sovereign to man and the state as sovereign."[116] By teaching this "alien" view to a "Biblical Christian," Olin would be "subjecting himself to damnation," and, consequently, the Court ruled the regulation was a "burden [to] his free exercise of religion."[117]

This ruling, one case among many in which Rushdoony's testimony played a significant role in the subsequent legal reasoning, points to the incredible force of presuppositional apologetics. To argue that orthodox Christianity is somehow prima facie at odds with compulsory education is anachronistic at best, requiring a considerable amount of interpretation—mostly distilled from very specific strains of twentieth-century American fundamentalist theology and popular historiography—and an essentialist understanding of what constitutes both *religion* and *Christianity*. But to further argue that state education is essentially *humanist* because of its meandering, indirect descent from the philosophy of John Dewey requires a similarly essentialist view of ideas and their transmission across time and through complex bureaucratic institutions. Rushdoony's ability to flatten these incredibly complex institutional and religious transformations into intelligible and reasonable witness-stand sound bites indicates presuppositionalism's remarkable power to simplify and clarify.

The Christian Rights Foundation

By the early 1980s, as a consequence of all of his networking, lecturing, and testifying, Rushdoony had established an impressive Rolodex of Christians who knew the ins and outs of the U.S. legal system, and he wanted to put them to use. In a letter to fellow Reconstructionist James B. Jordan, Rushdoony explained that he was using all of his lecture appearances as opportunities to drum up emotional and financial support for John Whitehead's legal cases involving homeschooling: "Chalcedon donates my time, travel expenses, and services; among other things, we help subsidize John Whitehead's work in the courts. This is a financial drain, as well as a personal drain; it also limits my ability to speak where I can bring funds for Chalcedon. But it is a necessity."[118] Rushdoony's support for Whitehead eventually led the two men to cooperate on the establishment of a Christian public-interest law firm dedicated to defending homeschoolers or any other issue they deemed a threat to the free practice of the Christian faith.

"I have asked John Whitehead," Rushdoony wrote to a potential financial supporter of the project, "to draw up papers for a group, titled Christian Rights Foundation, to fight such cases wherever they are."[119] Rushdoony wanted the foundation to participate in cases that most conservative evangelical Christians felt did not concern them: "Christians refuse to unite on these matters in existing groups; i.e., different kinds of Baptists will not work together; Arminians and Calvinists will not work together; neither will work with Catholics, nor charismatics and there is a division among charismatics."[120] This meant he wanted Whitehead to organize a foundation that would accept cases involving "heretical and non-Christian"[121] organizations such as Church of Scientology because Rushdoony believed that if such cases were lost, it "can destroy all churches and erode the First Amendment."[122]

As Whitehead drew up his plans for the advocacy firm, he also received support from Francis A. "Franky" Schaeffer V, the son of Francis A. Schaeffer IV, the world-famous evangelical apologist. The elder Schaeffer studied at Westminster Theological Seminary for two years under Cornelius Van Til. There, he learned an apologetic framework that he then popularized in a series of books and films advancing uniquely Christian critiques of Western culture that paralleled Rushdoony's work on law, politics, and social reform. The senior Schaeffer had started L'Abri ("the Shelter"), a sort of communal seminary and educational retreat for Christians interested in studying cultural and philosophical issues, in the Swiss Alps in the 1950s under the auspices of Carl McIntire's Independent Board of Presbyterian Foreign Missions.[123] The Shelter drew a constant flow of curiosity seekers, exhausted hippies, and Christian dropouts to Europe, where they could argue with Fran, as Schaeffer was known to his friends, and whet their apologetic and philosophical skills.[124] While running L'Abri with his wife, Edith, the elder Schaeffer authored a series of best-selling books on the Christian legacy of Western culture.

Franky, raised abroad in the cosmopolitan and intellectually stimulating context of his father's Swiss refuge, found much of the American evangelical and fundamentalist establishment to be parochial and behind the times when he and his father traveled to the United States in the 1970s. The Schaeffers came to the United States to encourage other evangelicals to stand

Franky Schaeffer (left) and John W. Whitehead (right) at Whitehead's Rutherford
Institute in 1990. The two men pioneered "Christian activism" in the late 1980s
and had a major influence on Franky's father, Francis A. Schaeffer IV.
Courtesy of John Whitehead and the Rutherford Institute.

against abortion, but they were shocked by the intellectual vapidity of leaders like Jerry Falwell and Pat Robertson.[125] "Most absurd of all," Schaeffer
later recalled, "I really knew *nothing* about the real America. I might as well
have been from Mars."[126] Schaeffer was an aspiring painter and filmmaker
who had inherited his father's love for Renaissance art. After a meeting in
which Pat Robertson breathlessly recounted burning a copy of a nude by
Italian modernist Modigliani—one of Francis Schaeffer's favorite modern
painters—the elder Schaeffer began to wonder "just *who* he was urging to
take power in the name of returning America to our 'Christian roots.'"[127]
Neither he nor Franky ever really felt at home among their American evangelical peers.

Still, in spite of his growing discomfort with the likes of Robertson and
others on the Religious Right, Franky Schaeffer, influenced by some of the
more radical L'Abri visitors, wanted to cultivate a more activist and con-

frontational strain among American evangelicals. Brash and combative, the younger Schaeffer thrived on confrontation and was impatient with the ignorance and lack of cultural relevance that he perceived among American evangelicals. In order to pull American evangelicals forward into a more confrontational form of cultural relevance, Franky pressed his respected father to use his fame to challenge young Christians. Working as a director and producer, Franky wrote his father's ideas in lightning with film versions of the books *How Should We Then Live?* and *What Ever Happened to the Human Race?* The latter was particularly significant and is frequently cited by evangelicals and scholars alike as a primary impetus behind Protestant resistance to the U.S. Supreme Court's landmark ruling legalizing abortion in *Roe v. Wade*.[128] Beyond his films, Franky Schaeffer also authored several highly polemical best-selling works that urged evangelical activism on political and social issues. Many of these works, most notably *A Time for Anger*, freely cited Rushdoony's work and recommended Chalcedon to Schaeffer's readers.[129] Relying on his father's fame and the success of his own films and books, Franky was determined to raise the money necessary to build a network of organizations capable of challenging the *Roe v. Wade* decision by dragging evangelicals and their resources into the public sphere.

In 1980 Schaeffer cold-called Whitehead after having read one of Whitehead's legal briefs. Whitehead, already pressed by Rushdoony to fight secularism in the courtroom, immediately recognized a kindred spirit in Schaeffer. The two men formed a tight bond and began working in earnest on a public-advocacy law firm that would not only defend the rights of homeschooling parents but also carve out more freedom for preachers and religious activists to engage in confrontational evangelistic tactics in public venues.

With encouragement and promises of support from both Rushdoony and Schaeffer, Whitehead drew up plans for an ambitious new foundation aimed at nothing less than reconstructing America's legal system in terms of a Christian heritage that Whitehead believed modern Americans had abandoned. The initial proposal for the foundation indicated that the "central purpose of the Christian Rights Foundation shall be to promote, assure and enhance the freedom of Christians in the exercise of their faith in accordance with the guarantees of the United States Constitution."[130] Organizationally, the foundation would have "branch offices across the United States that will effectively fight the legal battles necessary for reinstating a constitutional form of government."[131]

Whitehead's proposal relied heavily on ideas drawn from Rushdoony and the Schaeffers. It emphasized a return to constitutional values, moral reconstruction, and the importance of public education. The foundation would take as its primary duty to "reconstruct and revitalize America's legal heritage" by training "lawyers and interested laymen" how to participate in "legal and political processes."[132] This process of education and reconstruction would "guide the American public to an understanding of and desire for a true legal and constitutional system based upon the philosophy of those who drafted the American founding documents."[133] The proposal seamlessly combined the broad goals of Rushdoony's Christian Reconstruction with Schaeffer's vision of a more-aggressive, activist form of evangelicalism.

After the initial proposal for the Christian Rights Foundation floundered, Whitehead and Franky Schaeffer reworked the project and changed its name to the Rutherford Institute (TRI). The revised project was named for Scottish churchman Samuel Rutherford, the author of *Lex, Rex; or, the Law and the Prince* (1644). Rutherford's quickly banned book challenged the divine right of kings (that is, of *rex lex*—the king is the law), arguing instead that the king was subject to a greater law, a covenant established by God between the ruler and the ruled. The tract provided a theological framework for revolt against a tyrannical earthly power that failed to recognize the limits of divine law. Whitehead had previously highlighted Rutherford's argument, using it as the theoretical heart of his own book, *The Second American Revolution* (1982), which he published with support from the Schaeffers shortly before founding the Rutherford Institute. In the book, with Franky Schaeffer's encouragement, Whitehead used Rutherford's legal theology to justify Christian civil disobedience. Whitehead argued that *Lex, Rex* provided the moral foundation for the American colonies' first revolution against the English crown. Contemporary Christians, he insisted, must similarly adopt Rutherford's ideas as the moral foundation for their second revolution against the state's encroachment on religious freedom and assault on unborn life.

In 1982, with all of the necessary elements assembled, Whitehead incorporated the Rutherford Institute. As president of TRI, he assembled a board of directors made up of three other Christian lawyers and a cohort of nonlawyers. Among the nonlawyers, he included R. J. Rushdoony, Franky Schaeffer, and the reclusive but obscenely rich Howard Ahmanson. Ahmanson, then barely over thirty, was the heir to a savings-and-loan fortune estimated at $2.5 billion. Modest, humble, and reluctant to speak in public because of the awkward gestures and verbal ticks associated with his Tourette's syndrome, Ahmanson was a sharp organizer determined to use his vast wealth to further Christian causes. He made this commitment after encountering Rushdoony's writings as a young man.[134] When Ahmanson wrote a letter asking Rushdoony advice about professional counseling related to his Tourette's, Rushdoony dismissed the suggestion. "You have both intelligence of a high order, and money. You need now to put both to work. There is no better solution to problems and tensions than productive work. . . . The knowledge of Scripture and our application of it heals and strengthens us. . . . Get to Christ's work."[135] Charged with conviction and buoyed by Rushdoony's dominion wisdom, Ahmanson leaped into the Reconstructionist project.

Even with Schaeffer and Rushdoony fund-raising and Ahmanson's deep pockets, TRI operated on a shoestring budget. Chalcedon provided some of the initial capital needed to finance the formation of the foundation. With the support of Ahmanson, Rushdoony located the necessary funds to pay Whitehead's mortgage for a year after the young lawyer and his family relocated to Virginia to maximize his legal practice's impact on national issues.[136] After Whitehead secured tax-exempt status for Rutherford, Ahmanson agreed to contribute $25,000 per year and continued his support for nearly a decade.[137]

Slowly but surely, Whitehead used the notoriety of his board of directors and his own success in the courtroom to build a public-interest law firm that eventually became highly significant within American religious and political history. Historian R. Jonathan Moore has argued that the Rutherford Institute "represents a particularly important organization" because its genesis "helps to explain the rise of conservative Christian legal advocacy groups in late twentieth-century America."[138] Further, Whitehead developed legal and political tactics that many of "its younger peers imitated."[139] Although he would eventually abandon Reconstructionism for Franky Schaeffer's more radical brand of Christian activism, Whitehead nonetheless owed much of the initial impetus and theoretical foundation of the TRI to Rushdoony. If Whitehead and Schaeffer helped pioneer Christian legal activism in the 1980s, they did so by following paths blazed by Rushdoony in his effort to legalize Christian homeschooling.

Conclusion: Reconstruction Everywhere

The 1980s were the high watermark of Christian Reconstruction. Rushdoony's legal thinking and historical revisionism contributed to the reshaping of American education. His work, alongside the legal efforts of lawyers such as David Gibbs and John Whitehead, helped make homeschooling legal by shaping legal reasoning in small and large cases across the United

States. He found himself a regular guest on Pat Robertson's *The 700 Club* and D. James Kennedy's television broadcasts. Politicos such as Howard Phillips carried his ideas far beyond his small network of supporters in California. Greg Bahnsen, whom Rushdoony had cultivated since adolescence, had managed, however briefly, to challenge several seminaries to teach theonomy and consider the eschatological possibilities of postmillennialism. Although Bahnsen's direct impact was fleeting, his indirect influence has lingered for more than two decades, as his writings and recorded lectures remain popular in conservative Reformed circles. Further, his small group of loyalist RTS students continued to remake Reformed theology into the early 2000s.

Meanwhile, Gary North used the Institute for Christian Economics to flood America's Christian bookstores and academic libraries with Reconstructionist literature. Unlike Rushdoony, who had historically relied on connections with established Presbyterian and evangelical publishers to release his texts, North foresaw the power of the digital revolution taking place in the 1980s to bring books to market quickly and efficiently. Through the Institute for Christian Economics, North issued an endless stream of books, newsletters, and urgent fund-raising pleas to Christians. When Ron Sider, an evangelical critic of American consumption and advocate of a more-charitable, less-fundamentalist strain of evangelicalism, published *Rich Christians in an Age of Hunger* (1977), North agreed to debate him at Gordon-Conwell Theological Seminary in 1981.[140] Not content to simply debate Sider, North tapped David Chilton, a former student of Bahnsen's at RTS, to author a response to Sider's book. He gave Chilton three months to write *Productive Christians in an Age of Guilt Manipulators: A Biblical Response to Ronald J. Sider* (1981). At the debate, North propped the book up on the dais in front of him. Sider, surprised by the sudden appearance of a new polemic against his *Rich Christians*, asked North how long it had been in print. "One day," North deadpanned.[141] After the debate, he sold copies for a dollar. North kept the book in print throughout the decade, issuing a new edition every time Sider did the same with his book.[142]

By the early 1990s, North had so refined the publishing process that he could bring a book to press in a couple of months and print critical pamphlets in about a week.[143] In urgent situations, such as another Sider debate, he could produce books even faster. To ensure public access to ICE's voluminous output, North fraudulently sent boxes of books to university and college libraries with mailing slips indicating, "These books were paid for by an alumni [*sic*] who wishes to remain anonymous."[144] When an industrious pair of librarians uncovered the library-stacking scheme, North lamely responded that it was all the result of a "computer blunder."[145] Whether by hook, crook, or inventive, innovative publications schemes, ICE Reconstructionists were ready to bury their opponents under mounds of paper and no small amount of bluster.

At the height of their success, Rushdoony and his dominion men were offering a bold challenge to the mainstream of American evangelicalism. The sheer scope of their literary output and the ever-shriller tone of their theological assault commanded a grudging response, even in circles that would have preferred to ignore Reconstructionism.[146] But for all of their successes, the Reconstructionists could not agree with one another regarding the nature and meaning of Christian dominion. The movement was falling apart just as it approached the apex of its success.

CHAPTER SIX

American Heretics

Democracy, the Limits of Religion, and the End of Reconstruction

The tendency of institutions—church, state, and school—and of all
callings, is to absolutize themselves and to play god in the lives of men.
The answer of men to this problem has come to be "democracy."
Democracy, however, only aggravates the centralization of power into
institutional hands, because democracy has no solution to the problem
of human depravity and often fails even to admit the problem.
—R. J. RUSHDOONY, *The Institutes of Biblical Law*, 1:765

Who is she that looketh forth as the morning, fair as the moon,
clear as the sun, and terrible as an army with banners?
—Song of Solomon 6:10 (King James Version)

On October 4, 1982, the U.S. Congress "authorized and requested" President Ronald Reagan "to designate 1983 as a national 'Year of the Bible.'" Public Law 97-280 resolved that "our nation" needed "to study and apply the teachings of the Holy Scriptures" to the problems of the new decade. Fittingly, Reagan publicly fulfilled Congress's request at the National Prayer Breakfast in Washington, D.C., on February 3, 1983. In the official statement, Proclamation 5018, Reagan declared: "The Bible and its teachings helped form the basis for the Founding Fathers' abiding belief in the inalienable rights of the individual, rights which they found implicit in the Bible's teachings of the inherent worth and dignity of each individual."[1] Campus Crusade for Christ leader Bill Bright, who suggested the proclamation to Reagan in the first place, believed that such initiatives were leading to a civil revival in the United States.[2] Religious broadcasters and other Protestant leaders cheered the proclamation, viewing it as a symbolic victory over the forces of secularism and irreligion in the United States.[3]

Nancy DeMoss, president of the Arthur S. DeMoss Foundation, and Bright belatedly decided to celebrate the Year of the Bible with a major new program of evangelical outreach. DeMoss committed $15 million to the project. It would include the publication of a short book, *Power for Living*, supported by a major advertising blitz in national newspapers and on television and radio. DeMoss and Bright wanted a brief, punchy book that looked like any of a myriad of secular self-help books. It would be filled with personal testimonies and practical advice about the power of Christ in every believer's life. The only problem was that they settled on the project in August 1983 and wanted the book written, published, and distributed before the Year of the Bible ended.

DeMoss and Bright tapped American Vision to write and publish the book. Founded in 1978, suburban Atlanta–based American Vision published Reconstructionist-inspired literature, including Gary DeMar's highly popular homeschooling text, *God and Government* (1982). DeMar, a student of Greg Bahnsen at RTS Jackson and a longtime confidant of R. J. Rushdoony and Gary North, assembled a team of proven writers whom he could trust to produce quality Christian writing on a tight deadline. The team included David Chilton, Michael Gilstrap, and Ray R. Sutton. Reconstructionists all, DeMar's handpicked team lived in Tyler, Texas. They were members of the Westminster Presbyterian Church, taught in the church's Geneva Divinity School, and wrote books and produced ministry materials "on such subjects as law, government, economics, education, and social action" for North's Institute for Christian Economics.[4] The team wrote the 130-page booklet in a week.[5] *Power for Living* was implicitly Reconstructionist. It featured practical discussions of biblical law, elliptical references to Van Til's concept of presuppositionalism, and the implications of living a life in obedience to the ethical standards of Scripture.[6] By October, millions of copies were in the warehouse ready to ship. A multimillion-dollar marketing blitz kicked off with television ads featuring American singer and actor Pat Boone, former football player and then Dallas Cowboys head coach Tom Landry, and figure skater and Olympian Janet Lynn urging viewers to order their own free copy of the text.[7]

Before the Year of the Bible ended, however, rumors circulated that the DeMoss Foundation planned to destroy millions of copies of the American Vision version of the tract and distribute a revision. The Reconstructionist pamphlet troubled some of its DeMoss and Campus Crusade distributers. In November 1983, a new edition of *Power for Living* materialized after nearly 2.5 million copies of the first edition had been printed.[8] Although it retained sections of the DeMar-Chilton-Gilstrap-Sutton version, the revised edition bore the name of a single author: popular charismatic minister and writer Jamie Buckingham. Buckingham's version downplayed the legalism and conflict of worldviews implicit in the Reconstructionist text and instead emphasized personal experience and individual conversion.

The controversy over *Power for Living* reached a national audience. Because of the testimonies of the national figures included in it, wire services across the United States covered the dispute.[9] Newspapers quoted David Chilton as condemning the book for espousing a "very defective version of Christianity."[10] Sutton accused Buckingham of plagiarism.[11] Buckingham tried to downplay the controversy and insisted the new edition was simply a more nonconfrontational refinement of the first edition. Chilton, in return, angrily summed up his assessment of the kinder, gentler edition: "Buckingham's book and a lot of churches say, 'Come to Jesus and feel good and be happy.' The danger is that people would come to Mickey Mouse if they thought they would get a joy ride out of it."[12] By 2007, millions of copies of Buckingham's "Mickey Mouse" edition had been distributed in the United States, Germany, Mexico, and Japan.

The publishing history of *Power for Living* represents, in miniature, the status of Christian Reconstructionism in the 1980s and early 1990s. DeMoss and Bright knew exactly what they were getting when they hired American Vision to produce the book. The publisher's catalog was transparently Reconstructionist. DeMar, Chilton, and the other authors on the project were known quantities in evangelical circles because of their own extensive publication history. American Vision embodied the aggressive, in-your-face, militant cultural-warrior ethic that organizations such as the DeMoss Foundation and Campus Crusade for Christ wanted to avoid. In contrast, DeMoss and Bright represented the very pietistic strain of American evangelicalism that Reconstructionists despised—a form of Protestantism that emphasized conversion and personal experience over systematic theology and direct confrontation with America's secular culture. The resulting spat was predictable, yet it seemed to surprise everyone involved.

David Chilton, in a detailed comparison of the two versions of *Power for Living*, argued that the real fight that motivated the creation of a revised edition came down to two issues. First, as was the Reconstructionists' wont, he believed the DeMoss Foundation and Campus Crusade wanted "Reformation without confrontation."[13] Second, and more significantly, he recognized that the two versions reflected a deeper struggle between an Arminian strain of evangelicalism that emphasized a conversion-oriented, experience-centered view of Christianity and a Calvinist one that focused on the elect attempting "to apply the Bible to all of life."[14]

Throughout the 1980s and 1990s, Christian Reconstructionism influenced American evangelicalism in complex and subterranean ways. Very few Protestants in the United States had ever heard of Christian Reconstruction; fewer still self-identified as Reconstructionists. However, in spite of their lack of mainstream recognition and limited numbers, Reconstructionists' militant, aggressive vision of biblically based theonomy inspired Protestants across denominations. Reconstructionists not only made deep inroads into many small Calvinist groups, but they also influenced social conservatives in the Southern Baptist Convention and inspired the ministries of numerous Pentecostal and charismatic groups. Further, their focus on economics, law, and politics helped reshape conservative ideas in an era of right-wing political mobilization. Simultaneously, as it influenced religious and political conservatives, Reconstructionism became better known to many more Americans—evangelicals, secularists, and non-Protestants. To this new audience, largely unaware of the complex history of the movement, Reconstructionism appeared to be a sui generis antidemocratic, tyrannical, and personally invasive theocratic crusade. To these worried observers, Reconstructionism was an unprecedented movement intent on fusing church and state into a dangerous totalitarian union. In short, Reconstruction seemed like the ultimate American heresy.

Significantly, the theological and personal conflicts between Reconstructionists and the wider evangelical community coupled with institutional division to produce profound ignorance about the goals and mission of a generation of highly motivated young scholars cultivated and supported by Rushdoony. Unlike many evangelicals, especially those motivated by premillennialism, Rushdoony taught his followers to think in terms of generations, not individual lifetimes or decade-long election cycles. Not simply content to win one soul for Jesus at a time, Christian Reconstructionism called for capturing entire social and cultural systems for Christ. This sociological and political mission caught many evangelicals off guard, even as they asserted themselves into the mainstream of American political and cultural life during the 1970s.

The Tyler Church

When the DeMoss Foundation and Campus Crusade for Christ commissioned American Vision to produce *Power for Life*, they found themselves working with representatives of Christian Reconstructionism's so-called Tyler Theology. Headquartered in the Westminster Presbyterian Church, a small congregation located about 100 miles east of Dallas in Tyler, Texas, Tyler Theology embodied a complex mix of Rushdoony-style Reconstructionism, paramilitary survivalism, and aggressive theological polemics. Rev. Ray R. Sutton, a graduate of Dallas Theological Seminary, established Westminster in the late 1970s as a mission church to Tyler and slowly built the congregation into a central node in the Reconstructionist network. Although Sutton had graduated from one of the leading premillennialist seminaries in the evangelical movement and had no direct organizational connection to Rushdoony's Chalcedon Foundation, he had converted to theonomy based on his own reading of Scripture and through conversations with Reconstructionists.[15]

Sutton actively lobbied like-minded Christians to move to the 70,000-strong city of Tyler. After Gary North moved to Tyler in the late 1970s, Sutton managed to lure other Reconstructionists associated with Rushdoony's Chalcedon Foundation, including several of Greg Bahnsen's former RTS students, to join Westminster. As a critical mass of Reconstructionists descended on Tyler in the early 1980s, members of Westminster began a series of theological innovations that focused on the place of the church in the lives of dominion men. Instead of continuing Rushdoony's perspective that the family was the primary social instrument of God's dominion, the men at Tyler sought to downplay the family and emphasize the role of the church.

At Tyler, the church became the central organizing institution in the lives of the congregation. Sutton, North, and other leaders envisioned a powerful ecclesiastical structure with the ability to discipline its members and structure their lives according to the strictures biblical law. This contrasted sharply with Rushdoony's familial structure, and it was a difference that members of the Westminster Presbyterian Church took great pains to highlight. Through Geneva Divinity School, the "teaching ministry" of the church, and North's ICE, the Tyler church produced a seemingly endless proliferation of books, pamphlets, newsletters, and audiotapes designed to popularize their vision of a church-centered Christian Reconstruction of the United States of America.[16]

Westminster's church-centered perspective emerged clearly from the writings of a host of Tyler-based authors. The chief architects of the Tyler Theology were Greg Bahnsen's former students from the Reformed Theological Seminary in Jackson, Mississippi. Inspired by Bahnsen's articulation of theonomy and its noticeable distance from Rushdoony's family-centered model, the key architects behind the Tyler branch of Reconstructionism were James B. Jordan and David Chilton. With Sutton overseeing the church and North in charge of publishing and propagating the Tyler Theology, Jordan, Chilton, and other authors tapped by North articulated an innovative form of Reconstructionism that spoke directly to participants in the emerging New Christian Right.

In his writings during the 1980s, Chilton took aim at Rushdoony's Chalcedonian model of family-centered Reconstruction to offer a stark alternative. "*The center of Christian reconstruction is the church*," he insisted.[17] "The River of life," he concluded, "does not flow out from the doors of the chambers of Congresses and Parliaments. It flows from the restored Temple of the Holy Spirit, the church of Jesus Christ. Our goal is world domination under Christ's Lordship, a 'world takeover' if you will: but our strategy begins with reformation, reconstruction of the church. From that will flow social and political reconstruction, indeed a flowering of Christian civilization."[18]

Similarly, James B. Jordan developed this point quite rigorously, likening the church to a military unit. According to Jordan, the church instructs men in the offices of dominion through the threefold pedagogies of fear, drill, and education. In terms of fear, Jordan argued that the Bible sets a "court-enforced boundary. God threatened to kill anyone who got too far out of line. He established authorities in Church and in state with real power to enforce this. Fear is a very real factor in Christianizing a people, for fear shapes the minds and attitudes of people."[19] Second, church liturgy is a form of structured "drill": "The performance of ritual actions by our whole persons restructures our lives. Such ritual creates a context for understanding truth when we hear it."[20] Finally, education must be conducted in terms of the presuppositional constraints developed by Van Til and popularized by Rushdoony. Thus, just as the "military shapes men by means of fear (threat of real punishment), drill (ceremonial acts, such as marching), and instruction," so, too, will the "reestablishment of true government in the Church" lead to the recovery of these pedagogies in "society at large."[21] Jordan concluded with a clear contrast to Rushdoony's position that the family is the womb of the Kingdom: "The Church is the nursery of the Kingdom, and there can be no reformation in state, school, or family, until there is reformation in the Church."[22]

North promoted this ecclesiology as a unique innovation within the Reconstructionist movement. The Tyler Group distinguished itself from other versions of Reconstructionism by "its heavy accent on the church, with weekly Communion."[23] North specifically contrasted the Tyler Group's identity from Chalcedon's work in California, arguing in publication after publication that Rushdoonian Reconstruction "tended to stress the social issues before the ecclesiastical ones."[24] North's various newsletters also attempted to draw focus away from Rushdoony's work, noting that "the Christian Reconstruction movement has been appreciably altered by the work of scholars here at Geneva [Divinity School]. It is our conviction that at this point in history, the focus of our efforts must be directed at the Church."[25]

The Decentralized Church

As with all aspects of Reconstructionist theology, the Tyler Group's focus on the church had real-world consequences. Unlike Rushdoony, who focused most of his attention on ideas and family organization, North and the men at Tyler explicitly developed a sociological theory organized around the institution of the church. Within the context of the Tyler Theology, however, the "church" was not a monolithic, centralized hierarchy of ecclesiastical units working in unison across varied geographic regions. For theorists in the Tyler Group, decentralization and fragmentation among church groups was not a weakness; it was instead one of the primary political assets of Christianity. "Christianity is decentralized," North insisted, "indeed, 'fragmented' better describes our condition. If the Christians can assemble themselves into loosely organized but well-trained special-interest blocs, while today's centralized humanist culture is disintegrating, the result could be the creation of a new cultural synthesis, one based on Biblical law rather than some version of humanistic natural law."[26] Wise churches (located in the home) would then further decentralize their structures by delegating their ministries to their individual family units and, ultimately, to the individual members of the churches.[27]

To develop his argument, North adopted then-faddish pop-scientific rhetoric borrowed from nonlinear dynamics and chaos theory.[28] North claimed that decentralization would lead to a systemic "positive feedback loop" in which the gains made in one sphere of society would "feedback" into the other spheres, generating positive, ever-increasing levels of faith, obedience, and monetary prosperity.[29] The divine positive feedback loop of dominion means that godly men will multiply exponentially, and that their presence will make the state sphere more unruly over time.

God, in His infinite wisdom, understood that sinful men would try to consolidate and regulate this expansion through Babel-like centralization and, accordingly, God built a solution into His law-word: "As societies become larger and more complex, the civil government must remain decentralized in order to achieve its goal of creating social peace. . . . The more complex a society becomes, the less able the State's officials are to direct the society. . . . It is only by means of *self-government under God's law* that a complex and developing society can regulate itself."[30] In short, not only is a monolithic, centralized, top-down system sinful, but it also is not dynamic enough to bring about the Kingdom; therefore, God's law requires the decentralization of humanity to ensure that it increases and fills the earth.[31] Thus, "The international kingdom of God must be decentralized. No new tower of Babel will do Christians any good. . . . But person by person, church by church, occupation by occupation, nation by nation, the world is to be brought under the dominion of God."[32]

The positive feedback that leads to the expansion of dominion also creates the conditions that make centralized bureaucracy impossible because churches can engage in "brush fire wars" that "show the bureaucrats that they cannot stop the spread of the Christian fire by putting out one blaze. They have to put out hundreds of blazes."[33] Christians could make these brush fires even more effective if they would essentially "hide" their home churches from federal oversight by refusing to seek federal tax exemption.[34] Evoking the rhetoric of Martin Luther King Jr., North admitted that he "dreamed" of these brush fires. "*My dream*," he noted wistfully, "*would be the state's nightmare*."[35]

The brush fires of the emergent, decentralized church are made possible by an important godly historical mechanism: the free market. Capitalism is a primary element of God's plan precisely because it undermines the Babel-like unity of all social and cultural structures. In North's view, capitalism— through its endless mechanisms of production and consumption—erodes centralization. Echoing Karl Marx, North argued that capitalism undermined social classes such as the priesthood and aristocracy in medieval Europe and, in the process, destroyed the centralized structures of the feudal manor and the Roman church. Further, capitalism destroyed tribal familial networks and provided the conditions for the rise of the nuclear family and the development of individualism as a subject position.[36]

This logic led North to conclude that capitalism created the conditions necessary for allowing humans to conceive of themselves as discrete, atomized units (a precondition of the self-government of dominion men).

Capitalism also fractured the family from tribal and ethnic groupings into nuclear family units (similarly a requirement for the emergence of Christians as the third race of men). Finally, capital created the political conditions for decentralized federal or republican governance (the final judgment on Satanic Babel-like bureaucratic centralization). Soon, North predicted, the corrosive logic of capitalism will also decentralize American cities and, with them, the last vestiges of urban, liberal Christianity. "Capitalism made agriculture sufficiently productive to allow people to move to the city. But there are limits to this centralization. . . . As roads wear out (as they did after the fall of Rome), as urban pollution increases, as traffic jams of the 'free' roadways become intolerable to many, as the lifestyle of the urban dwellers becomes anathema to all but the very rich and the very poor, and as technology moves society back toward decentralized production, this centralization will change."[37] With the deterioration of the city, the great mainline churches—now burdened by excessive property taxes and decaying infrastructure—will collapse. North imagined a brave new world of crumbling Satanic megalopolises ringed by independent exurban fiefdoms ruled by vigilant, well-armed dominion men.

North's focus on the importance of the decentralized nature of the church, family, and state led him to make a number of increasingly bold predications about the economic and political future of the United States and the global economic system. North and his fellow churchmen at Tyler believed that the process of Christian Reconstruction could be accelerated during periods of intense social unrest and economic collapse. First, they foresaw the possibility that the Kingdom of God might be brought about by sudden shifts in the global economic and social system. Specifically, North made a series of predications regarding the sudden systematic collapse of such transient institutions as the U.S. federal government and the global banking system. Of his many predications, North most notoriously prophesied that the Y2K computer glitch would lead to the total collapse of the global economy, leaving Christians in the United States to pick up the pieces.[38] Second, in the event of any of these catastrophic collapses, decentralized churches operating independently from the federal government would step into the void left by the imploding state and provide societal stability.[39] When American society finally collapses under the combined weight of massive foreign debt, military overreach, and internal decadence, North and his followers at Tyler hoped to have a network of churches ready to step into the breach. To prepare Christians for this future event, he wrote book after book aimed at educating Christians on how to live debt free, avoid electronic surveillance, and develop the skills necessary for surviving economic collapse.

Survivalism

The Tyler Group's ecclesiastical mission, militaristic metaphors, and heated rhetoric were closely paralleled by a survivalist-inspired, hard-money social agenda that they believed would allow the church to survive and thrive in the wake of cataclysmic economic or military disaster. The group's emphasis on decentralization, gold, and guns was part of a much larger survivalist movement that influenced groups—religious and nonreligious alike—countrywide during the 1970s and 1980s and served as the precursor to the militia movements of the 1990s.[40] Survivalism, which sociologist Richard G. Mitchell has defined as the "creative transcendence of calamitous cultural change," emerged as an ad hoc social movement combining religious and secular sensibilities into a network of practical strategies intended to help individuals and families anticipate and overcome natural and man-made calamities.[41]

Gary North was at the cutting edge of the development of this survivalist ethos in the United States. The popularity of survivalist strategies and products emerged in the late 1970s just as North left Washington, D.C., and sought his post–Ron Paul identity. During the 1970s and early 1980s, North connected with this new survivalist impulse to build a cottage publishing industry, especially in the form of his aptly named *Remnant Review*, which commenced publication in 1974 as a four-page monthly newsletter. It outlined North's vision for an economically self-sufficient, off-the-grid Christian lifestyle that would allow a practical patriarch and his family to weather the coming lean times.

In the 1970s and early 1980s, North used his connections with grassroots conservatives and Washington insiders to build a robust network of commercial connections with a host of best-selling doom peddlers. Most notably, he built alliances between evangelical communities and Latter-day Saint (LDS) preparedness advocates. For a brief period immediately following his time on Texas Representative Ron Paul's staff, North wrote for Howard Ruff's *Ruff Times*, a digest of hard-money, no-debt preparedness strategies. Ruff, a Latter-day Saint, hired North not for his religious sensibilities but for his no-nonsense preparedness bona fides. During the economic downturn of the 1970s, Ruff, like many others on the Right, believed that America's departure from the gold standard in 1971 had led to the hyperinflation of the late 1970s and worsened the effects of the post–Iranian Revolution energy crisis on the United States. His *How to Prosper during the Coming Bad Years* (1979) became a *New York Times* best seller, and by the end of the 1970s, North's journalism in *Ruff Times* reached more than 80,000 subscribers.[42]

With his effortless blend of postmillennial eschatology, patriarchal vision, deurbanization, and procapitalist economics, North became a hit on the survivalist lecture circuit, and his non-Reconstructionist books and newsletters sold well. Through his connections with Ruff, North came into contact with other LDS preparedness activists. By the early 1980s, as concerns about domestic unrest and nuclear war once again peaked, North frequently appeared on the preparedness lecture circuit alongside the likes of not only Ruff but also Joel and Mark Skousen, well-known hard-money preparedness advocates who situated their work firmly within the "self-reliance" and "provident living" discourses of contemporary Latter-day Saints.[43]

As North's ideas circulated widely in conservative circles, he downplayed their Reconstructionist underpinning in order to appeal to a wide variety of secular, LDS, and premillennial preparedness advocates. For example, *Government by Emergency* (1983), a warning that governments usurp power during catastrophes, and his *Fighting Chance: Ten Feet to Survival* (1986), a passionate plea for backyard bomb shelters coauthored with scientist and homeschooling advocate Arthur Robinson, barely referenced anything beyond a bland Protestant tradition even as they developed complex preparedness schemes to address the national and international threats of the 1980s.

The result of North's endless stream of books, newsletters, fund-raising notes, and pleas to Reconstructionists was a small media empire. He made revenues estimated in the millions. Rumors circulated in Reconstructionist circles that he made land investments across the country designed to facilitate his own preparedness schemes and fund his business ventures. Other sources suggested that he used sales of his preparedness literature to fund the publishing projects of the Tyler branch of Christian Reconstruction.[44]

North brought this survivalist instinct directly into the Tyler church and cultivated survivalism in the wider Reconstructionist movement. While serving as editor for the *Journal of Christian Reconstruction*, North published a manifesto for Christian survivalism. In "A Biblical Basis for Survival Preparations," *Power for Living* coauthor Michael R. Gilstrap argued: "A Christian, of all people, *should* be a survivalist. . . . We must see from Biblical history and Biblical law that survival preparation is not an option. It is not a new fad of the rich. It is not simply the practice of the doom-and-gloomer. *It is a matter of faith.*"[45] Gilstrap declared that biblical patriarchs such as Noah,

Joseph, and Moses were prototypical survivalists who heard a warning from God, listened to His instructions, and then acted on faith to prepare for the future. As with ancient times, God, Gilstrap claimed, was again giving clear signs that the United States was now under judgment, and Christians "have a reason to survive." Why? Because Christians will regenerate the world following God's judgment. "Of all people," asserted Gilstrap,

> we are obligated to survive. This is God's world, not the devil's. We are not just another speck of dust in this vast universe, but part of the body of Christ—the new humanity. . . . Before there can ever be regeneration, there must be death. The judgment to come is that death. The Dark Angel of the Lord will bring death to western civilization. But if Christians do not survive, then someone or something else will gain temporary dominion in this world, and we will have to begin all over again. Just as Noah's sons went on to help shape the future history of the world, we must survive so that our children can help shape the future for God. *No one else will do it.* It is not only our privilege to survive if God wills, but in a sense it is our *duty* to survive so that our children *will* survive. *We must survive*—for the Lord.[46]

Here, Gilstrap and others at Tyler pushed Rushdoony's postmillennial vision toward its nightmarish logical end. Just as orthodox Protestant theology insists that an individual must die to him- or herself in order to be reborn in the body of Christ, Tyler's brand of survivalism insisted that a civilization must be destroyed in its entirety before it can be regenerated as a Christian civilization. The "body of Christ"—the church—must be prepared for this judgment, or it, too, will perish. Consequently, just as God destroyed humanity but saved the remnant of Noah to regenerate the world, Christian Reconstructionists must heed the warnings and prepare to rule in the wake of the coming destruction of humanity.

If Rushdoony had once emphasized the cultivation of an ideological and theological Remnant during the 1960s, then the Tyler Reconstructionists were now focused on building something far less abstract and much more militant. They were concerned with material survival in "the postcrash world." Gilstrap warned that Reconstructionists must get their priorities right: "Our foresightedness must extend not only to the crisis, but to the world on the other side of the crisis. Hopefully, in our case, to a world under God's Law."[47] Prepping for the "postcrash world" was a primary concern for some within the Tyler Group.[48] Rumors circulated that some in the church had begun to hoard firearms—for security, as an investment, or both—and the leaders of the church engaged in aggressive and dismissive attacks on their enemies.[49]

With the Tyler Group's focus on strict church discipline and respect for ecclesiastical authority, the church had a habit of excommunicating dissident members. In the mid-1980s, the church's membership peaked with about sixty families, but that number declined slowly as the fevered paranoia and harsh church discipline eroded support for Sutton's leadership. Journalist and religion scholar Diane Winston reported that "Church members lived in constant fear of excommunication for rebellious behavior. . . . Rebellion could take many forms: questioning a church elder, refusing to participate in a church activity, debating a church teaching."[50] Confusion and anger peaked when one deacon asserted that if the church insisted all members should put whitewall tires on their cars, "the congregants had better obey or face excommunication."[51] Matters became much worse when Gary North and other elders mishandled a significant sum of money given to the church by a wealthy widow.[52]

These membership issues, combined with the church's survivalist rhetoric, led to its slow unraveling. As one former church member wrote to Rushdoony,

> The things of greatest emphasis at Westminster are money,
> personal power and influence, infiltration of other churches,
> government, social associations, paramilitary equipment and
> training, an elite inner core group and other cultic trappings.
> They talk constantly of the Law, humanism, the coming collapse
> of all economies, governments, etc., but never of love of God for a
> sinful people. The fruits of the Spirit are not evident in them, nor
> has a single soul been won to the Lord by their ministry. What hap-
> pened is that some, coming out of other error or bad experience[,]
> are banding together in semi-secret hatred of all established orders.
> They would call themselves "Dominion Men" but are far more
> accurately characterized as Dostoyevsky's "Underground men."[53]

Another dissident who left the church similarly cited the stockpiling of guns as something he did not understand about the Tyler Group's theology, and his disagreement with the practice helped prompt his exit from the church.[54]

As the Tyler church imploded because of its hard-nosed theological brawling and survivalist paranoia, Rushdoony was going through one of his darkest personal periods as the president of the Chalcedon Foundation. His endless writing, researching, lecturing, and fund-raising tours were beginning to wear him down. When Jordan and North tried to bring Rushdoony to Tyler for a lecture, his anger with the church and its leaders eventually came to a head. In a particularly telling letter, Rushdoony registered his exhaustion and frustration in stark terms:

> Yesterday noon, I ate (as often) a cold meal, alone, because, when I sat down to eat, the phone rang. A pastor I have never met, with a weeping woman before him, called for counsel; he had called a year before in another case. For the same reason, I ate alone at night. In between, I spent a couple hours again on the phone in like matters. This goes on daily. Yet not even one in ten will contribute to Chalcedon.
>
> I will continue, only because the battle is the Lord's. But I will not go [to Tyler, Texas,] where people will not fight with their precious pocketbooks. They have guns and food to defend themselves, but the battle in the courts goes begging.
>
> In five and a half years, I have not been home all of any month. I am canceling all trips in April . . . staying home for my birthday and Dorothy's . . . and that is it.[55]

Rushdoony, now in his midsixties, was, in his own words, "a very fallible man."[56] He was a human being capable of shallow pettiness and arrogant pride. But he was also a man who was rarely home and missed his beloved wife, Dorothy, and his German shepherd, Juno.[57] He longed to surround himself with his grandchildren and great-grandchildren. He cared so deeply for his work that he missed meals and volunteered his time generously for people who volunteered nothing in return. His love of Jesus Christ was so profound that he willingly sacrificed his own health, happiness, and mental well-being—and that of his loved ones—for the "battle." The young men at Tyler, to whom Rushdoony had given so generously, were about to turn on him, and he was not in the emotional or spiritual state to handle the attack.

"Let the Lord Judge between Us"

The movement that Rushdoony had labored to build was in many ways thriving: Chalcedon was supporting John Whitehead's work in the courts to defend Christian homeschoolers; Rushdoony was lecturing far and wide and appearing before influential conservative groups, such as the Heritage Foundation; and his name freely circulated in evangelical circles as a man of God of significant influence. But members of those same circles rarely mentioned Rushdoony in public because of his controversial writings, and, for all of its successes, Chalcedon was still a one-man operation that had exhausted its seemingly inexhaustible founder.[58]

Rushdoony felt that many of the leading lights associated with the Tyler church—namely, James B. Jordan, Gary North, and Greg Bahnsen—were using his reputation to embellish their own. In brash, self-confident writings, many in the Tyler Group downplayed Rushdoony's work, insisting they had moved beyond his concept of Reconstruction. Some even implied that Greg Bahnsen had developed the idea of theonomy before Rushdoony.[59] Worse still, North exacerbated these tensions by quietly insinuating that his father-in-law was insane for living in California. North believed California was vulnerable to nuclear attack and ridiculed any conservative for remaining in such a liberal bastion. When James B. Jordan inquired about Rushdoony's anger with the Tyler Group, Rushdoony responded: "I am sure Tyler is loaded with stored foods, guns, and perhaps bomb shelters."[60] But, Rushdoony insisted, the battle would not be waged in some postapocalyptic future: "The battle is *now*, and people should not fear Moscow or hungry mobs, but the Lord. There is no bomb shelter to hide them from the wrath of God, or guns to hold him at bay."[61]

Tensions between Vallecito and Tyler exploded over an article North wrote for the *Journal of Christian Reconstruction*. After reading a draft of the essay, Rushdoony wrote: "I am returning your Economic Commentary on 'Walls and Wealth.' I am baffled that you could write a piece so bad. It smacks of fertility cults, not Scripture."[62] In the essay, North followed an interpretation developed by James B. Jordan to argue that the lamb's blood splashed on the top and sides of the door frame by the Hebrews during Passover represented the hymeneal blood of a deflowered virgin on her wedding night.[63] Rushdoony declared the argument "weird" and commanded North to "*destroy this*."[64] Rather than debate the theological point, North immediately turned on Rushdoony, seizing the opportunity to assert that the movement Rushdoony had started was now ready to surpass him. "To be quite frank," North sneered,

> some of the younger men in the movement are ready to make some
> fundamental innovations in the existing theonomy framework. No
> movement stays in the same mold forever. Chilton, Bahnsen, Jordan,
> and I are going to make our own independent innovations, and I
> will (God willing) finance us in this endeavor. We have 50 years of
> production ahead of us, we hope, and we're all likely to come up with

ideas that we don't even suspect today. And our younger disciples will no doubt go beyond us. That's what progress in theology is all about. Young men innovate.[65]

"Your letter," Rushdoony responded, "is written with your usual grace and courtesy. You are 'innovative,' and I am, as you make clear to many, over the hill, so the future of theonomy with some 'fundamental innovations' (that word again) is in the hands of 'Chilton, Bahnsen, and I.'"[66] The sarcastic letters set off a rapid exchange of correspondence that shuttled back and forth among Rushdoony, North, Jordan, and Tyler church pastor Ray Sutton. With each note, the temperature of the rhetoric increased, until Rushdoony eventually charged all three Tyler men with "blasphemy"[67] and demanded they "recant" their positions.[68]

Rushdoony's charge of blasphemy and his demand that the Tyler Group recant their argument put him in an awkward position that Gary North eagerly locked onto: "The previous letters seemed to imply, 'recant, or else.' Or else what? What, precisely, are you telling me? What are my options? If I don't recant—and I wish to say clearly that I am not now recanting—what then? You see, it's a question of authority and sanctions. If you have authority, you can impose sanctions. If you have no sanctions, you have no authority."[69] Not only was Rushdoony "over the hill"; the grand patriarch of Reconstructionism also was impotent, powerless to wield any authority over the men he had mentored and cultivated into the acid-witted and rock-ribbed theological adversaries he now faced.

Rushdoony's only recourse was to fire North as the *Journal of Christian Reconstruction*'s editor and terminate his relationship to Chalcedon, a move that North both anticipated and desired. He warned that if Rushdoony fired him, the Tyler Group would simply start a rival publication.[70] North taunted, "Let me know the next step. Soon."[71] Rushdoony took his son-in-law's advice and immediately fired North and Jordan, who also contributed to the journal. Not to be outdone, North sent letters to all of the journal's previous authors and subscribers to inform them of the "sad situation" at Chalcedon and tell them that a rival journal would begin publication in Tyler.[72]

Rushdoony ended the matter forever with one final note to Sutton. In it, he reluctantly admitted that Jordan and North apparently believed in their interpretation of Passover (although he implied North's belief might have been, at best, shallow). For Sutton, however, he reserved particularly harsh words: "You have made clear in telephone conversations twice that you do not like it [Jordan and North's interpretation], but you want unity, not truth apparently."[73] This was a particularly severe charge because, in theory, Sutton was the primary ecclesiastical and theological authority at Westminster Presbyterian Church. Sutton's failure to discipline North and Jordan was, for Rushdoony, a gross dereliction of his duty. Mustering the full measure of his sectarian anger, Rushdoony continued: "The gospel is not pragmatism."[74] In haste, he concluded the note: "Let the Lord judge between us. I commit judgment into His hands. Let me be."[75] Rushdoony never spoke to North, Jordan, or Sutton again.

Democracy as a Heresy

The schism between Chalcedon and the Tyler Group had complex implications for Christian Reconstruction. On one hand, North and the other young men at Tyler tried to bury Rushdoony's and Chalcedon's corpses with paper. As Howard Ahmanson told Rushdoony, "Gary acts as though you are already deceased—or should be."[76] This meant a veritable explosion of publication as North, Jordan, Chilton, Sutton, and many others produced book after book, newsletter after newsletter, and audiotape after audiotape in the hopes of convincing the world that they, and not the stodgy has-beens at Chalcedon, were the true dominion men of the Christian Reconstruction movement. Further, while Rushdoony specifically avoided responding to the output of the Tyler Group, he and his tiny staff at Chalcedon continued their own prodigious literary output and lecture itineraries. The result was that the two branches of Reconstruction engaged in agonistic but ultimately mutually beneficial publishing campaigns that saw the younger generation of Reconstructionists reaching new audiences while helping to sustain interest in Rushdoony's writings.[77]

On the other hand, the schism put a considerable amount of emotional stress on the individuals involved and on their organizational infrastructure. It strained Rushdoony's relationship with his daughter Sharon and his grandchildren. It also broke the strong bonds with several men whom Rushdoony had cultivated as his spiritual and intellectual heirs. North, Bahnsen, Chilton, and Jordan all had spent a portion of their formative years under Rushdoony's tutelage, and, especially in the case of North, Rushdoony's family had become their own. Beyond the sudden severing of strong personal ties among these men, the schism also caused discomfort among organizations and individuals active in the Reconstruction movement. Many complained that they felt they were being required to choose between Tyler and

Chalcedon, and they resented it. Some went so far as to try to intervene and heal the rift, but to no avail.

Beyond the schism between Tyler and Chalcedon, broader cultural and political changes in the United States were also influencing Christian Reconstructionism. First, the rise of the Religious Right as an amorphous but potent political force had helped elect two presidents, Jimmy Carter in 1976 and Ronald Reagan in 1980. Second, dramatic cultural shifts accelerated as changing attitudes toward abortion, sexuality, and individual liberty partially resonated with the concomitant rise of the Christian Right. Third, the resonance between the stated political and cultural aspirations of the Christian Right and the emergence of popular conservative sentiment during the early 1980s created a context in which the ideas of Rushdoony and other Reconstructionists circulated far beyond Reformed church circles and gained a certain amount of cultural traction. Consequently, just as the institutional and personal relationships among Reconstructionists disintegrated, Christian Reconstructionism emerged as an important component of the conservative realignment of political and religious culture in the United States during the 1980s.

For evangelicals and fundamentalists, social and political action has long proved a significant theological and practical problem. Neoevangelical Protestants in the post-Scopes era had struggled to reconcile their religious commitments to evangelism, the doctrine of individual salvation, and the imminent return of Christ with overt political and social activism. The emergence of the Christian Right in the 1970s and 1980s indicated that, on some level, many of these questions were being answered in practice: Christians had an obligation to evangelize to individuals, but this obligation could be furthered and mediated through mechanisms of governance beyond the church and family; salvation is a gift from God, but certain social environments are more conducive to winning souls than others; and yes, Christ will return soon, but that does not mean that a Christian may stand by idly as sin dominates the surrounding culture.

For his part, Rushdoony had labored to push these points since his time in Owyhee. Occasionally and fleetingly—especially in his interactions with Spiritual Mobilization, the William Volker Charities Fund, and J. Howard Pew—Rushdoony managed to use these revolutionary ideas to influence important institutions in political conservatism and among evangelicals. By the 1980s, he sensed that he was singularly responsible for this shift in evangelical and fundamentalist attitudes toward culture and politics. Specifically, he believed that his emphasis on biblical law as the condition for the establishment of Christ's postmillennial Kingdom on earth had challenged many evangelicals and fundamentalists to rethink their withdrawal from participation in the broader culture. This perception, while exaggerated, was not totally without warrant. In the 1980s, after nearly two decades of studiously ignoring Rushdoony, many influential church leaders and evangelical intellectuals suddenly realized that Rushdoony's ideas were everywhere. And this required explanation.

The Obscured Reformer

In *The Anointed*, their 2011 book about evangelical "experts" who challenge secular standards of knowledge production, historian Randall J. Stephens and physicist Karl W. Giberson profiled some of the leading historical and scientific revisionists working in conservative Christian circles. Well-known Protestant historical and scientific revisionists such as Dan Barton, the Christian "amateur" historian who tries to Christianize every American historical figure, and Ken Ham, the young-earth creationist behind Kentucky's Creation Museum, dominate Stephens and Giberson's book.[78] In a telling aside, the authors briefly mentioned Rushdoony's influence on revisionist historians like Barton: "Rushdoony toiled in obscurity. His work on God, Indians, law, and the Founders was unknown in his lifetime. *Christianity Today*, the most influential evangelical magazine of the twentieth century, seldom mentioned him or his work."[79] While Stephens and Giberson were certainly correct that *Christianity Today* rarely mentioned Rushdoony's work, it had little to do with his prima facie obscurity. Quite the opposite: because of his association with J. Howard Pew and the wide-ranging appeal of his grassroots ministry, Rushdoony was anything but obscure to the editors of the journal.

In response to Rushdoony's disastrous bid to leverage J. Howard Pew's patronage to bully *Christianity Today* into a more-conservative stance at odds with its editors' neoevangelical vision, the journal's editors adopted a gatekeeper stance aimed at carefully supervising the publication and transmission of Rushdoony's ideas. Although Rushdoony never personally submitted another article for the editors' review, his supporters did occasionally submit unsolicited manuscripts. Carl F. H. Henry, in his "irenic spirit," initially considered publishing such work, in one instance ordering an editor to "forget this is by Rushdoony. Does it have any merit?"[80] The reviewer concluded: "This has the form of scholarship but none of its content. . . . Rush's theology is not much better."[81] Other pieces followed, each with the inevitable rejection. Later, in 1975, the journal's editors purposefully removed all references to Rushdoony's ideas from Terrill I. Elniff's October 24 cover story, "The Reformers." The article discussed Puritan philosophies of government and jurisprudence, leaning heavily on Rushdoony's ideas and directly citing his works and those by other Reconstructionists. When the edited article ran without directly quoting Rushdoony or even "attributing the sources of indirect quotations" to him or other Reconstructionists in footnotes, Elniff was "embarrassed and not a little shocked."[82]

Elniff had inadvertently stumbled onto *Christianity Today*'s unwritten policy of ignoring Rushdoony whenever possible. As a de facto editorial policy, snubbing Rushdoony—an avowed enemy of the publication—made sense. Journalistically, however, this blackout had a significant unintended consequence: as Christian Reconstructionism's influence became more apparent in classrooms, courtrooms, and small churches, it caught many evangelical observers off guard. Rushdoony's subtle—and inconsistent—movement between withdrawal and engagement with other conservative Protestants and political activists created a context in which publications such as *Christianity Today* and prominent evangelical institutions in the mold of Fuller Seminary, Wheaton College, and Dallas Theological Seminary could ignore Reconstructionism even as they did nothing to undermine its influence in highly conservative Presbyterian circles, among homeschoolers, and in church polities across the United States. This lack of popular exposure helped nurture the interconnected misconceptions that Reconstructionism was either a dangerous foreign aberration with no roots in traditional American evangelicalism or that it had somehow leaped, fully formed and Athena-like, from Rushdoony's fevered brow. Neither characterization is accurate, but both served the important discursive function of emphasizing the sui generis otherness of Christian Reconstruction.

Dominion Theology

With the Tyler and Vallecito camps pumping out Reconstructionist-themed books, audiotapes, and lectures, Rushdoony and his tiny handful of acolytes saw their gradualist strategy begin to transform conservative Protestant thinking across the United States. Within a decade of the publication of *The Institutes of Biblical Law*, the book was a familiar citation for law school faculty at Oral Roberts University, Pat Robertson's CBN/Regent University, and Jerry Falwell's Liberty University. This widespread awareness of Rushdoony's ideas coincided with the explosion of religious broadcasting that was facilitated by cable and satellite television networks. Further, Federal Communications Commission regulatory changes allowed local television stations to broadcast paid religious programming as a public service.[83] Soon, not only were millions of Americans tuning into the likes of Jimmy Swaggart, Jerry Falwell, and many other television preachers, but they also were exposed to a kaleidoscopic mishmash of theological improvisation. In this theological Wild West, Rushdoony began making guest appearances on Pat Robertson's *The 700 Club* and D. James Kennedy's television broadcasts, while charismatic megaministries across the nation started fusing their traditional prosperity gospels with elements of Reconstructionist-style covenant theology.[84]

Robertson, the media and preaching mogul who hosted the widely viewed *700 Club* and founded the Christian Broadcasting Network and the Family Channel cable network, famously cultivated relationships with Rushdoony and other Reconstructionists. During the 1970s and early 1980s, Rushdoony had been a guest on Robertson's television program, where he discussed subjects ranging from psychology and philosophy to biblical law.[85] Robertson was a Baptist, but he was heavily influenced by charismatic practices such as a faith healing, speaking in tongues, and believing one's earthly prosperity is directly correlated to one's Christian faithfulness. In *The Secret Kingdom* (1982), Robertson and his coauthor, Bob Slosser, appropriated the concept of "The Law of Dominion" to frame a discussion of subduing the earth in terms of a "health and wealth" gospel of material success through Christian service. By the middle of the 1980s, Robertson had adopted language that sounded less charismatic and more Reconstructionist, going so far as to paraphrase Rushdoony's writing on the subject. "God's plan," Robertson told his television audience, "is for his people to take dominion. . . . What is dominion? Dominion is lordship. He wants his people to reign and rule with him."[86] While running for the Republican presidential nomination in 1987, Robertson freely admitted that he respected Reconstructionism when a reporter asked him about the subject. "The Lord intends his people to exercise dominion in his name," Robertson explained. "I admire many of these [Reconstructionist] teachings because they are in line with Scripture."[87] As critics in both the secular and evangelical media repeatedly pushed Robertson to elaborate on his understanding of dominion, he denounced the theocratic elements of Rushdoony's ideas as dangerous and out of step with American traditions—but not before he had already appropriated core elements of Reconstructionism's wider cultural vision into his popular ministry.[88]

If Robertson only unevenly assimilated aspects of the dominion mandate into his popular ministry, other major Protestant clergy offered more full-throated endorsements of Rushdoony's theology. Most notably, D. James Kennedy, Christian television broadcaster, author, and pastor of the mammoth Coral Ridge Presbyterian Church in Fort Lauderdale, Florida, embraced aspects of Rushdoony's ideas.[89] Kennedy used Rushdoony's concepts of dominion and his presuppositional approach to advocate for practical steps to take America back from secular humanists, ideas that are most clearly outlined in his small book *Reconstruction: Biblical Guidelines for a Nation in Peril* (1982).[90] As was the case with Robertson, Kennedy's acceptance of Rushdoony's ideas prompted critical reports and coverage in national news outlets, including the *Wall Street Journal*.[91] Kennedy denounced Rushdoony's concept of theocracy and insisted any attempt to associate him with Reconstructionism amounted to "the McCarthyite technique of guilt by association."[92]

In addition to Robertson's and Kennedy's hesitant appropriation of components of Reconstructionist thought, other popular ministries that used aspects of Rushdoony's ideas began to emerge within Pentecostal and charismatic congregations during the 1980s. The Reconstructionist emphasis on the dominion mandate and keeping the covenant, complete with its promises of wealth, health, and spiritual sanctification via reconstruction, fit neatly within traditional "health-and-wealth" prosperity gospel messages.[93] Further, Reconstructionism—especially in the militant and popular Tyler texts authored by North, Chilton, and others—encouraged wild speculation about dramatic spiritual battles between Christ's church and Satan's very real demonic forces that thrive on planet earth.[94] Reconstructionism's focus on the dominion mandate resonated with the "Latter Rain" tradition in North American Pentecostalism, which, since the middle of the twentieth century, has argued that miraculous manifestations of the Holy Spirit and spiritual warfare against demonic forces would precede the immediate coming of the Kingdom of God.[95] While these resonant themes certainly would not convince most charismatics to take up dominion rhetoric, they did influence a small but influential group of charismatic leaders.

In the 1980s, a number of major charismatic and Pentecostal preachers embraced this or that aspect of Reconstructionist thought and melded it with aspects of the eschatological thinking drawn from the Latter Rain tradition. For example, Bishop Earl Paulk Jr. of the 12,000-member Chapel Hill Harvester Church in suburban Atlanta, Georgia, "received a vision from God" telling him that Christians must use the church to "take rightful dominion" over the earth.[96] God would use the power of the Holy Spirit

to restore Christ's church in the here and now through a "five-fold minis-
try" led by "prophets" and "apostles."[97] Paulk's ministry became known as
"Kingdom Now," a social project that taught Christians to "demonstrate" the
Kingdom in their day-to-day lives.[98] Christ's sacrifice, Paulk argued, defeated
Satan, but Christians must finally finish the war against Satan's remaining
earthly forces.[99] Like Rushdoony, Paulk used Genesis 1:26–28 to argue that
God commands men to dominion.[100] He insisted that Christians must not
abstain from politics and wait for the rapture of the church; instead, they
must "edify all Democrats and Republicans in the gospel of the Kingdom and
point to the authority of Jesus Christ as the solution in all issues."[101] Paulk's
media outreach through books, television, and radio made him famous in
the 1980s, but sexual and fiscal scandal undid his ministry shortly before his
death in 2009.

Likewise, C. Peter Wagner, a leader in the church-growth movement and
cofounder of the New Apostolic Reformation movement of global missionary outreach, appropriated the dominion mandate into an aggressive missionary program aimed at Latin America, Africa, and parts of the developing world. In 1982, after developing "Signs, Wonders and Church Growth," a
course he cotaught at Fuller Seminary with Vineyard Christian Fellowship
founder John Wimber, Wagner developed "power evangelism," which Molly
Worthen has described as winning "coverts not by rational argument, but by
demonstrating God's power through healing, prophecy, or other miraculous
intervention."[102] Wagner's "power evangelism" emphasized asserting Christian principles in seven key areas of cultural production—religion, family,
education, media, government, the arts and entertainment, and business—
which he dubbed the "Seven Mountains Mandate."[103] Wagner's notion of
dominion combined Kuyper's concept of sphere sovereignty, Rushdoony's
idea of a cultural mandate to Christianize all realms of earthly existence,
and a Pentecostal message of spiritual warfare into a dynamic evangelistic
project.[104]

Recognizing the potential associated with the sudden high visibility of
the movement, in October 1987 Reconstructionists organized a conference
with leaders from several prominent charismatic ministries in Dallas, Texas.
Of the 100 participants, only a third were Reconstructionists; the remaining two-thirds included such notable charismatic pastors as Bob Mumford, Dennis Peacocke, Jay Grimstead, and Earl Paulk, among many others.[105] Intellectually, however, Reconstructionists dominated the meeting,
with Gary North and R. J. Rushdoony addressing the various panels.[106] One
Reconstructionist present noted the cooperation and general consensus

among all the participants, concluding: "This is what is making the Christian Reconstruction Movement so influential in the 1980s, although it is still embryonic. God is mixing the *light* of the Reformed Faith with the *heat* of the Charismatic Movement."[107]

By the end of the 1980s, Rushdoony reflected on the state of his movement and estimated that about 20 million Christians ascribed to some aspect of theonomic or Reconstructionist-inspired thinking.[108] More modestly, Gary North considered mailing lists and publication subscriptions to approximate that 25,000 to 40,000 Christians were involved in the movement.[109] Rushdoony's hyperbolically inflated number likely came from his willingness to include in his count the television audiences and parishioners in charismatic megachurches across the country. Although an estimation of the number of Reconstructionists or those influenced by Reconstructionist ideas is impossible to infer from the paucity of solid data, one thing is clear: Rushdoony's interconnected concepts of dominion, biblical law, and postmillennialism were reaching a wide audience and positively shaping popular ministries across the United States. Sometimes—as in the cases of Robertson, Kennedy, Paulk, and Wagner—Reconstructionism had a subtle, if indirect, influence. In other cases, however, Reconstructionism's impact was fundamentally negative. That is, many American evangelicals knew what "true" Christianity was, and Christian Reconstructionism was not it.

Theocracy and Democracy

The popularity of dominion rhetoric in numerous ministries prompted alarm across the evangelical spectrum. Televangelist Jimmy Swaggart, before his defrocking by the Assemblies of God following a prominent sexual scandal, began aggressively condemning "Kingdom Now" and "Dominion teaching" in his popular broadcast ministry.[110] "Whenever you hear Dominion teaching," Swaggart thundered in a 1987 broadcast of *Study in the Word*, "that is a form of modern liberation theology. Those who participate in this spirit are participating in the anti-Christ spirit."[111] Swaggart's condemnation pointed to a wide range of American evangelical and fundamentalist sentiment that was uneasy with this sudden interest in "dominion." This uneasiness developed just as politically and theologically conservative evangelicals began to explore the intellectual and organizational sources driving the synthesis of religion and politics that was at once so alluring and revolting in the 1980s.

It is no accident that in the 1980s, dominion became simultaneously a source of inspiration and controversy. Conservative Christians could point to their direct access to the White House in the Carter and Reagan administrations while basking in the victorious imagery of the Washington for Jesus rallies of 1980 and the symbolic coup of having 1983 declared the Year of the Bible. Yet abortion was legal, while faculty-led school prayer was not. More and more of the organizers of the Religious Right realized that the realities of Washington politics seriously constrained their influence over domestic policy at the federal level. By the middle of the 1980s, evangelicals needed to come to terms with both their victories and failures. As Pat Robertson geared up to challenge George H. W. Bush, the sitting vice president of an extremely popular president, for the presidential nomination of the Republican Party, the televangelist's calls for dominion could not be ignored. Dominion was everywhere: a network of activists, missionaries, and national church leaders were calling for Christians to "take dominion," although exactly what "dominion" meant was inchoate at best. Critics and champions of Rushdoony's dominion mandate began debating the problem of "dominionism" or "dominion theology" in order to understand the limits of evangelical political activism in the age of the Religious Right.

Fittingly, *Christianity Today* became the first national journalistic outlet to assess the growing influence of Christian Reconstructionism and spark an intense internal debate within American evangelicalism over the concept of the dominion mandate. In a 1987 cover story, "Democracy as Heresy," Rodney Clapp, an editor and essayist at *Christianity Today*, developed a narrative that has since become one of the most popular frameworks for assessing Rushdoony and his project of Christian Reconstruction.[112] The article dutifully noted that theonomy and postmillennialism were two of Reconstructionism's most significant departures from traditional evangelicalism, but rather than lingering on these arcane theological matters, the story deftly translated Reconstructionism's theological implications into the idiom of political dystopia:

> In the Reconstructed society, there will be no federal government.
> Nor will there be a democracy, which Reconstructionists regard as
> a "heresy." . . . Government will be republican, with the Bible as the
> charter and constitutional document. Government will occur at the
> state and local level, and society will center on families. The family
> will be ordered in a patriarchal fashion. . . . Parents will be responsible for the education of their children. Public, or "government,"
> education, is thought to rob the family of the right to shape its
> children by Biblical beliefs.[113]

Graphic artist Paul Turnbaugh created these caricatures of R. J. Rushdoony (left), Gary North (middle), and Greg Bahnsen (right) to accompany Rodney Clapp's February 20, 1987, *Christianity Today* exposé of Christian Reconstruction. Turnbaugh's images highlight the aggressive and sinister themes developed in Clapp's essay. Courtesy of Paul Turnbaugh.

Clapp portrayed a dystopian society built on Rushdoony's ideas. By focusing on the crimes and punishments enumerated in Rushdoony's *Institutes of Biblical Law* and the tensions between Rushdoony and North, Clapp's article presented a movement in which violence trumped benevolence, and theology—the exalted Queen of the Sciences—was little more than a generational grudge match. More conveniently, Rushdoony's focus on theonomy over autonomy and God's will over humanity's allowed Clapp to argue that Rushdoony's ideas were inherently antidemocratic. As the editor's note at the beginning of the story asked, "Do Reconstructionists really want to trade the freedoms of American democracy for the strictures of Old Testament theocracy?" Clapp's article answered the question with an emphatic *Yes!*, thus insinuating that at some fundamental level, Rushdoony was not only antidemocratic but also anti-American.[114]

In a single article, Clapp distilled the spirit of a decades-long theological fight into a fundamental accusation: Rushdoony was a heretic. But Clapp sidestepped condemning all Reconstructionists as religious heretics and instead portrayed them as political heretics out of touch with contemporary evangelicalism and, worse still, contemporary American political sensibilities.[115] In effect, Clapp's reporting brought an arcane subject out of the seminaries and the editor's office and into the contemporary debate over religion's place in American democracy in the era of the Religious Right. Secular concepts of force, violence, domination, and political legitimation replaced theological squabbling over pre/postmillennialism and presuppo-sitionalism to become the new metrics for measuring Rushdoony's theology.

Within a year of the publication of Clapp's watershed article, a series of critical assessments of Reconstructionism appeared in the popular evangeli-cal press. Most of this material replicated and amplified the theological argu-ments leveled against theonomy and postmillennialism common in premi-llennial criticism of Reconstruction. But this new material also increasingly focused on the concept of dominion that was so popular in charismatic circles and gaining attention in Protestant media across the country. As a result, evangelical publishers produced a large body of work that introduced a generation of Americans to Christian Reconstructionism while also popu-larizing a multiplicity of concomitant concepts—such as "dominion theol-ogy," "dominionism," and "dominionist"—to categorize this trend emerging in American evangelicalism.

Following immediately on the heels of Clapp's article, three representative books attacking the dominion mandate appeared in the evangelical press during a short one-year burst in 1988–89: Dave Hunt's *Whatever Happened to Heaven?* (1988), H. Wayne House and Thomas D. Ice's *Dominion Theology: Blessing or Curse?* (1988), and Hal Lindsey's *The Road to Holocaust* (1989). Significantly, these books—all by popular evangelical authors—developed the interpretive categories of "dominion theology" and "dominionism" to frame a wide-ranging discussion of evangelical political engagement. Since the publication of these three books, other authors in the evangelical and secular presses have repeatedly cited them, thereby solidifying their central role in forming popular conceptions of Christian Reconstructionism in the evangelical imagination. Each work exemplified three themes common to all subsequent work on Reconstructionism. First, the authors situated their discussion of evangelicals and politics firmly in the post-Reagan moment. Second, Reconstructionism bore the brunt of the authors' wrath, while the various charismatic appropriations of the dominion mandate were impor-tant to each text but not the primary object of attack. Finally, the authors unanimously concluded that "dominion"—however defined—has no place in contemporary evangelicalism.

In each book, concerns over the perceived failure of evangelical political activism weighed heavily on the authors' minds. Hunt, a popular and pro-lific dispensationalist, explicitly set his book within the context of the "Rea-gan years," a time "when evangelicals became more intrigued by periodic marches on Washington and getting their candidates voted into key offices" than by saving souls.[116] Similarly, House and Ice argued that the appeal of dominion grew out of the "political climate of the 1980s," an era of "disillusionment with big government" and "concern over America's moral decay."[117] Finally, Lindsey, who had once hosted Rushdoony at the JC Light and Power House, argued that Christians in the 1980s wrongly desired "a crown before a cross."[118]

Each text blamed the "unbiblical" political atmosphere of the 1980s on Reconstructionism. Hunt explained that Reconstructionists, despite their "many differences" with Pentecostals and mainstream evangelicals, fall under the blanket term "dominion theology" because they represent a new movement that "expect[s] to establish the kingdom prior to Christ's return."[119] Dominion theology, argued Hunt, is dangerous because it rejects the concept of the future rapture of Christ's church to heaven and instead encourages Christians to use the church to build heaven on earth now. Similarly, House and Ice used "dominion theology" to categorize the belief that "the church is to exercise rule over every area of society, people as well as institutions, before Christ returns."[120] They blamed Reconstructionists for popularizing this idea, noting that their ideas are so convincing that "Reconstructionists cannot be dismissed as a passing, and therefore irrelevant, sidecurrent to the course of evangelical thought."[121] Lindsey similarly attacked Reconstructionism, asserting that it confuses human political ambitions with godly sovereignty.[122]

Ultimately, each text warned that dominion theology was incompatible with mainstream evangelicalism. Lindsey told his readers, "No matter how appealing the idea of the Church taking over the world and establishing the Kingdom of God is, it is not what the Bible teaches."[123] Hunt explained that "dominionists" teach the "unbiblical hope that, by exerting godly influence upon government, society could be transformed."[124] Finally, in the most visionary admonition as to why evangelicals must reject dominion theology, House and Ice warned readers that dominion theology's "heavenization of earth" is dangerous to Christians and non-Christians alike. They argued that dominion theology could fuel non-Christians' fears that the "Christian takeover" proposed by Reconstructionists is nigh and resistance and persecution is necessary to avert the creation of a tyrannical theocracy.[125] This, they concluded, "could draw out a more severe reaction to Christianity than would have normally occurred."[126]

Many evangelicals in the 1980s viewed Christian Reconstruction as intriguing but also as a direct threat to their goal of preaching the Gospel. This threat emerged from the Reconstructionist or dominionist desire to Christianize all spheres of human life. Many evangelicals saw such a goal as not only impossible but also a danger to the very secular democratic system that allowed them to freely preach the Gospel. Reconstructionism, many concluded, may actually hurt the chances of non-Christians hearing the Gospel and lead to unneeded conflict between Christians and non-Christians. This latter point, first suggested by House and Ice and then seconded by many other evangelicals, is significant because it underscores that many evangelicals in the 1980s believed that voting their values was important, but this did not necessarily translate into a direct or concerted desire to "Christianize" the United States through political mechanisms. At best, many evangelicals believed that they should vote for people who shared their religious beliefs and against those who did not. Further, it points to the vast diversity of American evangelicalism. While Rushdoonian Christian Reconstruction motivated thousands of Americans, it terrified many, many others. In short, as theologically and socially conservative Protestants came to terms with their collective political power, many feared that their sisters and brothers in Christ were engaging in politics out of a hubristic and failed attempt to Christianize a chronically un-Christianizable world.

Anxieties of Influence

As interest in Christian Reconstruction surged during the late 1980s, Rushdoony studiously ignored most of the media-driven controversy. Instead, he turned his attention toward solidifying the influence of Reconstructionism at the grassroots of America's religious and political revival. As he had done at the Center for American Studies and in his association with J. Howard Pew, rather than ducking organizational controversy, Rushdoony wanted to provoke it. He was furious with other evangelical leaders whom he felt were seeking ecumenical and cooperative strategies at the expense of theological purity. He went so far as to indicate that he felt many in the emerging Christian Right were using his ideas without giving him the proper credit. To James B. Jordan, Rushdoony mused: "I was also told a couple of years ago that one 'scholar' said, 'Rushdoony is damned good to steal from' (re. ideas)."[127] His anxiety about whether scholars and activists on the Right were stealing from him only increased over the course of the 1980s. His concern was not simply a function of some petty desire for recognition; it was rooted in his fear that evangelical leaders might compromise too much on important issues. While it would be impossible to suggest that Rushdoony's ideas and writings alone motivated widespread evangelical reentry into politics and social activism, it is indisputable that he did indeed have a profound impact on a small number of figures who helped prompt this very shift. As Rushdoony's ideas intersected with these broader trends on the right, he was both pleased with and worried about the consequences of political success and the implications of Christians making compromises through a broader conservative social and political agenda. Compromise and failure to strictly hold the ground on biblical authority, he feared, could roll back the most significant gains he had made among evangelicals since founding the Chalcedon Foundation in 1965.

Council for National Policy

Rushdoony had never been popular with the political insiders of the American conservative movement. Regarding Rushdoony's earliest association with the William Volker Fund, Kenneth S. Templeton, one of the recruiters of the fund, recalled that the theologian was well known to fund staff in the early 1950s, but aside from Harold W. Luhnow and Ivan R. Bierly, who were infatuated with his ideas, the rest of the staff "avoided him like the plague" because of his sectarian religious ideas.[128] Similarly, movement organizers believed that Rushdoony's religious ideas had helped poison relationships at the Center for American Studies from the very beginning. When Rushdoony wandered outside the halls of conservative power during the 1970s, many activists knew his reputation and tried to avoid associating with him. Richard Viguerie, the powerful direct-mail pioneer, once condemned Rushdoony as "harsh, judgmental, [and] divisive" before he ever met the preacher.[129] As a result of this suspicion, Rushdoony's influence in direct political organizing at the national level was incredibly limited. Rushdoony resented being shut out of such organizing because he believed, with some merit, that his ideas had influenced political operatives at the local level, even if they preferred to abandon him at national events. Nowhere was this tension more clear than in his love-hate relationship with the secretive Council for National Policy (CNP).[130]

Few organizations on the right are more controversial and shrouded with the secretive vestments of conspiratorial intrigue than the CNP. Founded in 1981 by evangelical author, former JBS member, and then-head of the Moral Majority Tim LaHaye, the CNP reflected the new evangelical consensus that conservative Protestants must engage in direct political action and seek to influence public policy.[131] Gary North was present at the first organizational meeting of the CNP in Dallas. "That first meeting was a mess," North reported on his blog decades later. "Nobody had a clue as to what was going on, who was in charge, what the CNP was supposed to become."[132]

After some wrangling, those present agreed that the organization should serve as a conservative counterweight to the Council on Foreign Relations (CFR) and could maintain a similarly elite roster by charging new members $5,000 to join.[133] Upon realizing that few in the room could put up such a fee, the founding members quickly exempted themselves from the rule.[134] The expense of joining the organization assured that many of the members would come from the business community and from well-funded nonprofits with cash to burn. The CNP would then function as a networking organization that would put businesspeople, religious leaders, and intellectuals into contact with conservative policy makers and politicians.

Rushdoony was not invited to the initial planning sessions of the CNP. The secret meeting came just as the relationship between the Vallecito and Tyler branches of Reconstructionism began to fray. This exacerbated the strain between the two camps and angered Rushdoony because he knew most of the attendees and saw himself as a central actor who had developed part of the infrastructure that LaHaye, North, and the other organizers sought to mobilize. "A 'secret' meeting of top Christian leaders," lamented Rushdoony, "most of whom are to some degree indebted to me, left me out; none present including Gary [North], opened their mouth *at the meeting* to say: Rush should have been invited."[135] Although North did not mention Rushdoony at the initial meeting, he did nominate his father-in-law for future membership. James B. Jordan reported to Rushdoony that the first meeting did not necessarily reflect the best and brightest Christian intellectuals: "Gary said that you must be included. Gary feels that the Christian element in the meeting is small-minded and immature. It was apparently organized by Tim LaHaye. Gary thinks these guys are just playing games, trying to become another 'Christian' CFR."[136] In the early 1980s, the CNP accepted Rushdoony's nomination, and in 1982 he sat on the organization's Board of Governors.[137] After leaving the board, he remained an active member throughout the 1980s, regularly attending its organizational meetings. Eventually, however, he came to agree with North's assessment of the CNP and saw the domination of business interests and Christian leaders in the mold of LaHaye as the group's ultimate failing.

During the CNP's regular meetings, Rushdoony associated closely with Howard Phillips, founder of the Conservative Caucus, a powerful New Right grassroots lobbying group. Rushdoony had "played a critically important role" in Phillips's life when he led the conservative activist away from Judaism to evangelical Christianity and helped shape the beliefs of Phillips's children through his taped sermons.[138] Philips would later insist that Rushdoony would become the "most influential man of the 21st century" for his pioneering activism.[139] In 1991 Phillips founded the ultraconservative U.S. Tax Payers Party (now known as the Constitution Party) and carefully modeled its platform on Rushdoony's ideas.[140] At the CNP, the two served on panels addressing problems related to public education.[141] Through Phillips and the panels, Rushdoony networked with other CNP members, most of whom he ultimately dismissed as "true believers in politics."[142]

In spite of the general political orientation—and, therefore, secular persuasion—of many participating in the CNP meetings, Rushdoony did find them beneficial as he hobnobbed with some of the principal moneymen and religious leaders of the Right. Especially useful were the connections he made with like-minded Protestant ministers who flew just below the horizon of national politics and widespread notoriety but who were fighting battles similar to the ones waged by Chalcedon. After one such meeting, he noted: "Made some excellent contacts, especially with Pastor Hodges of Baton Rouge, La., concerned with Christian Schools for blacks."[143] In numerous other meetings, he encountered churchmen on the front lines of the battle against state education. The meetings were also excellent for fundraising, as Rushdoony discovered during a Dallas meeting during which he obtained $60,000 from supporters of Chalcedon's legal work.[144]

In spite of the CNP's utility, however, Rushdoony generally disliked the meetings and stopped attending them in the late 1980s. Part of his disgust derived from the fact that he believed that the CNP and many of its members were stealing his ideas and using them without proper credit. For instance, during a meeting in Phoenix in 1984, the participants watched a taped speech from televangelist Pat Robertson and heard floor speeches from U.S. representative Newt Gingrich and Herbert Titus, the Harvard-educated law professor turned Reconstructionist who would helm Robertson's CBN (now Regent) University law school. All three men, Rushdoony noted, "called for the reconstruction of America, religious renewal, etc., a program 'close' to Chalcedon's but without regeneration and God's law mentioned, nor Chalcedon. More than a few [of those attending the meeting] saw the parallel to our work."[145] Rushdoony knew Robertson well from his appearances on *The 700 Club*, and Titus had contributed to the appendixes to *The Institutes of Biblical Law*.[146] Further, Titus was associated with many of Chalcedon's legal activities during the 1970s and 1980s and explicitly credited Rushdoony with shaping his view of the law.[147] General awareness of these connections led one participant at the CNP meeting to observe, "Everyone steals from Rushdoony."[148]

Rushdoony, although clearly bitter that two men whom he knew well and counseled on the importance of biblical law did not publicly acknowledge his influence, was angry for deeper reasons than some petty personal slight might imply. He was concerned that men such as Robertson and Titus had downplayed his influence as a symptom of a broader evangelical desire to compromise on matters of doctrine in order to cooperate with secular and non-Christian conservatives. "Month in and month out," Rushdoony insisted in a letter, "I find my materials, illustrations, and footnotes used, sometimes verbatim, with no credit, because I am 'controversial.' So is the Lord."[149] In short, he interpreted a failure to directly cite his influence as a manifestation of Christian cowardice and cultural retreat in order to avoid controversy.

Rushdoony feared that participants in the CNP meetings were politicians and activists first and Christians second. Their concern was moral and ethical in a generic sense, not in an explicitly Christian sense. While Robertson, Titus, and others would have certainly disputed this point, Rushdoony's sectarian definition of orthodox Christianity made it nearly impossible for any evangelical Christians to live up to his standards. Further, Rushdoony's antipluralist and antidemocratic sentiments ensured that he interpreted any language similar to his own as essentially identical to his own. From Rushdoony's perspective, CNP participants simultaneously stole his ideas and denied their fundamental truth.

Cobelligerents

In the end, it is impossible to assess whether or not this or that political operative at CNP meetings stole Rushdoony's ideas or simply couched their political projects in a generalized Christian rhetoric that simultaneously echoed Reconstructionist concepts while still adhering to a pluralistic, majoritarian view of social organization. Most evidence would suggest the latter. Nonetheless, when Rushdoony detected strands of his theology in others' ideas, he was often correct.

Nowhere was Rushdoony's profound, if indirect, effect on well-known ministries of the 1980s more apparent than on the highly influential writings of the popular evangelical theologian Francis A. Schaeffer IV. Rushdoony and Schaeffer had been reading one another's work for years and shared many basic theological ideas. Schaeffer had studied under Van Til at Westminster Theological Seminary.[150] Both Schaeffer and Rushdoony shared a profound fondness for the Reformed theologies of Dutchmen Abraham Kuyper and Herman Dooyeweerd.[151] Rushdoony even briefly worked with

Schaeffer's son Franky on legal issues related to John W. Whitehead's Rutherford Institute.

Rushdoony had a distant, complex influence on the genesis of Schaeffer's *A Christian Manifesto* (1981), one of the minister's most important texts. The *Manifesto* has long been considered a touchstone in the history of contemporary Protestantism in the United States for its impassioned insistence that evangelicals and fundamentalists must understand that their faith in Christ "not only has personal results, but also governmental and legal results."[152] In his history of the rise of the Religious Right, William Martin pointed out that the *Manifesto* influenced a generation of evangelicals to engage in civil disobedience campaigns to protest U.S. abortion laws.[153] Similarly, one Schaeffer biographer argued that the book "substantially helped create a new Evangelical Right in America" by fusing Schaeffer's pro-life activism with political conservatives to create a coalition "which was able to exercise considerable political clout during the Reagan era."[154] The book shaped Christian activist Randall Terry's highly controversial anti-abortion ministry, Operation Rescue, which used elaborately staged acts of civil disobedience to protest outside of abortion clinics.[155] The *Manifesto* sold nearly 300,000 copies in its first year, remains in print, and continues to influence evangelical activists into the twenty-first century.[156]

Schaeffer's fusion of activism, theology, and politics owed a certain debt to the ideas and actions of Rushdoony and the grassroots infrastructure of the Chalcedon Foundation. After reading the *Manifesto*, Rushdoony angrily confided in his journal: "Read Francis Schaeffer: *A Christian Manifesto*, another book using some of my material, with phone calls for citations, with no mention of me: for most writers, I am useful but unmentionable! Not faith but timidity is the mark of too many Christians today, including able men like Francis."[157] Unlike his unverifiable concern that CNP members were stealing from him, Rushdoony's influence on the *Manifesto* went far beyond a few unacknowledged sources. Rushdoony directly contributed to the very origin of the book: the inspiration for the *Manifesto* emerged from a meeting of the Christian Legal Society, which Schaeffer attended in April 1981.[158] Rushdoony's legal activism helped pave the way for the formation of the society during the 1970s, and many organizing the event were Reconstructionist-connected lawyers and activists. Most notably, John W. Whitehead and Herbert Titus, longtime associates of Chalcedon who could trace their understanding of the law directly to Rushdoony's *Institutes*, attended the conference. Schaeffer warmly cited them in the text as the two most critical legal influences on his reasoning.

After the Christian Legal Society meeting, Schaeffer hired Whitehead as his legal research assistant and asked him to shape the legal substance of the text. By this point in his career as a legal activist, Whitehead had begun to abandon Rushdoony's more hardline theocratic stance, a fact that likely contributed to the Schaeffers' willingness to work with him.[159] Whitehead researched and wrote the entire first draft of the manuscript that Schaeffer and his son Franky later reworked.[160] According to Whitehead, about 40 percent of the final text is directly from his original draft.[161]

In spite of the organizational and personal connections, at its heart, the *Manifesto* is not a Reconstructionist text. Instead, it is a complex work that, like all cultural objects, is polyvocal—a malleable alloy of Kuyperian sphere sovereignty, Van Tillian presuppositionalism, and Rushdoonian antistatism, all forged in the mold of the unique form of Christian activism that Whitehead and the Schaeffers developed in the 1980s. Although a concise synthesis of nearly 400 years of a specific Anglo-American strain of Reformed social thinking, the text ultimately focuses on twentieth-century concerns grounded in the political implications of the "antithesis" between Christian and secular worldviews. At the outset of the *Manifesto*, Schaeffer made it clear that American culture has shifted "*away from* a world view that was at least vaguely Christian . . . toward something completely different—*toward* a world view based upon the idea that the final reality is impersonal matter or energy shaped into its present form by impersonal chance" in which man—and not God—becomes the measure of all things.[162] These two perspectives "stand as totals in complete antithesis to each other."[163] Consequently, anyone who embraces the humanistic view that impersonal chance dominates the universe cannot ultimately cooperate with Christians to create a better world.[164]

Non-Christians, however, are not totally useless within the absolutist binary structure of Schaeffer's antithesis. As sales of the *Manifesto* soared and many of Schaeffer's other books topped best-seller lists, he used his status as an evangelical *agent provocateur* to push Jerry Falwell and other Christian Right leaders to "use pagans to do your work."[165] His reasoning in the *Manifesto* and public lectures from this time helped prompt the formation of the Moral Majority, a panreligious and pandenominational organization, and other similar groups. Schaeffer proposed that socially and theologically conservative Christians had ceded too much to the humanists because of a misguided and naïve commitment to purity. Instead of this suicidal pursuit of purity, he suggested that an evangelical might work with a "cobelligerent," "a person who may not have any sufficient basis for taking the right position but takes the right position on a single issue." The cobelligerent then becomes a person "I can join with . . . without any danger as long as I realize that he is not an ally and all we're talking about is a single issue."[166]

In the end, Schaeffer and Rushdoony might also rightly be understood as cobelligerents. As any number of historians and theologians have pointed out, it is impossible to conflate the systems of Rushdoony and Schaeffer.[167] The two men did share similar ideas that they developed through mutual and often oppositional engagement with one another's work. Schaeffer, it seems, was more deeply influenced by Rushdoony than vice versa.[168] During the 1960s, Schaeffer and many at his L'Abri fellowship read Rushdoony carefully, especially his historical work on the Christian origins of the United States.[169] After close study of Rushdoony's eschatology, Schaeffer rejected most aspects of Rushdoony's system but retained components of the latter's critique of history and culture.[170] Notably, Schaeffer neither appealed to Genesis's "dominion mandate" to authorize his political agenda nor believed in theocratic rule in any context.[171] He found any talk of alliances between church and state distressing, refusing to speak in churches that displayed the Christian or U.S. flags.[172] Francis Schaeffer helped persuade John Whitehead to abandon Rushdoony's theocratic project and warned many others against Reconstructionism's postmillennial utopianism.[173] Franky Schaeffer later went so far as to claim that his father thought that Rushdoony was "clinically insane."[174] Rushdoony, however, remained publicly loyal to the Schaeffers despite his anger over Francis's failure to publicly acknowledge his influence. Late in life, when reflecting on their relationship, Rushdoony concluded of Schaeffer: "We were friends, we differed at points but never argued about them."[175]

Conclusion: The Ayatollah of the Religious Right

In a 1987 television documentary, journalist and former Democratic political operative Bill Moyers posed a stark question to R. J. Rushdoony: would he willingly execute homosexuals, witches, incorrigible children, unchaste women, and other sinners? Unfazed, Rushdoony responded: "I wouldn't. . . . I'm saying this is what God requires. I'm not saying that everything in the Bible I like. Some of it rubs me the wrong way. But I'm simply saying this is what God requires."[176] Moyers's documentary, the final installment of a three-part series titled *God and Politics*, aired on PBS and exposed many Americans to Reconstructionism. Moyers opened the program with a monologue explaining that even though "the press says the political influence of the religious right is fading," the growth of Reconstructionism and Kingdom Now suggested otherwise.[177] To understand the Christian Right, Moyers explained, Americans must also understand these controversial theologies.

Clapp's *Christianity Today* profile of Reconstructionism, Moyers's *God and Politics*, and the wave of "dominionism"-themed evangelical books in 1988 and 1989 brought Christian Reconstructionism to the attention of many Americans and prompted widespread interest in the movement in nonevangelical sources. A number of liberal groups—especially Americans United for the Separation of Church and State, People for the American Way, and Public Research Associates—spent a considerable amount of their resources documenting the influence of conservative evangelicals on American politics, and they began paying close attention to Christian Reconstruction by monitoring the activities of the Chalcedon Foundation and the Institute for Christian Economics.[178] Investigative reporters pored over documents searching for any and every connection between local, state, and national political figures and Reconstructionist thinkers. They were easy to find. Rushdoony's relationships with organizations ranging from tiny Christian colleges to the nationally prominent Council for National Policy assured that at one time or another, he or one of his acolytes had come into contact with this or that public figure.

Terms such as "dominionism" and "dominion theology" crept into popular press accounts discussing the Religious Right. These terms developed in evangelical and fundamentalist circles as second-order classificatory categories to index a host of interrelated theologies that appealed to Genesis to legitimate social reform—ranging from Reconstructionism to Kingdom Now and beyond. But by the late 1980s, journalists and researchers began adopting such terms from the evangelical literature to point to a network of religiously motivated political activity. As one journalist observed, "Dominion theology has become the *central unifying ideology for the Christian Right.*"[179] In the mid-1990s, the categories became more precise, as some coverage distinguished between a "hard" dominionism that calls for the "literal reimposition of Biblical law" and a "soft" dominionism that advocates "more limited systems of Christian control."[180]

If, in the 1980s, the challenge of Christian Reconstructionism prompted evangelicals to reflect on who was actualizing a proper evangelical political theology, by the late 1990s and early 2000s, "dominionism" not only had similarly challenged nonreligious audiences to reflect on the limits of religious participation in U.S. democracy but also had prompted some to question the political limits of Christianity itself. The 1990s saw spasmodic outbreaks of tit-for-tat conflicts between government forces and advocates of religiously motivated violence—Christian Identity race warriors in the Pacific Northwest and Branch Davidian apocalypticists in Waco, Texas; the Oklahoma City bombing; grisly public assassinations of clinicians who performed abortions. Against this tumultuous backdrop, understanding "dominionism" gained a certain existential urgency for some observers. But while evangelicals used "dominion" labels to facilitate the critique and expulsion of what they perceived as theological and eschatological aberrations, many secular pundits and journalists abandoned nuance and instead identified "dominionism" as the unifying ideology behind all politically engaged conservative Protestants.

Many critics of "dominion theology" turned to a readymade set of tropes that exhibit a latent tendency to orientalize and exoticize conservative religious adherents. Rushdoony, with his foreign name and patriarchal demeanor, bore the brunt of this discursive wrath. Most prominently, critics honed in on Rushdoony's focus on religious law to liken him unfavorably to Islamic extremists. This trend began in the wake of al Qaeda's first attempt to bomb the World Trade Center in 1993 and then intensified after the attacks on New York, Washington, D.C., and Pennsylvania in September 2001. For example, one pre-9/11 interviewer, in an in-depth profile of the Reconstructionist patriarch, characterized Rushdoony as "the Ayatollah of holy rollers."[181] After the September 11, 2001, al Qaeda attacks, reporting on Rushdoony became more vicious. One profile labeled him a "Christian Jihadi."[182] Even Francis Schaeffer's son Franky entered the mix, declaring Rushdoony and his ilk equivalent to the Taliban.[183]

Along with Islamicizing Reconstructionism, critics also classified the movement as fascist. Much of this work relied on the popular appropriation of the Frankfurt School's analysis of right-wing psychology typified by German critical theorist Theodor Adorno's concept of the "authoritarian personality."[184] One of the most popular works in this mold was journalist Chris Hedges's *American Fascists* (2008). Hedges's best seller warned readers: "Christian reconstructionism . . . has, like all fascist movements, a belief in magic along with leadership adoration and a strident call for moral and physical supremacy of a master race, in this case American Christians. It also has, like fascist movements, an ill-defined and shifting set of beliefs, some of which contradict one another."[185] Journalist Max Blumenthal relied on German psychoanalyst Eric Fromm's theory of why humans seek to escape the obligations of freedom for the security of authoritarianism to single out Rushdoony and dominionism as the wellspring of the Republican Party's most religiously authoritarian aspects.[186] In a similar vein, another popular account by New York University media professor Mark Crispin Miller asserted links between George W. Bush's White House and Rushdoony. Miller claimed that Reconstructionism was not "genuinely Christian," arguing that it should instead be labeled "Christo-fascism."[187]

At the end of the twentieth century, a consensus had emerged between a vast swath of American evangelicalism and among some secularists angry with the mingling of religion and politics: Rushdoony and his Christian Reconstructionists were not "real" American Christians because such Christians would accept democratic pluralism and abjure any hint of theocracy. After 2001, as paranoia over the fusion of religion and politics peaked, it became possible to suggest—via the discursive tropes of Islamicization and fascification—that anyone sympathetic to Rushdoony's ideas might not even be a real American.

To a Thousand Generations
Governance and Reconstruction

Man is a sinner.
—R. J. RUSHDOONY in John W. Whitehead,
Slaying Dragons, 146

I the Lord thy God am a jealous God, visiting the iniquity of
the fathers upon the children unto the third and fourth generation of
them that hate me, and shewing mercy unto thousands of them that
love me and keep my commandments.
—Deuteronomy 5:9–10 (King James Version)

During the 1990s, R. J. Rushdoony's health rapidly deteriorated. His hearing and eyesight began to fail. In a visit to his doctor in 1986, he learned that an ear infection would likely leave him mostly deaf.[1] Further treatment revealed that his lifelong habit of sleeping "2½–4 hours only" a night was related to chronic infections and other ear disorders he had experienced since he was three years old.[2] Tests run in 1990 indicated that Rushdoony was suffering from high cholesterol and had developed type-2 diabetes.[3] He continued to testify in court cases after the diagnosis, but his appearances became rarer until they ceased in the late 1990s.[4]

Aside from Rushdoony's failing health, a series of other setbacks related to the Chalcedon/Tyler split weakened the overall progress of Christian Reconstruction during the 1990s. Two of the movement's most promising younger theologians, Greg Bahnsen and David Chilton, died suddenly in 1995 and 1997, respectively. They had published, lectured, and preached with a vengeance during the 1980s, but both men had extensive health issues that caught up with them as they drove themselves to follow the productive models set by Rushdoony and Gary North.

Furthermore, North did little to try to reconcile the Vallecito/Tyler split and instead spent much of the 1990s authoring direct attacks on his father-in-law's legacy. He accused Rushdoony of supporting Unitarianism, aired dirty laundry about Rushdoony's first marriage and the subsequent divorce, highlighted his associations with Holocaust denier and neo-Nazi David L. Hoggan, and charged that Rushdoony "was not really in charge" of the *Chalcedon Report*.[5] "In recent years," North informed ICE donors, "as [Rushdoony] has grown older . . . and increasingly deaf, he has tended to hand over much of Chalcedon's operations to inexperienced people without any theological training."[6]

As North mocked Chalcedon and attempted to undermine its donor support, his own work with ICE declined. In the late 1990s, he published a series of newsletters and position papers popularizing his concerns over the Y2K computer glitch.[7] The programming error, some warned, might lead to major problems on January 1, 2000, when many computer systems would incorrectly roll over to January 1, 1900. North warned ICE supporters that the glitch could crash banking systems and destroy government computer databases. He advised his readers that if they prepared, global collapse would provide the right moment for Christian men to step forward and impose dominion through their local churches.[8] In other words, the Kingdom was at hand.

With the millennium winding down, North took his message to a whole new audience with multiple appearances on Art Bell's late-night, conspiracy-themed radio show, *Art Bell Coast to Coast AM*.[9] He told Bell's infinitely credulous audience that the calendar-related programming error built into many computer operating systems would lead to possibly catastrophic worldwide problems, affecting everything from the global financial system to electrical grids and air traffic control. Bell's prudent audience, North advised, should take the necessary steps to prepare for the disaster. Not surprisingly, he soft-pedaled his ideas regarding the post-disaster rule of a theocratic elite, but he did manage to plug his books and newsletters.

North's predictions, of course, were wrong, but perhaps more damaging than his prophetic failure were entries on numerous Internet sites and message boards reposting alleged e-mail exchanges between North and some of his critics.[10] These posts suggested that North was motivated by rank opportunism, not real conviction. One claimed that North was sending out nearly 250,000 pieces of mail a month documenting his scenario.[11] If any portion of this massive output included subscribers to North's *Remnant Review*—which cost $129 for an annual subscription—he was likely making hundreds of thousands of dollars (or more) from the imagined crisis. After his hopes for the emergent Kingdom failed to materialize, North shuttered ICE in 2001

R. J. Rushdoony and his second wife, Dorothy, in 1991. During the
1990s, Rushdoony's health failed, and his intense schedule of writing,
lecturing, and testifying in court cases slowed. R. J. Rushdoony died on
February 8, 2001. Following Rushdoony's death, Dorothy confided to a
family friend: "My husband was my life. What shall I do without him?"
Dorothy Barbara Ross Rushdoony died of heart failure on October 30,
2003. Courtesy of the Chalcedon Foundation.

and turned most of his attention to financial advice work, opening the website *Specific Answers* and continuing to publish the *Remnant Review*.

Even as Gary North slid into self-parody with his hyperbolic warnings
of societal collapse and his repeated attacks on a man too old, tired, and
uninterested to defend himself, the larger idea of Christian Reconstruction,
especially the wider concept of "dominion theology," was more popular and
reaching a wider audience than ever before. Parents were taking Rushdoony's
writings on education seriously. The emergence of the Christian Right saw
many evangelicals and fundamentalists adopting variations on Reconstructionist theologies. With Christ's second millennium giving way to a third,
the disintegration of the organizational structures of Christian Reconstructionism seemed to have little impact on its influence on an assemblage of
interlocking religious and political issues.

In spite of his illnesses and the institutional Sturm und Drang of the 1990s,
Rushdoony's mind remained sharp and he focused on solidifying his larger

theological legacy. He continued to write and deliver an occasional lecture or sermon into his eighties. His last years were incredibly prolific, even for a man with failing eyesight who stubbornly coaxed every word from an inkwell and dip pen. Once crisp, precise cursive now staggered and looped across the page. But he wrote on everything from *magick*—in the Aleister Crowley sense—to Christ's Sermon on the Mount, producing manuscripts that his publishing house, Ross House Books, will be editing and printing throughout the first few decades of the twenty-first century.

Eventually, as it must to all sinners, death came to R. J. Rushdoony. Doctors diagnosed Rushdoony with prostate cancer. His intense daily regimen of reading and writing flagged. By 1998, Rushdoony, now eighty-two, regularly found himself too ill to read or write. He needed surgery for cataracts and regular therapy for his cancer. On February 6, 1998, he confided in his journals: "Did nothing, which is difficult for me."[12] Shortly thereafter, his journal entries became sporadic. In the spring of 2000, he reported three heart attacks in a single week.[13] His entries abruptly ended in the fall of 2000. His final journal entry noted that he "wrote on 'The Necessary Future.'"[14] With his family huddled around his deathbed, he preached his last sermon: "The victory is ours and so we must fight. May He give you all strength to fight the battle. We have a battle to fight and an obligation to win. We have a certain victory. We are ordained to victory. I can't talk much more."[15] He died on February 8, 2001.

Following Rushdoony's death, financial support for the Chalcedon Foundation plateaued. Public records for the Chalcedon Foundation indicate that gifts to the organization peaked just before Rushdoony's death and have not increased substantially since. Before 2001, the foundation's assets never totaled much more than $1 million, and they remained largely stagnant during the 1990s. The departure of Howard Ahmanson Jr., the Home Savings bank heir, from Chalcedon's board of directors in the mid-1990s precipitated the fiscal stagnation. Although Ahmanson was a close friend of the Rushdoony family, his political and philanthropic aspirations ultimately made an intimate relationship with Rushdoony and the Chalcedon Foundation a major public-relations liability. Politicians began returning his contributions; art museums and other beneficiaries questioned his motivations for funding their projects.[16]

Ahmanson's departure illustrates how Reconstructionism became a victim of its own success. While Rushdoony openly courted controversy, many of his followers realized they could not maintain their places in polite society by openly adhering to the project of Reconstruction.[17] As a result of Rushdoony's ill health, financial setbacks, and the premature deaths of theologians such as Bahnsen and Chilton, the 1990s and early 2000s marked an era of change for Rushdoony's Chalcedon Foundation and North's ICE. Even as public awareness of Reconstructionism grew during this period, declining public support and the factional disputes among various Reconstructionist camps seriously weakened Christian Reconstructionism as a coherent movement.

The Legacy of Reconstruction

Rushdoony's precarious position within the wider American conservative movement and within American evangelicalism became obvious as assessments of his life rolled in during the days and years following his death. Gary North set aside his vicious criticism of Rushdoony to highlight his father-in-law's influence on twentieth-century intellectual and political history. "The death of Rousas John Rushdoony on February 8 at the age of 84," wrote North, "will not be perceived as newsworthy by the American media." But, North continued, "being a newsworthy event is rarely the same as being a significant event."[18] For North, Rushdoony's significance lay in his "fringe ideas," which "[flew] in the face of politically correct reality."[19] Ultimately, North concluded that his father-in-law spent his life "marshaling logic and footnotes on the sidelines of respectable culture" but may be "seen in retrospect as [a] pioneer."[20]

Within the broader evangelical movement, *Christianity Today* briefly acknowledged Rushdoony as the "founder of the Christian homeschooling movement and an intellectual catalyst of the Christian Right."[21] Similarly, *Christian Century* noted that he was "preeminent in the Christian Reconstructionist movement that challenged the Religious Right, often calling on them to consider such extreme stances as advocating the execution of homosexuals."[22] Aside from these passing references to his legacy, few national periodicals noted his death.

In the conservative press, reassessments of Rushdoony's legacy began appearing during the mid-2000s. Many of these judgments were ambivalent if cautiously positive. Writing in the pages of the theologically and socially conservative Catholic journal *First Things*, William Edgar honored Rushdoony's "extraordinary brilliance" and "encyclopedic knowledge of human affairs" but wondered if "Rushdoony's particular brand of reconstruction might not outlast his death."[23] Several years later, another writer in *First Things* answered Edgar by arguing that Rushdoony ranked "somewhere between the Free Mumia movement and the Spartacist Youth League on the totem pole of political influence in America."[24] More generously, a writer in the *American Conservative*, a magazine founded by former Nixon aide Patrick J. Buchanan, labeled Rushdoony "an eccentric outsider" in the conservative movement who "left behind a commanding legacy."[25]

For all of the ambivalence among conservatives about Rushdoony's legacy, it is telling that the Intercollegiate Studies Institutes—a venerable organization of midcentury fusionist conservatism—chose to enshrine Rushdoony and Christian Reconstructionism in its *American Conservatism: An Encyclopedia* (2006). In it, Rushdoony is honored as the father of a movement that "has united Christians of different backgrounds, offering them an objective standard of ethics, an optimistic vision of national renewal, and a radically theistic interpretation of all disciplines."[26] In short, the encyclopedia suggested that Rushdoony's project—for all of its rough edges, "politically incorrect" mandates, and theological harshness—was part of the larger conservative movement, but it was never limited to it.

By and large, these retroactive and mostly self-serving assessments of Rushdoony and Reconstructionism are beside the point. Rushdoonian Christian Reconstruction was never a centralized movement. Thus its legacy cannot be assessed based on head counts or exposés of this politician or that businessperson who once read one of Rushdoony's books. Rushdoony's vision of Reconstruction emerged at the confluence of American evangelicalism and a conservative milieu in which pastors, intellectuals, activists, and rank-and-file adherents sought to come to terms with the problems of an active, powerful, and centralized federal bureaucracy. Christian Reconstructionism informed and was informed by a wider cultural concern for withholding, withdrawing, and contesting the power of an intrusive state. In this sense, Reconstruction will have a durable, if discrete, legacy in American culture in three interconnected areas. First, through its educational philosophy, Christian Reconstruction has already contributed an aggressive, patriarchal antistatism to conservative evangelical understandings of education. Next, the movement has developed a specific strain of Christian libertarianism rooted in Reconstructionist economic ideas that has interacted constructively with more-mainstream movements, such as the Tea Party. Finally, and most significantly, Reconstructionism has played a major but underappreciated role in forming popular ideas of what makes religion *good* and *bad* in the United States.

The modern state was Rushdoony's white whale. It haunted his ministry and prodded him toward activism. His antistatist theology will remain his major contribution to American culture, especially in the form of his assault on state-funded education. His work as an expert witness and key organizer of the legal infrastructure behind the conservative evangelical wing of the homeschooling movement will linger for decades. While it is certainly true that most conservative Christian homeschoolers are not Reconstructionists, it is also true that many of the key intellectual and legal leaders in the movement have some connection to Rushdoony's movement. Many of these leaders took up Rushdoony's concept of antistatist dominion families and developed them into a set of ideas and practices that have grown to dominate some corners of the homeschooling movement.

Nowhere is the persistent effect of Reconstructionist antistatism more evident than in the various popular patriarchal ministries that grew up with the homeschooling movement. Rushdoony's concept of an imperial Christianity spread through dominion families shaped the thinking of a large number of activists in the Christian patriarchy, or "Quiverfull" movement.[27] Quiverfull is a decentralized Protestant movement that emphasizes raising large families led by a male father and his female helpmeet. Proponents of Quiverfull also regulate male/female sexuality by carefully cultivating specific understandings of normative gender roles and using "courtship" or "purity" culture to structure premarital social contact between girls and boys.[28] Although there are many streams of thought contributing to Quiverfull that cannot accurately be described as Reconstructionist—such as the writings of antifeminist and anti–birth control Christian author Mary Pride—as journalist Kathryn Joyce has documented, Rushdoony's theology had a direct influence on the movement.[29]

These associations were most clearly evidenced in Doug Phillips's now-defunct Vision Forum ministry.[30] Phillips—husband of Beall Phillips, father of eight children, and son of Rushdoony's close friend and political confidante, Howard Phillips—ran the popular patriarchal ministry until the fall of 2013, when he publicly acknowledged an inappropriate relationship with a woman other than his wife.[31] The for-profit wing of the ministry sold a number of products, including homeschooling material and books on Christian courtship and Quiverfull family management. Vision Forum stressed "the necessity of building large family dynasties, generations of families with six, eight, ten or more children" that will "raise a godly seed for Christ and the salvation of America."[32] While Phillips spoke of "dominion vision" in an explicitly Rushdoonian sense, he downplayed Reconstructionist language in the ministry.[33] Parents looking for quality homeschooling products and gender-specific toys for their children—guns and swords for boys, tea sets, dolls, and aprons for girls—encountered a generically "Christian" catalog that subtly cultivated a form of "Christian self-government" through male headship and female submission. Vision Forum maintained close ties with a number of homeschooling advocates. Most prominently, the Phillips family was friendly with Michelle and Jim Bob Duggar, matriarch and patriarch of a nineteen-child family whose Quiverfull lifestyle is featured prominently in a popular cable television series on The Learning Channel.[34]

Along with Doug Phillips's Vision Forum, high-profile homeschooling reform organizations such as Rev. E. Ray Moore's Exodus Mandate have played a central role in bringing Reconstructionist themes to America's homeschooling culture. Founded in 1997, Exodus Mandate has worked to "encourage and assist Christian families to leave government schools for the Promised Land of Christian schools or homeschooling."[35] Moore, a former army chaplain and pastor active in the Southern Baptist Convention (SBC), has explicitly acknowledged his debt to Reconstructionism.[36] Dr. Bruce N. Shortt, one of Moore's allies in his fight against public education, has been promoted by the Chalcedon Foundation, and his book, *The Harsh Truth about Public Schools* (2004), was published by Rushdoony's Ross House Books. Since 2004, Moore and Shortt have teamed up with others in the SBC to promote an "exit strategy" from the public schools. The resolution they proposed for the SBC's 2007 annual meeting called for the formation of an alternative K-12 school system to be administered by Christian churches. Echoing Rushdoony's writings from nearly half a century earlier, the resolution stated: "[E]ducation is not theologically neutral, and for generations . . . [children] have been discipled primarily by an anti-Christian government school system."[37] Although the 2007 resolution was not adopted, Moore and his supporters have pushed for similar resolutions in subsequent annual meetings of the SBC.[38]

Outside of the United States, Reconstructionist antistatist ideas related to education have also found small audiences. Although no systemic international studies of Christian Reconstructionism exist, journalists and some scholars have recorded anecdotal evidence of homeschooling advocates around the world using Rushdoony's writings.[39] Rushdoony likely laid the foundation for some of these connections when he lectured in the British Isles and Australia on a few occasions in the 1980s and early 90s and found some limited support for his ideas.

More prominently, Reformed theologians in South Africa took a keen interest in Rushdoony's development of Reformed thought.[40] After the fall of apartheid, educational reform in South Africa's school became a contentious national issue, as various Christian, Muslim, and secular factions argued over proposed changes. In the late 1990s and early 2000s, South Africa's Department of Education developed a new policy of "religion education" designed to recognize diversity, discourage discrimination, and emphasize learning about multiple religious traditions.[41] "In response to the new curriculum," religious studies scholar David Chidester noted, "some Christians in South Africa, especially those with ideological, organizational, and financial links with conservative Christian groups in the United States, vigorously objected to the policy of religion education."[42] Not surprisingly, Chidester highlighted how homeschooling organizations in the country resisted the state intervention in family-based education by directly appealing to Rushdoony's framework of discrimination mediated through biblical law.[43]

Beyond homeschooling and educational reform, Reconstructionism's unapologetically dehumanizing theology of homosexuality has found a tiny but troubling international audience.[44] Most notably, Scott Lively, an American minister, has lobbied hard to pass draconian legislation in Uganda to outlaw homosexuality. Lively coauthored *Pink Swastika* (1995), an antigay screed that argued Nazism and the Holocaust were the products of a homosexual conspiracy in Germany. Lively adopted elements of Rushdoony's legal reasoning in his "pro-family" ministry that seeks to criminalize homosexuality in Uganda and other parts of Africa.[45] Lively has also influenced antihomosexual ministries in Russia and other parts of the former Soviet Union, which have, in turn, taken an interest in Rushdoony's writings on the matter.[46] As American attitudes toward homosexuality and patriarchal relationships change—especially as younger generations of evangelicals abandon their open hostility to homosexuality—it is quite likely that Rushdoony will become more popular abroad as "pro-family" activists seek more welcoming audiences outside of the United States.[47] Similarly, Rushdoony is likely to become something of politically incorrect folk hero in the more marginal areas of the American right wing that will likely hang on to his ideas out of aesthetic temperament and sheer malice for years to come.[48]

Gary North, R. J. Rushdoony's estranged son-in-law, speaking in June 2013 at
Ron Paul's annual barbecue in Lake Jackson, Texas. Courtesy of
Gage Skidmore, https://flic.kr/p/eZfFFs.

Libertarianism and Economics

Although the connections between antistatism, education, and patriarchy
are complex, Reconstructionist emphasis on biblical law in opposition to
state government will likely have staying power in the United States—and
even garner limited international appeal—well into the twenty-first century.
This is, in part, guaranteed by the recent resurgence in libertarianism that
coincided with the economic downturn of 2008 and the subsequent growth
in popularity of the Tea Party and a host of national figures such as former
Texas representative and former Gary North employer Ron Paul. While it
would be inaccurate to characterize Paul or the Tea Party as influenced by
Reconstructionism, it would be accurate to note that they are resonant and
mutually reinforcing antistatist phenomena.

Rushdoony and Gary North both anticipated the fusion of conservative
politics, laissez-faire economics, and conservative Protestant religiosity as
early as the late 1960s. Rushdoony articulated hardline libertarian principles
—such as maintaining the gold standard, the limitation of the state to police
and military functions, and an end to publicly funded services—for the
remainder of his life. In the summer of 1980, Rushdoony clearly articulated
his libertarian impulse in a Chalcedon Position Paper titled "The Meaning

of Theocracy." "Few things," he wrote, "are more commonly misunderstood than the nature and meaning of theocracy. It is commonly assumed to be a dictatorial rule by self-appointed men who claim to rule for God. In reality, theocracy in Biblical law is the closest thing to a radical libertarianism that can be had."[49] To his mind, a reconstructed theocracy built on the foundation of theonomy and dominion would lead to the development of truly free dominion men beholden to no authority but God. Likewise, North, through his various economic commentaries on the Bible, developed into something of an economic guru for libertarian-minded conservative Christians. His *Remnant Review* newsletter and *Specific Answers* website brought his synthesis of Christianity and Austrian economics to the masses.

As economist Timothy D. Terrell and political scientist Glenn Moots have noted, "Christian Reconstruction is in no small sense the gateway for libertarianism and Austrian economics to make its way into the thinking of the religious right. While there are clearly points of disagreement, libertarianism's link to Christian Reconstruction is much stronger than its link to other groups within the religious right."[50] Similarly, political scientist Michael Lienesch and economist Laurence R. Iannaccone have both documented how Reconstructionist sources came to dominate popular evangelical economic writing in the 1980s.[51] The resulting literature has given Reconstruction an outsized influence on the economic arguments of conservative Protestants and prepared the way for subtle incursions of Reconstructionist ideas into wider economic debates on the American right.

Ever the entrepreneurial innovator, North in 2013 set out to capitalize on this confluence of libertarianism and conservative Christianity by launching the Ron Paul Curriculum, an online homeschooling portal created by North and libertarian historian Thomas E. Woods.[52] In a promotional video for the curriculum, North told parents:

> At the end of this program your child should be able to do the following: speak in public and speak confidently, write effectively, run a website, operate a YouTube channel, understand mathematics, understand basic science, start a home business, defend the free-market system intellectually, understand the history of Western civilization, understand American history, understand the U.S. Constitution and how it has been hijacked, understand the interaction between literature and historical development, understand Christianity's influence in the West, [and] understand Austrian-school economics.[53]

Most books in the curriculum are free in the public domain; only providentially significant works, such as Austrian economist Friedrich von Hayek's *Road to Serfdom*, will require purchase. Lectures are recorded and streamed online. Message boards for parents to discuss pedagogy and lessons are accessible through a paywall.

While the effectiveness and solvency of North's venture remain to be seen, the Ron Paul Curriculum stands as one of Reconstructionism's more perplexing monuments—antistatism, Christian education, and libertarianism all wrapped up in a tidy bow of base opportunism and ugly HTML coding. A movement that began as an open rebellion against midcentury liberalism and the homogenization of public education has grown into its own commercial maturity. The Internet has streamlined the basic principles of Reconstructionism into a sleek, bulleted list that is largely indistinguishable from any other nominally "conservative" social project. Rushdoony's dream of Christian education is now a product to be marketed by exploiting the popularity of perennial presidential candidate Ron Paul. The homeschool curriculum, once the idealized dominion of mothers and fathers in a domestic setting, can now be outsourced to cyberspace, complete with talking heads droning on about Christian liberty in streaming YouTube videos. It is *Reconstruction 2.0*.

Good Religion, Bad Religion

The previous chapters have documented the ways in which Reconstructionism informed critical debates in the rise of the American conservative and libertarian movements while also functioning reciprocally as both a theological foil and catalyst for evangelical Protestants. In many ways, Rushdoony's subtle influence on evangelicals was largely negative. That is, by the 1980s, Rushdoony and his followers had provoked a significant backlash against their eschatological and legal writings. This prompted many evangelicals—some of the most prominent leaders of the movement—to address the challenges raised by Reconstructionism by reshaping their public ministries in small but significant ways. When figures such as Pat Robertson, D. James Kennedy, and Francis Schaeffer felt compelled to publicly denounce theocracy and condemn church/state mergers, they did so with Rushdoony lingering in the shadows. Nowhere was this clearer than in the "dominion theology" debates of the 1980s and 1990s, a controversy that still echoes into the twenty-first century regarding Francis Schaeffer's relationship to Rushdoony.[54]

In the end, Rushdoony's ultimate, confounding legacy may have little to do with the reform movements he inspired or his intellectual output and that of his followers. Instead, the interest in Christian Reconstructionism prompted by evangelical infighting and secular journalistic reports of the "dominionist" sympathies of GOP party leaders or the post-Obama Tea Partiers all suggest that Rushdoony and Reconstructionism have become nodes in a vast, shifting discursive network that codes public imaginings of "good" and "bad" forms of public religiosity. This concern over Reconstructionism—whether in the 1980s or the 2010s—is analogous to the media's interest in "cults" during the 1960s and 1970s. As religious studies scholar Sean McCloud has shown, popular journalistic interest in "cults" peaked during the 1960s as Americans came to terms with a shifting religious landscape.[55] Boundaries between "mainstream" and "fringe" religious movements emerged in the press because, McCloud argued, "the American religious fringe functioned for journalists as a 'negative reference group' in a process of identity construction. . . . As a negative reference group, the cultic margins helped to define what writers and editors desired or perceived themselves, their readers, and American culture as a whole to be."[56] The struggle to identify the limits of Christian Reconstructionism vis-à-vis evangelicalism and conservatism similarly reflects an attempt to identify and differentiate a "negative reference group" against which a more acceptable sort of public religiosity might be constructed.

This process of negation amounts to a subtle but profound assertion of a normative understanding of the proper limits of religion and citizenship in the United States. These normative assumptions belie an underinvestigated tendency that dominates both journalism and scholarship. As religious scholar Robert A. Orsi has pointed out in a harsh critique of the academic study of religion, "Both in content and method, Religious Studies has long been occupied with 'good' religion."[57] He further noted that this tendency to seek the "good" in religion is hardly limited to scholars. Journalists, Orsi explained, tend to seek out traditions marked by exuberant worship, hateful rhetoric, and violent tendencies precisely because they are incompatible with this search for "good" religion. Such outsider traditions are "valuable as others, as the unassimilable and intolerable. . . . So long as the point of religious scholarship, even implicitly or unconsciously, is to seal the borders of our own worlds of meaning and morals," then the business of religion and its study is the creation of marginalized others.[58]

The obsessive, ritualized exposure and condemnation of Reconstructionism falls neatly into the patterns identified by McCloud and Orsi. In popular reporting and in quite a bit of scholarship, the theology of R. J. Rushdoony has become a Rorschach test for the social anxieties of any number of progressives, conservatives, and Christians. No longer simply a theological controversy within conservative evangelicalism, Christian Reconstructionism has become a screen upon which critics project competing interpretations of the proper place of religion in American society. By using Reconstructionism to embody "bad" religion, such narratives reify the normative and naïve assumption that "good" American evangelicalism simply seeks to bring the light of Christ's Gospel to a fallen world. Similarly, "good" secularists can highlight the dangers of Reconstructionism as they try to carve out a space where Americans can live free from religious tyranny.

Such saccharine discourses conveniently ignore that both evangelicalism and secularism are culturally constituted systems of exclusion facilitated by powerful institutional, legal, and governmental mechanisms. Rushdoony, unlike many of the fundamentalists and evangelicals of his generation, fully grasped the reciprocal relationship between knowledge (epistemological structures) and power (governance in all of its complexity) and recognized how they conspired to constitute the limits of citizenship and who could govern whom. He intuited the relationship between the nation-state and total warfare and acknowledged that the intensification of global capitalism posed both problems and unlimited opportunities for American Protestantism.

Reconstructionism is hardly an aberration or a sui generis phenomenon; it did not develop in a vacuum. Reconstructionism is part and parcel of America's twentieth-century legacy. Rushdoony and the Reconstructionist project he cultivated cut to the very heart of a brutal century dominated by the technocult of the modern state and a global autophagic capitalist order. If his vision of the world is disturbing, it is because it grew from cultural soil fertilized with the rotting offal of modernity: three world wars (two hot, one cold); industrialized genocide; mass revolutions; the rise of omnipresent governmental and corporate surveillance systems; corrupt political regimes; skyrocketing domestic crime; and corporate piracy. Rushdoony's political theology spoke to all of these issues and offered prescriptive, often nauseatingly violent responses to deal with a century that was, in so many ways, an unmitigated disaster for a significant portion of humanity. And in the process, he led a grassroots movement in the United States—he influenced a generation of preachers, challenged conservative seminaries and small liberal-arts colleges to rethink the way they taught Christianity, and helped thousands of American families free themselves from what they perceived as the shackles of state education. He prodded a generation of American Christians to use biblical law to wage holy war on a godless order—a gauntlet many activists and politicians took up with a hearty, *"Deus vult!"* Rushdoony decreed that life itself is warfare. I know of no clearer assessment of the twentieth century.

NOTES

Abbreviations

BGC   Archives of the Billy Graham Center, Wheaton College Archives and Special Collections, Wheaton, Ill., Collection 8, box 20, folder 42

C&C   *Christianity and Civilization*

C&S   *Church and State*

CAS   Group Research File on the Center for American Studies (box no. 56), Group Research, Inc., Records, 1955–1996, Rare Book and Manuscript Library, Columbia University, New York, N.Y.

CGS   C. Gregg Singer Papers, Historical Center of the Presbyterian Church in America, St. Louis, Mo.

CR   *Chalcedon Report*

CT   *Christianity Today*

FF   *Faith and Freedom*

FFAOL   *Faith for All of Life*

HEK   Howard E. Kershner Papers, Special Collections and University Archives, University of Oregon Libraries, Eugene, Ore.

IFAS   Institute for First Amendment Studies Records, 1980–1999, Digital Collections and Archives, Tufts University, Medford, Mass.

IHS   Institute for Humane Studies Library, Institute for Humane Studies, George Mason University, Fairfax, Va.

ISI   Intercollegiate Studies Institute Library, Intercollegiate Studies Institute, Wilmington, Del.

JCI   James C. Ingebretsen Papers, Special Collections and University Archives, University of Oregon Libraries, Eugene, Ore.

JCR   *Journal of Christian Reconstruction*

JHP   J. Howard Pew Papers, Hagley Museum and Library, Wilmington, Del.

KJV   King James Version

Newsletter   Chalcedon Foundation *Newsletter*

PFAW   Center for Right-Wing Studies and People for the American Way Archive of Conservative Video Broadcasting, University of California, Berkeley, http://crws.berkeley.edu/video-archive/primary-source-documents

PG   *Presbyterian Guardian*

PRA   Political Research Associates Library, Political Research Associates, Somerville, Mass.

RJR   Rousas John Rushdoony Library, Chalcedon Foundation, Vallecito, Calif.

WTC   William Terry Couch Papers, Southern Historical Collection, Louis Round Wilson Special Collections Library, University of North Carolina at Chapel Hill

WTJ   *Westminster Theological Journal*

WVCR   William Volker and Company Records, Western Historical Manuscript
Collection, Kansas City, Mo.

WVF   Group Research File on the Volker Fund (box no. 327), Group Research, Inc.,
Records, 1955–1996, Rare Book and Manuscript Library, Columbia University,
New York, N.Y.

Introduction

1. R. J. Rushdoony to Emil Schwab, January 15, 1945, RJR.

2. Ibid.

3. R. J. Rushdoony to Chester A. Green, January 10, 1945, RJR.

4. R. J. Rushdoony to Emil Schwab, January 15, 1945, RJR.

5. "Rushdoony *Leeper* Transcript."

6. McIlhenny, "The Austin T.E.A. Party."

7. Ibid., 212. McIlhenny noted that the activism associated with the *Leeper* case facilitated a "watershed" moment, which saw Texas, long a holdout against homeschooling, change course in its resistance to home education (ibid., 212–13).

8. Duigon, "Homeschooling's Greatest Courtroom Victory." See also Schwartz and Sharpe, "J. Shelby Sharpe Remembers Rush."

9. There were other groups as well. As historian Milton Gaither has noted, Christian conservatives such as Rushdoony made up one of several tributaries of the homeschooling movement. Other key leaders included the decidedly leftist John Holt. See Gaither, *Homeschool*, 121–28.

10. Rushdoony, *Philosophy of the Christian Curriculum*, 113.

11. Rushdoony, *Messianic Character of American Education*, 282–83; emphasis in the original.

12. Rushdoony, *Institutes of Biblical Law*, 1:40.

13. For an in-depth discussion of the demographic and policy changes influencing the rise of the homeschooling movement in the United States, see Gaither, *Homeschool*, 85–94.

14. Reconstructionism is an unapologetically male-centered—and arguably misogynistic—movement. As a result, most references to "man" or "men" in this book are quite deliberate and reflect Rushdoony's particular theological project. Women, in Rushdoony's vision, are secondary or derivative instruments of godly governance and are consequently downplayed, silenced, or otherwise rendered invisible in most Reconstructionist literature.

15. Rushdoony, *Institutes of Biblical Law*, 1:235, 425.

16. Genesis 1:26–28 (KJV).

17. Rushdoony, *Institutes of Biblical Law*, 1:14.

18. Rushdoony, "Dominion Man," MP3, n.d.

19. Brown, "Theology, Apologetics, Ethics," *CT*, March 1, 1974, 70.

20. Iannaccone, "Heirs to the Protestant Ethic?," 349.

21. "Who's Who on the Right," 60.

22. See, respectively, Clarkson, *Eternal Hostility*; Juergensmeyer, *Terror in the Mind of God*; and Miller, *Cruel and Unusual*.

23. See, for example, Wilder, "Rick Perry's Army of God"; Lizza, "Leap of Faith"; and Goldberg, "A Christian Plot for Domination?"

24. See, respectively, "The Books and Beliefs Shaping Michele Bachmann"; Bill Keller, "Asking Candidates Tougher Questions about Faith," *New York Times Magazine*, August 25, 2011; and Cafferty, "How Much Does It Worry You if Both Michele Bachmann and Rick Perry Have Ties to Dominionism?"

25. McGirr, *Suburban Warriors*; Dochuk, *From Bible Belt to Sun Belt*; and Worthen, *Apostles of Reason*. A notable exception includes the work of ethnographer and religion scholar Julie Ingersoll. See Ingersoll, "Mobilizing Evangelicals"; and Ingersoll, *Building God's Kingdom*.

26. See Miller, *Billy Graham*; and Flippen, *Jimmy Carter*.

27. For representative treatments of Reconstructionism, see Martin, *With God on Our Side*, 353–54; Williams, *God's Own Party*, 225–26; and Miller, *Age of Evangelicalism*, 141–42.

28. Hendershot, *What's Fair on the Air*, 13. Hendershot's work is a significant contribution to such literature. Also, Ribuffo, *Old Christian Right*; Diamond, *Roads to Dominion*; and Schoenwald, *A Time for Choosing*, have carefully documented the surprisingly "mainstream" significance of the purportedly "extreme" elements of the Right.

29. Mulloy, *The World of the John Birch Society*, 2.

30. McGirr, *Suburban Warriors*; Lassiter, *Silent Majority*; Turner, *Bill Bright*; Dochuk, *From Bible Belt to Sun Belt*; Nickerson, *Mothers of Conservatism*.

31. This narrative approach is inspired, in part, by Turner, *Bill Bright*; and Burns, *Goddess of the Market*.

32. For a summary of the contours of this definitional debate, see Stone, *On the Boundaries of American Evangelicalism*, 1–23.

33. Nash, *The Conservative Intellectual Movement*; Burns, "In Retrospect"; and Phillips-Fein, "Conservatism."

34. See Latour, "Powers of Association"; and Latour, "From Object to Things." This approach is also indebted to Stone, *On the Boundaries of American Evangelicalism*.

35. Latour, "Powers of Association," 272–73.

36. This concept of milieu is inspired by Campbell, "The Cultic Milieu."

37. R. J. Rushdoony journal entry for August 1, 1953, RJR.

38. R. J. Rushdoony journal entries for May 12, 1951, and September 19, 1951, RJR.

39. On Sharon swearing, see R. J. Rushdoony journal entry for February 24, 1954, RJR.

40. Rebecca Rouse, "A Daughter's Memories," *FFAOL* (September/October 2005): 31.

41. R. J. Rushdoony to John Kistler, March 3, 1990, RJR.

Chapter 1

1. R. J. Rushdoony to Dave Stowe, January 2, 1946, RJR.

2. Ibid.

3. Ibid.

4. Ibid.

5. See Rushdoony, *The American Indian*.

6. For an overview situating Kantorowicz's concept of "political theology" in its historical context, see Kahn, "Political Theology," 77–101.

7. McCarthy et al., *Armenian Rebellion at Van*, 6–7.

8. Ibid., chapters 4 and 5.

9. Y. K. Rushdouni did not standardize and simplify his surname until he and his family immigrated to the United States of America in 1916. The original spelling of "Rushdouni" is retained for this discussion of the Rushdouni family in Armenia.

10. Larson, "Oral History Interview," 14–16, RJR.

11. M. Rushdoony, "Biographical Sketch of My Father," 22.

12. M. Rushdoony, "The Vision of R. J. Rushdoony."

13. M. Rushdoony, "Biographical Sketch of My Father," 22.

14. Rushdouni, "Letter Dated Van, 7th June 1915," 49.

15. Ibid.

16. McCarthy et al., *Armenian Rebellion at Van*, 200–206.

17. Rushdouni, "Narrative by Mr. Y. K. Rushdouni," 65.

18. M. Rushdoony, "Biographical Sketch of My Father," 22.

19. Larson, "Oral History Interview," 3–4, RJR.

20. M. Rushdoony, "Biographical Sketch of My Father," 23.

21. Bulbulian, *Fresno Armenians*, 48.

22. Ibid., 48, 99.

23. Maibaum, "Armenians in California," 27.

24. Larson, "Oral History Interview," 19–20, RJR.

25. Ibid.

26. Ibid., 36.

27. Ibid., 32.

28. Ibid.

29. Ibid., 48.

30. *Natsihi*, 18. Jerusha K. Lofland's blog, Heresy in the Heartland, pointed me to this link.

31. Jeri, "Voiceless Women."

32. Williams, "Ordination Ceremony of Rousas John Rushdoony," May 14, 1944, RJR. Years later, after seeing Rushdoony on a PBS special hosted by Bill Moyers in which Rushdoony defended, among other things, his support for the death penalty for many of the offenses listed in the Old Testament, Williams wrote to Rushdoony: "It seemed last night utterly implausible that it was I whom you asked to preach the ordination sermon for you in the Presbyterian Church in Chinatown in S.F." (George Huntston Williams to R. J. Rushdoony, December 30, 1987, RJR).

33. Williams, "Ordination Ceremony," RJR.

34. Ibid., 2, RJR.

35. R. J. Rushdoony to Ernst H. Kantorowicz, March 22, 1945, RJR.

36. For Rushdoony's solitary fishing trips, see Stewart C. Potter, "The Man from Owyhee," *CR* 429 (April 2001): 24.

37. R. J. Rushdoony to George Huntston Williams, February 26, 1945, RJR.

38. R. J. Rushdoony to George Huntston Williams, December 20, 1944, RJR.

39. R. J. Rushdoony to Orval Clay, December 15, 1944, RJR.

40. Ibid.

41. *Arda Rushdoony v. R. J. Rushdoony*, order modifying final decree of divorce, no. 29,666, Superior Court of the State of California in and for the County of Santa Cruz, vol. 62, p. 251, October 31, 1962.

42. During the late 1940s, Rushdoony repeatedly recorded his dissatisfaction with Arda's

contribution to the mission and to their family. A representative journal entry noted: "Chores, prepared church for Girls Scout meeting at noon. Cared for children in afternoon. Cleaned church again (4th time in week) after meeting. Cared for children in evening together with Lorraine Manning (8 months) while Arda and May *played* in basketball game. . . . Studied after midnight" (R. J. Rushdoony journal entry for December 6, 1947, RJR; emphasis in the original). Such references slowly disappeared from his journals until the late 1950s, when considerable personal tensions eventually led Rousas and Arda to divorce.

43. R. J. Rushdoony to George Huntston Williams, November 9, 1949, RJR.

44. R. J. Rushdoony to George Huntston Williams October 5, 1945; R. J. Rushdoony to Lorna Logan, April 4, 1946, RJR; and R. J. Rushdoony to James Laurie, October 15, 1949, RJR.

45. R. J. Rushdoony to Emil Schwab, January 15, 1945, RJR.

46. R. J. Rushdoony to Orval Clay, December 15, 1944, RJR.

47. The following biographical material about Kantorowicz is drawn from Cantor, "Nazi Twins," 79–117; and Malkiel, "Ernst H. Kantorowicz," 146–219.

48. Malkiel, "Ernst H. Kantorowicz," 203.

49. On Williams's relationship with Kantorowicz, see ibid., 203 (n. 42).

50. This account of Rushdoony and Kantorowicz's conversation is recounted in Larson, "Oral History Interview," 41–43, RJR. Rushdoony recalls that they were discussing a "book," but both the content of his description and the date of the conversation suggest that the two discussed Kantorowicz's "'King's Advent.'" It is also possible they were discussing aspects of Kantorowicz's soon to be published *Laudes Regiae* (1946).

51. On Kantorowicz's rattan porch furniture, see Cantor, "Nazi Twins," 98–99. The phrase *adventus regis* refers to the liturgical reception of a king by the civil and religious officials of medieval cities and towns. Kantorowicz, "'King's Advent,'" 210.

52. Larson, "Oral History Interview," 43, RJR.

53. For examples, see R. J. Rushdoony to Orval Clay, December 15, 1944; R. J. Rushdoony to George Huntston Williams, February 26, 1945; and R. J. Rushdoony to Ernst H. Kantorowicz, March 22, 1945, RJR.

54. R. J. Rushdoony to Ernst H. Kantorowicz, March 22, 1945, RJR.

55. John Scoon to R. J. Rushdoony, March 21, 1945, RJR.

56. Ibid.

57. R. J. Rushdoony to Ernst H. Kantorowicz, May 20, 1946, RJR.

58. Cantor, "Nazi Twins," 84. See also Kantorowicz, *Frederick the Second*.

59. Kantorowicz, *King's Two Bodies*.

60. Malkiel, "Ernst H. Kantorowicz," 218.

61. M. Rushdoony, "Biographical Sketch of My Father," 25.

62. Years later, Rushdoony formalized his dissent from secular, professional historiography in a series of historical studies that in many ways owed a deep debt to Kantorowicz. For a summary of Rushdoony's rejection of humanistic and scientific historiography, see Rushdoony, *Nature of the American System*, v–vii.

63. R. J. Rushdoony to George Huntston Williams, June 12, 1947, RJR.

64. Ibid.

65. R. J. Rushdoony to Kantorowicz, March 22, 1945, RJR. The phrase "Ichabod, the glory is departed" references 1 Samuel 4:21.

66. R. J. Rushdoony to Orval Clay, February 24, 1945, RJR.

67. Rushdoony, "Christian Missions and Indian Culture," 12. Rushdoony's multiple references to "crisis" reflect the early influence of Reinhold Niebuhr, the highly influential Union Theological Seminary theologian and cultural critic. Rushdoony was a subscriber to Niebuhr's journal, *Christianity and Crisis*, and frequently cited Niebuhr, *Leaves from the Notebook of a Tamed Cynic* (1929), in his correspondence. He had apparently read Niebuhr extensively during his days at PSR. After Rushdoony embraced the thinking of Cornelius Van Til, he turned against Niebuhr and rejected him as a theological liberal.

68. Rushdoony, "Christian Missions and Indian Culture," 3.

69. R. J. Rushdoony to Orval Clay, February 24, 1945, RJR.

70. Larson, "Oral History Interview," 43, RJR; R. J. Rushdoony to Gilbert Lovell, March 12, 1946, RJR; and M. Rushdoony, "Biographical Sketch of My Father," 26.

71. Larson, "Oral History Interview," 33, RJR.

72. Ibid.

73. In assessing the influence of Van Til's criticism of Barth and Brunner, Phillip R. Thorne insisted: "Without a doubt the history of Barth's reception by American Evangelicals must begin with Dr. Cornelius Van Til. . . . Not only was he one of the earliest, most prolific and well read of Fundamentalist Evangelical interpreters, Van Til was the most influential." Thorne, *Evangelicalism and Karl Barth*, 33. Gregory G. Bolich reached a similar conclusion regarding the importance of *The New Modernism*: "Under Van Til . . . the work of Barth was declared off limits to a generation of evangelicals. Van Til's general conclusions, as well as many of his specific criticisms, became the primary response of the American conservative community to Karl Barth." Bolich, *Karl Barth*, 66–67. Bolich was careful, however, to point out that many conservatives rejected Van Til's analysis as a mere "caricature" of Barth's theology (ibid., 71, 70–73). Van Til's biographer, John R. Muether, noted that Van Til helped set the tone for Barth's reception in the United States partly because he had the advantage of reading Barth in the original German years before many of the Swiss's key writings appeared in English. Muether, *Van Til*, 121. Finally, historian George Marsden described Van Til as "one of the few in the fundamentalist fold equipped philosophically and linguistically to deal with the complexities of European dialectic theologies." He concluded: "Few fundamentalists read [*The New Modernism*], but many repeated the title." Marsden, *Reforming Fundamentalism*, 101.

74. As John M. Frame summarizes, Van Til did not clearly define *presupposition*: "Van Til uses the term *presupposition* to indicate the role that divine revelation ought to play in human thought. I do not believe that he ever defines the term. I have tried to define it for him as a 'basic heart-commitment.' For the Christian, that commitment is to God as he reveals himself in his Word. Non-Christians substitute something else . . . as that to which they are ultimately committed and that which governs all of life, including thought." *Cornelius Van Til*, 136.

75. Or, in Van Til's words, "Christian method of apologetic argument, in agreement with its own basic conception of the starting point, must be by presupposition. To argue by presupposition is to indicate what are the epistemological and metaphysical principles that underlie and control one's method." Van Til, *Apologetics*, 61.

76. R. J. Rushdoony to Lorna Logan, April 4, 1946, RJR.

77. Ibid.

78. Holifield, *Theology in America*, 8–9.

79. Balmer and Fitzmier, *The Presbyterians*, 5.

80. Fosdick, "Shall the Fundamentalists Win?," 776.

81. Machen, *Christianity and Liberalism*, 15–16.

82. Hankins, *Jesus and Gin*, 1–4.

83. Longfield, *Presbyterian Controversy*, 162–73.

84. Muether, *Cornelius Van Til*, 67–71.

85. See Brasich, "Parallel Lines Never Intersect," 26–48; and Worthen, *Apostles of Reason*, 84–87.

86. Longfield, *Presbyterians and American Culture*, 65–67.

87. Noll, "Common Sense Traditions," 220.

88. Ibid., 221–22.

89. Ibid., 224.

90. Van Til encountered Kuyper in his theology and religion classes at Calvin College in Grand Rapids, Michigan. Calvin College was founded by the Christian Reformed Church, which in turn has its roots in the Dutch Reformed churches. For Van Til's introduction to Kuyper, see Muether, *Van Til*, 44–46.

91. Ibid., 24–25; Marsden, *Reforming Fundamentalism*, 78–79. For Kuyper's influence in the United States, see Bolt, *A Free Church, A Holy Nation*.

92. Muether, *Van Til*, 25.

93. Ibid. As Muether explains, Kuyper believed that Christians and non-Christians could work together in spite of their irreconcilable worldviews because of the work of common grace. Since non-Christians can never be truly epistemologically self-conscious and ultimately rely on Christian presumptions, there is room for cooperation on projects designed to better the human condition. Van Til reformulated this view of common grace to argue that it provides a check on any "absolute expression" of human depravity in history. See ibid., 154–55.

94. Roberts, "Cornelius Van Til," 124.

95. Van Til, *Defense of the Faith*, 35, 23–30; and Roberts, "Cornelius Van Til," 122.

96. Roberts, "Cornelius Van Til," 119.

97. Ibid.

98. Van Til, *Defense of the Faith*, 27. Rushdoony eventually translated this into a political vocabulary to assert that all aspects of social reality are equal to one another. Therefore no aspect of society can be reduced to another, and conversely, no aspect can claim superiority over another. See Rushdoony, *One and the Many*.

99. Frame, *Cornelius Van Til*, 76.

100. Van Til, "My Credo," 5. For less-fanciful accounts of Satan's challenge to Eve, see Van Til, *Defense of the Faith*, 33–35; and Van Til, *Apologetics*, 56–57.

101. Van Til, "My Credo," 5–6.

102. Van Til, *Apologetics*, 57.

103. Roberts, "Cornelius Van Til," 124.

104. Ibid.

105. Frame, *Cornelius Van Til*, 135.

106. Ibid.

107. Roberts, "Cornelius Van Til," 124; and Van Til, *Defense of the Faith*, 32–33.

108. "Santa Cruz Church Formed," *PG*, July 15, 1958.

109. Watson, "Theonomy," 7–8.

110. R. J. Rushdoony journal entries for July 4, 1953; October 2, 1953; and February 21, 1953, RJR.

111. R. J. Rushdoony journal entry for April 12, 1957, RJR.

112. R. J. Rushdoony journal entry for December 24, 1956, RJR.

113. R. J. Rushdoony journal entry for January 19, 1956, RJR.

114. R. J. Rushdoony journal entries for January 24, 1957; March 23, 1957; and May 5, 1957, RJR.

115. R. J. Rushdoony journal entries for May 25, 1957; June 3, 1957; June 26, 1957; and June 29, 1957, RJR.

116. *Arda Rushdoony v. R. J. Rushdoony*, complaint in divorce, no. 29,666, Superior Court of the State of California in and for the County of Santa Cruz, April 21, 1958.

117. *Arda Rushdoony v. R. J. Rushdoony*, final decree of divorce, no. 29,666, Superior Court of the State of California in and for the County of Santa Cruz, vol. 53, p. 242, July 6, 1959.

118. *Arda Rushdoony v. R. J. Rushdoony*, order modifying final decree of divorce, no. 29,666, Superior Court of the State of California in and for the County of Santa Cruz, vol. 62, p. 251, October 31, 1962.

119. *Arda Rushdoony v. R. J. Rushdoony*, complaint in divorce, no. 29,666, Superior Court of the State of California in and for the County of Santa Cruz, April 21, 1958.

120. Decades later, Rushdoony confided in his journal that Arda had engaged in "extensive fornication after the divorce" and noted that some unnamed similar offense had "preceded that step" of the divorce. R. J. Rushdoony journal entry for June 20, 1984, RJR. Whether this unnamed offense weighed more heavily on him than her mental state is not clear.

Chapter 2

1. Memorandum, SAC (Special Agent in Charge), San Francisco to Director, FBI, March 27, 1964, "Rousas John Rushdoony (SOCAP) Espionage-R," 65-68503-3.

2. Letter, SAC (Special Agent in Charge), San Francisco to Director, FBI, January 24, 1964, "Rousas John Rushdoony (SOCAP) Espionage-R," 65-68503-1.

3. Greenberg, *Surveillance in America*, 12.

4. Rushdoony's subscription to a communist publication and his reception of Klan material made him especially notable in 1964, the year the FBI initiated COINTELPRO (Counter Intelligence Program) against "White Hate Groups" in the United States. See, Cunningham, *There's Something Happening Here*, 6–13 and 87–92.

5. Memorandum, SAC (Special Agent in Charge), San Francisco to Director, FBI, August 13, 1964, "Rousas John Rushdoony (SOCAP) Espionage-R," 65-68503-7, 4.

6. Ibid., 1, 7.

7. Burns, *Goddess of the Market*, 138–40.

8. Nash, *The Conservative Intellectual Movement*, xiii.

9. Ibid.

10. For a lucid critical appraisal of Nash's argument, see Burns, "In Retrospect." A number of recent histories—including Murphy, *The Rebuke of History*; Phillips-Fein, *Invisible Hands*; and Lichtman, *White Protestant Nation*—have challenged Nash's organizational argument, but

these studies confirm the *perception* among contemporary conservative activists that they were an embattled, isolated minority without institutional support. On the latter point, see Doherty, *Radicals for Capitalism*; and Burns, *Goddess of the Market*.

11. William T. Couch to Fred D. Wieck, May 12, 1964, folder 138, WTC.

12. See Phillips-Fein, *Invisible Hands*, 68–86, for the various atheist, Catholic, and Protestant convictions influencing midcentury probusiness activism.

13. On the American Liberty League, see Wolfskill, *Revolt of the Conservatives*. For the NAM, see Phillips-Fein, *Invisible Hands*, 13–15; and Lichtman, *White Protestant Nation*, 62–65, 85–87. Doenecke, *Storm on the Horizon* and *Not to the Swift*, cover the rise and fall of the America First Committee and isolationist sentiment before and during the Cold War.

14. For Peale's and other notable churchmen's association with SM, see George, *God's Salesman*, 171–72; Fones-Wolf, *Selling Free Enterprise*, 223; and Lichtman, *White Protestant Nation*, 80.

15. Roy, *Apostles of Discord*, 286 and 288; and Phillips-Fein, *Invisible Hands*, 70–77.

16. Hollinger, *After Cloven Tongues of Fire*, 89.

17. For a concise summary of Fifield's appeal to the eighth commandment, see Doherty, *Radicals for Capitalism*, 271–74.

18. From the masthead of *FF*, December 1953.

19. Toy, "Spiritual Mobilization," 80 (n. 9).

20. Ibid. Spiritual Mobilization repeatedly attacked the Social Gospel in its publications, especially because of renewed interest in the movement in Congregational circles. See, for notable examples, Opitz and Bennett, "Dear Dr. Bennett, Dear Dr. Opitz," *FF*, April 1953; Johnson, "The Social Gospel Debate," *FF*, December 1953; and Riley, "Not by Bread Alone," *FF*, March 1957.

21. From Spiritual Mobilization's founding "Credo" quoted in Fifield, "Dr. Fifield's Farewell," *FF* 10, no. 1 (1959): 2.

22. Doherty, *Radicals for Capitalism*, 271.

23. Toy, "Faith and Freedom," 153–61.

24. Roy, *Apostles of Discord*, 286.

25. For representative articles, see, respectively, Opitz, "One is Still a Crowd," *FF*, October 1954; Mises, "The Alleged Injustice of Capitalism," *FF*, June 1950; and Rothbard, "Not Worth a Continental," *FF*, February 1950.

26. Heard wrote a regular "Seeking New Ideas with Gerald Heard" column through 1958. Supportive profiles of Heard's teachings included Ashby, "Exploration into Gerald Heard," *FF*, June 1956; and Ingebretsen, "Pause for Reflection," *FF*, September 1956.

27. Toy, "Spiritual Mobilization," 77.

28. R. J. Rushdoony to William Johnson, March 14, 1950, RJR.

29. Ibid.

30. Rushdoony, "Noncompetitive Life," *FF*, June 1950.

31. R. J. Rushdoony to William Johnson, March 14, 1950, RJR.

32. Ibid.

33. Ibid.

34. R. J. Rushdoony to Herbert C. Cornuelle, October 10, 1950, RJR.

35. Herbert Cornuelle to R. J. Rushdoony, August 30, 1950, RJR.

36. F. A. Harper to R. J. Rushdoony, October 18, 1950, RJR. Ultimately, the Volker Fund, citing its long-standing "non-denominational" policy, rejected offering any assistance to the *Herald*. See Herbert C. Cornuelle to R. J. Rushdoony, May 20, 1952, RJR.

37. For Ingebretsen's religious convictions, see Ingebretsen, *Apprentice to the Dawn*. Ingebretsen's father was an LDS apostate who carefully insulated his children from religious influence (26). As result, in his undergrad days at Stanford University in the 1930s, Ingebretsen was thoroughly convinced that religion was "balderdash" (27). Further, in describing his reason for heading Spiritual Mobilization, Ingebretsen noted, "I didn't come to Spiritual Mobilization as a preacher: I came as a lawyer and libertarian. Fighting the forces that wanted to abolish the free enterprise system was my mission, not promoting Christ!" (27–28). Ingebretsen eventually became a follower of Gerald Heard (45–76). Heard, a confidant of Aldous Huxley, was interested in psychic phenomena and experimentation with LSD. For a summary of Ingebretsen's religious ideas, see Doherty, *Radicals for Capitalism*, 274–85. For a study of Heard and Ingebretsen's drug use, see Toy, "The Conservative Connection."

38. James C. Ingebretsen to R. J. Rushdoony, April 10, 1952, JCI.

39. R. J. Rushdoony to James C. Ingebretsen, April 15, 1952, JCI. If Rushdoony did not think much of Crane, he was more positive about Mullendore's pastor, W. Clarence Wright. Rushdoony described Wright as "one of our outstanding men in the Church. . . . He has received copies [of the *Herald*], and has given [money]" (ibid.).

40. Robert Glover Shoemaker to R. J. Rushdoony, October 5, 1950, RJR.

41. R. J. Rushdoony to Samuel G. Craig, October 11, 1950, RJR.

42. R. J. Rushdoony to James C. Ingebretsen, April 15, 1952, HEK.

43. Ibid.

44. R. J. Rushdoony to C. Ralston Smith, May 10, 1952, RJR.

45. R. J. Rushdoony to James C. Ingebretsen, April 15, 1952, HEK.

46. For example, Rushdoony's future publisher, Dr. Samuel G. Craig, the theologically conservative president of the Presbyterian and Reformed Publishing Company, offered Rushdoony everything short of his direct support. That such "support" did Rushdoony little good was not lost on the aspiring editor. Samuel G. Craig to R. J. Rushdoony, September 20, 1950, RJR.

47. "Two Churches Organized in California," *PG*, June 15, 1958, 86.

48. Ibid. It is important to note that Van Til was not a PCUSA member. This angered some in Rushdoony's church.

49. R. J. Rushdoony journal entry for December 3, 1956, RJR.

50. "Two Churches Organized in California," *PG*, June 15, 1958, 86.

51. R. J. Rushdoony journal entry for October 8, 1957, RJR.

52. "Two Churches Organized in California," *PG*, June 15, 1958, 86.

53. "Charter Roll 100 at Santa Cruz," *PG*, February 10, 1959, 48.

54. Later in the decade, the OPC investigated Rushdoony for violating church law by preaching outside of his official presbytery when he led Bible studies in the Northern and Southern California Presbyteries every Sunday. Frustrated, he eventually left the OPC. M. Rushdoony, "Biographical Sketch," 27–28; and North, *Tithing and the Church*, 152–56.

55. R. J. Rushdoony journal entry for November 29, 1961, RJR.

56. Marriage License, August 1, 1932, Brooke County, West Virginia, http://www.wvculture

.org/vrr/va_mcdetail.aspx?Id=11753047. Their marriage license listed their ages as twenty-one, suggesting Dorothy was born in 1911. When Dorothy Barbara Rushdoony died in 2003, her gravestone listed her birth year as 1916, which does not match the age indicated on her marriage license to Thomas Kirkwood.

57. Rushdoony's journals indicate that Thomas Kirkwood Jr., or Tommy, was likely a source of friction between Thomas Sr. and Dorothy. Tommy was in his teens when his parents separated. He was frequently in trouble for skipping school. He also broke into people's homes and likely stole money from the Kirkwoods and Rushdoony. Thomas Sr. struggled to discipline the boy, and he and Dorothy disputed custody of their son following the divorce. After Dorothy's marriage to Rushdoony, references to Tommy quickly disappear from Rushdoony's journals, an indication that he severed ties from the family. R. J. Rushdoony journal entries for October 19, 1960; March 19, 1962; April 20, 1962; and October 8, 1963, RJR.

58. "Two Churches Organized in California," PG, June 15, 1958.

59. "Santa Cruz, Calif.," PG, May 1962, 79; and M. Rushdoony, "Biographical Sketch of My Father," 27.

60. R. J. Rushdoony journal entry for March 20, 1962, RJR.

61. McVicar, "Aggressive Philanthropy."

62. Mark 6:1 (KJV).

63. Cornuelle, Mr. Anonymous.

64. A Statement of Policy, 10. See also Doherty, Radicals for Capitalism, 185–86.

65. In 2013 dollars, this would total more than $54 million in targeted gifts. This figure combines the Volker Fund's charitable budgets in the categories "Education" and "Humane Studies" from 1952 to 1962. This included large, non-ideologically driven donations to the University of Kansas City and other midwestern institutions. It also included substantial grants to ideologically aligned organizations and individuals through such mechanisms as the Basic Books project ($727,236); the Council for Basic Education ($266,729); the National Book Foundation ($79,487); the Mont Pèlerin Society ($16,479); the Foundation for Economic Education ($5,800); and the Intercollegiate Society of Individualists ($4,300). Many of these organizations also benefited from indirect but considerable donations via funded symposia and other grants not reflected in these totals. See "Table 2, William Volker Fund—Summary of Grants, by Category"; "Table 3, William Volker Fund—Selected Grantees, Education Category"; and "Table 4, William Volker Fund—Selected Grantees, Human Studies Category," WVF.

66. See Nash, Conservative Intellectual Movement, xiii.

67. Doherty, Radicals for Capitalism, 186.

68. Nash, Conservative Intellectual Movement, 182–83.

69. For biographical overviews of Nock and his eccentric place on the American Right, see Wreszin, The Superfluous Anarchist; and Wills, Confessions of a Conservative, 26–29.

70. Nock outlined this argument in the libertarian cult classic Our Enemy the State (1946).

71. Nock, "Isaiah's Job," 642. Nock had already espoused the outline of his theory of the Remnant in a 1924 introduction to The Selected Works of Artemus Ward, reprinted as Nock, "Artemus Ward."

72. Nock, "Isaiah's Job," 642.

73. Ibid.

74. Ibid., 643.

75. Nock, *Memoirs of a Superfluous Man.*

76. Ibid., 121.

77. Biographers have noted Nock's influence on Rand. See Burns, *Goddess of the Market,* 71–72; and Heller, *Ayn Rand and the World She Made,* 268–69.

78. Buckley, "National Review," 201–2.

79. R. J. Rushdoony to Herbert C. Cornuelle, October 10, 1950, RJR.

80. "The Institute for Humane Studies: Founding and Objective," n.d., IHS.

81. F. A. Harper, "Institute for Humane Studies: Extracted from 'The Concept and Preliminary Proposal,' August 1961," 7, WTC.

82. "Some Key Points in 'Concept' Appraisals," n.d., IHS. Context clues indicate these quotations were recorded during a meeting (or a series of meetings) in the early 1960s before the Volker Fund rejected Harper's IHS proposal.

83. "The Idea of the Institute: An Introduction to the Institute for Humane Studies," n.d., IHS.

84. R. J. Rushdoony to Ivan R. Bierly and F. A. Harper, n.d., RJR. In R. J. Rushdoony to F. A. Harper, November 18, 1961, RJR, Rushdoony noted, "I should like to pursue my remarks concerning liberty as a product," indicating the former response was probably authored in October or November of 1961.

85. Several versions of this essay exist. Two slightly different drafts (one dated circa January 3, 1962, and another dated February 26, 1963) are available in folder 141, WTC. A copy of the February 26, 1963 draft is also available in box 15, HEK.

86. Ivan R. Bierly to William Terry Couch, January 3, 1962, folder 141, WTC.

87. R. J. Rushdoony, "The Strategy of Fabian Socialism," February 26, 1963, HEK.

88. R. J. Rushdoony, "The Strategy of Fabian Socialism," ca. January 3, 1962, 3, folder 141, WTC.

89. Ibid., 12.

90. Harold W. Luhnow, "Mr. Anonymous of Kansas City, Missouri," 23, mimeograph typescript, September 15, 1948, folder 67, WVCR; and Doherty, *Radicals for Capitalism,* 160–61.

91. Doherty, *Radicals for Capitalism,* 161.

92. Eow, "Fighting a New Deal," 145.

93. R. J. Rushdoony, "The Strategy of Fabian Socialism," ca. January 3, 1962, 15, folder 141, WTC.

94. Ibid., 14.

95. Nash, *The Conservative Intellectual Movement,* 182.

96. Ibid., xiii.

97. Brent Bozell, Buckley's brother-in-law, first labeled this threefold conservative synthesis "fusionist" in a highly critical *National Review* article. Bozell, "Freedom or Virtue." Bozell picked up the term from a suggestive passage in a January 16, 1962, *National Review* article, "The Twisted Tree of Liberty," in which Meyer refers to "the fusion that is contemporary conservatism." Meyer, *Conservative Mainstream,* 41. Nash has since popularized the term in *The Conservative Intellectual Movement* and established it as a central but highly problematic category in the historiography of the American Right.

98. Phillips-Fein, *Invisible Hands,* 43

99. Nobel Prize winners who received Volker support included Hayek, Friedman, James Buchanan, Gary Becker, Ronald Coase, and George Stigler.

100. By most accounts, Luhnow adhered to some idiosyncratic form of Christian Science or

New Thought. Templeton described Luhnow as a "science of mind guy" from a "nominally" Baptist background who opened all board meetings with a prayer. Kenneth S. Templeton, telephone interview by author, March 20, 2007. Luhnow was also a teetotaler who forbade smoking in the Volker offices. Gary North, Rushdoony's future son-in-law who interned at CAS in 1963, remembered that as he prepared to meet Luhnow for the first time, Rushdoony "warned me that Luhnow was a science of mind disciple, and not to laugh if he said something preposterous." Gary North, e-mail to author, March 17, 2007.

101. Anonymously authored "Defensive Memo #7: Institute for Humane Studies: History and Progress," April 20–22, 1962; document in author's possession.

102. Doherty, *Radicals for Capitalism*, 294. Doherty cites a Volker associate as recalling "Bierly [made] sly references to what a shame it was that certain of his Volker colleagues weren't going to church, and that Rothbard was attempting to craft a libertarian natural rights theory that wasn't explicitly theological" (ibid., 671–72 [n. 5]). Rothbard seems to have been a lightning rod for Bierly's religiously inspired wrath.

103. For details on the fund's collapse, see Doherty, *Radicals for Capitalism*, 294; and McVicar, "Aggressive Philanthropy," 200–202.

104. H. W. Luhnow to Members and Executive Staff of the William Volker Fund, 15 March 1962; available in folder 132, WTC and RJR.

105. The *San Francisco Examiner* reported that the Center for American Studies formed with $10 million that "would have gone to the University of Kansas City." "New Study Center for Burlingame," *San Francisco Examiner*, August 13, 1963, WVF. The end result was a series of lawsuits, eventually settled out of court with no public record, which ultimately saw more than $10 million of the fund's money going to the Hoover Institution at Stanford University. See "10.5 Million May Go to Conservatives—A Case Study," *Group Research Report*, April 20 1977, 15, WVF.

106. As one early CAS memo noted, "So long as this remains the William Volker Fund, the fact of its long history of fund-granting will be an important road block to contributions to its programs." I. R. Bierly, "Administrative, Policy, Budget Matters for the Center for 12 Months after June 1, 1963," May 14, 1963, 10, folder 133, WTC.

107. Harold W. Luhnow press release to the *Kansas City Star*, August 11, 1963, folder 133, WTC.

108. Harold W. Luhnow to all staff members of the Center for American Studies, July 30, 1963, folder 133, WTC.

109. In an effort to garner support for the publication, Couch cast a wide net to find scholars, public figures, and businessmen who might be interested in the encyclopedia. For his troubles, he often received responses that noted the vagueness of the proposed encyclopedia. For example, Henry Hazlitt, an editor at *Newsweek* and a major figure in the development of American libertarianism, responded to Couch's inquiries for help on the project with confusion: "I am in some doubt about the exact scope of your proposed 'Encyclopedia of Americana.'" Henry Hazlitt to William T. Couch, August 16, 1963, folder 139, WTC. Former Yale professor Ralph H. Gabriel was far more blunt in his assessment of the project: "I do not see how an encyclopedia of Americana can be developed on any such base as suggested in your letter." Ralph H. Gabriel to William T. Couch, August 16, 1963, folder 139, WTC. The encyclopedia (sometimes also referred to as the "Bicentennial Encyclopedia") was to be modeled on Couch's previous work with Collier's and the University of Chicago, but it never developed beyond the preliminary

stages. It was to function as a supplement and support for the center's proposed "Vital Issues" series. The series was to serve as study guides of basic issues in politics, history, religion, and philosophy. "Revised Memorandum of Suggestions," October 19, 1962, folder 133, WTC. The earliest proposed volumes were to be authored by center staffers Rushdoony, Miller, Bierly, and Hoggan. "Administrative, Policy, Budget Matters for the Center for 12 Months after June 1, 1963," May 14, 1963, 10, WTC.

110. Rushdoony, *Intellectual Schizophrenia*. Rushdoony received his first grant from the fund "to write a book on educational problems and principles" in 1959. Harold W. Luhnow to P. M. Schuhmann, March 18, 1959, RJR.

111. After receiving grants and making connections with Volker staffers at the Carleton College conference, Rushdoony was eventually invited to directly participate in conferences sponsored by the fund. Kenneth S. Templeton to Rousas John Rushdoony, June 29, 1960, RJR.

112. For example, in 1958 Bierly wrote to Rushdoony, "[Y]our letter of December 1 challenges me to a moment of contemplation" regarding the relationship between religion and the law. Expanding on the point, Bierly noted: "I am increasingly conscious of my almost total lack of history and philosophy, to say nothing of specific religious training." I. R. Bierly to R. J. Rushdoony, December 3, 1958, RJR. Rushdoony was more than happy to provide Bierly with the historical, philosophical, and theological training that he lacked. To this end, Rushdoony sent Bierly long letters summarizing his ideas, citing Van Til, and generally plugging his understanding of presuppositional apologetics. R. J. Rushdoony to Ivan R. Bierly, November 23, 1961, RJR; and R. J. Rushdoony to Ivan R. Bierly, January 14, 1962, RJR. Finally, as late as 1963, when their relationship was strained by Rushdoony's Calvinism, Bierly nonetheless commended Rushdoony for convincing him "of the relevance of Christian faith to scholarship in the West. . . . Rush has been tremendously challenging and helpful to me in the process of the development of my own consciousness of this need today." I. R. Bierly to William T. Couch, March 13, 1963, folder 132, WTC.

113. Meyer, "Richard M. Weaver," 243.

114. Murphy, *Rebuke of History*, 162.

115. For a lengthy discussion of Milione's relationship with the ISI, see Edwards, *Educating for Liberty*.

116. Forster and Epstein, *Danger on the Right*, 275.

117. The text was a spiral-bound mimeograph of a series of lectures Rushdoony had conducted for the ISI at St. Mary's College of California and the University of Washington. At the two colleges, Rushdoony appeared with speakers that included such midcentury conservative pioneers as Hans F. Sennholz, Felix Morley, and the Volker Fund's I. R. Bierly. "ISI Summer Schools, 1962," *ISI Campus Report* (Winter 1963–1964), ISI.

118. Richard M. Weaver to I. R. Bierly, February 7, 1963, folder 132, WTC.

119. I. R. Bierly to Richard M. Weaver, February 12, 1963, folder 132, WTC.

120. William T. Couch to A. N. J. den Hollander, March 24, 1964, folder 138, WTC.

121. Richard M. Weaver to I. R. Bierly, February 23, 1963, folder 132, WTC.

122. I. R. Bierly to Richard M. Weaver, February 27, 1963, folder 132, WTC.

123. Ibid.

124. William T. Couch to I. R. Bierly, March 4, 1963, folder 132, WTC.

125. Ibid.

126. I. R. Bierly to William T. Couch, March 13, 1963, folder 132, WTC.

127. William T. Couch to A. N. J. den Hollander, March 24, 1964, folder 138, WTC.

128. William T. Couch to Fred Wieck, September 5, 1963, folder 138, WTC.

129. For these quotations, see, respectively, ibid. and William T. Couch to Ivan R. Bierly, n.d., folder 138, WTC.

130. William T. Couch to A. N. J. den Hollander, March 24, 1964, folder 138, WTC.

131. Most notably, Couch was involved in a heated public controversy over the publication of Grodzins's *Americans Betrayed* (1949). The book discussed the internment and forced evacuation of Japanese Americans from the West Coast and concluded that the program was rooted partly in New Deal policies and blatantly racist. Couch, then at Chicago, agreed to publish the book over the objection of Grodzins's academic advisers and in violation of the rules governing the publication of graduate assistant research he conducted in California. Couch saw the book's publication as a moral imperative and ultimately ran afoul of the university's chancellor, who dismissed him from the press in 1950. Murray, "The Rights of Research Assistants and the Rhetoric of Political Suppression"; and Hughes, "How to Fire a Professor."

132. C. J. Miller, "Suggested Statement of Purpose and Perspective," May 28, 1963, folder 133, WTC.

133. Ibid.

134. David Hoggan, "The American Conservative Concept in Relation to the American Studies Program," May 28, 1963, folder 133, WTC.

135. William T. Couch to I. R Bierly, May 29, 1963, folder 133, WTC.

136. Ibid.

137. William T. Couch to I. R. Bierly, July 9, 1963, folder 133, WTC.

138. Ibid.

139. Ibid.

140. William T. Couch to I. R. Bierly, July 8, 1963, folder 133, WTC.

141. Ibid.

142. Ibid.

143. William T. Couch to A. N. J. den Hollander, March 24, 1964, folder 138, WTC.

144. Memo directed to all staff members, August 8, 1963; available in folder 133, WTC and RJR.

145. Ibid.

146. Couch seems to have penned the phrase, and his signature is appended to nearly two dozen form letters containing it. The letters were sent to various scholars and public figures associated with the growing American conservative movement in an effort to generate interest in the center's proposed "Encyclopedia of Americana." Recipients of the letters included such important figures as William F. Buckley Jr., Frank Meyer, Howard E. Kershner, Victor Milione, Carl F. H. Henry, William J. Baroody, Cleanth Brooks, and Aaron Director. The various letters are available in folders 137 and 139, WTC.

147. I. R. Bierly to R. J. Rushdoony and David L. Hoggan, September 30, 1963, RJR. Bierly closed the note by further asserting his control over Rushdoony and Hoggan: "I would appreciate it personally very much if each of you would make a point of stopping in to visit with me each time you stop in the Library here—or at least frequently, as I do want to keep in contact closely with you."

148. I. R. Bierly to R. J. Rushdoony, December 20, 1963, RJR.

149. "Center for American Studies: Grants Made during the Year: FY Ending 6-30-64," 1, CAS.

150. Ibid. and "Volker Fund, The William—Supplement," April 29, 1968, 11, WVF. For Pat McCarran Sr.'s biography, see Edwards, *Pat McCarran*; and Ybarra, *Washington Gone Crazy*.

151. See Simonelli, *American Fuehrer*; and Dawidowicz, "Lies about the Holocaust." Because of Hoggan's connections with neo-Nazi groups in West Germany, the FBI and CIA tracked his activities. Before his death in 1988, Hoggan struggled with alcohol abuse and had several brushes with law enforcement. In one notably tragic case, Hoggan, in a drunken rage, nearly beat his wife to death with a portable television set. "Historian Jailed as Wife Beater," *The Times* (San Mateo), December 11, 1969, 26.

152. McVicar, "Aggressive Philanthropy."

Chapter 3

1. R. J. Rushdoony to Gary North, January 9, 1964, RJR.

2. Larson, "Oral History Interview," 52, RJR.

3. M. Rushdoony, "Books, My Father's Treasure," *CR* 439 (March 2002): 9.

4. Ibid.

5. Potter, "The Man from Owyhee," *CR* 429 (April 2001): 24.

6. M. Rushdoony, "Books, My Father's Treasure."

7. Ibid., 10.

8. Rushdoony, *Newsletter* 2 (October 1965).

9. These details about North's exposure to Rushdoony's book are from Gary North, e-mail to the author, December 10, 2008.

10. Society of Former Special Agents of the FBI, "Samuel W. North, Jr.," 185.

11. Gary North, "It All Began with Fred Schwarz." Interestingly, while serving in the bureau's L.A. office, Samuel North was an investigator who worked on the Martin Luther King Jr. assassination case. Society of Former Special Agents of the FBI, "Samuel W. North, Jr.," 185. Gary North recalled that his father "was one of the four Los Angeles FBI agents who discovered evidence that identified James Earl Ray as King's assassin." North, "It All Began with Fred Schwarz."

12. North and DeMar, *Christian Reconstruction*, ix. North appears to have written Rushdoony for the first time in March of 1962. Although I could not find a copy of North's original letter, Rushdoony's response, dated March 16, 1962, RJR, indicates that North wrote to Rushdoony to inquire about the latter's effort to reconcile Christian principles with libertarian economic theory.

13. North, "It All Began with Fred Schwarz."

14. "ISI Summer Schools, 1962," 4, ISI.

15. North, "It All Began with Fred Schwarz."

16. North had contacted Baldy Harper in 1961 when the CAS was still formally organized as the Volker Fund, but he was not officially hired until the fund was restructured into the CAS and I. R. Bierly had replaced Harper as the head of the organization. Gary North, e-mail to the author, March 17, 2007.

17. North, "It All Began with Fred Schwarz."

18. First, North noted, "I am a conservative. I would also regard myself as a fundamentalist, in that I hold to the traditional orthodox view of Jesus Christ as divine and Lord of the World."

Gary North to Thomas Braden, November 9, 1963, RJR. Second, in terms of dispensational-ism, he noted, "Too bad I'm not a post-millennialist." Gary North to R. J. Rushdoony, March 12, 1964, RJR.

19. Gary North to R. J. Rushdoony, July 23, 1964, RJR. Stefan T. Possony was an influential midcentury conservative intellectual, economist, and military strategist who worked at the Hoover Institution and later helped conceptualize the Strategic Defense Initiative, or so-called Stars Wars program, of the 1980s.

20. McGirr, *Suburban Warriors*; and Nickerson, *Mothers of Conservatism*.

21. McGirr, *Suburban Warriors*, 6–7.

22. Nickerson, "Moral Mothers and Goldwater Girls," 60.

23. Ibid., 58.

24. Ibid., 59.

25. Ibid., 58.

26. Nickerson, *Mothers of Conservatism*, 2. This feminine do-it-yourself aesthetic in educa-tion correlated to the masculine do-it-yourself projects related to home preparedness and security in the age of the bomb shelter; see Lichtman, "Do-It-Yourself Security."

27. Schoenwald, "We Are an Action Group," 28.

28. Nickerson, "Moral Mothers and Goldwater Girls," 59–60.

29. Nickerson, *Mothers of Conservatism*, 2.

30. McGirr, *Suburban Warriors*, 232–35; and Spruill, "Gender and America's Right Turn."

31. Nickerson, "Women, Domesticity, and Postwar Conservatism," 20.

32. Nickerson, "Domestic Threats," 283.

33. Quoted in ibid.

34. Rushdoony, *The Foundations of Social Order*.

35. Ibid.

36. Ibid., 54.

37. Ibid.

38. Ibid., 53.

39. Ibid., 56.

40. Ibid.

41. Worthen, "Chalcedon Problem," 407.

42. Ibid., 408.

43. Rushdoony, *The Foundations of Social Order*, 2.

44. Twelve Southerners, *I'll Take My Stand*, xv.

45. Kirk, *Conservative Mind*, 7–8, 414–15.

46. Weaver, *Ideas Have Consequences*, 29–31.

47. Dochuk, *From Bible Belt to Sun Belt*, 66–76; Moreton, *To Serve God and Wal-Mart*, 49–66.

48. Rose, *Powers of Freedom*, 65.

49. Quoted in Schoenwald, "We Are an Action Group," 31.

50. This point has been made by a number of scholars. See, for example, McGirr, *Suburban Warriors*, 225–37; and Nickerson, *Mothers of Conservatism*, 167–68.

51. Kintz, *Between Jesus and the Market*.

52. On the anthropological concept of "nurturance," see Collier et al., "Is there a Family?"; and Ginsburg, *Contested Lives*.

53. Taves, "Sexuality in American Religious History," 41.

54. Lassiter, "Inventing Family Values," 13–28.

55. May, *Homeward Bound*, ix.

56. Ibid., xii–xvi, 14–15, 137.

57. Self, *All in the Family*, 19.

58. Cohen, "Is There an Urban History of Consumption?," 92.

59. O'Mara, "Uncovering the City in the Suburb," 60–67.

60. McGirr, *Suburban Warriors*, 39.

61. Dochuk, *From Bible Belt to Sun Belt*, 20.

62. Lipsitz, *Possessive Investment in Whiteness*, 6; Cohen, "Is There an Urban History of Consumption?," 93–94.

63. Federal investment had this effect across the Sunbelt, but the spending "that poured into California created the nation's largest urban military-industrial complex" (McGirr, *Suburban Warriors*, 26).

64. Hise, *Magnetic Los Angeles*, 126–37.

65. May, *Homeward Bound*; Self, *All in the Family*.

66. McGirr, *Suburban Warriors*, 40–42; Nickerson, *Mothers of Conservatism*, 37–50.

67. See McGirr, *Suburban Warriors*, chapter 3.

68. As noted, the JBS served "as a kind of matchmaker, where lone individuals with broad visions could join each other and help turn an ideology into a movement" (Schoenwald, *A Time for Choosing*, 63).

69. Diamond, *Roads to Dominion*, 53.

70. John Birch Society, *Blue Book*, vii.

71. Ibid., 22.

72. Ibid., 26.

73. Ibid., 26–27.

74. See Fenster's suggestion that conspiracy theories function as a form of "hyperactive semiosis" in *Conspiracy Theories*, xvii and chapter 4.

75. R. J. Rushdoony to Robert Welch, January 4, 1966, RJR.

76. Rushdoony, "Public Schools," 81–94; and Scott Stanley Jr., to R. J. Rushdoony, February, 21, 1966, RJR. *American Opinion* paid Rushdoony $175 for another article on the school prayer amendment in response to the Supreme Court's rulings in *Engel v. Vitale* (1962) and *Abington School District v. Schempp* (1963); Margot Shields to R. J. Rushdoony, December 15, 1966, RJR.

77. Marian P. Welch to R. J. Rushdoony, February 28, 1966, RJR, indicated that JBS staffers were reading Rushdoony's *The Religion of Revolution* (1965), a pamphlet that was circulating widely among those on the right in the 1960s.

78. Marian P. Welch to R. J. Rushdoony, February 28, 1966, RJR.

79. See "Dues Schedule," available in John Birch Society, *Blue Book*.

80. Rushdoony paid his dues on April 14, 1966. Carole J. McKinney to R. J. Rushdoony, April 20, 1966, RJR; and Mary White to R. J. Rushdoony, May 18, 1966, RJR.

81. Rushdoony, *Nature of the American System*, 140.

82. Ibid.

83. Ibid., 156.

84. R. J. Rushdoony to Marius and Marguerite, January 25, 1965, RJR.

85. Ibid.

86. R. J. Rushdoony to J. Vard Loomis, December 5, 1965, RJR. Rushdoony authored this letter *before* he paid the home chapter fees and became an unofficial member of the JBS, but one is left to consider how honest this assertion is given the strong ties Rushdoony cultivated with the society.

87. Worthen, "Chalcedon Problem," 403.

88. R. J. Rushdoony to Marius and Marguerite, January 25, 1965, RJR.

89. Gaston, Keltner, and Adair Attorneys at Law to Los Angeles County Clerk, April 20, 1965; and U.S. Treasury Department, Internal Revenue Service to Chalcedon, Inc., May 18, 1965, RJR.

90. Gaston, Keltner, and Adair Attorneys at Law to Chief of the Audit Division of Los Angeles County, September 12, 1965, RJR.

91. R. J. Rushdoony draft of a letter to H. J. Grant, n.d. [drafted in response to Gaston, Keltner, and Adair Attorneys at Law to R. J. Rushdoony, September 14, 1965], RJR.

92. Ibid.

93. Ibid.

94. Ibid.

95. Dochuk, *From Bible Belt to Sun Belt*, 54.

96. Ibid., 55; see also Moreton, *To Serve God and Wal-Mart*, 145–72.

97. Swartz, *Moral Minority*, 15.

98. Larson, "Oral History Interview," 52. Walter Knott's association with right-wing politics and fundamentalist religion is well documented; see Hosier, *Walter Knott*; McGirr, *Suburban Warriors*, 98–146; and Dochuk, *From Bible Belt to Sun Belt*, 175–206.

99. Rushdoony, *Newsletter* 9 (June 1966): 2; and Rushdoony, *Newsletter* 7 (December 1965): 3.

100. Larson, "Oral History Interview," 52, RJR.

101. M. Rushdoony, "My Recollection of Chalcedon's First Forty Years," *FFAOL* (September/October 2005): 4.

102. Rushdoony, *Newsletter* 1 (October 1965): 1.

103. Ibid., 2.

104. Ibid.

105. Ibid.; emphasis in the original.

106. Rushdoony, *Newsletter* 2 (October 1965): 1.

107. Ibid.

108. M. Rushdoony, "My Recollection of Chalcedon's First Forty Years," 30.

109. Rushdoony, *CR* 55 (March 1970): 1.

110. Ibid., 3.

111. Philips, "Dorothy Rushdoony, Chalcedon Matriarch, Dies."

112. M. Rushdoony, "My Recollection of Chalcedon's First Forty Years," 30.

113. Rushdoony wrote to Robert Welch that his largest audience was college students. He listed his second-largest audience as ministers. R. J. Rushdoony to Robert Welch, March 21, 1966, RJR.

114. This number is based on entries in Rushdoony's ledger and his year-end summaries of his speaking engagements in his *Newsletter* and the *Chalcedon Report*.

115. Illustrative titles include "This Christian Republic" (September 13, 1964); "Psalm 2: Conspiracy and History" (October 25, 1964); "Revolutionary Art" (April 10, 1967); and "The Soviet View of Money" (April 11, 1967).

116. Robert D. Norton to R. J. Rushdoony, March 12, 1965, RJR.

117. Forster and Epstein, *Danger on the Right*, 170.

118. R. J. Rushdoony to Robert D. Norton, March 30, 1965, RJR.

119. Robert D. Norton to R. J. Rushdoony, March 12, 1965, RJR.

120. Ibid.

121. Yuba County is located in north-central California about forty miles north of Sacramento.

122. Antonia Fiske to R. J. Rushdoony, February 27, 1965, RJR; Antonia Fiske to R. J. Rushdoony, March 23, 1965, RJR; and Antonia Fiske to R. J. Rushdoony, April 8, 1965, RJR.

123. Antonia Fiske to R. J. Rushdoony, April 8, 1965, RJR.

124. Rushdoony, *Newsletter* 4 (January 1966): 4.

125. Ibid.

126. Rushdoony, *Newsletter* 40 (December 1968); and Rushdoony, *CR* 44 (April 1969). Although the name of the publication changed, the numbering remained constant.

127. These numbers are drawn from Rushdoony, *Newsletter* nos. 4, 15, 29, and 41 (January 1966, December 1966, January 1968, and January 1996, respectively). The sum for his correspondence and books read does not include 1965.

128. See, respectively, Rushdoony *Newsletter* nos. 4, 6, 11, and 12 (January 1966, March 1966, August 1966, and September 1966).

129. Rushdoony, *Newsletter* 13 (October 1966): 1.

130. The pamphlet was originally distributed through Leonard Read's organization, the Pamphleteers. Read used the organization to publish libertarian-themed literature, which it cheaply distributed to a wide array of conservative audiences throughout Southern California. Notable works brought to press by the Pamphleteers, Inc., included the first U.S. edition of Ayn Rand's *Anthem*, Rose Wilder Lane's *Give Me Liberty!*, and a translation of Frederic Bastiat's *The Law*.

131. Rushdoony, *Preparation for the Future*, 22.

132. The August 1965 Watts Riots obviously motivated Rushdoony to write *Preparation for the Future*, although he does not directly reference the uprising in the text. Rushdoony moved his family to Woodland Hills about a week after the riots. It is impossible to conceive that the event did not weigh heavily on his mind as he moved to a city poised so precariously on the edge of racial and political chaos.

133. Ibid., 22.

134. Ibid., 23.

Chapter 4

1. Rushdoony, *Newsletter* 20 (May 1, 1967): 2.

2. Ibid.

3. Self, *All in the Family*.

4. Johnson, "President Lyndon B. Johnson's Remarks at the University of Michigan."

5. Flamm, *Law and Order*, 6.

6. Gill, *Embattled Ecumenism*, 65–66, 216–17, 297–302.

7. Ibid., 193.

8. "Law and Order, 1966."

9. Ibid.

10. Ibid.

11. Miller, *Billy Graham and the Rise of the Republican South*, 129.

12. Ibid.

13. Rushdoony, *Newsletter* 23 (August 1967): 3.

14. This section follows John R. Stone's suggestion that the twentieth-century evangelical movement should be seen as a shifting "collection of changing constituencies," a coalition of allies drawn together in the impermanent flux of theological positions, institutional organizations, emotional sentiments, and individual constituents. See Stone, *On the Boundaries of American Evangelicalism*, 7.

15. Martin, *With God on Our Side*, 42.

16. Marsden, *Reforming Fundamentalism*, 158.

17. "Volker Fund, The William," report dated November 12, 1963, 3, 8, WVF; Board, "Moving the World with Magazines," 141 (n. 37); and Shipps, "Christianity Today," 171–72;

18. Board, "Moving the World with Magazines," 130.

19. Dochuk, *From Bible Belt to Sun Belt*, 118.

20. Martin, *With God on Our Side*, 40.

21. Ibid.

22. Swartz, *Moral Minority*, 22.

23. Ibid., 18.

24. Henry, *The Uneasy Conscience of Modern Fundamentalism*, 2–3.

25. These two phrases are normally used interchangeably and appear to have been coined by Harold John Ockenga during an address in the late 1940s. See Marsden, *Reforming Fundamentalism*, 146; and Dorrien, *The Remaking of Evangelical Theology*, 56.

26. Dorrien, *The Remaking of Evangelical Theology*, 56.

27. Ibid., 55.

28. On the latter point, see Coffman, *Christian Century*, 182–216.

29. Board, "Moving the World with Magazines," 131. Board noted that many critics believe that after Henry's departure as editor, the magazine ceased speaking for evangelicals in Washington and instead began to simply "speak to" evangelicals when it began publishing across the street from NAE headquarters. Board disputed this interpretation of the magazine's history, but he indicates that some critics of the magazine believe it.

30. Ibid., 130.

31. Henry, *Confessions of a Theologian*, 147.

32. Ibid., 167.

33. J. Marcellus Kik to Rousas J. Rushdoony, February 7, 1956, RJR.

34. R. J. Rushdoony to J. Marcellus Kik, February, 25, 1959, RJR.

35. On the journal's intended audience, see Shipps, "Christianity Today," 171; and Henry, *Confessions of a Theologian*, 144.

36. R. J. Rushdoony, "Do-It-Yourself Religion," *CT*, November 11, 1957. Kik solicited other reviews from Rushdoony, but it is not clear how many Rushdoony wrote at Kik's request. J. Marcellus Kik to R. J. Rushdoony, May 20 1957, RJR.

37. R. J. Rushdoony, "Ecumenism and the Lord's Table," *CT*, September 30, 1957. As the title implies, the article is a critique of various ecumenical liturgical experiments that Rushdoony believed "obscure[d] the essential meaning of the sacrament" by placing too much emphasis on the supposed unity of humanity as a precondition for the power of the ritual (13).

38. William Young, "Apologetic," *CT*, November 23, 1959; and Robert D. Knudsen, "Current Mood of Our Century: Alienation," *CT*, October 13, 1961.

39. J. Marcellus Kik to R. J. Rushdoony, January 30, 1959, RJR.

40. Virginia Ramey Mollenkott, "A Biblical Approach to Modern Literature," *CT*, February 16, 1959.

41. R. J. Rushdoony to J. Marcellus Kik, February 25, 1959, RJR.

42. Ibid.

43. J. Marcellus Kik to R. J. Rushdoony, March 12, 1959, RJR.

44. Henry, *Confessions of a Theologian*, 147.

45. Hendershot, *What's Fair on the Air*, 105.

46. R. J. Rushdoony to L. Nelson Bell, October 30, 1961, RJR.

47. Ibid.

48. R. J. Rushdoony to C. Gregg Singer, September 28, 1965, folder 24, CGS.

49. Ibid.

50. Dochuk, "Blessed by Oil, Cursed with Crude," 60–61.

51. Ibid. See also Phillips-Fein, *Invisible Hands*, 70–77; and Lichtman, *White Protestant Nation*, 173–74, 215–16.

52. Toy, "National Lay Committee and the National Council of Churches," 196.

53. Phillips-Fein, *Invisible Hands*, 70–77.

54. Lichtman, *White Protestant Nation*, 194.

55. Pew was on the editorial board of the John Birch Society magazine *American Opinion*. See Berlet, "Von Mises Rises from the Scrap Heap of History." Also, according to Charles H. Craig to R. J. Rushdoony, October 4, 1965, RJR, Pew was an active member in the JBS.

56. Howard E. Kershner to J. Howard Pew, January 26, 1966, JHP.

57. J. Howard Pew to R. J. Rushdoony, November 26, 1965, JHP.

58. R. J. Rushdoony to J. Howard Pew, December 2, 1965, RJR.

59. Undated letter from C. Gregg Singer to J. Howard Pew, CGS.

60. R. J. Rushdoony journal entry for February 14, 1966, RJR.

61. J. Howard Pew to Howard E. Kershner, January 24, 1966, JHP.

62. Phillips-Fein, *Invisible Hands*, 77.

63. See Henry, *Confessions of a Theologian*, 162.

64. Bell used all manner of dissimulation to hide from Henry that Pew or his surrogate, Howard Kershner, secretly reviewed editions of the journal. Henry, *Confessions of a Theologian*, 160–62.

65. R. J. Rushdoony, "The Mediator: Christ or the Church?," 1; and R. J. Rushdoony, "The Witness of Jesus Christ," 4, JHP.

66. J. Howard Pew to R. J. Rushdoony, March 3, 1966, RJR.

67. J. Howard Pew to Dr. L. Nelson Bell, March 3, 1966, JHP.

68. R. J. Rushdoony to C. Gregg Singer, March 15, 1966, CGS.

69. R. J. Rushdoony, "The Mediator: Christ or the Church?," 2; Rushdoony, "The Witness of the Apostles," 3, JHP.

70. Ibid.

71. Carl F. H. Henry to R. J. Rushdoony, April 5, 1966, RJR.

72. Ibid.

73. Ibid.

74. R. J. Rushdoony to Dr. Carl F. Henry, April 19, 1966, RJR.

75. Carl F. H. Henry to R. J. Rushdoony, April 26, 1966, BGC.

76. R. J. Rushdoony to J. Howard Pew, April 19, 1966, RJR.

77. Gary North, e-mail to author, March 17, 2007.

78. Shipps, "Christianity Today," 174–75.

79. Rushdoony, "The Mediator: Christ or the Church?," 2, JHP.

80. Ibid., 6.

81. Miller, *Billy Graham and the Rise of the Republican South*, 44.

82. Ibid., 45.

83. See, for instance, chapter 2 of Henry, *Uneasy Conscience of Modern Fundamentalism*.

84. Swartz, *Moral Minority*, 21.

85. Miller, *Billy Graham and the Rise of the Republican South*, 49.

86. Ibid.

87. Goldwater, "Extremism in the Defense of Liberty," 33.

88. Flamm, *Law and Order*, 1–2.

89. Larson, "Oral History Interview," 44, RJR.

90. Here, Rushdoony developed the idea that men are God's vicegerents on earth who must "seek . . . first the kingdom of God." This, according to Rushdoony, could happen only as men disciplined themselves to the commandments of Scripture. Rushdoony, *By What Standard?*, 89–90.

91. Rushdoony, *Intellectual Schizophrenia*, 100.

92. Rushdoony, *Nature of the American System*, 6; emphasis in the original.

93. Rushdoony, *This Independent Republic*, 10; emphasis in the original.

94. Ibid., 15–16; and Rushdoony, *Nature of the American System*, 10. On conservative intellectuals' hostility to democracy, see Nash, *Conservative Intellectual Movement*, 49–56, 206–18.

95. Rushdoony, *This Independent Republic*, 84, 96, 135–40.

96. Ibid., 84.

97. Rushdoony, *Christianity and the State*, 11.

98. M. Rushdoony, "My Recollection of Chalcedon's First Forty Years," 5.

99. R. J. Rushdoony, *CR* 58 (June 1970): 2.

100. R. J. Rushdoony, *Newsletter* 20 (May 1967): 3.

101. R. J. Rushdoony, *CR* 69 (May 1971): 1.

102. North and DeMar, *Christian Reconstruction*, xi–xii.

103. Gary North, e-mail to author, December 10, 2008.

104. RJR ledgers, January 30, 1969, RJR.

105. R. J. Rushdoony to Gary North, March 17, 1981, RJR.

106. This suggests that Rushdoony wrote the body of the *Institutes* in less than three years. Year-end summary for 1970 in his journals, RJR.

107. Rushdoony, *Institutes of Biblical Law*, 1:60. This section treats the entire three volumes of the *Institutes* and several related publications, such as *Salvation and Godly Rule*, as representing a coherent vision of biblical law.

108. Ibid.

109. Ibid. "All known religious beliefs . . . present a common quality: they presuppose the classification of things . . . into two classes" of the sacred and profane. Durkheim, *Elementary Forms of Religious Life*, 36.

110. Rushdoony wrote at some length on the clothing requirements outlined in biblical law. He argued that specific garment restrictions had been superseded by Christ's new covenant, but the symbols remained relevant for Christians. See Rushdoony, *Institutes of Biblical Law*, 1:22–23. In one of his more dizzying passages, Rushdoony discussed biblical restrictions against mixing linen and wool in garment weaving (Deuteronomy 22:11). He connected the restriction to biblical prohibitions against the "unequal yoking" of an ass and ox to plow fields (Deuteronomy 22:11) with marriage prohibitions discussed by Saint Paul (2 Corinthians 6:14). He then moved on to a wide-ranging discussion of hybridization in modern genetic science; condemned homosexuality and bestiality; warned against interracial and intercultural marriages; and criticized "man's rash interference with the balance of nature" through the use of DDT. Rushdoony, *Institutes of Biblical Law*, 1:253–256.

111. On Ann Landers, see Rushdoony, *Institutes of Biblical Law*, 1:295, 419, 426, and 483.

112. Exodus 20:13–14 (KJV). See, respectively, Rushdoony, *Institutes of Biblical Law*, 1:219–332 and 1:333–447.

113. Exodus 20:16 (KJV). This chapter on bearing false witness is one of the most controversial in the *Institutes*. In one section, Rushdoony argued that witnesses had exaggerated the numbers of Jews and other minorities killed by the Nazis during World War II. He suggested that such charges amounted to a violation of the ninth commandment (Rushdoony, *Institutes of Biblical Law*, 1:586). In the passage, Rushdoony suggested that, at most, thousands of Jews died and German scientists tortured only tens, or perhaps hundreds, of victims. His argument has roundly been condemned as a form of Holocaust denial. See, for example, Trueman, *Histories and Fallacies*, 30 (n. 4). Rushdoony's historical analysis was based on "atrocious, secondhand, and unverified" sources (ibid.), which were likely rooted in his personal relationship with David L. Hoggan. During the late 1960s, Rushdoony actively lobbied for the publication of Hoggan's anonymous *Myth of the Six Million* (1973), one of the first works of Holocaust denial published in the United States. Rushdoony appealed directly to Hays Craig, his friend and publisher at Presbyterian and Reformed Publishing Company and the Craig Press. Charles H. Craig to R. J. Rushdoony, n.d., RJR. The Craig Press did publish Hoggan's *The Myth of the "New History"* (1965), a critical assault on historiographic methods that Hoggan believed vilified Germany and wrongly blamed the Reich for World War II. While controversial, the book was largely ignored by the historical establishment. Craig was far less responsive to the manuscript that eventually became *Myth of the Six Million*. Craig rejected the manuscript, citing a mass of contradictory evidence. Years later, Rushdoony backtracked from his support of Hoggan's work. R. J. Rushdoony to "Wayne," November 14, 1992, RJR. He also wrote that he never intended to enter a "debate over numbers" but only meant to insist "that in all such matters what the ninth commandment requires is the truth, not exaggeration, irrespective of the cause one seeks to serve." Rushdoony, "Exaggeration and Denial," *CR* 422 (September 2000): 2.

114. "The commandment is very clear: we are not too bear false witness against our neighbor but this does not mean that our neighbor is ever entitled to the truth from us, or any word from us about matters of no concern to them, or of [a] private nature to us. No enemy or criminal has any right to knowledge from us which can be used to do us evil. Scripture does not condemn Abraham and Isaac for lying in order to avoid rape and murder." Rushdoony, *Institutes of Biblical Law*, 1:543. This passage has led critics to charge that Reconstructionism amounts to a "stealth theology" that encourages its followers to lie about their actions and wage secret cam-

paigns to take over American political institutions. See Clarkson, "Christian Reconstruction"; Miller, *Cruel and Unusual*, 279; and Urban, *Secrets of the Kingdom*, 40.

115. Rushdoony, *Institutes of Biblical Law*, 1:544; 566–67; see also Rushdoony, *Roots of Reconstruction*, 302–6.

116. Rushdoony, *Institutes of Biblical Law*, 1:77 and 1:235. He listed eighteen crimes, but one, violating the Sabbath, was superseded by Jesus.

117. Exodus 20:3 (KJV).

118. Rushdoony, *Institutes of Biblical Law*, 1:227.

119. Ibid.

120. Ibid.

121. Genesis 1:26–28 (KJV).

122. Rushdoony, *Institutes of Biblical Law*, 1:14.

123. Balmer and Fitzmier, *Presbyterians*, 5–6; and Holifield, *Theology in America*, 39.

124. Holifield, *Theology in America*, 39–40.

125. Ibid.

126. Reformed divines, especially in the *Westminster Confession of Faith*, distinguished between the ceremonial, judicial, and moral aspects of biblical law. Traditionally, Christians have seen Jesus's sacrifice as annulling the ceremonial laws associated with the ancient YHWH cult of the Hebrews. Further, with the end of the theocracy of the ancient Jewish kings, Christians generally hold that the judicial aspects of the law no longer apply to modern civil governments. What remains is the moral spirit of the law to govern individual action and religious obligation. Rushdoony rejected this parsing of the law, arguing: "In what respect is 'Thou shalt not steal' valid as moral law, and not valid as civil or judicial law? If we insist on this distinction, we are saying that the state is free to steal, and is beyond law, whereas the individual is under the law." Rushdoony, *Institutes of Biblical Law*, 1:551. Rushdoony therefore recognized some aspects of the traditional rejection of ceremonial law related to temple rites (although he personally followed Jewish dietary laws throughout his life), but he insisted that the civil and moral law of the Old Testament were inseparable.

127. Rushdoony, "Dominion Man."

128. Rushdoony, *Newsletter* 1 (October 1965): 1; emphasis in the original.

129. Rushdoony, *Institutes of Biblical Law*, 1:240. For a strikingly similar line of argument, see Foucault, *Security, Territory, Population*, 122.

130. See Harris, *Fundamentalism and Evangelicals*, 234–42; and Skillen and McCarthy, "Sphere Sovereignty," 397–418.

131. Rushdoony, *Messianic Character of American Education*, 219.

132. Rushdoony, *Revolt against Maturity*, 17.

133. Ibid., 17–18.

134. Rushdoony, *Institutes of Biblical Law*, 1:341.

135. Rushdoony, *Salvation and Godly Rule*, 604.

136. Ibid., 338.

137. Ibid.

138. Ibid., 345.

139. Ibid., 605.

140. Ibid., 604.

141. Rushdoony, *Institutes of Biblical Law*, 1:345.

142. Ibid., 2:131; and Rushdoony, *Salvation and Godly Rule*, 607.

143. Rushdoony, *Institutes of Biblical Law*, 2:131.

144. Ibid., 1:357.

145. Rushdoony, *Salvation and Godly Rule*, 606.

146. See, respectively, Graziano, *Millennial New World*, 22–31, and Boyer, *When Time Shall Be No More*, 68–75.

147. Graziano, *Millennial New World*, 22.

148. For a concise summary of this consensus, see Balmer, *Making of Evangelicalism*, 27–42.

149. Boyer, *When Time Shall Be No More*, 80.

150. Marsden, *Fundamentalism and American Culture*, 49.

151. Ibid.

152. Balmer, *Blessed Assurance*, 50–51.

153. Balmer, *Making of Evangelicalism*, 36.

154. Hendriksen, *More than Conquerors*, 14.

155. Ibid.

156. Rushdoony's son Mark noted, "My father's eschatology . . . crystallized by the mid-1950s. He had very early studied premillennialism as it was widely espoused, but was horrified at what he thought resembled fantastic fairy-tale exegesis. He then turned to amillennial writers but never felt comfortable with that position, either. . . . He . . . considered himself a postmillennialist after reading Roderick Campbell's *Israel and the New Covenant*." M. Rushdoony, "Biographical Sketch of My Father," 26.

157. Campbell, *Israel and the New Covenant*, 297.

158. Ibid., 30.

159. Ibid., 298; emphasis in the original.

160. Rushdoony, "Introduction," in Kik, *An Eschatology of Victory*, viii–ix; emphasis in the original. Rushdoony edited this significant text by Kik, which reprinted Kik's *Matthew Twenty-Four: An Exposition* (1948), a postmillennial interpretation of Jesus's prophetic statements recorded in the Gospel of Matthew. Kik's *Matthew Twenty-Four* influenced Campbell. See Campbell, *Israel and the New Covenant*, 78 (n. 10).

161. Rushdoony, *Institutes of Biblical Law*, 3:110.

162. Ibid.

163. Ibid.

164. Kuyper, *Lectures on Calvinism*, 78–81.

165. Ibid., 80.

166. Rushdoony, *Institutes of Biblical Law*, 1:357.

167. Matthew 6:33 (KJV).

168. Rushdoony, *Institutes of Biblical Law*, 1:444. Rushdoony draws the phrases "terminal truths" and "death of man philosophy" from Foucault, *Madness and Civilization*, ix.

169. Rushdoony, *Salvation and Godly Rule*, 606.

170. On "counter governance," see Foucault's discussion of "revolts of conduct" and "counter-conducts" in *Security, Territory, Population*, 191–226.

171. Worthen, *Apostles of Reason*, 207; and Shires, *Hippies of the Religious Right*, 165.

172. Lindsey seems to have borrowed the image from J. Vernon McGee's *Thru the Bible* series.

173. Turner, *Bill Bright*, 131; Stowe, *No Sympathy for the Devil*, 69; and Shires, *Hippies of the Religious Right*, 153–54.

174. John Dart, "Youthful Evangelists Make Impact on American Religious, Social Scene," *Sarasota Herald-Tribune*, July 21, 1971, B3.

175. Isserman and Kazin, *America Divided*, 246; and Eskridge, *God's Forever Family*, 76–77.

176. Whitehead, *Slaying Dragons*, 143.

177. Direct quotations from this exchange appear in Whitehead, *Slaying Dragons*, 145; italicized questions paraphrase the same text.

178. On the Right, see Williams, *God's Own Party*; on the Left, see Swartz, *Moral Minority*.

179. The phrase "Christian anti-liberalism" is from Bivens, *Fracture of Good Order*.

Chapter 5

1. Harold O. J. Brown, "Theology, Apologetics, Ethics," *CT*, March 1, 1974, 70.

2. Gaston, Keltner, and Adair Attorneys at Law to R. J. Rushdoony, September 14, 1965, RJR.

3. Draft answers to H. J. Grant of the Internal Revenue Service, n.d. [ca. August 1965], RJR.

4. Ibid.; emphasis in the original.

5. Watson, "Theonomy," 16.

6. Ibid., 23.

7. Smith, "His Truth Is Marching On."

8. Howell Raines, "Reagan Backs Evangelicals In Their Political Activities." *New York Times*, August 23, 1980, 8; Martin, *With God on Our Side*, 217; and Lichtman, *White Protestant Nation*, 344.

9. North, "The Intellectual Schizophrenia of the New Christian Right," 12.

10. Balmer, "Rove of the Religious Right, a Eulogy."

11. Crespino, "Civil Rights and the Religious Right," 105.

12. Ibid.

13. R. J. Rushdoony journal entry for January 18, 1982, RJR.

14. R. J. Rushdoony journal entry for January 26, 1982, RJR.

15. Ibid.

16. Ibid.

17. Ibid.

18. These rulings, in turn, relied on the court's logic in *Cantwell v. Connecticut* (1940) and *Everson v. Board of Education* (1947).

19. Board of School Commissioners of Baltimore City rule cited in *School District of Abington Township, Pennsylvania v. Schempp*, 374 U.S. 203 (1963).

20. Balmer, "Religion in Twentieth-Century America," 398.

21. For the relationship between the *Green* ruling and other important rulings and how they prompted varied Christian legal responses, see Martin, *With God on Our Side*, 168–73; and Moore, *Suing for America's Soul*, 24–33. Balmer developed his racialized argument to challenge the typical narrative that evangelicals created a political infrastructure to respond to *Roe v. Wade*. His suggestion that *Green* prompted the emergence of the Religious Right suggests that the movement's motivation was not to save unborn babies but to discriminate against African Americans. He based this assessment on comments regarding the *Green* case made by

Paul Weyrich in a meeting of conservatives in the 1990s. This anecdote is fully recounted in Balmer, *Thy Kingdom Come*, 13–14. Balmer's argument is intriguing, and its implications are, as historian Milton Gaither has noted, "deliciously scandalous" but not entirely convincing (*Homeschool*, 112). The racial implications behind *Green* were, it is true, the motivation of *some* evangelicals to enter politics; the larger legal context, however, cannot be reduced to *Green* no matter what Weyrich may have boasted.

22. Gaither, *Homeschool*, 111.

23. See Mason, *Reading Appalachia from Left to Right*.

24. Martin, *With God on Our Side*, 139.

25. Teles, *Rise of the Conservative Legal Movement*, 22–57.

26. Ibid., 221.

27. Beginning in the 1970s, Christian Reconstruction and theonomy emerged as an infrequent topic in theses and dissertations produced at seminaries and Christian colleges across the United States. The vast bulk of this material was produced in Baptist and Reformed affiliated institutions. Watson, "Theonomy," exemplifies much of the research done during the 1970s and 1980s. Following the publication of Rodney Clapp, "Democracy as Heresy," *CT*, February 20, 1987, interest in Reconstructionism exploded (the significance of Clapp's article is addressed in chapter 6). ProQuest Dissertations and Theses indexing indicates no less than thirty theses defended from 1988–2000 citing Rushdoony, Bahnsen, and other Reconstructionist texts. Some of these documents only make passing citations to Reconstructionist work, but many display careful engagement with Reconstructionism. Exemplary titles include Weyl, "Patriotic Pastors" (1989); Abbott, "A Critical Analysis of the Meaning of the Kingdom of God in the Theology of the Christian Reconstruction Movement" (1990); Hatfield, "Critiques of the Major Tenets of Christian Reconstructionism" (1991); Burgin, "The Use of the Bible in the Christian Reconstruction Movement" (1993); Cunningham "Theonomy" (1996); and McCune "An Evaluation of Theonomic Assertions Respecting Matthew 5" (1997).

28. For law-journal articles citing Rushdoony and his legal influence, see Whitehead and Conlan, "Establishment of the Religion of Secular Humanism"; Smolin, "State Regulation of Private Education"; Ingber, "Religion or Ideology"; and Backer, "Theocratic Constitutionalism."

29. "Who's Who on the Right," 60.

30. North, "Concept of Property in Puritan New England, 1630–1720."

31. Robert A. Nisbet to the Chairman of Chalcedon, Inc., February 16, 1967, RJR. Nisbet later served on North's Ph.D. dissertation committee.

32. Edwin S. Gaustad to the Chairman of Chalcedon, Inc., March 1, 1967, RJR. Gaustad later chaired North's Ph.D. dissertation committee.

33. Warren I. Cohen to the Chairman of Chalcedon, Inc., February 27, 1967, RJR.

34. Ibid.

35. North began irregular contributions to *The Freeman* in the late 1960s and by 1970 was a fixture in the publication. His articles were aimed at the libertarian readers of the magazine but contained indications of his theological presuppositions. His numerous contributions included analyses of Marx's theory of labor ("Marx's View of the Division of Labor"), critiques of the state's intervention in individual economic failure ("Statist Bureaucracy in the Modern Economy"), and critical assessments of the economic implications of feminism ("The Feminist Mistake: The Economics of Women's Liberation"). On occasion, North produced articles that clearly revealed a heavy reliance on Rushdoony's theological project, such as "The Theology

of the Exponential Curve." He later edited and compiled the early years of his *Freeman* articles into the single volume *An Introduction to Christian Economics*.

36. Gary North to R. J. Rushdoony, October 28, 1971, RJR.

37. Ibid.

38. Ibid.

39. R. J. Rushdoony journal entry for October 25, 1971, RJR.

40. Gary North to R. J. Rushdoony, October 28, 1971, RJR.

41. Ibid.

42. Ibid.

43. Ibid.

44. North, "Confessions of a Washington Reject," *JCR* (Summer 1978): 76.

45. North, "John W. Robbins, R.I.P." Ron Paul apparently subscribed to North's *Remnant Review* before he hired him, but it is unclear what he knew about North's political and religious commitments beyond his libertarian economic views. For Paul's subscription, see North, "It All Began with Fred Schwarz."

46. North, "John W. Robbins, R.I.P."

47. Gary North, "Confessions of a Washington Reject."

48. Ibid., 85.

49. Ibid., 86.

50. North, "It All Began With Fred Schwarz."

51. Ibid.

52. Ibid. In an interview with a Tyler reporter, North indicated that the reasoning behind this decision was more complex than this quip suggests. "Tyler is one of the most important Christian centers in the United States," North told the reporter. "It's decentralized. It's not one group. Tyler is going to be the mobilization center for evangelism and the reconstruction movement over the next 20 years." Wayne Roper, "Support of Theology Influenced Gary North in Move to Tyler," *Tyler Courier-Times-Telegraph*, December 12, 1982, sec. 1, 8.

53. Gary North, ed., *Theology of Christian Resistance*, *C&C* (Winter 1983); and Gary North, ed., *Tactics of Christian Resistance*, *C&C* (Summer 1983).

54. Bahnsen, "Life of Dr. Greg L. Bahnsen," 9.

55. "Here and There in the Orthodox Presbyterian Church," *PG*, April 25, 1959, 127.

56. Bahnsen, "Life of Dr. Greg L. Bahnsen," 9; Watson, "Theonomy," 13.

57. As with Rushdoony's divorce, most of the information about Bahnsen's divorce comes from Bahnsen's perspective. According to Greg L. Bahnsen Jr., Cathie Wade repeatedly violated the "marriage covenant" and abandoned the family in 1989 despite his father's heroic attempts to salvage the marriage. Bahnsen, "Life of Dr. Greg L. Bahnsen," 21.

58. Ibid., 13.

59. Ibid.

60. Ibid.

61. "Chalcedon Scholars," *CR* 96 (August 1973): 3.

62. North's "An Economic Commentary on the Bible" series began in *CR* 94 (June 1973). Bahnsen's series commenced in *CR* 99 (November 1973).

63. R. J. Rushdoony to Greg [Bahnsen], September 20, 1978, RJR; James B. Jordan to the Faculty of Reformed Theological Seminary, Jackson, Mississippi, May 31, 1984, RJR.

64. Matthew 5:17 (KJV); Bahnsen, *Theonomy*, 39–86.

65. For Bahnsen's respective development of these themes, see Bahnsen, *Theonomy*, 62–81, 279–306, 1–38, 157–81.

66. Ibid., 149.

67. Bahnsen, "Foreword," xii.

68. R. J. Rushdoony to Dale B. Hartman II, September 5, 1978, RJR.

69. Ibid.

70. R. J. Rushdoony to Greg [Bahnsen], September 20, 1978, RJR.

71. Ibid.

72. Ibid.

73. James B. Jordan to the Faculty of Reformed Theological Seminary, Jackson, Mississippi, May 31, 1984, RJR.

74. Ibid.

75. Bahnsen, "Life of Dr. Greg L. Bahnsen," 18.

76. In the early 1990s, after declining enrollment and financial strain forced the closure of Newport Christian High School, Bahnsen accepted a position at the Southern California Center for Christian Studies. There, he did oversee graduate study of about 100 students (ibid., 24).

77. These numbers are drawn from a WorldCat survey, January 2014.

78. Randy Booth, telephone interview with the author, June 27, 2014.

79. This summary of Paul Hill's antiabortion activism is synthesized from Juergensmeyer, *Terror in the Mind of God*, 20–24; Ingersoll, *Building God's Kingdom*, chapter 10; North, *Lone Gunners for Jesus*; and "The Writings of Paul Jennings Hill."

80. Ingersoll, *Building God's Kingdom*, chapter 10.

81. For North's defense of Operation Rescue, see *Trespassing for Dear Life*. Rushdoony resigned from the Rutherford Institute's board in March 1989 after Whitehead wrote an editorial criticizing evangelicals who did not support Operation Rescue's civil disobedience tactics. Rushdoony argued that Whitehead's editorial suggested that "all who disagree with Operation Rescue" are "cowards who stand on the sidelines" of the contentious issue. "More than a few people who have been active in [the] pro-life [movement], and active in *lawful* demonstrations, are offended by this," Rushdoony explained. R. J. Rushdoony to John Whitehead and the Board of Trustees of the Rutherford Institute, March 24, 1989, RJR.

82. North, *Lone Gunners for Jesus*, 2, 3, 14.

83. See, for example, "The Great Debate"; "Dr. Gordon Stein (Atheist) vs. Dr. Greg Bahnsen (Jesus follower)"; and "MP3-Bahnsen," Covenant Media Foundation's extensive MP3 library of Bahnsen's lectures and debates.

84. Dissertations and theses containing significant engagement with Bahnsen's ideas include Lazor, "Convergence in Sexual Ethics?" (1983); Boa, "A Comparative Study of Four Christian Apologetic Systems" (1985); Child, "Biblical Law in the Theology of R. J. Rushdoony" (1985); Abbott, "A Critical Analysis of the Meaning of the Kingdom of God in the Theology of the Christian Reconstruction Movement" (1990); Gabbert, "An Historical Evaluation of Christian Reconstructionism" (1991); Hatfield, "Critiques of the Major Tenets of Christian Reconstructionism" (1991); Burgin, "The Use of the Bible in the Christian Reconstruction Movement" (1993); Cunningham, "Theonomy" (1996); Sullivan, "The Ethics of Obscenity/Pornography" (1996); McCune, "An Evaluation of Theonomic Assertions Respecting Matthew 5." (1997); and McConnel, "The Historical Origins of the Presuppositional Apologetics of Cornelius Van Til" (1999).

85. Frame, "Bahnsen at the Stein Debate."

86. Whitehead, *Slaying Dragons*, 110.

87. Ibid., 115–17; and Moore, *Suing for America's Soul*, 37.

88. Whitehead, *Slaying Dragons*, 119; emphasis in the original.

89. Ibid., 119–20.

90. Ibid., 146.

91. Ibid., 146; R. J. Rushdoony to Otto Scott, April 28, 1977, RJR. Rushdoony also made several references to Whitehead's visits in his personal journals. Whitehead recalled that he only visited Vallecito once. John W. Whitehead, interview with author, June 4, 2014.

92. Larson, "Oral History Interview," 70, RJR.

93. Many historians have documented this trend of the state absorbing functions traditionally maintained by the family. See, for example, Demos, *Little Commonwealth*, 183.

94. Rushdoony, *Institutes of Biblical Law*, 1:40.

95. Ibid., 1:185.

96. Gaither, *Homeschool*, 134–40.

97. Ibid., 4.

98. Most prominently, *Vision Forum* distributed Rushdoony's works until it closed in 2013 because of the sexual impropriety of its founder, Doug Phillips, whose father, Howard Phillips, was a Rushdoony disciple.

99. Journalist Jeff Sharlet has argued that these lectures, which reconceptualize Western history from a presuppositional Van Tillian perspective, may be Rushdoony's greatest legacy. See Sharlet, "Through a Glass, Darkly." See also "Unschooling," in Sharlet, *The Family*. Klein *From History to Theory*, 152, makes a similar point.

100. Gaither, *Homeschool*, 137.

101. R. J. Rushdoony to George Pearson, n.d., RJR.

102. Ibid.

103. See Grover, *Ohio's Trojan Horse*, for a conservative Christian perspective on the implications of *Ohio v. Whisner, et al.*

104. R. J. Rushdoony to Nelson Bunker Hunt, April 15, 1976, RJR.

105. R. J. Rushdoony journal entry for April 7, 1976, RJR.

106. See Rushdoony, "Introduction," in Grover, *Ohio's Trojan Horse*, xiii–xiv; and 41–55.

107. "Important Note," *CR* 133 (September 1976): 4; R. J. Rushdoony, "The New War of Religion," *CR* 149 (January 1978): 2; and R. J. Rushdoony, "We Are at War," *CR* 159 (November 1978): 2.

108. R. J. Rushdoony to Nelson Bunker Hunt, April 15, 1976, RJR.

109. This count is based on entries in Rushdoony's journals; it is likely he testified in more cases. He was indirectly involved in many more.

110. R. J. Rushdoony journal entry for April 12, 1983, RJR.

111. R. J. Rushdoony journal entry for February 4, 1983, RJR.

112. Ibid.

113. R. J. Rushdoony journal entry for February 22, 1983, RJR.

114. *State ex rel. Nagle v. Olin*, 64 Ohio St. 2d 341 1980. See also, Smolin, "State Regulation of Private Education," 1022.

115. *State ex rel. Nagle v. Olin.*

116. Ibid.

117. Ibid.

118. R. J. Rushdoony to Jim [James B. Jordan], March 12, 1981, RJR.

119. R. J. Rushdoony to Howard Ahmanson, September 8, 1980, RJR.

120. Ibid.

121. Ibid.

122. Ibid.

123. Worthen, *Apostles of Reason*, 210.

124. Duriez, *Francis Schaeffer*, 17.

125. Frank Schaeffer, *Crazy for God*, 314–20 and 330–35.

126. Ibid., 314.

127. Ibid., 335.

128. Martin, *With God on Our Side*, 239; and Williams, *God's Own Party*, 155.

129. See, for instance, Franky Schaeffer, *Time for Anger*, 205. Watson noted that in some of his other works, "Schaeffer did not give the credit to the theonomists which was due them." Watson, "Theonomy," 36.

130. John W. Whitehead, "Proposal: Christian Rights Foundation," September 3, 1980, RJR.

131. Ibid.

132. Ibid.

133. Ibid.

134. Peter Larsen, "Part 1: Burden of Wealth," *The Orange County Register*, August 8, 2004.

135. R. J. Rushdoony to Howard Ahmanson, January 12, 1981, RJR.

136. In a letter requesting $75,000 from Ahmanson to "get the foundation going," Rushdoony noted: "We are financing all the preliminary work, because we feel the survival of all of us depends on it." R. J. Rushdoony to Howard Ahmanson, September 8, 1980, RJR. Later, Rushdoony asked Ahmanson to contribute $100,000 per year to keep the foundation operating. R. J. Rushdoony to Howard Ahmanson, March 23, 1982, RJR.

137. John W. Whitehead, "re: Organizational Board Meeting of the Rutherford Institute," July 20, 1982, RJR.

138. Moore, *Suing for America's Soul*, 5.

139. Ibid.

140. North, "David Chilton."

141. Ibid.

142. Ibid.

143. For example, when the faculty of Westminster Theological Seminary published *Theonomy: A Reformed Critique* in 1990, North responded with *Theonomy: An Informed Response* in 1991.

144. Lee and Forschler, "Bearing Gifts," revealed North's library-stacking tactic. The authors, after some investigation, found no such anonymous donors existed, a fact that might have prompted many of the libraries to return the unsolicited books. Historian Randall Balmer and others mocked ICE's "inventive trickery." Randall H. Balmer, "Commentary: I Wish I'd Thought of That!," *Christian News*, February 8, 1992. See also "Christian Reconstructionists Hope to Stack Library Stacks, Duo Argues," *C&S*, January 1993.

145. Gary North, "A Mistake but No Crook," *Christian News*, February 8, 1993.

146. On the harsh rhetoric of North and other Reconstructionists, see Shupe, "Christian Reconstructionism and the Angry Rhetoric of Neo-Postmillennialism."

Chapter 6

1. Reagan, "Proclamation 5018."

2. Turner, *Bill Bright*, 200.

3. Williams, *God's Own Party*, 203.

4. Chilton, "Between the Covers of *Power for Living*," 1.

5. Ibid.

6. For clearly Reconstructionist themes, see Chilton et al., *Power for Living*, 27, 84–90, 119–27.

7. Chilton, "Between the Covers of *Power for Living*," 1.

8. Buckingham, *Power for Living*. See Wayne Roper, "Tylerites Touch Millions with 'Power for Living,'" *Tyler Courier-Times-Telegraph*, December 25, 1983, for information on the original printing of Chilton et al. *Power for Living*.

9. "Theological Book Feud," *Gettysburg Times*, February 6, 1984, 3, Newspapers.com.

10. "Religious Book Sparks Heated Debate," *Salina Journal*, February 6, 1984, 7, Newspapers.com.

11. "Theological Feud," *Baytown Sun*, February 6, 1986, 18, Newspapers.com.

12. "Campaign Leads to Squabbles," *Salina Journal*, February 18, 1984, 17, Newspapers.com.

13. Chilton, "Between the Covers of *Power for Living*," 4.

14. Ibid.

15. Watson, "Theonomy," 23–24.

16. Ibid., 25.

17. Chilton, *Paradise Restored*, 214.

18. Ibid.

19. Jordan, "Introduction," *C&C* (1985): xi.

20. Ibid.

21. Ibid., xii.

22. Ibid.

23. North, "Publisher's Preface," xix.

24. Watson, "Theonomy," 26.

25. Ibid.

26. North, *Backward Christian Soldiers*, 225.

27. North, *Unconditional Surrender*, 376.

28. For brief overviews of the appropriation of nonlinear dynamics into humanistic and popular discourses, see Hayles, "Complex Dynamics in Literature and Science"; and Best and Kellner, *Postmodern Adventure*, 100–149.

29. North, *Liberating Planet Earth*, 136–38, 146–48.

30. North, *Unconditional Surrender*, 256; emphasis in the original.

31. Centralization is a component of "Satan's social order" because Satan, like a human being, "is a limited creature" who substitutes bureaucratic centralization for "God's omniscience and omnipotence." North, *Liberating Planet Earth*, 155.

32. North, *Unconditional Surrender*, 348.

33. North, "The Escalating Confrontation with Bureaucracy," *C&C* (Summer 1983): 180.

34. See North, *Backward Christian Soldiers*, 199.

35. Ibid., 188; emphasis in the original.

36. This summary is from North, "Market Decentralization and Covenantal Organization."

37. Ibid., 2.

38. See Boston, "Apocalypse Now," *C&S*, March 1999; and McCullagh, "There's Something about Gary North."

39. This point is explicitly developed in North, "Confirmation, Confrontation, and Caves," *C&C* (Winter 1983).

40. For a report directly linking survivalist activity to the Tyler church, see Chismar and Rausch, "The New Puritans and Their Theonomic Paradise." It is important to note that Chismar later retracted key passages of this article in an embarrassing public apology, but he did not retract any of his comments about the activities of survivalists discussed in the story; see Chismar, "A Correction."

41. Mitchell, *Dancing at Armageddon*, 3.

42. "Profit of Doom Ruff Huffs and Puffs."

43. On the peaking of nuclear war concerns, see Rose, *One Nation Underground*, 214–24. For North's relationship with the Skousens, see North, "Gary North Presents: Racing to the Year 2000—Planning for Personal Stability in the Midst of Change," Conference Program, IFAS. Mark and Joel are nephews of the important LDS conservative author, activist, and educator Willard Cleon Skousen, a Brigham Young University professor, John Birch Society member, and author of the now-classic conservative texts *The Naked Communist* (1958) and *The 5000-Year Leap* (1981). Interest in the Skousens (especially Cleon and Mark) has increased during the 2000s because Glenn Beck, an LDS convert and popular conservative radio talk-show host, has promoted their work. See Zaitchik, "Meet the Man Who Changed Glenn Beck's Life."

44. Burgin, "Use of the Bible in the Christian Reconstruction Movement," 41–42, hints at these rumors.

45. Gilstrap, "Biblical Basis for Survival Preparation," *JCR* (Summer 1981): 197; emphasis in the original. Rushdoony also believed that Christians must prepare for the future, and it is difficult to believe that Gilstrap authored his essay without first consulting Rushdoony's *Preparation for the Future*.

46. Gilstrap, "Biblical Basis for Survival Preparation," 202–3; emphasis in the original.

47. Ibid., 203.

48. After Rushdoony fired North as editor of the *Journal*, Douglas F. Kelly, the new editor, published an essay rebuking survivalism among Reconstructionists; see Martin Selbrede, "You Can't Split Rotten Wood," *JCR* (Winter 1982–1983).

49. James Jordan argued that machine guns "like rare stamps, art, and other similar things, are skyrocketing in value" and that prudent Christians would invest in them, not stockpile them for a coming battle. James B. Jordan to R. J. Rushdoony, March 16, 1981, RJR.

50. Winston, "Reconstructionist Movement Remains Misunderstood," *News-Herald* (Del Reo, Texas), December 26, 1987, 4A.

51. Ibid. This assertion was infamous in Reconstructionist circles, and stories about it circulated for years. Chilton, "The Work of the Ecclesiastical Megalomania"; and David Chilton to Jim [James B. Jordan], July 7, 1986, RJR. James Jordan later insisted that no one ever made such an absurd claim. James B. Jordan to the *Chalcedon Report*, December 12, 1991, RJR.

52. No legal repercussions came from this event, but the controversy troubled many in the movement. After leaving the Tyler church, David Chilton remembered: "There was a widow in the church . . . a little bit eccentric. She had quite a bit of money. She had it in gold and silver and precious stones and things like that. And she didn't trust banks. . . . So instead the elders of

the church took her money or took her valuables for safekeeping. . . . And somehow that money just disappeared. . . . And this was in the tens of thousands of dollars. . . . They eventually gave her a few rusty tools and things they scraped together and that was all they gave her." Chilton, "The Work of the Ecclesiastical Megalomania."

53. Richard Hinds to R. J. Rushdoony, October 10, 1981, RJR.

54. John A. Nelson to Ray R. Sutton and Bob Dwelle, April 4, 1981, RJR.

55. R. J. Rushdoony to James B. Jordan, March 12, 1981, RJR.

56. R. J. Rushdoony to John Kistler, March 3, 1990, RJR.

57. John W. Whitehead, telephone interview by author, February 26, 2012.

58. R. J. Rushdoony to James B. Jordan, March 12, 1981, RJR.

59. To this, Rushdoony responded: "*Let* people think of Bahnsen as the senior thinker. I am fighting for a cause, not trying to promote myself." Ibid.

60. R. J. Rushdoony to James B. Jordan, March 12, 1981, RJR.

61. R. J. Rushdoony to James B. Jordan, March 12, 1981, RJR; emphasis in the original. In a March 16, 1981, letter to Rushdoony, Jordan responded that Tyler was not stockpiling guns, although "most people own one or two." Also, "no one here has a bomb shelter, and no one except Gary talked about putting one in."

62. R. J. Rushdoony to Gary North, July 3, 1981, RJR.

63. See Jordan, "Slavery in Biblical Perspective," 89.

64. R. J. Rushdoony to Gary North, July 3, 1981, RJR; emphasis in the original. North revised and lengthened the article, eventually publishing it as North, "The Marriage Supper of the Lamb," *C&C* (1985).

65. Gary North to R. J. Rushdoony, July 8, 1981, RJR.

66. R. J. Rushdoony to Gary North, July 13, 1981, RJR.

67. R. J. Rushdoony to Gary North, July 20, 1981, RJR.

68. Gary North to R. J. Rushdoony, August 9, 1981, RJR.

69. Ibid.

70. The rival publication was *Christianity & Civilization*, published by the Geneva Divinity School at Tyler.

71. Gary North to R. J. Rushdoony, August 9, 1981, RJR.

72. Letter from Gary North to all former *Journal of Christian Reconstruction* authors, August 21, 1981, RJR.

73. R. J. Rushdoony to Ray R. Sutton, September 25, 1981, RJR.

74. Ibid.

75. Ibid.

76. Journal entry for April 25, 1989, RJR.

77. Watson, "Theonomy," 25; and Barron, *Heaven on Earth*, 42.

78. See Stephens and Giberson, *The Anointed*, chapters 1 and 2.

79. Ibid., 80.

80. Undated exchange between Carl F. H. Henry and a reviewer identified as "Jim," BGC.

81. Ibid. Henry also considered several other pieces of Rushdoony's writing but ultimately rejected them. "Evaluation of Manuscript," March 8, 1973, BGC.

82. Terrill I. Elniff to R. J. Rushdoony, 23 October 1975, RJR.

83. Williams, *God's Own Party*, 161.

84. Marley, *Pat Robertson*, 56; and R. J. Rushdoony journal entry for February 24, 1982, RJR.

85. Marley, *Pat Robertson*, 56

86. "Televangelist Summaries, May 1986," 53, PFAW. For Robertson's other recorded references to the dominion mandate, see "Televangelist Summaries, June 1986," 76, PFAW. Robertson also had frequent conversations with lawyer John Whitehead during the early 1980s.

87. Rodney Clapp, "Democracy as Heresy," *CT*, February 20, 1987, 21.

88. Despite his frequent invocation of "dominion," Robertson's connections to Christian Reconstruction were more nuanced than his critics often recognize. As religion scholar Justin Watson has noted in his study of the Christian Coalition, Robertson's references to dominion were often "devoid of political references. Demands for Christian control of social and political institutions have apparently been read into Robertson's 'Law of Dominion' in view of his later entry into politics." Watson, *Christian Coalition*, 117. Similarly, historian David John Marley pointed out that Robertson ultimately remained truer to his Baptist background than to any vision of political dominion. "While he might occasionally say things that resonated with fans of Rushdoony, Robertson's Baptist roots showed when he praised religious pluralism. . . . Robertson's hopes that Christians will hold sway over the government are based on the democratic idea of majority rule. If religious conservatives are the largest single group of Americans, their ideas should naturally find expression in the nation's laws. Dominionist [such as Rushdoony] do not view democracy as God ordained, especially if it keeps his laws from being enacted." Marley, *Pat Robertson*, 58–59. Robertson's tendency to speak off the cuff and his willingness to bend theological boundaries have given credence to simplistic attempts to portray him as a popular expositor of "dominion theology" even though his ideas are often more nuanced—or confused—than such portrayals allow.

89. Stephens and Giberson, *The Anointed*, 80–81.

90. For direct references to Rushdoony and his ideas on education, see Kennedy, *Reconstruction*, 14–15. The final chapter, "Biblical Guidelines for Work," does not cite Rushdoony but uses his concept of dominion.

91. Anson Shupe, "Prophets of a Biblical America," *Wall Street Journal*, April 12, 1989.

92. "Letters to the Editor: Christians, Not Revolutionaries," *Wall Street Journal*, May 3, 1989. In his editorial, Kennedy further insisted: "In fact, in my numerous discussions with these two men, in public and in private, I have never even discussed that aspect of their theology" (ibid.). This is singularly difficult to believe given that Kennedy authored a book entitled *Reconstruction* that clearly cites major aspects of Rushdoony's ideas. Further, Kennedy and Rushdoony sought to implement some of the ideas developed in *Reconstruction* when they corresponded about creating a Christian legal advocacy group in the early 1980s. D. James Kennedy to R. J. Rushdoony, May 14, 1981, RJR.

93. As historian Kate Bowler has noted, E. W. Kenyon, a pioneering voice in the prosperity gospel, believed that "Christ's resurrection united humanity's spiritual nature with God's own, restoring their spiritual vision and legal rights to dominion over the earth." Bowler, *Blessed*, 17–18. Later advocates of the tradition emphasized that "sin transferred legal dominion of the earth to Satan," but grace provides the mechanism for restoring dominion and therefore wealth, health, and power to humans. Ibid., 97.

94. See, for example, North, *Unholy Spirits*, the updated and expanded version of his *None Dare Call It Witchcraft*.

95. For a summary treatment of the Latter Rain tradition and its relationship to the dominion mandate, see Anderson, *To the Ends of the Earth*, 204–5.

96. Paulk, *That the World May Know*, xii; and Paulk, *Satan Unmasked*, 36.

97. Barron, *Heaven on Earth*, 71.

98. Ibid.

99. Paulk, *Satan Unmasked*, 27.

100. Ibid., 24.

101. Barron, *Heaven on Earth*, 73.

102. Worthen, *Apostles of Reason*, 145–46. See also "About C. Peter Wagner."

103. Wagner appropriated the Seven Mountain concept from Lance Wallnau; see Wagner, *Wrestling with Alligators*, 263.

104. See Wagner, *Dominion*, for a full exposition of the merger of Pentecostal and Reconstructionist themes.

105. Morecraft, "The Christian Reconstruction Dialogue."

106. Ibid.

107. Ibid., 7.

108. Shupe, "The Reconstructionist Movement," 882.

109. Ibid.

110. North, "Chilton, Sutton, and Dominion Theology," 1.

111. "Televangelist Summaries, June 1987," 94, PFAW. See also "Televangelist Summaries, June 1986," 122, PFAW; and "Televangelist Summaries, October 1986," 134, PFAW. Swaggart initially embraced Reconstructionist literature by distributing copies of Gary DeMar's three-volume *God and Government*, which he promoted as the "best series" on "America's spiritual history." Johnson, "Reformed Fundamentalism in America," 240. Swaggart abandoned the movement when he realized it was postmillennial.

112. Rodney Clapp, "Democracy as Heresy," *CT*, February 20, 1987.

113. Ibid., 19.

114. Ibid.

115. Gary North authored a caustic response to Clapp that addressed many of the article's criticisms. See North, "Honest Reporting as Heresy." North charges that *Christianity Today* initially agreed to run an article on Reconstructionism by John Hannah of Dallas Theological Seminary but eventually rejected it, telling him "that they had hoped for an essay that went into the details about the Reconstructionists' in-fighting" (328). Given *Christianity Today's* past relationship with Rushdoony, this is entirely plausible.

116. Hunt, *Whatever Happened to Heaven?*, 8.

117. House and Ice, *Dominion Theology*, 21. Ice was formerly a Reconstructionist with connections to the Tyler church. North, "Publisher's Foreword," xxx. Consequently, his work with House represents a sophisticated and fair-minded engagement with Reconstructionist literature. As a result, Gary North launched his ICE publishing machine into high gear to attack House and Ice. He enlisted Greg Bahnsen and Kenneth Gentry, Bahnsen's former RTS student, to write *House Divided* as a response. True to form, North published the book less than a year after the House and Ice text.

118. Lindsey, *Road to Holocaust*, 274.

119. Hunt, *Whatever Happened to Heaven?*, 223.

120. House and Ice, *Dominion Theology*, 419.

121. Ibid., 16.

122. Lindsey, *Road to Holocaust*, 25.

123. Ibid., 274.

124. Hunt, *Whatever Happened to Heaven?*, 8.

125. House and Ice, *Dominion Theology*, 253.

126. Ibid., 338.

127. R. J. Rushdoony to James B. Jordan, March 13, 1981, RJR.

128. Kenneth S. Templeton, telephone interview by author, March 20, 2007.

129. Lofton and Ortiz, "Remembering Rushdoony."

130. The popular press largely ignored the CNP during the 1980s. A handful of investigative journalists did take note of the organization and documented its meetings, members, and activities as they related to domestic and foreign policy. Most notably, Russ Bellant set the standard for later reporting on the CNP with his chapter on the organization in *The Coors Connection*. Bellant argued that the origins of the organization "are not found in mainstream conservatism or the traditional Republican Party but in the nativist and reactionary circles of the Radical Right, including the John Birch Society" (43), and that it threatened to undermine democratic pluralism in the United States and abroad. He documented the CNP's relationship to Christian Reconstructionism and how it influenced foreign policy in the Middle East and Latin America. Bellant's book influenced other like-minded researchers, including Frederick Clarkson, Sara Diamond, and Skipp Porteous, who would situate the CNP as an important secretive organization at the heart of the rise of the New Right in the 1980s. By the late 1990s and early 2000s, journalists in publications such as the *New York Times* and *The Nation* took notice of the CNP and its relationship to the Republican Party and the wider conservative movement. Because of the organization's secret membership lists and private meetings, most of the coverage focuses on the secretive mysteriousness of the organization.

131. Adam Clymer, "Conservatives Gather in Umbrella Council for a National Policy," *New York Times*, May 20, 1981; and Bellant, *The Coors Connection*, 36–37.

132. North, "Writing Conspiracy History."

133. Ibid. North cites a $5,000 membership fee, but Bellant indicated that individuals paid $2,000 for a one-year membership; $5,000 bought one membership on the CNP Board of Governors. See Bellant, *The Coors Connection*, 36. Regardless, the fee was significant.

134. North, "Writing Conspiracy History."

135. R. J. Rushdoony to James B. Jordan March 12, 1981, RJR; emphasis in the original.

136. James B. Jordan to R. J. Rushdoony, March 16, 1981; and Gary North to R. J. Rushdoony, March 25, 1981, RJR.

137. Council for National Policy Board of Governors contact list for 1984, CNP File, PRA; and Member Participants list for the Dallas, Texas, August 17–18, 1984 meeting of the Council for National Policy, CNP File, PRA.

138. Schwartz and Phillips, "Howard Phillips Remembers Rush."

139. Ingersoll, chapter 7 in *Building God's Kingdom*.

140. Ibid.

141. R. J. Rushdoony journal entry for May 21–23, 1983, RJR.

142. R. J. Rushdoony journal entry for May 19, 1981, RJR.

143. Ibid.

144. R. J. Rushdoony journal entry for August 17, 1984, RJR. Other meetings seem to have also led to significant fund-raising, but Rushdoony did not record them in detail.

145. R. J. Rushdoony journal entry for January 27, 1984, RJR. Titus's ties to Reconstructionism

were especially strong. His previous career as a left-wing law professor at various state institutions in the West prompted Robertson to see the lawyer as "a mover and shaker" in the evangelical community who could get CBN University's School of Law accredited by the American Bar Association. Marley, *Pat Robertson*, 58, 256. Robertson later fired Titus, in part because of the latter's relationship to Christian Reconstructionism when the movement became a liability in the late 1980s and early 1990s. Robertson believed that Reconstruction made Titus "very narrow minded and [he] had a very narrow definition of what a Christian is." Ibid., 58.

146. Titus, "The Constitutional Law of Privacy," in Rushdoony, *The Institutes of Biblical Law*, 2:710–26.

147. Titus attributed his awareness of modern jurisprudence's indebtedness to biblical law to R. J. Rushdoony. Titus, "Impact of Rushdoony."

148. R. J. Rushdoony journal entry for January 27, 1984, RJR.

149. R. J. Rushdoony to James B. Jordan, March 12, 1981, RJR.

150. Duriez, *Francis Schaeffer*, 40.

151. Irving Hexham, "The Evangelical Response to the New Age," 322 (n. 16).

152. Schaeffer, *Christian Manifesto*, 20.

153. Martin, *With God on Our Side*, 321. This point was also developed earlier in Diamond, *Roads to Dominion*, 246–47.

154. Duriez, *Francis Schaeffer*, 191.

155. Ibid., 192–93. See also Williams, *God's Own Party*, 223–24.

156. Diamond, *Roads to Dominion*, 246.

157. R. J. Rushdoony journal entry for December 1, 1981, RJR. Far less concerned with polite opinion was Gary North, who recognized some of Rushdoony's citations in the text and essentially charged Schaeffer with plagiarizing Rushdoony's ideas for more than twenty years. See North and Chilton, "Apologetics and Strategy" *C&C* (Summer 1983): 124–26. Further, Schaeffer did cite some Reconstructionist authors in the text, most notably using articles from the *Journal of Christian Reconstruction*; see Schaeffer, *Christian Manifesto*, 141 (n. 2); 141–42 (n. 7).

158. Schaeffer, *Christian Manifesto*, 10–11.

159. John W. Whitehead, telephone interview by author, February 26, 2012.

160. Whitehead, "Crazy for God."

161. John W. Whitehead, telephone interview by author, February 26, 2012.

162. Schaeffer, *A Christian Manifesto*, 18; emphasis in the original.

163. Ibid.

164. Schaeffer is explicit that secular conservatives are just as bad as secular liberals: "As Christians we must stand absolutely and totally opposed to the whole humanist system, *whether it is controlled by conservative or liberal elements*." Ibid., 77–78; emphasis in the original.

165. Martin, *With God on Our Side*, 197.

166. Duriez, *Francis Schaeffer*, 192. See also Martin, *With God on Our Side*, 197–204.

167. See Hankins, "The New Yorker and Evangelicalism"; and Hexham, "The Evangelical Response to the New Age."

168. If, as Molly Worthen has argued, Schaeffer's primary insight was, "The danger of abandoning God's inerrant word could be made plain to American evangelicals through a history lesson" and cultural criticism (Worthen, *Apostles of Reason*, 209), then it is fair to note that Rushdoony came to this same conclusion some twenty years before Schaeffer published 1968's *The God Who Is There*, the first major public statement of Schaeffer's cultural apologetic.

Rushdoony's engagement with modernist literature, pornography, modern art, and existential philosophy stretched back into the late 1940s and early 1950s. Rushdoony rarely cited Schaeffer in any of his research, but his journals indicate that he read nearly everything Schaeffer wrote.

169. Edgar, "The Passing of R. J. Rushdoony"; and Hankins, *Francis Schaeffer*, 193–94.

170. Hankins, *Francis Schaeffer*, 193.

171. Schaeffer, *Christian Manifesto*, 120–21.

172. John W. Whitehead, telephone interview by author, February 26, 2012.

173. John W. Whitehead, telephone interview by author, June 6, 2014.

174. Frank Schaeffer, *Crazy for God*, 333. Franky Schaeffer's charge that his father believed Rushdoony was "clinically insane" may be true, but it probably reflects a retrospective assessment of Rushdoony's ideas rather than any statement made openly by his father. First, Schaeffer relied on Rushdoony's ideas, and they had shared citations and sources since the late 1960s. Furthermore, Schaeffer regularly used Rushdoony's books in his study groups at L'Abri (Edgar, "The Passing of R. J. Rushdoony"). It is fair to suggest that it is unlikely Schaeffer would have sought guidance from and paid such intellectual respect to a madman. Second, Schaeffer and Rushdoony did correspond occasionally. In one telling letter from the late 1970s, Schaeffer told Rushdoony of his latest round of cancer tests and warmly thanked him and Gary North for their support (Francis A. Schaeffer to R. J. Rushdoony, November 20, 1978, RJR). Further, attesting to their intimate association, Rushdoony also knew some of the last words Schaeffer ever spoke: "Please, Father, take me home. I'm very tired." R. J. Rushdoony to John Kistler, March 3, 1990, RJR. This latter point strongly implies that Rushdoony was present at Schaeffer's bedside near the end of his life, or that Schaeffer's friends or family were close enough with Rushdoony to relay such a story to him. Either way, it suggests that Schaeffer's feelings for Rushdoony were far more complex than Franky Schaeffer implies.

175. R. J. Rushdoony to John Kistler, March 3, 1990, RJR.

176. Public Affairs Television and Bill Moyers, *God and Politics*, 5. Direct quotations are from the official transcript of the original broadcast (December 23, 1987). The program was widely reviewed in the popular press. See, for example, Tom Shales, "Of Democracy and the New Theocracy," *Washington Post*, December 23, 1987, D3.

177. Public Affairs Television, *God and Politics*, 2.

178. Americans United published one of the first secular exposés of Reconstructionism. See Rob Boston, "Thy Kingdom Come: Christian Reconstructionists Want to Take Dominion over America," *C&S*, September 8, 1988. Norman Lear's People for the American Way and Public Research Associates collected extensive files on the Chalcedon Foundation and the Institute for Christian Economics during the 1980s and 1990s. PRA-affiliated reporters such as Frederick Clarkson and Sara Diamond pioneered most of the secular coverage of Reconstructionism. See Clarkson, "Christian Reconstruction"; and Diamond, *Spiritual Warfare*.

179. Diamond, *Spiritual Warfare*, 138, emphasis in the original.

180. Berlet and Lyons, *Right-Wing Populism in America*, 247; and Berlet, "How We Coined the Term 'Dominionism.'"

181. Marghe Covino, "Grace under Pressure: The World According to Rev. R. J. Rushdoony," *Sacramento News and Review*, October 20, 1994, 17.

182. Sharlet, "Through a Glass, Darkly," 36.

183. Frank Schaeffer, *Crazy for God*, 333.

184. See Adorno, *The Authoritarian Personality*.

185. Hedges, *American Fascists*, 11.

186. Blumenthal, *Republican Gomorrah*, 7–13 and 17–22. The text liberally appropriates Fromm, *Escape from Freedom*.

187. Miller, *Cruel and Unusual*, 264.

Conclusion

1. R. J. Rushdoony journal entry for May 23, 1986, RJR.

2. R. J. Rushdoony journal entry for June 20, 1986, RJR.

3. R. J. Rushdoony journal entry for March 28, 1990, RJR.

4. Rushdoony's last recorded stint as an expert witness seems to have been in a trial involving pastor Royal Blue of the Redding Baptist Church in Sacramento, California, on April 11, 1988. As late as October 1998, Rushdoony gave a recorded deposition for an unnamed trial in Texas. Rushdoony journal entry for October 11, 1998, RJR.

5. Most of these charges came in North's ICE Position Papers: North, "Rumor #213"; and "Clarifying the So-called 'Hitler Connection.'" In the short *Baptized Patriarchalism*, North attacked Rushdoony as a father, husband, and pastor and discussed private details about Rushdoony's first marriage.

6. North, "Rumor #213."

7. For North's place relative to other Y2K doom peddlers, see Rob Boston, "Apocalypse Now," *C&S*, March 1999; McMinn, "Y2K, the Apocalypse, and Evangelical Christianity"; and Cowan, "Confronting the Failed Failure."

8. See, for example, his claim that a post-Y2K world would destroy feminism because it would further decentralize American society and allow for the reassertion of the kinds of gender-based divisions of labor found in preindustrial economic regimes: North, Institute for Christian Economics cover letter, March 1998.

9. In total, North appeared on the show at least four times. North, Institute for Christian Economics cover letter, January 1999.

10. Some of these exchanges have been archived by Lorenz, "Wolves in Sheep's Clothing."

11. Ibid.

12. R. J. Rushdoony journal entry for February 6, 1998, RJR.

13. R. J. Rushdoony journal entry for March 26, 2000, RJR.

14. R. J. Rushdoony journal entry for November 19, 2000, RJR.

15. M. Rushdoony, "R. J. Rushdoony's Final Sermon," *CR* 429 (April 2001): 33.

16. Peter Larsen, "Part 1: Burden of Wealth," *Orange County Register*, August 8, 2004.

17. R. J. Rushdoony to James B. Jordan, March 12, 1981, RJR.

18. North, "R. J. Rushdoony, R.I.P."

19. Ibid.

20. Ibid.

21. "Briefs: North America," *CT*, April 2, 2001, 25.

22. "People," *Christian Century*, April 11, 2001, 13.

23. Edgar, "The Passing of R. J. Rushdoony."

24. Douthat, "Theocracy, Theocracy, Theocracy."

25. Bramwell, "Defining Conservatism Down."

26. Schultz, "Rushdoony, Rousas John (1916–2001)," 754. See also Samson, "Christian Reconstruction."

27. The movement appeals to Psalms 127:3–5 (KJV): "Lo, children are an heritage of the Lord: and the fruit of the womb is his reward. As arrows are in the hand of a mighty man; so are children of the youth. Happy is the man that hath his quiver full of them: they shall not be ashamed, but they shall speak with the enemies in the gate."

28. On normative gender roles, see E. Ludy, *God's Gift to Women*; and L. Ludy, *Set-Apart Femininity*. On courtship, see Harris, *I Kissed Dating Goodbye*; and Botkin and Botkin, *It's (Not That) Complicated*.

29. Joyce, *Quiverfull*, 19–30. See also Pride, *The Way Home*; and Hess and Hess, *A Full Quiver*.

30. Shively, "Happily Ever After," 67–70.

31. The nature of the improper relationship remains unclear, though Phillips insisted they "did not 'know' each other in the Biblical sense." Phillips, "Statement of Resignation." Long before this scandal, Phillips was close to Chalcedon and preached at Rushdoony's funeral. Schwartz and Phillips, "Howard Phillips Remembers Rush."

32. Joyce, *Quiverfull*, 4.

33. Ibid., 24.

34. Lee, "Duggar Family's Close Relationship with Vision Forum Founder Doug Phillips"; and "Vision Forum Ministries Closing Its Doors."

35. "Christian Children Need Christian Education."

36. Moore, *Let My Children Go*.

37. Unruh, "Christians Need Exodus from 'Pharaoh's System.'"

38. In 2014 Moore declared his candidacy for lieutenant governor of South Carolina.

39. For a Canadian perspective on the influence of Reconstruction, see McDonald, *The Armageddon Factor*.

40. Hexham, *The Irony of Apartheid*, 165 (n. 2), 194–95.

41. Chidester, "Religion Education in South Africa," 434.

42. Chidester, *Wild Religion*, 80.

43. Ibid., 80–82.

44. Aside from Rushdoony's notorious condemnation of homosexuality in *Institutes of Biblical Law*, other notable Reconstructionist works on the subject include Bahnsen, *Homosexuality*; and Chilton, *Power in the Blood*. Both works emphasized Rushdoony's account of human nature and law; neither focus on the death penalty.

45. "Scott Lively"; and Alan Cowell, "Ugandan Lawmakers Pass Measure Imposing Harsh Penalties on Gays," *New York Times*, December 20, 2013.

46. "Scott Lively"; and Kaoma, *Globalizing the Culture Wars*.

47. "Generations at Odds."

48. Rushdoony's status as a politically incorrect folk hero and inspiration to marginal hate groups is already apparent in the Kinist movement. Kinism is a religiously inspired white-supremacist movement in the American South that rejects violence for a kinder, gentler form of hate rooted in ideas like Rushdoony's "unequal yoking" doctrine. See Anti-Defamation League, "Kinism." Mark Rushdoony has noted that his father did not support Kinist views of race and

was not against interracial marriage, having performed at least one during his ministry. "Mark Rushdoony Says That His Father, R. J. Rushdoony, Was Not a Kinist."

49. Rushdoony, *Roots of Reconstruction*, 63.

50. Moots and Terrell, "One Protestant Tradition's Interface with Austrian Economics," 95.

51. Lienesch, *Redeeming America*; and Iannaccone, "Heirs to the Protestant Ethic?"

52. "Ron Paul Curriculum: The Story of Liberty, K-12."

53. North, "Ron Paul Curriculum." Thanks to Keith Padgett for pointing me to this source.

54. See Lizza, "Leap of Faith."

55. McCloud, *Making the American Religious Fringe*.

56. Ibid., 6–7.

57. Orsi, "Snakes Alive," 105.

58. Ibid., 111–12. Susan Harding makes a similar argument in "Representing Fundamentalism."

BIBLIOGRAPHY

Archival Collections

Berkeley, Calif.
    University of California, Berkeley
        Center for Right-Wing Studies and People for the American Way (PFAW) Archive
        of Conservative Video Broadcasting, http://crws.berkeley.edu/video-archive/
        primary-source-documents, June 27, 2014
Chapel Hill, N.C.
    Southern Historical Collection, Louis Round Wilson Special Collections Library,
    University of North Carolina
        William Terry Couch Papers
Eugene, Ore.
    Special Collections and University Archives, University of Oregon Libraries
        Ingebretsen, James C., Papers
        Kershner, Howard E., Papers
Fairfax, Va.
    Institute for Humane Studies, George Mason University
        Institute for Humane Studies Library
Kansas City, Mo.
    Western Historical Manuscript Collection, University of Missouri–Kansas City
        William Volker and Company Records
Medford, Mass.
    Digital Collections and Archives, Tufts University
        Institute for First Amendment Studies Records, 1980–1999
New York, N.Y.
    Rare Book and Manuscript Library, Columbia University
        Group Research, Inc. Records, 1955–1996
            Group Research File on the Center for American Studies
            Group Research File on the Volker Fund
St. Louis, Mo.
    The Historical Center of the Presbyterian Church in America
        C. Gregg Singer Papers, Manuscript Collection
Somerville, Mass.
    Political Research Associates
        Political Research Associates Library
Vallecito, Calif.
    Chalcedon Foundation
        Rousas John Rushdoony Library

Wheaton, Ill.

    Wheaton College Archives and Special Collections

        Archives of the Billy Graham Center

Wilmington, Del.

    Hagley Museum and Library

        J. H. Pew Papers

    Intercollegiate Studies Institute

        Intercollegiate Studies Institute Library

Books, Dissertations, and Theses

Abbott, Stephen Lee. "A Critical Analysis of the Meaning of the Kingdom of God in the Theology of the Christian Reconstruction Movement." Ph.D. diss., Southwestern Baptist Theological Seminary, 1990.

Adorno, Theodor W. *The Authoritarian Personality*. New York: Harper, 1950.

Anderson, Allan Heaton. *To the Ends of the Earth: Pentecostalism and the Transformation of World Christianity*. New York: Oxford University Press, 2013.

Bahnsen, Greg L. *Homosexuality: A Biblical View*. Grand Rapids, Mich.: Baker Book House, 1978.

——— . *Theonomy in Christian Ethics*. Nutley, N.J.: Craig Press, 1977.

——— . *Van Til's Apologetic: Readings and Analysis*. Phillipsburg, N.J.: P&R, 1998.

Balmer, Randall, and John R. Fitzmier. *The Presbyterians*. Westport, Conn.: Praeger, 1994.

Balmer, Randall H. *Blessed Assurance: A History of Evangelicalism in America*. Boston: Beacon Press, 1999.

——— . *The Making of Evangelicalism: From Revivalism to Politics and Beyond*. Waco, Tex.: Baylor University Press, 2010.

——— . *Thy Kingdom Come: An Evangelical's Lament*. New York: Basic Books, 2006.

Barker, William S., and W. Robert Godfrey, eds. *Theonomy: A Reformed Critique*. Grand Rapids, Mich.: Zondervan, 1990.

Barron, Bruce. *Heaven on Earth? The Social and Political Agendas of Dominion Theology*. Grand Rapids, Mich.: Zondervan, 1992.

Bellant, Russ. *The Coors Connection: How Coors Family Philanthropy Undermines Democratic Pluralism*. Boston: South End Press, 1991.

Best, Steven, and Douglas Kellner. *The Postmodern Adventure: Science, Technology, and Cultural Studies at the Third Millennium*. New York: Guilford Press, 2001.

Bivins, Jason C. *The Fracture of Good Order: Christian Antiliberalism and the Challenge to American Politics*. Chapel Hill: University of North Carolina Press, 2003.

Blumenthal, Max. *Republican Gomorrah: Inside the Movement That Shattered the Party*. New York: Nation Books, 2009.

Boa, Kenneth Dale. "A Comparative Study of Four Christian Apologetic Systems." Ph.D. diss., New York University, 1985.

Bolich, Gregory G. *Karl Barth and Evangelicalism*. Downers Grove, Ill.: Intervarsity Press, 1980.

Bolt, John. *A Free Church, a Holy Nation: Abraham Kuyper's American Public Theology*. Grand Rapids, Mich.: William B. Eerdmans Publishing, 2001.

Botkin, Anna Sofia, and Elizabeth Botkin. *It's (Not That) Complicated: How to Relate to Guys in a Healthy, Sane, and Biblical Way*. Centerville, Tenn.: Western Conservatory, 2011.

Bowler, Kate. *Blessed: A History of the American Prosperity Gospel*. New York: Oxford University Press, 2013.

Boyer, Paul S. *When Time Shall Be No More: Prophecy Belief in Modern American Culture*. Studies in Cultural History. Cambridge, Mass.: Belknap Press of Harvard University Press, 1992.

Brasich, Adam S. "'Parallel Lines Never Intersect': The Influence of Dutch Reformed Presuppositionalism on American Christian Fundamentalism." M.A. thesis, Florida State University, 2013.

Buckingham, Jamie. *Power for Living*. N.p.: Arthur S. DeMoss Foundation, 1983.

Bulbulian, Berge. *The Fresno Armenians: History of a Diaspora Community*. Fresno: The Press at California State University, Fresno, 2000.

Burgin, James Erman. "The Use of the Bible in the Christian Reconstruction Movement: A Christian Ethical Analysis." Ph.D. diss., Southwestern Baptist Theological Seminary, 1993.

Burns, Jennifer. *Goddess of the Market: Ayn Rand and the American Right*. New York: Oxford University Press, 2009.

Calvin, John. *Calvin's Institutes*. Edited by Donald K. McKim. Abridged ed. Louisville: Westminster John Knox Press, 2001.

Campbell, Roderick. *Israel and the New Covenant*. Philadelphia: Presbyterian and Reformed, 1954.

Chidester, David. *Wild Religion: Tracking the Sacred in South Africa*. Berkeley: University of California Press, 2012.

Child, John Graham. "Biblical Law in the Theology of R. J. Rushdoony: A Systematic Theological Analysis and Appreciation." M.Th. thesis, University of South Africa, 1985.

Chilton, David. *Paradise Restored: A Biblical Theology of Dominion*. Tyler, Tex.: Dominion Press, 1985. PDF e-book, http://www.garynorth.com/freebooks/docs/pdf/paradise_restored.pdf. June 27, 2014.

———. *Power in the Blood: A Christian Response to AIDS*. Brentwood, Tenn.: Wolgemuth & Hyatt, 1988.

———. *Productive Christians in An Age of Guilt Manipulators: A Biblical Response to Ronald J. Sider*. 3rd ed. Tyler, Tex.: Institute for Christian Economics, 1990. PDF e-book, http://www.garynorth.com/ProductiveChristians.pdf. June 27, 2014.

Chilton, David, Gary DeMar, Victoria T. deVries, Michael Gilstrap, and Ray Sutton. *Power for Living*. Atlanta: Vision Forum, 1983.

Clarkson, Frederick. *Eternal Hostility: The Struggle between Theocracy and Democracy*. Monroe, Maine: Common Courage Press, 1997.

Coffman, Elesha J. *The Christian Century and the Rise of the Protestant Mainline*. New York: Oxford University Press, 2013.

Cornuelle, Herbert C. *"Mr. Anonymous": The Story of William Volker*. Caldwell, Idaho: Caxton Printers, 1951.

Cunningham, David. *There's Something Happening Here: The New Left, the Klan, and FBI Counterintelligence*. Berkeley: University of California Press, 2005.

Cunningham, Harold Gardiner. "Theonomy: An Attempt at Reconstruction." Ph.D. diss., Queen's University of Belfast, 1996.

DeMar, Gary. *God and Government*. 3 vols. Atlanta: American Vision, 1990.

Demos, John. *A Little Commonwealth: Family Life in Plymouth Colony*. New York: Oxford University Press, 2000.

Diamond, Sara. *Roads to Dominion: Right-Wing Movements and Political Power in the United States*. New York: Guilford Press, 1995.

——. *Spiritual Warfare: The Politics of the Christian Right*. Boston: South End Press, 1989.

Dochuk, Darren. *From Bible Belt to Sunbelt: Plain-Folk Religion, Grassroots Politics, and the Rise of Evangelical Conservatism*. New York: W. W. Norton & Company, 2010.

Doenecke, Justus D. *Not to the Swift: The Old Isolationists in the Cold War Era*. Lewisburg, Pa.: Bucknell University Press, 1979.

——. *Storm on the Horizon: The Challenge to American Intervention, 1939–1941*. Lanham, Md.: Rowman and Littlefield Publishers, 2000.

Doherty, Brian. *Radicals for Capitalism: A Freewheeling History of the Modern American Libertarian Movement*. New York: PublicAffairs, 2007.

Dorrien, Gary J. *The Remaking of Evangelical Theology*. Louisville: Westminster John Knox Press, 1998.

Duriez, Colin. *Francis Schaeffer: An Authentic Life*. Wheaton, Ill.: Crossway Books, 2008.

Durkheim, Émile. *The Elementary Forms of the Religious Life*. Edited by Mark S. Cladis. Translated by Carol Cosman. Oxford World Classics. Oxford, UK: Oxford University Press, 2001.

Edwards, Jerome E. *Pat McCarran, Political Boss of Nevada*. Reno: University of Nevada Press, 1982.

Edwards, Lee. *Educating for Liberty: The First Half-Century of the Intercollegiate Studies Institute*. Washington, D.C.: Regnery, 2003.

Eow, Gregory Teddy. "Fighting a New Deal: Intellectual Origins of the Reagan Revolution, 1932–1952." Ph.D. diss., Rice University, 2007.

Eskridge, Larry. *God's Forever Family: The Jesus People Movement in America*. New York: Oxford University Press, 2013.

Fenster, Mark. *Conspiracy Theories: Secrecy and Power in American Culture*. Minneapolis: University of Minnesota Press, 1999.

Flamm, Michael W. *Law and Order: Street Crime, Civil Unrest, and the Crisis of Liberalism in the 1960s*. New York: Columbia University Press, 2005.

Flippen, J. Brooks. *Jimmy Carter, the Politics of Family, and the Rise of the Religious Right*. Athens: University of Georgia Press, 2011.

Fones-Wolf, Elizabeth A. *Selling Free Enterprise: The Business Assault on Labor and Liberalism, 1945–60*. Urbana: University of Illinois Press, 1994.

Forster, Arnold, and Benjamin R. Epstein. *Danger on the Right*. New York: Random House, 1964.

Foucault, Michel. *Madness and Civilization: A History of Insanity in the Age of Reason*. Translated by Richard Howard. New York: Mentor, 1965.

——. *Security, Territory, Population: Lectures at the Collège de France, 1977–78*. Edited by Michel Senellart, François Ewald, Alessandro Fontana, and Arnold I. Davidson. Translated by Graham Burchell. Lectures at the Collège de France. New York: Palgrave Macmillan, 2007.

Frame, John M. *Cornelius Van Til: An Analysis of His Thought*. Phillipsburg, N.J.: P&R, 1995.

Fromm, Erich. *Escape from Freedom*. New York: Holt, Rinehart and Winston, 1976.

Gabbert, Michael Dennis. "An Historical Evaluation of Christian Reconstructionism Based on the Inherent Inviability of Selected Theocratic Models." Ph.D. diss., Southwestern Baptist Theological Seminary, 1991.

Gaither, Milton. *Homeschool: An American History*. New York: Palgrave Macmillan, 2008.

George, Carol V. R. *God's Salesman: Norman Vincent Peale and the Power of Positive Thinking*. New York: Oxford University Press, 1993.

Gill, Jill K. *Embattled Ecumenism: The National Council of Churches, the Vietnam War, and the Trials of the Protestant Left*. DeKalb: Northern Illinois University Press, 2011.

Ginsburg, Faye D. *Contested Lives: The Abortion Debate in an American Community*. Berkeley: University of California Press, 1989.

Grant, George. *The Changing of the Guard: Biblical Blueprints for Political Action*. Fort Worth, Tex.: Dominion Press, 1987. PDF e-book, http://www.garynorth.com/freebooks/docs/pdf/the_changing_of_the_guard.pdf. June 27, 2014.

Graziano, Frank. *The Millennial New World*. New York: Oxford University Press, 1999.

Greenberg, Ivan. *Surveillance in America: Critical Analysis of the FBI, 1920 to the Present*. Lanham, Md.: Lexington Books, 2012.

Grodzins, Morton. *Americans Betrayed: Politics and the Japanese Evacuation*. Reprint ed. Chicago: University of Chicago Press, 1974.

Grover, Alan N. *Ohio's Trojan Horse: A Warning to Christian Schools Everywhere*. Greenville, S.C.: Bob Jones University Press, 1977.

Hankins, Barry. *Francis Schaeffer and the Shaping of Evangelical America*. Grand Rapids, Mich.: Wm. B. Eerdmans, 2008.

———. *Jesus and Gin: Evangelicalism, the Roaring Twenties, and Today's Culture Wars*. New York: Palgrave Macmillan, 2010.

Harris, Harriet A. *Fundamentalism and Evangelicals*. Oxford Theological Monographs. New York: Clarendon Press, 1998.

Harris, Joshua. *I Kissed Dating Goodbye*. Updated ed. Sisters, Ore.: Multnomah Books, 2003.

Hatfield, William Charles. "Critiques of the Major Tenets of Christian Reconstructionism." Th.D. diss., Mid-America Baptist Theological Seminary, 1991.

Hedges, Chris. *American Fascists: The Christian Right and the War on America*. New York: Simon and Schuster, 2008.

Heller, Anne C. *Ayn Rand and the World She Made*. New York: Doubleday, 2009.

Hendershot, Heather. *What's Fair on the Air? Cold War Right-Wing Broadcasting and the Public Interest*. Chicago: University of Chicago Press, 2011.

Hendriksen, William. *More than Conquerors: An Interpretation of the Book of Revelation*. Grand Rapids, Mich.: Baker Book House, 1940.

Henry, Carl F. H. *Confessions of a Theologian: An Autobiography*. Waco, Tex.: Word Books, 1986.

———. *The Uneasy Conscience of Modern Fundamentalism*. 1947. Reprint ed. Grand Rapids, Mich.: Wm. B. Eerdmans, 2003.

Hess, Rick, and Jan Hess. *A Full Quiver: Family Planning and the Lordship of Christ*. Brentwood, Tenn.: Wolgemuth & Hyatt, 1990.

Hexham, Irving. *The Irony of Apartheid: The Struggle for National Independence of Afrikaner Calvinism against British Imperialism*. New York: Edwin Mellen, 1981.

Hise, Greg. *Magnetic Los Angeles: Planning the Twentieth-Century Metropolis*. Creating the North American Landscape. Baltimore: Johns Hopkins University Press, 1999.

Hoggan, David L. *The Myth of the "New History": The Techniques and Tactics of the New Mythologists of American History*. Nutley, N.J.: Craig Press, 1965.

[Hoggan, David L.]. *The Myth of the Six Million*. 2nd ed. Los Angeles: Noontide Press, 1973.

Holifield, E. Brooks. *Theology in America: Christian Thought from the Age of the Puritans to the Civil War*. New Haven, Conn.: Yale University Press, 2003.

Hollinger, David A. *After Cloven Tongues of Fire: Protestant Liberalism in Modern American History*. Princeton, N.J.: Princeton University Press, 2013.

Hosier, Helen Kooiman. *Walter Knott, Keeper of the Flame*. Fullerton, Calif.: Plycon Press, 1973.

House, H. Wayne, and Thomas D. Ice. *Dominion Theology: Blessing or Curse?* Portland, Ore.: Multnomah Press, 1988.

Hunt, Dave. *Whatever Happened to Heaven?* Eugene, Ore.: Harvest House, 1988.

Ingebretsen, James C. *Apprentice to the Dawn: A Spiritual Memoir*. Los Angeles: Philosophical Research Society, 2003.

Ingersoll, Julie. *Building God's Kingdom: Christian Reconstruction in America*. New York: Oxford University Press, forthcoming.

Isserman, Maurice, and Michael Kazin. *America Divided: The Civil War of the 1960s*. New York: Oxford University Press, 2012.

Kantorowicz, Ernst Hartwig. *Frederick the Second, 1194–1250*. New York: R. R. Smith, 1931.

——. *The King's Two Bodies: A Study in Mediaeval Political Theology*. Princeton, N.J.: Princeton University Press, 1957.

——. *Laudes Regiae: A Study in Liturgical Acclamations and Mediaeval Ruler Worship*. Berkeley: University of California Press, 1946.

Kaoma, Kapya. *Globalizing the Culture Wars: U.S. Conservatives, African Churches, and Homophobia*. Somerville, Mass.: Political Research Associates, 2009.

Kennedy, D. James. *Reconstruction: Biblical Guidelines for a Nation in Peril*. Fort Lauderdale, Fla.: Coral Ridge Ministries, 1982.

Kik, J. Marcellus. *An Eschatology of Victory*. Phillipsburg, N.J.: Presbyterian and Reformed, 1971.

——. *Matthew Twenty-Four: An Exposition*. Swengel, Pa.: Bible Truth Depot, 1948.

Kintz, Linda. *Between Jesus and the Market: The Emotions That Matter in Right-Wing America*. Durham, N.C.: Duke University Press, 1997.

Kirk, Russell. *The Conservative Mind: From Burke to Santayana*. Chicago: H. Regnery, 1953.

Klein, Kerwin Lee. *From History to Theory*. Berkeley: University of California Press, 2011.

Kuyper, Abraham. *Lectures on Calvinism*. New York: Cosimo Classics, 2007.

John Birch Society. *The Blue Book of the John Birch Society*. Boston: Western Islands, 1961.

Jordan, James B. "Slavery in Biblical Perspective." M.A. thesis, Westminster Theological Seminary, 1980.

Joyce, Kathryn. *Quiverfull: Inside the Christian Patriarchy Movement*. Boston: Beacon Press, 2009.

Juergensmeyer, Mark. *Terror in the Mind of God: The Global Rise of Religious Violence*. 2nd ed. Berkeley: University of California Press, 2001.

Lazor, Joseph M. "Convergence in Sexual Ethics? Roman Catholic and Protestant Approaches in the United States Today." Ph.D. diss., University of Ottawa, 1983.

Lichtman, Allan J. *White Protestant Nation: The Rise of the American Conservative Movement.* New York: Atlantic Monthly Press, 2008.

Lienesch, Michael. *Redeeming America: Piety and Politics in the New Christian Right.* Chapel Hill: University of North Carolina Press, 1993.

Lindsey, Hal. *The Late Great Planet Earth.* Grand Rapids, Mich.: Zondervan, 1970.

——. *The Road to Holocaust.* New York: Bantam Books, 1989.

Lipsitz, George. *The Possessive Investment in Whiteness: How White People Profit from Identity Politics.* Revised ed. Philadelphia: Temple University Press, 2006.

Lively, Scott, and Scott Abrams. *The Pink Swastika: Homosexuality in the Nazi Party.* Keizer, Ore.: Founders, 1995.

Longfield, Bradley. *The Presbyterian Controversy: Fundamentalists, Modernists, and Moderates.* New York: Oxford University Press, 1991.

——. *Presbyterians and American Culture: A History.* Louisville: Westminster John Knox Press, 2013.

Ludy, Eric. *God's Gift to Women: Discovering the Lost Greatness of Masculinity.* Sisters, Ore.: Multnomah Books, 2003.

Ludy, Leslie. *Set-Apart Femininity: God's Sacred Intent for Every Young Woman.* Eugene, Ore.: Harvest House Publishers, 2008.

Machen, J. Gresham. *Christianity and Liberalism.* Grand Rapids, Mich.: Wm. B. Eerdmans, 1946.

Marley, David John. *Pat Robertson: An American Life.* Lanham, Md.: Rowman & Littlefield, 2007.

Marsden, George M. *Fundamentalism and American Culture.* 2nd ed. New York: Oxford University Press, 2006.

——. *Reforming Fundamentalism: Fuller Seminary and the New Evangelicalism.* Grand Rapids, Mich.: W. B. Eerdmans, 1987.

Martin, William C. *With God on Our Side: The Rise of the Religious Right in America.* New York: Broadway Books, 1996.

Mason, Carol. *Reading Appalachia from Left to Right: Conservatives and the 1974 Kanawha County Textbook Controversy.* Ithaca, N.Y.: Cornell University Press, 2009.

May, Elaine Tyler. *Homeward Bound: American Families in the Cold War Era.* New York: Basic Books, 1988.

McCarthy, Justin, Esat Arslan, Cemalettin Taşkıran, and Ömer Turan. *The Armenian Rebellion at Van.* Utah Series in Turkish and Islamic Studies. Salt Lake City: University of Utah Press, 2006.

McCloud, Sean. *Making the American Religious Fringe: Exotics, Subversives, and Journalists, 1955–1993.* Chapel Hill: University of North Carolina Press, 2004.

McConnel, Timothy Irwin. "The Historical Origins of the Presuppositional Apologetics of Cornelius Van Til." Ph.D. diss., Marquette University, 1999.

McCune, Lorne A. "An Evaluation of Theonomic Assertions Respecting Matthew 5." Ph.D. diss., Dallas Theological Seminary, 1997.

McDonald, Marci. *The Armageddon Factor: The Rise of Christian Nationalism in Canada.* Toronto: Random House Canada, 2010.

McGirr, Lisa. *Suburban Warriors: The Origins of the New American Right.* Politics and Society in Twentieth-Century America. Princeton, N.J.: Princeton University Press, 2001.

Meyer, Frank S. *The Conservative Mainstream*. New Rochelle, N.Y.: Arlington House, 1969.

Miller, Mark Crispin. *Cruel and Unusual: Bush/Cheney's New World Order*. New York: W. W. Norton & Company, 2004.

Miller, Steven P. *The Age of Evangelicalism: America's Born-Again Years*. New York: Oxford University Press, 2014.

————. *Billy Graham and the Rise of the Republican South*. Politics and Culture in Modern America. Philadelphia: University of Pennsylvania Press, 2009.

Mitchell, Richard G. *Dancing at Armageddon: Survivalism and Chaos in Modern Times*. Chicago: University of Chicago Press, 2002.

Moreton, Bethany. *To Serve God and Wal-Mart: The Making of Christian Free Enterprise*. Cambridge, Mass.: Harvard University Press, 2010.

Moore, E. Ray. *Let My Children Go: Why Parents Must Remove Their Children from Public School NOW*. Greenville, S.C.: Ambassador-Emerald International, 2002.

Moore, R. Jonathan. *Suing for America's Soul: John Whitehead, the Rutherford Institute, and Conservative Christians in the Courts*. Emory University Studies in Law and Religion. Grand Rapids, Mich.: William B. Eerdmans, 2007.

Moore, R. Laurence. *Selling God: American Religion in the Marketplace of Culture*. New York: Oxford University Press, 1994.

Muether, John R. *Cornelius Van Til: Reformed Apologist and Churchman*. American Reformed Biographies. Phillipsburg, N.J.: P&R, 2008.

Mulloy, D. J. *The World of the John Birch Society: Conspiracy, Conservatism, and the Cold War*. Nashville, Tenn.: Vanderbilt University Press, 2014.

Murphy, Paul V. *The Rebuke of History: The Southern Agrarians and American Conservative Thought*. Chapel Hill: University of North Carolina Press, 2001.

Nash, George H. *The Conservative Intellectual Movement in America, since 1945*. New York: Basic Books, 1976.

The Natsihi: Annual Publication of Whitworth College. Spokane, Wash.: Whitworth College, 1941. PDF e-book, http://cdm16004.contentdm.oclc.org/cdm/compoundobject/collection/p15238coll1/id/688/rec/1. June 27, 2014.

Nickerson, Michelle M. "Domestic Threats : Women, Gender, and Conservation in Cold War Los Angeles, 1945–1966." Ph.D. diss., Yale University, 2003.

————. *Mothers of Conservatism: Women and the Postwar Right*. Politics and Society in Twentieth-Century America. Princeton, N.J.: Princeton University Press, 2012.

Niebuhr, Reinhold. *Leaves from the Notebook of a Tamed Cynic*. 1929. Reprint, Hamden, Conn.: Shoestring Press, 1956.

Nock, Albert Jay. *Memoirs of a Superfluous Man*. Chicago: Regnery, 1964.

————. *Our Enemy, the State*. Caldwell, Idaho: Caxton Printers, 1946.

North, Gary. *Backward Christian Soldiers: An Action Manual for Christian Reconstruction*. Tyler, Tex.: Institute for Christian Economics, 1984. PDF e-book, http://www.garynorth.com/freebooks/docs/pdf/backward_christian_soldiers.pdf. June 27, 2014.

————. *Baptized Patriarchalism: The Cult of the Family*. Tyler, Tex.: Institute for Christian Economics, 1995. PDF e-book, http://www.garynorth.com/freebooks/docs/pdf/baptized_patriarchalism.pdf. June 27, 2014.

————. "The Concept of Property in Puritan New England, 1630–1720." Ph.D. diss., University of California, Riverside, 1972.

———. *Government by Emergency*. Fort Worth, Tex.: American Bureau of Economic Research, 1983.

———. *An Introduction to Christian Economics*. Nutley, N.J.: Craig Press, 1973. PDF e-book, http://www.garynorth.com/freebooks/docs/pdf/intro_to_christian_economics.pdf. June 27, 2014.

———. *Liberating Planet Earth: An Introduction to Biblical Blueprints*. Biblical Blueprint Series 1. Fort Worth, Tex.: Dominion Press, 1991. PDF e-book, http://www.garynorth.com/freebooks/docs/pdf/liberating_planet_earth.pdf. June 27, 2014.

———. *Lone Gunners for Jesus: Letters to Paul J. Hill*. Tyler, Tex.: Institute for Christian Economics, 1994.

———. *The Sinai Strategy: Economics and the Ten Commandments*. Tyler, Tex.: Institute for Christian Economics, 1986. PDF e-book, http://www.garynorth.com/freebooks/docs/pdf/the_sinai_strategy.pdf. June 27, 2014.

———. *Tithing and the Church*. Tyler, Tex.: Institute for Christian Economics, 1994. PDF e-book, http://www.garynorth.com/freebooks/docs/pdf/tithing_and_the_church.pdf. June 27, 2014.

———. *Trespassing for Dear Life: What Is Operation Rescue Up To?* Fort Worth, Tex.: Dominion Press, 1989. PDF e-book, http://www.garynorth.com/freebooks/docs/pdf/trespassing_for_dear_life.pdf. October 5, 2014.

———. *Unconditional Surrender: God's Program for Victory*. Tyler, Tex.: Institute for Christian Economics, 1994. PDF e-book, http://www.garynorth.com/freebooks/docs/214a_47e.htm. June 27, 2014.

———. *Unholy Spirits: Occultism and New Age Humanism*. Tyler, Tex.: Institute for Christian Economics, 1988. PDF e-book, http://www.garynorth.com/freebooks/docs/pdf/unholy_spirits.pdf. June 27, 2014.

———, ed. *Theonomy: An Informed Response*. Tyler, Tex.: Institute for Christian Economics, 1991. PDF e-book, http://www.garynorth.com/freebooks/docs/pdf/theonomy_an_informed_response.pdf. June 27, 2014.

North, Gary, and Gary DeMar. *Christian Reconstruction: What It Is, What It Isn't*. Tyler, Tex.: Institute for Christian Economics, 1991. PDF e-book, http://www.garynorth.com/freebooks/docs/pdf/christian_reconstruction.pdf. June 27, 2014.

Paulk, Earl. *Satan Unmasked*. Atlanta: K Dimension, 1984.

———. *That the World May Know*. Atlanta: K Dimension, 1987.

Phillips, Kevin. *American Theocracy: The Peril and Politics of Radical Religion, Oil, and Borrowed Money in the 21st Century*. New York: Viking, 2006.

Phillips-Fein, Kim. *Invisible Hands: The Making of the Conservative Movement from the New Deal to Reagan*. New York: W. W. Norton & Company, 2009.

Pride, Mary. *The Way Home: Beyond Feminism, Back to Reality*. Fenton, Mo.: Home Life Books, 2010.

Public Affairs Television and Bill Moyers. *God and Politics: On Earth as It Is in Heaven*. New York: Public Affairs Television, 1987.

Ribuffo, Leo P. *The Old Christian Right: The Protestant Far Right from the Great Depression to the Cold War*. Philadelphia: Temple University Press, 1983.

Robinson, Arthur, and Gary North. *Fighting Chance: Ten Feet to Survival*. Cave Junction, Ore.: Oregon Institute of Science and Medicine, 1986.

Rose, Kenneth D. *One Nation Underground: The Fallout Shelter in American Culture.* New York: New York University Press, 2004.

Rose, Nikolas S. *Powers of Freedom: Reframing Political Thought.* New York: Cambridge University Press, 1999.

Roy, Ralph Lord. *Apostles of Discord: A Study of Organized Bigotry and Disruption on the Fringes of Protestantism.* Boston: Beacon Press, 1953.

Ruff, Howard J. *Famine and Survival in America.* N.p.: Ruff, 1974.

———. *How to Prosper during the Coming Bad Years.* New York: Times Books, 1979.

Rushdoony, Rousas John. *The American Indian.* Vallecito, Calif.: Ross House Books, 2013.

———. *By What Standard? An Analysis of the Philosophy of Cornelius Van Til.* Philadelphia: Presbyterian and Reformed, 1959.

———. *Christianity and the State.* Vallecito, Calif.: Ross House Books, 1986.

———. *The Death of Meaning.* Vallecito, Calif.: Ross House Books, 2002.

———. *The Foundations of Social Order: Studies in the Creed and Councils of the Early Church.* 3rd ed. Vallecito, Calif.: Ross House Books, 1998.

———. *The Institutes of Biblical Law.* 3 vols. Nutley, N.J.: Craig Press, 1973; Vallecito: Ross House Books, 1982–1999.

———. *Intellectual Schizophrenia: Culture, Crisis, and Education.* International Library of Philosophy and Theology: Philosophical, and Historical Studies. Phillipsburg, N.J.: Presbyterian and Reformed, 1980.

———. *The Messianic Character of American Education: Studies In the History of the Philosophy of Education.* Nutley, N.J.: Craig Press, 1963.

———. *The Myth of Over Population.* Fairfax, Va.: Thoburn Press, 1975.

———. *The Mythology of Science.* Vallecito, Calif.: Ross House Books, 2001.

———. *The Nature of the American System.* Fairfax, Va.: Thoburn Press, 1978.

———. *The One and the Many: Studies in the Philosophy of Order and Ultimacy.* Nutley, N.J.: Craig Press, 1971.

———. *The Philosophy of the Christian Curriculum.* Vallecito, Calif.: Ross House Books, 1985.

———. *The Politics of Pornography.* New Rochelle, N.Y.: Arlington House, 1974.

———. *Preparation for the Future.* Mountainview, Calif.: Bern's Print Shop, 1966.

———. *The Religion of Revolution.* Victoria, Tex.: Trinity Episcopal Church, 1965.

———. *Revolt against Maturity: A Biblical Psychology of Man.* Fairfax, Va.: Thoburn Press, 1977.

———. *The Roots of Reconstruction.* Vallecito, Calif.: Ross House Books, 1991.

———. *Salvation and Godly Rule.* Vallecito, Calif.: Ross House Books, 1983.

———. *This Independent Republic: Studies in the Nature and Meaning of American History.* Vallecito, Calif.: Ross House Books, 2001.

———. *To Be as God: A Study of Modern Thought since the Marquis de Sade.* Vallecito, Calif.: Ross House Books, 2003.

———. *Van Til.* International Library of Philosophy and Theology: Modern Thinkers Series. Philadelphia: Presbyterian and Reformed, 1960.

———. *The Word of Flux: Modern Man and the Problem of Knowledge.* Vallecito, Calif.: Ross House Books, 1965.

Schaeffer, Francis A. *A Christian Manifesto.* Revised ed. Westchester, Ill.: Crossway Books, 1982.

———. *How Should We Then Live? The Rise and Decline of Western Thought and Culture.* Old Tappan, N.J.: F. H. Revell, 1976.

Schaeffer, Francis A., and C. Everett Koop. *Whatever Happened to the Human Race?* Old Tappan, N.J.: F. H. Revell, 1979.

Schaeffer, Frank. *Crazy for God: How I Grew up as One of the Elect, Helped Found the Religious Right, and Lived to Take All (or Almost All) of It Back.* New York: Carroll & Graf, 2008.

Schaeffer, Franky. *A Time for Anger: The Myth of Neutrality.* Westchester, Ill.: Crossway Books, 1982.

Schoenwald, Jonathan M. *A Time for Choosing: The Rise of Modern American Conservatism.* New York: Oxford University Press, 2001.

Self, Robert O. *All in the Family: The Realignment of American Democracy since the 1960s.* New York: Hill and Wang, 2012.

Sharlet, Jeff. *The Family: The Secret Fundamentalism at the Heart of American Power.* New York: HarperCollins, 2008.

Shires, Preston. *Hippies of the Religious Right: From the Counterculture of Jerry Garcia to the Subculture of Jerry Falwell.* Waco, Tex.: Baylor University Press, 2007.

Shively, Elizabeth Lauren. "Happily Ever After: Gender, Romance, and Relationships in the Christian Courtship Movement." Ph.D. diss., Ohio State University, 2012.

Shortt, Bruce N. *The Harsh Truth about Public Schools.* Vallecito, Calif.: Ross House Books, 2004.

Simonelli, Frederick J. *American Fuehrer: George Lincoln Rockwell and the American Nazi Party.* Urbana: University of Illinois Press, 1999.

Skousen, W. Cleon. *The 5,000-Year Leap: The 28 Great Ideas That Changed the World.* 1981; reprint, [Washington, D.C.]: National Center for Constitutional Studies, 2007.

————. *The Naked Communist.* Salt Lake City, Utah: Ensign, 1958.

Stone, Jon R. *On the Boundaries of American Evangelicalism: The Postwar Evangelical Coalition.* New York: St. Martin's Press, 1997.

Sullivan, Joel Lee. "The Ethics of Obscenity/Pornography: Biblical Principles of Law and Interpretation." M.A. thesis, Regent University, 1996.

Swartz, David R. *Moral Minority: The Evangelical Left in an Age of Conservatism.* Philadelphia: University of Pennsylvania Press, 2012.

Teles, Steven Michael. *The Rise of the Conservative Legal Movement: The Battle for Control of the Law.* Princeton Studies in American Politics. Princeton, N.J.: Princeton University Press, 2008.

Thorne, Phillip R. *Evangelicalism and Karl Barth: His Reception and Influence in North American Evangelical Theology.* Pittsburgh: Pickwick Publications, 1995.

Trueman, Carl R. *Histories and Fallacies: Problems Faced in the Writing of History.* Wheaton, Ill.: Crossway, 2010.

Turner, John G. *Bill Bright and Campus Crusade for Christ: The Renewal of Evangelicalism in Postwar America.* Chapel Hill: University of North Carolina Press, 2008.

Twelve Southerners. *I'll Take My Stand; The South and the Agrarian Tradition.* New York: Harper, 1930.

Urban, Hugh B. *The Secrets of the Kingdom: Religion and Concealment in the Bush Administration.* New York: Rowman & Littlefield, 2007.

Van Til, Cornelius. *Apologetics.* Phillipsburg, N.J.: Presbyterian and Reformed, 1976.

————. *The Case for Calvinism.* International Library of Philosophy and Theology. Philadelphia: Presbyterian and Reformed, 1964.

———. *Christian Apologetics.* Edited by William Edgar. 2nd ed. Phillipsburg, N.J.: Presbyterian and Reformed, 2003.

———. *The Defense of the Faith.* 3rd ed., rev. Philadelphia: Presbyterian and Reformed, 1995.

———. *An Introduction to Systematic Theology: Prolegomena and the Doctrines of Revelation, Scripture, and God.* Edited by William Edgar. 2nd ed. Phillipsburg, N.J.: Presbyterian and Reformed, 2007.

———. *Karl Barth and Evangelicalism.* Philadelphia: Presbyterian and Reformed, 1964.

———. *The New Modernism: An Appraisal of the Theology of Barth and Brunner.* Philadelphia: Presbyterian and Reformed, 1946.

Viereck, Peter. *Conservatism Revisited: The Revolt against Ideology.* New Brunswick, N.J.: Transaction Publishers, 2005.

Wagner, C. Peter. *Dominion! How Kingdom Action Can Change the World.* Grand Rapids, Mich.: Chosen, 2008.

———. *Wrestling with Alligators, Prophets, and Theologians: Lessons from a Lifetime in the Church.* Ventura, Calif.: Regal, 2010.

Watson, David. "Theonomy: A History of the Movement and an Evaluation of Its Primary Text." M.A. thesis, Calvin College, 1985.

Weaver, Richard M. *Ideas Have Consequences.* Chicago: University of Chicago Press, 1948.

Weyl, Franklin D. "Patriotic Pastors: A Study of Christian Influences on Colonial America, the United States Constitution, and the United States Form of Government, with Recommendations for Today." M.A. thesis, CBN University, 1989.

Whitehead, John W. *The Separation Illusion: A Lawyer Examines the First Amendment.* Milford, Mich.: Mott Media, 1977.

———. *Slaying Dragons: The Truth behind the Man Who Defended Paula Jones.* Nashville, Tenn.: Thomas Nelson Publishers, 1999.

William Volker Fund. *A Statement of Policy.* Burlingame, Calif.: William Volker Fund, n.d.

Williams, Daniel K. *God's Own Party: The Making of the Christian Right.* New York: Oxford University Press, 2010.

Wills, Garry. *Confessions of a Conservative.* Garden City, N.J.: Doubleday, 1979.

Wolfskill, George. *The Revolt of the Conservatives: A History of the American Liberty League, 1934–1940.* Boston: Houghton Mifflin, 1962.

Worthen, Molly. *Apostles of Reason: The Crisis of Authority in American Evangelicalism.* New York: Oxford University Press, 2013.

Wreszin, Michael. *The Superfluous Anarchist: Albert Jay Nock.* Providence, R.I.: Brown University Press, 1972.

Ybarra, Michael. *Washington Gone Crazy: Senator Pat McCarran and the Great American Communist Hunt.* Hanover, N.H.: Steerforth Press, 2004.

Articles, Book Chapters, Websites, and Other Media

"About C. Peter Wagner." Wagner Leadership Institute, 2009, http://www.wagnerleadership.org/Peter.htm. June 27, 2014.

Anti-Defamation League. "Kinism: A Racist and Anti-Semitic Religious Movement." Anti-Defamation League, 2013, http://www.adl.org/assets/pdf/combating-hate/Kinism-Racist -and-Anti-Semitic-Religionfinal2.pdf. June 27, 2014.

Backer, Larry Catá. "Theocratic Constitutionalism: An Introduction to a New Global Legal Ordering." *Indiana Journal of Global Legal Studies* 16, no. 1 (2009): 85–172.

Bahnsen, David L., Jr. "The Life of Dr. Greg L. Bahnsen." In *The Standard Bearer: A Festschrift for Greg L. Bahnsen*, 9–28. Nacogdoches, Tex.: Covenant Media Press, 2002.

Bahnsen, Greg L. "Foreword." In *Debate over Christian Reconstruction*, edited by Gary DeMar. Fort Worth, Tex.: Dominion Press, 1988. PDF e-book, http://www.garynorth.com/freebooks/docs/pdf/debate_over_christian_reconstruction.pdf. June 27, 2014.

Balmer, Randall H. "By the Way: The Rove of the Religious Right, a Eulogy." *Religion Dispatches*, December 22, 2008, http://www.religiondispatches.org/archive/politics/899/by_the_way%3A_the_rove_of_the_religious_right,_a_eulogy/. June 27, 2014.

———. "Religion in Twentieth-Century America." In *Religion in American Life: A Short History*, by Jon Butler, Grant Wacker, and Randall H. Balmer, 309–427. Oxford, UK: Oxford University Press, 2003.

Berlet, Chip. "How We Coined the Term 'Dominionism.'" Talk to Action: Reclaiming Citizenship, History, and Faith, August 31, 2011, http://www.talk2action.org/story/2011/8/31/17047/5683/. June 27, 2014.

———. "Von Mises Rises from the Scrap Heap of History." *ZMagazine*, May 2009, http://www.zcommunications.org/von-mises-rises-from-the-scrap-heap-of-history-by-chip-berlet. June 27, 2014.

Board, Stephen. "Moving the World with Magazines: A Survey of Evangelical Periodicals." In *American Evangelicals and the Mass Media: Perspectives on the Relationship between American Evangelicals and the Mass Media*, edited by Quentin J. Schultze, 119–42. Grand Rapids, Mich.: Academie Books/Zondervan, 1990.

"The Books and Beliefs Shaping Michele Bachmann." *Fresh Air*. NPR, August 9, 2011, http://www.npr.org/templates/transcript/transcript.php?storyId=139084313. June 27, 2014.

Bozell, L. Brent. "Freedom or Virtue." *National Review*, September 1962.

Bramwell, Austin. "Defining Conservatism Down." *American Conservative*, August 29, 2005. http://www.amconmag.com/article/2005/aug/29/00007/. October 4, 2014.

Buckley, William F. "National Review: Credenda and Statement of Principles." In *Conservatism in America since 1930: A Reader*, edited by Gregory L. Schneider, 201–5. New York: New York University Press, 2003.

Burns, Jennifer. "Review: In Retrospect: George Nash's *The Conservative Intellectual Movement in America since 1945.*" *Reviews in American History* 32, no. 3 (September 2004): 447–62.

Cafferty, Jack. "How Much Does It Worry You if Both Michele Bachmann and Rick Perry Have Ties to Dominionism?" Cafferty File: CNN.com Blogs, August 17, 2011, http://caffertyfile.blogs.cnn.com/2011/08/17/17612/. June 27, 2014.

Campbell, Colin. "The Cult, the Cultic Milieu and Secularization." *A Sociological Yearbook of Religion in Britain* 5 (1972): 119–36.

Cantor, Norman F. "The Nazi Twins: Percy Ernst Schramm and Ernst Hartwig Kantorowicz." In *Inventing the Middle Ages: The Lives, Works, and Ideas of the Great Medievalists of the Twentieth Century*, 79–117. New York: W. Morrow, 1991.

Chidester, David. "Religion Education in South Africa." In *International Handbook of the Religious, Moral, and Spiritual Dimensions in Education*, edited by Marian De Souza, Gloria Durka, Kathleen Engebretson, Robert Jackson, and Andrew McGrady, 433–48. Dordrecht, Netherlands: Springer, 2007.

Chilton, David. "Between the Covers of Power for Living." *Biblical Economics Today*, March 1984.

———. "Ecclesiastical Megalomania." *Trinity Review*, May 1994.

Chismar, Douglas E. "A Correction." *Christian Century*, November 9, 1983.

Chismar, Douglas E., and David A. Rausch. "The New Puritans and Their Theonomic Paradise." *Christian Century*, August 1983.

"Christian Children Need Christian Education." Exodus Mandate, n.d. http://exodusmandate. org/?page_id=1378. October 4, 2014

Clarkson, Frederick. "Christian Reconstruction: Theocratic Dominionism Gains Influence." In *Eyes Right! Challenging the Right Wing Backlash*, edited by Chip Berlet, 59–80. Boston: South End Press, 1995.

Cohen, Lizabeth. "Is There An Urban History of Consumption?" *Journal of Urban History* 29, no. 2 (January 1, 2003): 87–106.

Collier, Jane, Michelle Rosaldo, and Sylvia Yanagisako. "Is There a Family? New Anthropological Views." In *The Gender/Sexuality Reader: Culture, History, Political Economy*, edited by Roger N. Lancaster and Micaela Di Leonardo, 71–81. New York: Routledge, 1997.

Cowan, Douglas E. "Confronting the Failed Failure: Y2K and Evangelical Eschatology in Light of the Passed Millennium." *Nova Religio* 7, no. 2 (November 1, 2003): 71–85.

Crespino, Joseph. "Civil Rights and the Religious Right." In *Rightward Bound: Making America Conservative in the 1970s*, edited by Bruce J. Schulman and Julian E. Zelizer, 90–105. Cambridge, Mass.: Harvard University Press, 2008.

Dawidowicz, Lucy S. "Lies about the Holocaust." In *What Is the Use of Jewish History? Essays*, edited by Neal Kozodoy, 84–100. New York: Schocken Books, 1992.

Douthat, Ross. "Theocracy, Theocracy, Theocracy." *First Things: A Monthly Journal of Religion and Public Life*, August 2006.

"Dr. Gordon Stein (Atheist) vs Dr. Greg Bahnsen (Jesus Follower)." YouTube, June 9, 2013, http://www.youtube.com/watch?v=anGAazNCfdY. June 27, 2014.

Duigon, Lee. "Homeschooling's Greatest Courtroom Victory." Chalcedon.edu, April 23, 2012, http://chalcedon.edu/research/articles/homeschoolings-greatest-courtroom-victory/#_edn1. June 27, 2014.

Edgar, William. "The Passing of R. J. Rushdoony." *First Things: A Monthly Journal of Religion and Public Life*, August/September 2001.

Fosdick, Harry Emerson. "Shall the Fundamentalists Win?" In *American Sermons: The Pilgrims to Martin Luther King, Jr*, edited by Michael Warner, 775–86. New York: Library of America, 1999.

Frame, John M. "Bahnsen at the Stein Debate." The Works of John Frame and Vern Poythress, n.d., http://www.frame-poythress.org/bahnsen-at-the-stein-debate/. June 27, 2014.

"Generations at Odds: The Millennial Generation and the Future of Gay and Lesbian Rights." Public Religion Research Institute, August 9, 2011. http://publicreligion.org/ research/2011/08/generations-at-odds/. October 4, 2014.

Goldberg, Michelle. "A Christian Plot for Domination?" The Daily Beast, August 14, 2011, http://www.thedailybeast.com/articles/2011/08/14/dominionism-michele-bachmann-and -rick-perry-s-dangerous-religious-bond.html. June 27, 2014.

Goldwater, Barry. "Extremism in the Defense of Liberty Is No Vice." In *Landmark Speeches of the American Conservative Movement*, edited by Peter Schweizer and Wynton C. Hall, 30–41. College Station: Texas A&M University Press, 2007.

"The Great Debate: Greg Bahnsen vs. Gordon Stein." Vimeo, January 13, 2012, http://vimeo.com/34998731. June 27, 2014.

Hankins, Barry. "The *New Yorker* and Evangelicalism." *American Spectator*, August 15, 2011, http://spectator.org/archives/2011/08/15/the-new-yorker-and-evangelical. June 27, 2014.

Harding, Susan. "Representing Fundamentalism: The Problem of the Repugnant Cultural Other." *Social Research* 58, no. 2 (Summer 1991): 373–93.

Hayles, N. Katherine. "Complex Dynamics in Literature and Science." In *Chaos and Order: Complex Dynamics in Literature and Science*, edited by N. Katherine Hayles, 1–36. Chicago: University of Chicago Press, 1991.

Hexham, Irving. "The Evangelical Response to the New Age." In *Perspectives on the New Age*, edited by James R. Lewis and J. Gordon Melton, 152–63. Albany: State University of New York Press, 1992.

Hughes, Frank. "How to Fire a Professor: A Case History in 'Academic Freedom.'" *Freeman* 2, no. 5 (December 3, 1951): 145–48.

Iannaccone, Laurence R. "Heirs to the Protestant Ethic? The Ethics of American Fundamentalists." In *The Fundamentalism Project: Fundamentalisms and the State*, vol. 3, edited by Martin E. Marty and R. Scott Appleby, 342–66. Chicago: University of Chicago Press, 1996.

Ingber, Stanley. "Religion or Ideology: A Needed Clarification of the Religion Clauses." *Stanford Law Review* 41, no. 2 (January 1, 1989): 233–333.

Ingersoll, Julie. "Mobilizing Evangelicals: Christian Reconstructionism and the Roots of the Religious Right." In *Evangelicals and Democracy in America: Religion and Politics*, vol. 2, edited by Steven Brint and Jean Reith Schroedel, 179–208. New York: Russell Sage Foundation, 2009.

Jeri. "Voiceless Women: Arda J. Rushdoony." Heresy in the Heartland, August 3, 2013, http://heresyintheheartland.blogspot.com/2013/08/voiceless-women-arda-j-rushdoony.html. June 27, 2014.

Johnson, Lyndon B. "President Lyndon B. Johnson's Remarks at the University of Michigan, May 22, 1964." LBJ Presidential Library, http://www.lbjlib.utexas.edu/johnson/archives.hom/speeches.hom/640522.asp. June 27, 2014.

Kahn, Victoria. "Political Theology and Fiction in *The King's Two Bodies*." *Representations* 106, no. 1 (May 2009): 77–101.

Kantorowicz, Ernst Hartwig. "The 'King's Advent' and the Enigmatic Panels in the Doors of Santa Sabina." *Art Bulletin* 26, no. 4 (December 1944): 207–31.

Lassiter, Matthew D. "Inventing Family Values." In *Rightward Bound: Making America Conservative in the 1970s*, edited by Bruce J. Schulman and Julian E. Zelizer, 13–28. Cambridge, Mass.: Harvard University Press, 2008.

Latour, Bruno. "From Object to Things: How to Represent the Parliament of Nature?" University of Berkeley Art Museum & Pacific Film Archive, October 17, 2005, http://www.bampfa.berkeley.edu/podcasts/ATC/latour. June 27, 2014.

———. "The Powers of Association." In *Power, Action, and Belief: A New Sociology of Knowledge?*, edited by John E. Law, 264–80. Sociological Review Monograph 32. London: Routledge & Kegan Paul, 1986.

"Law and Order 1966." NAE: Policy Resolutions & Documents, http://www.nae.net/fullresolutionlist/620-law-and-order-1966. June 27, 2014.

Lee, Earl, and Scott Forschler. "Bearing Gifts: How Librarians Deal with Gift Books and Gift Givers–A Detective Story." *Journal of Information Ethics*, vol. 1 (Fall 1992): 52–59.

Lee, Morgan. "Duggar Family's Close Relationship with Vision Forum Founder Doug Phillips and Wife Highlighted after Scandal." *Christian Post*, November 13, 2013, http://www.christianpost.com/news/duggar-familys-close-relationship-with-vision-forum-founder-doug-phillips-and-wife-highlighted-after-scandal-108697/. June 27, 2014.

Lichtman, Sarah A. "Do-It-Yourself Security." *Journal of Design History* 19, no. 1 (Spring 2006): 39–55.

Lizza, Ryan. "Leap of Faith." *New Yorker*, August 15, 2011.

Lofton, John, and Chris Ortiz. "Remembering Rushdoony." The American View, 2009, http://archive.theamericanview.com/index.php?id=1409. June 27, 2014.

Lorenz, Mike. "Wolves in Sheep's Clothing: Gary North, Y2K, and Hidden Agendas." Sweet Liberty. http://www.sweetliberty.org/garynorth.htm. October 4, 2014.

Maibaum, Matthew. "Armenians in California." *Patterns of Prejudice* 19, no. 1 (1985): 25–32.

Malkiel, Yakov. "Ernst H. Kantorowicz." In *On Four Modern Humanists: Hofmannsthal, Gundolf, Curtius, Kantorowicz*, edited by Arthur R. Evans. Princeton, N.J.: Princeton University Press, 1970.

"Mark Rushdoony Says That His Father, R. J. Rushdoony, Was Not a Kinist." Theonomy Resources, August 12, 2010, http://theonomyresources.blogspot.com/2010/08/mark-rushdoony-says-that-his-father-r-j.html. October 5, 2014.

McCullagh, Declan. "There's Something about Gary North." *Wired*, January 7, 1999, http://www.wired.com/culture/lifestyle/news/1999/01/17193. September 10, 2010.

McIlhenny, Ryan. "The Austin T.E.A. Party: Homeschooling Controversy in Texas, 1986–1994." In *Inequity in Education: A Historical Perspective*, edited by Debra Meyers and Burke Miller, 211–34. Lanham, Md.: Lexington Books, 2009.

McMinn, Lisa. "Y2K, the Apocalypse, and Evangelical Christianity: The Role of Eschatological Belief in Church Responses." *Sociology of Religion* 62, no. 2 (June 20, 2001): 205–20.

McVicar, Michael J. "Aggressive Philanthropy: Progressivism, Conservatism, and the William Volker Charities Fund." *Missouri Historical Review* 105 (July 2011): 191–12.

———. "'Let Them Have Dominion': 'Dominion Theology' and the Construction of Religious Extremism in the U.S. Media." *Journal of Religion and Popular Culture* 25, no. 1 (January 1, 2013): 120–45.

Meyer, Frank S. "Richard M. Weaver: An Appreciation." *Modern Age* 14, no. 3/4 (Summer/Fall 1970): 243–48.

Moots, Glenn, and Timothy D. Terrell. "One Protestant Tradition's Interface with Austrian Economics: Christian Reconstruction as Critic and Ally." *Journal of Markets and Morality* 9, no. 1 (Spring 2006): 91–114.

Morecraft, Joseph C. "The Christian Reconstruction Dialogue: Dallas, Texas, October 14–17, 1987." *Counsel of Chalcedon* (December 1987): 6–8.

"MP3-Bahnsen." Covenant Media Foundation, n.d, http://www.cmfnow.com/mp3-bahnsen.aspx. June 27, 2014.

Murray, Stephen O. "The Rights of Research Assistants and the Rhetoric of Political

Suppression: Morton Grodzins and the University of California Japanese-American Evacuation and Resettlement Study." *Journal of the History of the Behavioral Sciences* 27, no. 2 (April 1991): 130–56.

Nickerson, Michelle M. "Moral Mothers and Goldwater Girls." In *The Conservative Sixties*, edited by David R. Farber and Jeff Roche, 50–62. New York: Peter Lang, 2003.

———. "Women, Domesticity, and Postwar Conservatism." *Magazine of History* 17, no. 2 (2003): 17–21.

Nock, Albert Jay. "Artemus Ward." In *On Doing the Right Thing, and Other Essays*, 1–24. New York: Harper & Brothers, 1928.

———. "Isaiah's Job." *Atlantic Monthly*, June 1936.

Noll, Mark A. "Common Sense Traditions and American Evangelical Thought." *American Quarterly* 37, no. 2 (Summer 1985): 216–38.

North, Gary. "Chilton, Sutton, and Dominion Theology." *Institute for Christian Economics Position Papers*, January 1987. PDF e-file, http://www.garynorth.com/freebooks/docs/a_pdfs/newslet/position/8701.pdf. June 27, 2014.

———. "Clarifying the So-called 'Hitler Connection.'" *Institute for Christian Economics Position Papers*, November 1992. PDF e-file, http://www.garynorth.com/freebooks/docs/a_pdfs/newslet/position/9209.pdf. June 27, 2014.

———. "David Chilton: Free Books to Download." Gary North's Specific Answers, n.d., http://www.garynorth.com/public/6597.cfm. June 27, 2014.

———. "The Feminist Mistake: The Economics of Women's Liberation." *The Freeman* 21, no. 1 (January 1971): 3–14.

———. Institute for Christian Economics cover letter. I.C.E., March 1998, http://www.reformed-theology.org/ice/newslet/coverletters/cover98.03.htm. June 27, 2014.

———. Institute for Christian Economics cover letter. I.C.E., January 1999, http://www.reformed-theology.org/ice/newslet/coverletters/cover99.01.htm. June 27, 2014.

———. "It All Began with Fred Schwarz." LewRockwell.com, December 16, 2002, http://www.lewrockwell.com/north/north145.html. June 27, 2014.

———. "John W. Robbins, R.I.P." LewRockwell.com, August 14, 2008, http://www.lewrockwell.com/blog/lewrw/archives/22356.html. June 27, 2014.

———. "Market Decentralization and Covenantal Organization," *Christian Reconstruction* 8, no. 6 (November/December 1989). PDF e-file, http://www.garynorth.com/freebooks/docs/a_pdfs/newslet/cr/8911.pdf. June 27, 2014.

———. "Marx's View of the Division of Labor." *The Freeman* 19, no. 1 (January 1969): 28–35.

———. "Publisher's Foreword." In *House Divided: The Break-Up of Dispensational Theology*, by Greg L. Bahnsen, and Kenneth L. Gentry, ix–xliv. Tyler, Tex.: Institute for Christian Economics, 1989. PDF e-book, http://www.garynorth.com/freebooks/docs/pdf/house_divided.pdf. June 27, 2014.

———. "R. J. Rushdoony, R.I.P." LewRockwell.com, February 10, 2001, http://www.lewrockwell.com/north/north33.html. June 27, 2014.

———. "Ron Paul Curriculum: Introduction." YouTube, April 9, 2013, http://www.youtube.com/watch?v=dei_bt22lIY#t=132. June 27, 2014.

———. "Rumor #213: Rushdoony Has Gone Unitarian." *Institute for Christian Economics Position Papers*, 1994. PDF e-file, http://www.garynorth.com/freebooks/docs/a_pdfs/newslet/position/9408.pdf. June 27, 2014.

———. "Statist Bureaucracy in the Modern Economy." *The Freeman* 20, no. 1 (January 1970): 16–28.

———. "The Theology of the Exponential Curve." *The Freeman* 20, no. 5 (May 1970): 293–310.

———. "Writing Conspiracy History: Lists Are Not Enough." LewRockwell.com, March 1, 2002. http://www.lewrockwell.com/north/north95.html. October 4, 2014.

O'Mara, Margaret Pugh. "Uncovering the City in the Suburb: Cold War Politics, Scientific Elites, and High-Tech Spaces." In *The New Suburban History*, edited by Kevin M. Kruse and Thomas J. Sugrue, 57–79. Chicago: University of Chicago Press, 2006.

On Earth as It Is in Heaven. VHS. *God and Politics*, vol. 3. New York: Public Affairs Television, 1987.

Orsi, Robert A. "Snakes Alive: Resituating the Moral in the Study of Religion." In *Women, Gender, Religion: A Reader*, edited by Elizabeth A. Castelli and Rosamond C. Rodman, 98–118. New York: Palgrave, 2001.

Philips, Doug. "Dorothy Rushdoony, Chalcedon Matriarch, Dies." Doug's Blog: A Daily Log and Online Journal from Doug Philips, February 11, 2003, http://www.visionforum.com/hottopics/blogs/dwp/2003/11/602.aspx. April 19, 2010.

———. "Statement of Resignation." Vision Forum Ministries, October 30, 2013, http://www.visionforumministries.org. June 27, 2014.

Phillips-Fein, Kim. "Conservatism: A State of the Field." *Journal of American History* 98, no. 3 (December 1, 2011): 723–43.

Potok, Mark. "The Year in Hate 2004." Southern Poverty Law Center, http://www.splcenter.org/get-informed/intelligence-report/browse-all-issues/2005/spring/the-year-in-hate-2004. June 27, 2014.

"Profit of Doom Ruff Huffs and Puffs." *Time*, April 23, 1979.

Reagan, Ronald. "Proclamation 5018–Year of the Bible, 1983." Ronald Reagan Presidential Library & Museum, February 3, 1983, http://www.reagan.utexas.edu/archives/speeches/1983/20383b.htm. June 27, 2014.

Roberts, Wesley A. "Cornelius Van Til." In *Reformed Theology in America: A History of Its Modern Development*, edited by David F. Wells, 119–32. Grand Rapids, Mich.: W. B. Eerdmans, 1985.

"Ron Paul Curriculum: The Story of Liberty, K-12." Ron Paul Curriculum, http://www.ronpaulcurriculum.com. June 27, 2014.

"Rushdoony Leeper Transcript: Texas Homeschool Trial." *R. J. Rushdoony*. N.d, http://rushdoony.sitewave.net/rushdoony-leeper-transcript-texas-homeschool-trial/. June 27, 2014.

Rushdoony, Mark Rousas. "A Biographical Sketch of My Father." In *A Comprehensive Faith: An International Festschrift for Rousas John Rushdoony*, edited by Andrew Sandlin, 21–29. San Jose, Calif.: Friends of Chalcedon, 1996.

———. "The Vision of R. J. Rushdoony." Pocket College: Equipping the Saints to Advance the Kingdom, http://www.pocketcollege.com/beta/index.php?title=Rushdoony,_Dr._R._J. June 27, 2014.

Rushdoony, Rousas John. "Christian Missions and Indian Culture." *Westminster Theological Journal* 12, no. 1 (May 1949): 1–12.

———. "Dominion Man." MP3. N.d. Contemporary Cultural Ethics.

Rushdouni, Y. K. "Letter Dated Van, 7th June 1915, from Y. K. Rushdouni; Published in the

'Manchester Guardian,' 2nd August, 1915." In *The Treatment of Armenians in the Ottoman Empire, 1915–16; Documents Presented to Viscount Grey of Fallodon, Secretary of State for Foreign Affairs*, edited by James Bryce Bryce, 48–51. 2nd ed. Beirut: G. Doniguian & Sons, 1972.

———. "Narrative by Mr. Y. K. Rushdouni, Published Serially in the Armenian Journal 'Gotchnag,' of New York." In *The Treatment of Armenians in the Ottoman Empire, 1915–16; Documents Presented to Viscount Grey of Fallodon, Secretary of State for Foreign Affairs*, edited by James Bryce Bryce, 52–70. 2nd ed. Beirut: G. Doniguian & Sons, 1972.

Samson, Steven Alan. "Christian Reconstruction." In *American Conservatism: An Encyclopedia*, edited by Bruce Frohnen, Jeremy Beer, and Jeffery O. Nelson. Wilmington, Del.: ISI Books, 2006.

Schoenwald, Jonathan M. "We Are an Action Group: The John Birch Society and the Conservative Movement in the 1960s." In *The Conservative Sixties*, edited by David R. Farber and Jeff Roche, 21–36. New York: Peter Lang, 2003.

Schultz, Roger. "Rushdoony, Rousas John (1916–2001)." In *American Conservatism: An Encyclopedia*, edited by Bruce Frohnen, Jeremy Beer, and Jeffery O. Nelson. Wilmington, Del.: ISI Books, 2006.

Schwartz, Andrea, and Howard Phillips. "Howard Phillips Remembers Rush." Law and Liberty Podcast, March 28, 2011, http://chalcedon.edu/blog/2011/3/28/law-and-liberty-podcast -howard-phillips-remembers-rush/. June 27, 2014.

Schwartz, Andrea, and J. Shelby Sharpe. "J. Shelby Sharpe Remembers Rush." Law and Liberty Podcast, May 9, 2011, http://chalcedon.edu/blog/2011/5/9/law-and-liberty-podcast-j-shelby -sharpe-remembers-rush/. June 27, 2014.

"Scott Lively." PRA.org, http://www.publiceye.org/publications/globalizing-the-culture-wars/ scott-lively.php. June 27, 2014.

Sharlet, Jeff. "Through a Glass, Darkly: How the Christian Right Is Reimagining American History." *Harper's Magazine*, December 2006.

Shipps, Kenneth W. "Christianity Today, 1956–." In *The Conservative Press in Twentieth-Century America*, edited by Ronald Lora and William Henry Longton, 171–80. Historical Guides to the World's Periodicals and Newspapers. Westport, Conn.: Greenwood Press, 1999.

Shupe, Anson D., Thomas Robbins, and Susan J. Palmer. "Christian Reconstructionism and the Angry Rhetoric of Neo-Postmillennialism." In *Millennium, Messiahs, and Mayhem: Contemporary Apocalyptic Movements*, 195–206. New York: Routledge, 1997.

Sies, Mary Corbin. "North American Suburbs, 1880–1950: Cultural and Social Reconsiderations." *Journal of Urban History* 27, no. 3 (March 1, 2001): 313–46.

Skillen, James W., and Rockne M. McCarthy, eds. "Sphere Sovereignty, Creation Order, and Public Justice." In *Political Order and the Plural Structure of Society*, 397–418. Atlanta: Scholars Press, 1991.

Smith, Chris. "His Truth Is Marching On: Rousas John Rushdoony and the Rise of Christian Conservatives." *California Magazine*, Fall 2012, http://alumni.berkeley.edu/news/california -magazine/fall-2012-politics-issue/his-truth-marching. June 27, 2014.

Smolin, David M. "State Regulation of Private Education: Ohio Law in the Shadow of the United States Supreme Court Decisions." *University of Cincinnati Law Review* 54, no. 3 (1986): 1003–34.

Society of Former Special Agents of the FBI. "Samuel W. North, Jr." In *Society of Former Special Agents of the FBI*, 185. Paducah, Ky.: Turner Publishing, 1997.

Spruill, Marjorie J. "Gender and America's Right Turn." In *Rightward Bound: Making America Conservative in the 1970s*, edited by Bruce J. Schulman and Julian E. Zelizer, 71–89. Cambridge, Mass.: Harvard University Press, 2008.

Stowe, David W. *No Sympathy for the Devil: Christian Pop Music and the Transformation of American Evangelicalism*. Chapel Hill: University of North Carolina Press, 2011.

Taves, Ann. "Sexuality in American Religious History." In *Retelling U.S. Religious History*, edited by Thomas A. Tweed, 27–56. Berkeley: University of California Press, 1997.

Titus, Herbert. "The Impact of Rushdoony on Jurisprudence." Sermonaudio.com, February 2, 2005, http://www.sermonaudio.com/sermoninfo.asp?SID=220572324. June 27, 2014.

Toy, Eckard V. "The Conservative Connection: The Chairman of the Board Tool LSD before Timothy Leary." *American Studies* 21 (January 1980): 65–77.

———. "The National Lay Committee and the National Council of Churches: A Case Study of Protestants in Conflict." *American Quarterly* 21, no. 2 (Summer 1969): 190–209.

———. "Spiritual Mobilization: The Failure of an Ultraconservative Ideal in the 1950s." *Pacific Northwest Quarterly* 61 (April 1970): 77–86.

Unruh, Bob. "Christians Need Exodus from 'Pharaoh's System.'" *World Net Daily*, May 5, 2007, http://www.wnd.com/2007/05/41462/. June 27, 2014.

Van Til, Cornelius. "My Credo." In *Jerusalem and Athens: Critical Discussions on the Theology and Apologetics of Cornelius Van Til*, edited by E. R. Geehan, 3–21. Phillipsburg, N.J.: Presbyterian and Reformed, 1971.

"Vision Forum Ministries Closing its Doors." Duggar Family Blog: Updates and Pictures Jim Bob and Michelle Duggar 19 Kids and Counting, November 13, 2013, http://duggarsblog. blogspot.com/2013/11/vision-forum-ministries-closing-its.html. June 27, 2014.

Whitehead, John W. "Crazy for God: An Interview with Frank Schaeffer." *Oldspeak*, October 23, 2007, http://www.rutherford.org/publications_resources/oldspeak/crazy_for_god_an_interview_with_frank_schaeffer. June 27, 2014.

Whitehead, John W., and John Conlan. "The Establishment of the Religion of Secular Humanism and Its First Amendment Implications." *Texas Tech Law Review* 10 (1979–1978): 1–66.

"Who's Who on the Right." *Newsweek*, February 2, 1981.

Wilder, Forrest. "Rick Perry's Army of God." *Texas Observer*, August 3, 2011, http://www.texasobserver.org/cover-story/rick-perrys-army-of-god. January 30, 2014, and June 27, 2014.

Worthen, Molly. "The Chalcedon Problem: Rousas John Rushdoony and the Origins of Christian Reconstructionism." *Church History* 77, no. 2 (June 2008): 399–437.

"Writings of Paul Jennings Hill." Armyofgod.com. http://www.armyofgod.com/Paulhillindex.html. October 5, 2014.

Zaitchik, Alexander. "Meet the Man Who Changed Glenn Beck's Life." Salon.com, September 16, 2009, http://www.salon.com/2009/09/16/beck_skousen/. June 27, 2014.

INDEX

and law and order, 128–29; and the death penalty, 130–31; as form of covenant theology, 132, 257 (n. 126); and marriage, 133–34; and postmillennialism, 138–39; and economics, 153, 155; and churches, 182, 184, 188. *See also* Theonomy

Bierly, Ivan R., 62, 83, 207, 246 (n. 112), 247 (n. 147), 248 (n. 16); and sectarianism at the Volker Fund and Center for American Studies, 66–77 passim, 245 (n. 102)

Billings, Robert, 144–45

Blumenthal, Max, 215

Board, Stephen, 112

Bob Jones University (BJU), 145, 148

Bookstores. *See* Christian bookstores; Patriot bookstores

Boyer, Paul, 135

Bozell, Brent, 76–77, 244 (n. 97)

Bray, Michael, 160

Bright, Bill, 139, 178–80

Brown, Harold O. J., 142

Brunner, Emil, 34, 238 (n. 73)

Buchanan, Patrick J., 147, 222

Buckingham, Jamie, 180

Buckley, William F., Jr., 60–61, 247 (n. 146); and the Intercollegiate Society of Individualists (ISI), 63, 70; and fusionism, 65, 86, 244 (n. 97)

Bush, George H. W., 202

Bush, George W., 6, 216

Calvin, John, 36, 130

Calvin College, 98, 239 (n. 90)

Calvinism, 53, 84, 154, 161. *See also* Center for American Studies (CAS): sectarian tensions in; Dutch Reformed Calvinism; Neo-Calvinism

Calvin Theological Seminary, 136

Campbell, Roderick, 137, 258 (nn. 156, 160)

Campbell University, 155

Campus Crusade for Christ, 139, 144, 178, 179, 180, 182

Cantor, Norman F., 30

Capitalism, 70, 230; and Christianity, 49–50, 52, 68, 119, 188; versus socialism, 62, 63; and

decentralization, 185–86. *See also* Austrian economics

Carleton College, 53–54, 57, 59, 246 (n. 111)

Carter, Jimmy, 8, 144, 149, 195, 201

Catawba College, 116

Catholicism, 10, 49, 64, 66, 69, 70–71, 75, 135, 161, 171, 221; and anti-Catholicism, 48, 71, 73

CBN University. *See* Regent University

Center for American Studies (CAS), 14, 67, 79, 83, 84, 85, 90, 97, 206, 207, 245 (n. 105), 248 (n. 16); sectarian tensions in, 68–77 passim, 245 (nn. 100, 106)

Chalcedon, Inc. *See* Chalcedon Foundation

Chalcedon College, 98, 110, 118, 143, 144. *See also* Chalcedon Foundation

Chalcedon Foundation, 3, 5–6, 15, 80, 106, 144, 158, 159, 160, 173, 182, 207, 209, 211, 214, 221, 272 (n. 178), 274 (n. 31); founding of, 87; theological reasoning behind, 87–89, 126; family-centered ministry of, 94, 101, 139; relationship with John Birch Society, 94–97; funding of, 98–99, 104, 110, 143, 209, 220; and Christian Reconstruction, 100; and biblical law, 128–29; and educational reform, 148–53, 167–70, 224; support of Gary North, 150–52, 163; support of Greg L. Bahnsen, 157, 161, 163; support of John W. Whitehead, 175; tensions with Tyler Group and Gary North, 183–84, 190–95, 217–19. *See also* Chalcedon College; Rushdoony, Rousas John, works of: *Chalcedon Report* (journal); Rushdoony, Rousas John, works of: *Newsletter* (journal)

Chaos theory, 184

Chapel Hill Harvester Church, 199

Charismatic movement, 16, 171, 180; relationship with Christian Reconstructionism, 181, 198–201, 204. *See also* Pentecostalism

Chidester, David, 225

Chilton, David, 176, 199, 266–65 (n. 52); as Greg L. Bahnsen's student, 160; and *Power for Living* controversy, 179, 180, 183; and Tyler rivalry with R. J. Rushdoony, 192–94;

death of, 217, 221; on homosexuality, 274
(n. 44)

Chinese Presbyterian Church (San Francisco, Calif.), 24

Christian Anti-Communist Crusade (CACC), 63

Christian bookstores, 176

Christian Crusade, 78

Christian Freedom Foundation (CFF), 63, 117, 118, 119. *See also* Kershner, Howard E.

Christianity Today (journal), 15, 109–10, 122, 123; and neoevangelicalism, 111–21; coverage of Christian Reconstruction and R. J. Rushdoony, 5, 142, 196–97, 202–4, 214, 221, 269 (n. 115)

Christian Knights of the Ku Klux Klan, 46

Christian Legal Society, 211–12

Christian Manifesto, A (Schaeffer), 211–12

Christian Reconstruction: and homeschooling, 1–3, 163, 166–67, 170, 175, 223–25, 227–28; and educational reform, 4–5, 7, 97, 102, 163, 165–70, 174, 175, 224–25; and governance, 4–5, 15, 19, 92, 99–100, 132–34, 139; and dominion, 4–5, 15–16, 129, 131, 143, 150, 175, 177, 182, 197–205, 213, 215–16, 223–24, 268 (n. 88); definition of, 4–5, 100, 226–27; and the Chalcedon Foundation, 5–6, 99–100; political influence of, 5–7, 181, 195, 197, 201, 205–10, 221–22, 226–28; media coverage of, 6–7, 198–99, 203–6, 213–16, 221–22, 228–29, 269 (n. 115); scholarly study of, 7–8, 163, 235 (nn. 25, 27), 260 (n. 27), 262 (n. 84), 272 (n. 178); as rejection of neoevangelicalism, 8, 121, 122, 128, 138–39, 195; as family project, 15, 100–101, 130–31, 139, 182–83, 202, 225; as Protestant feudalism, 15, 125, 185; and the charismatic movement, 16, 181, 198–201, 204; origin of phrase, 100; and gender roles, 126, 131–34, 223–24, 234 (n. 14); and postmillennialism, 136–39; theological influence of, 157–59, 181, 197, 199–201, 210–13; and violence, 160–61; rejection by other Christians, 163, 201–6, 216, 228–31; as antidemocratic movement,

181, 194–95, 202–6, 210; as liberation theology, 201; as "stealth" theology, 256 (n. 114)

Christian Right, 5, 6, 16, 17, 126; and Christian Reconstructionism, 143–45, 183, 195, 206, 214, 219, 221. *See also* Religious Right

Christian Rights Foundation, 170–74

Church of Scientology, 171

Civil disobedience, 108–9, 161, 174, 211, 262 (n. 81)

Civil War, 135

Clapp, Rodney, 202–4, 214, 260 (n. 27), 269 (n. 115)

Clark, Gordon, 154

Clarkson, Frederick, 270 (n. 130), 272 (n. 178)

Clay, Orval, 28

Coast Federal Savings and Loan Association, 103

Cobelligerents, 212–13

Cohen, Warren I., 151–52

Common Core State Standards Initiative, 16–17

Common sense philosophy, 37. *See also* Evidentialist apologetics

Communism, 14, 47, 52, 55, 65, 85, 90, 92, 95, 97. *See also* Anticommunism

Confession of Chalcedon, 87; and governance, 88. *See also* Council of Chalcedon

Conservatism: and the Christian Right, 5–7, 143–49, 195; as milieu, 9–11, 14, 16, 49, 78, 84, 97, 122, 222; and fusionism, 14, 19, 65, 70, 86, 87, 222, 244 (n. 97); and Southern California, 14, 48, 50, 79–80, 82, 84, 86, 85, 90–91, 97, 124, 143; and "law and order," 15, 108–11, 124, 141; and antistatism, 45, 59, 60, 87, 89, 223, 226, 228; contested meaning of, 47–48, 50, 72–74, 77–78; and anticommunism, 48, 65, 108, 151; and the Remnant, 59–64; Center for American Studies (CAS) contested definitions of, 73–77; and female activists, 84–86, 102; and the family, 91–92

Conservative Caucus, 208

Conspiracy theories, 92, 94–96, 102, 218, 225

Constitution Party, 209

Coral Ridge Presbyterian Church, 199

Cornell University, 54, 62

Cornuelle, Herbert C., 54

Couch, William T., 68, 71–78, 245 (n. 109); 247 (nn. 131, 146)

Council for National Policy (CNP), 145–46; founding of, 207–8, 270 (nn. 130, 133); R. J. Rushdoony's relationship with, 209–11, 214

Council of Chalcedon, 87–89, 97. *See also* Confession of Chalcedon

Covenant theology, 132–33, 137, 174, 199, 256 (n. 110), 257 (n. 126)

Craig, Charles H. ("Hays"), 256 (n. 113)

Craig, Samuel G., 242 (n. 46)

Craig Press. *See* Presbyterian and Reformed Publishing Company (P&R)

Crane, Jasper, 50, 54–55, 242 (n. 39)

Creation Mandate, 5, 131. *See also* Dominion mandate

Creation Museum, 196

Crespino, Joseph, 146

Crowley, Aleister, 220

Dallas Theological Seminary, 136, 163, 182, 197, 269 (n. 115)

Darwin, Charles: evolutionary theory of, 30, 36

Death penalty, 4, 129, 274 (n. 44); in biblical law, 130–31, 141, 236 (n. 136)

DeMar, Gary, 160, 179–80, 269 (n. 111)

Democracy, 63, 89, 124, 125, 206, 214, 216, 268 (n. 88), 270 (n. 130); as heresy, 141, 202–3. *See also* Christian Reconstruction: as antidemocratic movement

Democratic Party, 200, 213

DeMoss, Nancy: and *Power for Living* controversy, 179–80

Diamond, Sara, 270 (n. 130), 271 (n. 153), 272 (n. 178)

Disaster preparedness, 187–88. *See also* Rushdoony, Rousas John, works of: *Preparation for the Future*; Survivalism

Dochuk, Darren, 8, 9, 94, 98, 117

Doherty, Brian, 60, 63

Dominion, 4–5, 16, 101, 143, 175, 177; and

biblical law, 15, 125–26, 131–34, 139, 141, 198, 201, 214, 227; as family project, 125–26, 129, 131, 133–34, 137, 139, 153; woman as helpmeet in, 133, 143, 152–53, 223; and the church, 182–85; as unbiblical concept, 205

Dominionism. *See* Dominion Theology

Dominion man, 5, 15, 132–33, 177, 182, 185, 186, 190, 194, 227

Dominion Mandate, 4, 125, 131–33, 141, 198–200, 202, 204, 213

Dominion Theology, 5, 202, 204–5, 214–15, 219, 228, 268 (n. 88)

Duck Valley Indian Reservation, 1, 3, 13, 18, 25, 31, 32, 44, 81, 91

Dutch Calvinism, 36, 38–39, 136, 138, 210, 239 (n. 90)

Duggar, Jim Bob, 224

Duggar, Michelle, 224

Durkheim, Émile, 129

Earhart Foundation, 151, 152

Edgar, William, 221

Education: Christian education, 1–3, 20, 40, 43, 48, 80, 92–93, 98, 141, 166, 167, 169, 183, 224–23, 228; R. J. Rushdoony's criticism of public education, 4–5, 68–69, 82, 113, 165–67, 209; public education, 7, 16, 135, 224, 228; government regulation of, 141, 143–48, 168, 170. *See also* Homeschooling; Humanism

Eisenhower, Dwight D., 85

Elniff, Terrill I., 197

Engel v. Vitale, 147–48, 250 (n. 76)

Epistemology, 19–20, 38, 40–41, 45, 78, 87, 90, 106, 139, 154, 155, 165, 230, 239 (n. 93)

Equal Rights Amendment, 86

Evangelical universalism, 123, 127

Eve (biblical figure), 4, 41–42, 133

Evidentialist apologetics, 37–38

Exodus Mandate, 224

Fabian Society, 62–63

Faith and Freedom (journal), 50–55, 55, 113, 119

Falwell, Jerry, 145–46, 172, 197, 198, 212

Family: and familialism, 15, 90–95, 165–67;

and profamily activism, 86, 145, 225; and education, 86, 165–66, 224–25; and antifeminism, 85–86, 223, 260 (n. 35), 273 (n. 8); nuclear family, 91–93, 107, 137, 185–86; and nurturance, 92; and demographic changes, 93–94. *See also* Christian Reconstruction: as family project; Dominion: as family project

Federal Bureau of Investigation (FBI), 82, 248 (nn. 151, 11); investigation of Rousas John Rushdoony, 46–48

Federal Housing Administration, 94

Federal Reserve System: R. J. Rushdoony's criticism of, 57

Feudalism, 15, 125, 185

Fifield, James, 50–53, 63. *See also* Spiritual Mobilization (SM)

First Amendment, 146, 171

Fiske, Antonia, 103

Fitzmier, John R., 36

Flamm, Michael W., 108

Flanagan, Grayce, 82, 84, 101

Fosdick, Harry Emerson, 36

Foundation for Economic Education (FEE), 44, 54, 56, 68, 103, 117, 119, 243 (n. 65); R. J. Rushdoony's criticism of, 63–64; relationship with Gary North, 152, 155

Foundation for Law and Society, 169

Frame, John M., 41, 42, 156, 238 (n. 74)

Frankfurt School, 215

French Revolution, 38

Fresno, Calif.: Armenian community of, 21–22

Friedan, Betty, 86

Fromm, Eric, 215

Fuller Theological Seminary, 111, 136, 197, 200

Fundamentalist/Modernist controversy, 36–45 passim, 112–13, 117

Fusionism, 14, 65, 70, 86, 87, 151, 222, 244 (n. 97). *See also* Conservatism

Gaither, Milton, 148, 166, 234 (n. 9), 260 (n. 21)

Gaston, Keltner, and Adair, Attorneys at Law, 97

Gaustad, Edwin S., 151–52, 260 (n. 32)

Geneva Divinity School (Tyler, Tex.), 176, 182, 184. *See also* Tyler Theology; Westminster Presbyterian Church (Tyler, Tex.)

Gentry, Kenneth, 160, 269 (n. 117)

Gibbs, David C., 168–69, 175

Giberson, Karl W., 196

GI Bill, 94, 98

Gilstrap, Michael R.: and *Power for Living* controversy, 179–80; and survivalism, 188–89, 266 (n. 45)

Gingrich, Newt, 209

Goldwater, Barry, 117, 144; and the 1964 presidential election, 95, 97, 123–24, 149

GOP, 6, 149, 229. *See also* Republican Party; Young Republicans

Gordon College, 98

Gordon-Conwell Theological Seminary, 163, 176

Graham, Billy, 5, 8, 109; and neoevangelicalism, 109–27 passim

Graziano, Frank, 135

Great Depression, 50, 93

Great Society, 93, 107, 108

Green v. Connally, 145–48, 259–60 (n. 21)

Gregory the Illuminator, 20

Grimstead, Jay, 220

Gun Owners of America, 168

Ham, Ken, 196

Hargis, Billy James, 78

Harper, F. A. ("Baldy"), 54, 248 (n. 16); and the Institute for Humane Studies (IHS), 61–63, 244 (n. 82)

Harvard University, 24, 68, 98, 209

Hayek, Friedrich A., 64, 66, 228, 244 (n. 99)

Hazlitt, Henry, 64, 245 (n. 109)

Heard; Gerald, 52, 54, 241 (n. 26), 242 (n. 37)

Hedges, Chris, 215

Hendershot, Heather, 8–9, 115

Hendriksen, William: and postmillennialism, 136–37

Henry, Carl. F. H., 15, 196, 247 (n. 146), 253 (n. 29), 254 (n. 64), 267 (n. 81); and neoevangelicalism, 110–23 passim

Herberg, Will, 65

Heritage Foundation, 145, 191

Hill, Paul Jennings, 160–61, 262 (n. 79)

Hinduism, 140–41

Hoggan, David L., 68, 245–46 (n. 109), 247 (n. 147), 248 (n. 151); and sectarianism at the Volker Fund and Center for American Studies, 73–77; and Holocaust denial, 218, 256 (n. 113)

Hollinger, David A., 50

Holt, John, 234 (n. 9)

Holy Spirit (biblical concept), 40, 199

Homeschooling, 4, 8, 16, 139, 173, 175, 179, 188, 197, 227, 228; and R. J. Rushdoony, 2, 4, 16, 144, 163–67, 169, 170, 221, 223–25; court cases related to, 2, 167–70, 234 (n. 7); as movement, 4, 167, 221, 223, 234 (n. 9); and John W. Whitehead, 163, 165, 170–71, 173, 191

Homosexuality, 146, 164, 225, 256 (n. 110); and the death penalty, 4, 131, 213, 221, 274 (n. 44)

Hoover Institution on War, Revolution, and Peace, 77, 245 (n. 105), 249 (n. 19)

House, H. Wayne, 204–6, 269 (n. 117)

Humanism, 23, 106, 123, 190, 165, 190, 199, 212; and statism, 99, 100, 125, 127, 139, 184; and law, 123, 131, 106, 148; as religion, 168, 170

Hunt, Dave, 204–5,

Hunt, Nelson Bunker, 169

Hutchinson, B. E., 50

Huxley, Aldous, 52, 54, 242 (n. 37)

Iannaccone, Laurence R., 227

Ice, Thomas D., 204–6, 269 (n. 117)

Independent Board of Presbyterian Foreign Missions, 171

Ingebretsen, James C., 51, 54, 56, 242 (n. 37). See also *Faith and Freedom* (journal)

Ingersoll, Julie, 235 (n. 25)

Institute for Christian Economics (ICE), 151, 160, 169, 214, 221, 272 (n. 178); origin of, 155; publishing efforts of, 176–77, 179, 182, 264 (n. 144), 269 (n. 117); conflict with Chalcedon Foundation, 218, 273 (n. 5)

Institute for Humane Studies (IHS), 61–63

Intercollegiate Society of Individualists (ISI), 63, 66, 70–73, 82, 83, 152, 155, 157, 243 (n. 65), 246 (n. 117)

Intercollegiate Studies of Institute (ISI), 151, 222

Internal Revenue Service (IRS), 76, 97, 99, 143, 145, 147, 148. *See also* Taxes

International Monetary Fund, 154

Jackson Theological Seminary, 103

Jarman, W. Maxey, 111

Jesus Christ (JC) Light and Power Company, 139, 141, 164

Jesus Christ (JC) Light and Power House, 140, 205

Jesus People, 140, 141

John Birch Society (JBS), 8, 15, 78, 126, 207, 250 (n. 68), 266 (n. 43), 270 (n. 130); and housewife activism, 85–86, 92, 102; and conspiracies, 94–95, 102; R. J. Rushdoony's relationship with, 95–97, 250 (n. 76), 251 (n. 86); J. Howard Pew's relationship with, 118, 254 (n. 55). *See also* Welch, Robert

Johnson, Lyndon Baines, 107

Johnson, William, 51–52. See also *Faith and Freedom* (journal)

Jordan, James B., 170, 206, 208; and Reformed Theological Seminary, Jackson, Mississippi (RTS), 159–60; and the Westminster Orthodox Presbyterian Church in Tyler, Texas, 183, 191–94, 266 (nn. 49, 51), 267 (n. 61)

Joyce, Kathryn, 233

Kanawha County, W.Va.: textbook controversy, 148

Kant, Immanuel, 38

Kantorowicz, Ernst H., 13, 19, 24, 28–31, 37, 45

Kennedy, D. James, 150, 165, 176; and Christian Reconstructionism, 198–99, 201, 228, 268 (n. 92)

Kerr, Ruth, 156

Kershner, Howard E., 63, 118, 247 (n. 146), 254 (n. 64). *See also* Christian Freedom Foundation (CFF)

Kik, J. Marcellus: and R. J. Rushdoony's relationship with *Christianity Today*, 113–21 passim, 253 (n. 36); and postmillennialism, 258 (n. 160)

King, Martin Luther, Jr., 82, 185, 248 (n. 11)

Kingdom Now, 200–201, 214. *See also* Dominion theology; Paulk, Earl, Jr.

Kinism, 274–75 (n. 48)

Kirk, Russell, 71, 91

Kirkwood, Dorothy. *See* Rushdoony, Dorothy

Kirkwood, Thomas, 57, 243 (nn. 56, 57)

Knott, Walter, 14, 99, 251 (n. 98)

Knott's Berry Farm, 14, 99

Kuyper, Abraham, 138, 210; influence on Van Til, 38–39, 239 (nn. 90, 93); and the antithesis, 116, 169; and sphere sovereignty, 133, 200, 212

Labour Party, 62–63

L'Abri, 171, 172, 213, 272 (n. 174)

LaHaye, Tim, 207–8

Landers, Ann, 130

Lane, Rose Wilder, 252 (n. 130)

Lassiter, Matthew D., 9

Latter-day Saints, 51, 153, 187–88

Latter Rain movement, 199

"Law and order," 15, 108–10, 124, 140–41

Leeper, Cheryl, 2

Leeper, Gary, 2

Leeper et al. v. Arlington ISD et al., 2

Leo I (pope), 87

Liberalism (politics), 14, 16, 47, 65, 85, 90, 107–9, 149, 228

Liberalism (theology), 23, 34, 36–37, 53–55, 111–23 passim, 156, 186

Libertarianism, 19, 56, 58, 60, 103, 150, 153, 245 (nn. 102, 109), 252 (n. 130); and Christian Reconstructionism, 20, 82, 222, 226–28, 248 (n. 12), 260 (n. 35), 261 (n. 45); and conservatism, 47, 49, 59, 64, 152; and Spiritual Mobilization (SM), 51–54, 242 (n. 37); and fusionism, 65; and Center for American Studies (CAS), 67, 79; theocracy as, 222

Liberty University, 197

Lienesch, Michael, 227

Lindsey, Hal, 139–40, 164, 204–5, 258 (n. 172)

Lively, Scott, 225

Los Angeles Chamber of Commerce, 63

Luhnow, Harold W., 79, 121, 207, 244–45 (n. 100); and management of the William Volker Charities Fund, 58–59, 65–68, 75–76, 77. *See also* William Volker Charities Fund

Machen, J. Gresham, 34, 36–37, 57, 113, 156

Marsden, George, 135, 238 (n. 73)

Marshner, Connie, 145–46

Martin, William, 211

Marx, Karl, 23, 30, 109, 185, 260 (n. 35)

May, Elaine Tyler, 93

McCarran, Pat, Sr., 76

McCarran, Sister Mary Margaret Patricia, 76

McCloud, Sean, 229–30

McGirr, Lisa, 8, 9, 84, 94

McIntire, Carl, 115, 171

Meese, Ed, 146

Meyer, Frank S., 65, 77, 244 (n. 97), 247 (n. 146)

Milione, Victor, 63, 70–73, 75. *See also* Intercollegiate Society of Individualists (ISI)

Militia movement, 150, 187

Miller, C. John, 74–76, 246 (n. 109)

Miller, Mark Crispin, 216

Miller, Steven P., 123

Mises, Ludwig von, 51, 66, 75, 82, 103

Mitchell, Richard G., 187

Mobilization for Spiritual Ideals. *See* Spiritual Mobilization (SM)

Monroe, Marilyn, 140

Mont Pèlerin Society, 66, 243 (n. 65)

Moore, E. Ray, 224, 274 (n. 38)

Moore, R. Jonathan, 175

Moots, Glenn, 227

Moral Majority, 145, 207, 212

Morley, Felix, 83, 246 (n. 117)

Moyers, Bill, 213–14, 236 (n. 32), 272 (n. 176)

Muether, John R., 238 (n. 73), 239 (n. 93)

Mullendore, William C., 50, 54, 242 (n. 39)

Mulloy, D. J., 8–9

Mumford, Bob, 200

Murray, Madelyn, 147

Murray v. Curlett, 147

Nash, George, 47, 65, 244 (n. 97)

National Association for the Advancement of Colored People, 145

National Association of Evangelicals (NAE), 108, 111, 112, 144, 253 (n. 29)

National Association of Manufacturers, 49

National Book Foundation (NBF), 65

National Council of the Churches of Christ (NCC), 108, 117, 118, 122

National Lay Committee of the National Council of the Churches of Christ, 117

National Prayer Breakfast, 178

National Rifle Association, 169

Neoevangelicalism, 8, 15, 110, 112, 113, 119, 195; R. J. Rushdoony's criticisms of, 114–16, 121–22, 127–28, 196

New Apostolic Reformation, 200

New Deal, 10, 49–52, 60, 61, 65, 68, 84, 107, 247 (n. 131)

New York University, 216

Nickerson, Michelle M., 9, 85–86

Niebuhr, Reinhold, 238 (n. 67)

Nisbet, Robert A., 151–52

Nixon, Richard, 117, 124, 222

Noah (biblical figure), 188–89

Nobel Prize, 66, 244 (n. 99)

Nock, Albert Jay, 60–61, 63, 87. *See also* Remnant (concept)

Noll, Mark A., 37–38

North, Gary, 15, 121, 127–28, 144; internship at Center for American Studies (CAS), 76, 79, 245 (n. 100); early association with R. J. Rushdoony, 79, 82–84, 150–52, 248 (nn. 12, 18); education of, 82, 84, 152–53, 260 (nn. 31, 32); and Christian economics, 82, 150–51, 153; Institute of Christian Economics (ICE), 151, 155, 160, 176, 179; courtship of Sharon Rushdoony, 152–53; as a congressional staff member, 154–55; and congressman Ron Paul, 154–55, 228, 261 (n. 45); move

to Tyler, Texas, 155, 182, 190, 261 (n. 52); lecturing and speaking engagements of, 176, 188, 194; publishing efforts of, 176–77, 179, 182, 264 (n. 144), 269 (n. 117); Church-centered theology, 182; and the decentralized church, 184–86; and the Y2K computer bug, 186, 218, 273 (nn. 7–9); and predictions of social collapse, 186–87; and disaster preparedness, 187–88, 266 (n. 43), 267 (n. 61); tensions with R. J. Rushdoony and the Chalcedon Foundation, 191–94, 208, 217–19, 266 (n. 48)

North, Peggy, 82, 101

North, Samuel W., Jr., 82, 248 (n. 11)

Norton, Robert D., 103

Ockenga, Harold John, 111–12, 253 (n. 25)

Ohio v. Whisner, et al., 168–69

Olin, James, 170

Operation Rescue, 161, 211, 262 (n. 81)

Opitz, Edmund A., 51, 60–61, 103, 152

Oral Roberts University, 197

Orsi, Robert A., 229–30

Orthodox Presbyterian Church (OPC), 99, 113, 150, 156–57, 159, 160, 161; R. J. Rushdoony's relationship with, 57, 118, 242 (n. 54)

Owyhee, Nev., 18, 25–28, 31, 32, 33, 34, 40, 43, 47, 49, 52, 53, 56

Pacific School of Religion (PSR), 23, 28, 37, 40, 124, 159, 238 (n. 67)

Pamphleteers, 252 (n. 130)

Passover (biblical concept), 192–93

Patriotic bookstores, 82, 84, 86

Paul, Ron, 150, 154–55, 187, 226, 228, 261 (n. 45). *See also* Ron Paul Curriculum

Paulk, Earl, Jr., 199–201. *See also* Kingdom Now

Peacocke, Dennis, 200

Peale, Norman Vincent, 50, 52

Pentecostalism, 153, 158, 181, 199–200, 205. *See also* Charismatic movement

People for the American Way (PFAW), 214, 272 (n. 178)

Perry, Rick, 6–7

Pew, J. Howard, 15, 50, 91, 110, 111; relationship with R. J. Rushdoony, 116–22, 195, 196, 206, 254 (n. 55)

Pew Charitable Trusts, 117

Phillips, Beall, 223

Phillips, Doug, 223–24, 263 (n. 98)

Phillips, Howard, 145–47, 176, 208–9, 223, 263 (n. 98)

Phillips-Fein, Kim, 66, 119

Porteous, Skipp, 270 (n. 130)

Possony, Stefan T., 83, 84, 249 (n. 19)

Postmillennialism, 109, 125, 141, 156, 163, 176, 204, 258 (nn. 156, 160), 269 (n. 111); and the Social Gospel, 50; and Christian Reconstructionism, 134–36, 157, 158, 196, 201, 202, 213; and dominion, 137–39; and preparedness, 188–89

Pratt, Lawrence D., 168–69

Premillennialism, 98, 109, 112, 135–36, 182, 188; R. J. Rushdoony's criticism of, 35, 136, 139–40, 258 (n. 156)

Presbyterian and Reformed Publishing Company (P&R), 157, 242 (n. 46), 256 (n. 113)

Presbyterian Church in America (PCA), 160–61

Presbyterian Church (U.S.A.) (PCUSA), 14, 36, 43, 117; R. J. Rushdoony's criticism of, 54–55; Rushdoony leaves, 56–57, 113

Presuppositional Apologetics, 53, 69, 72, 74, 78, 87, 90, 97, 98; Cornelius Van Til's concept of, 19, 34–35, 38–41, 68, 75, 79, 81, 127–28, 162, 169, 179, 183, 238 (n. 73), 246 (n. 112)

Preterism, 136–37

Pride, Mary, 223

Princeton Theological Seminary, 34, 37, 136, 138

Proclamation 5018, 178

Prosperity gospel, 52, 198–99, 268 (n. 93)

Public Law 97-280, 178

Public Research Associates (PRA), 214, 272 (n. 178)

Puritanism, 135, 151, 197

Quayle, Dan, 154

Quiverfull movement, 223–24, 274 (n. 27)

Race: and violence, 105; and IRS regulations of churches, 145–48, 259–60 (n. 21)

Rand, Ayn, 60, 61, 64, 87, 252 (n. 130)

Raynolds, George C., 21

Read, Leonard, 63–64, 152, 252 (n. 130)

Reagan, Ronald, 117, 124, 201, 204, 211; and 1980 presidential election, 17, 150, 195; and *Green v. Connally* controversy, 144–47; and the "Year of the Bible," 178

Reconstruction. *See* Christian Reconstruction,

Reconstructionism. *See* Christian Reconstruction

Reformed Christianity, 34–39, 74–75, 131–32, 135–37; and Greg L. Bahnsen, 155–63 passim, 176

Reformed Theological Seminary, Jackson, Miss. (RTS): Greg L. Bahnsen's tenure at, 157–61, 176, 179, 182, 182, 269 (n. 117);

Regent University, 197, 209, 271 (n. 145)

Religious Right, 6, 8, 144, 172, 195, 202–3; origin of, 147–50, 259–60 (n. 21); legacy of R. J. Rushdoony in, 211, 213–14, 221, 227. *See also* Christian Right

Religious Roundtable, 144

Remnant (concept), 14, 48, 59, 189; and Albert J. Nock, 60–61, 87; R. J. Rushdoony's criticism of, 61–64; and the Chalcedon Foundation, 82, 90, 94, 101, 105

Remnant (group), 103

Republican Party, 6, 22, 85, 103, 107, 109, 124, 144, 145, 149, 150, 198, 200, 202, 215, 270 (n. 130). *See also* GOP; Young Republicans

Robbins, John W., 154

Roberts, Wesley A., 42

Robertson, Pat, 150, 172, 176, 197, 228, 271 (n. 145); and dominion theology, 198–99, 201, 202, 268 (nn. 86, 88); and the Council for National Policy (CNP), 209, 210

Robinson, Arthur, 188

Rockwell, George Lincoln, 77

Roe v. Wade, 173, 259 (n. 21)

Ron Paul Curriculum, 227–28

Roosevelt, Franklin D., 49, 51

Ross House Books, 220, 224

Rothbard, Murray, 52, 62, 66, 152, 245 (n. 102)

Ruff, Howard, 155, 187–88

Rushdoony, Arda June (née Gent): early relationship with R. J. Rushdoony, 23, 25, 236–37 (n. 42); as missionary, 26–27; divorce from Rousas John Rushdoony, 43–44, 56, 118, 240 (n. 120)

Rushdoony, Dorothy Barbara Kirkwood (née Ross), 57, 101, 118, 191, 243 (nn. 56, 57)

Rushdoony, Haig, 22

Rushdoony, Joanna, 12, 27, 44

Rushdoony, Mark, 12, 27, 43, 80; recollections of the Chalcedon Foundation, 97, 99, 100, 101, 126, 258 (n. 156), 274–75 (n. 48)

Rushdoony, Martha, 12, 27, 43, 44

Rushdoony, Rebecca, 12, 26, 44

Rushdoony, Ronald, 12, 26, 44

Rushdoony, Rose (R. J. Rushdoony's sister), 22

Rushdoony, Rousas John: missionary on Duck Valley Reservation, 1, 13, 18–19, 24–29, 31–32, 40, 44–45, 53, 81, 91; as expert witness, 1–2, 148, 167–70, 191, 217, 223, 273 (n. 4) and foundation of Chalcedon Foundation, 3, 14–15, 80, 86–87, 96–102, 104, 143–44; early development of Christian Reconstruction, 4–5, 82, 100; and the William Volker Charities Fund, 8, 14, 44, 46–47, 53–72 passim, 77, 97, 103, 150, 195, 207; and the John Birch Society (JBS), 8, 15, 92–97, 102, 118, 250 (n. 76); extremism of, 8–10, 14, 48, 77–78, 215, 221; temperament of, 11–13, 140, 190–91, 193–94, 210; as a father and grandfather, 11–13, 140, 191, 194; lecturing and speaking tours of, 12, 14, 43, 44, 46–47, 69, 71–72, 82–83, 86, 97, 101–4, 124, 128–29, 143, 164–67, 170, 191, 194, 220, 225, 246 (n. 117), 251 (n. 115); relationship with Cornelius Van Til and presuppositionalism, 13, 14, 34–37, 40–43, 45, 56, 69, 75, 80, 84, 104, 113–14, 127–28, 169, 183, 246 (n. 112); move to Santa Cruz, Calif., 14, 43, 56; and Spiritual Mobilization

(SM), 14, 44, 49–50, 53–54, 56, 63, 113, 195; sectarianism of, 14, 48, 53, 69–78 passim, 79, 113, 193–94, 207, 210; and Greg L. Bahnsen, 15, 128, 155–63, 176, 192–94, 217, 269 (n. 27), 267 (n. 59); and John W. Whitehead, 15, 150, 161, 163–65, 170–75, 191, 211–13, 263 (n. 91), 264 (n. 136); antistatist reflections on Indian reservations, 18–19, 26–28, 31–32, 44–45, 91; at University of California, Berkeley, 19, 23–25, 28, 45, 114, 159; education of, 19–23; marriage to Arda June Gent, 23, 25–27, 43–44, 56, 236–37 (n. 42), 240 (n. 120); at Pacific School of Religion (PSR), 23, 28, 37, 40, 124, 159, 238 (n. 67); missionary in San Francisco, 24; move to Owyhee, Nev., 24; divorce from Arda June Rushdoony, 44, 47, 56, 118, 218, 237 (n. 42), 240 (n. 120), 261 (n. 57); marriage to Dorothy Ross Kirkwood, 57, 118, 243 (n. 57); views on democracy, 63, 89, 125, 141, 181, 194, 202–3, 214, 216; early relationship with Gary North, 76, 79, 82–84, 152–53, 245 (n. 100); move to Woodland Hills, Calif., 79–80, 82, 98–99, 128, 252 (n. 132); reading habits of, 80–82; interpretation of the Council of Chalcedon, 87–89; writing habits of, 101, 220; and failed San Luis Obispo land deal, 143; move to Vallecito, Calif., 143–44; and the Rutherford Institute (TRI), 161, 174–75, 262 (n. 81); and homeschooling, 165–67; relationship with Francis and Franky Schaeffer, 171, 210–13, 228, 271–72 (n. 168), 272 (n. 174); and Howard Ahmanson, 174–75, 194, 220, 264 (n. 136); disputes with Gary North, 182, 190–94, 203, 208, 217–18, 266 (n. 48), 269 (n. 115); theological disputes with Westminster Presbyterian Church (Tyler, Tex.), 182–84, 190–94; failing health and death of, 217–18, 219–20; and Holocaust denial, 218, 256 (n. 113); and Jewish dietary laws, 257 (n. 126)

—works of: The Institutes of Biblical Law, 4, 106, 129, 130, 142, 153, 158, 166, 178, 197, 203, 209, 211, 222, 255 (n. 106), 256

(TRI), 171–75; relationship with Francis and Franky Schaeffer, 171–75, 211–12

Whitworth College, 23

Williams, George Huntston, 13, 24, 28, 30, 31, 236 (n. 32)

William Volker & Co., 46–47

William Volker Charities Fund, 14, 44, 46–47, 53, 54, 91, 97, 103, 111, 121, 150, 195, 207; and secrecy, 8, 58–59; hires R. J. Rushdoony as consultant, 57–58, 68; origin of, 58; scope of charitable giving, 58, 243 (n. 65), 245 (n. 106); religion in, 65–66, 70–72, 242 (n. 36); termination of, 66–67, 77, 79. *See also* Luhnow, Harold W.; Remnant (concept)

Wills, Garry, 65

Wilson, Francis Graham, 83

Wimber, John, 200

Winston, Diane, 190

Women for America, Inc., 14, 80, 84, 86, 90, 92, 101, 129, 140

Woods, Thomas E., 227

Worthen, Molly, 8, 89, 200, 271 (n. 168)

Year of the Bible (1983), 178–79

Young Republicans, 103

YouTube, 227–28

Y2K computer glitch, 186, 218, 273 (n. 8)

Zwingli, 36